RECORDS
of the
ACCOUNTING OFFICERS
of the
DEPARTMENT *of the* TREASURY

Inventory 14
(Revised)

COMPILED BY
William F. Sherman

—WITH—

ADDITIONS AND INDEX BY
Craig R. Scott, CGRS

HERITAGE BOOKS
2010

HERITAGE BOOKS

AN IMPRINT OF HERITAGE BOOKS, INC.

Books, CDs, and more—Worldwide

For our listing of thousands of titles see our website
at
www.HeritageBooks.com

Published 2010 by
HERITAGE BOOKS, INC.
Publishing Division
100 Railroad Ave. #104
Westminster, Maryland 21157

Other Heritage Books by Craig Roberts Scott, CGRS:

Index to the Fairfax County, Virginia Register of Marriages, 1853–1933
Constance K. Ring and Craig R. Scott

New Jerusalem Lutheran Church Cemetery
Marty Hiatt and Craig R. Scott

Scott Family Finding Aids, Volume #1, Marriages, 1700–1900

The 'Lost' Pensions: Settled Accounts of the Act of 6 April 1838

International Standard Book Numbers
Paperbound: 978-1-888265-06-4
Clothbound: 978-0-7884-8552-7

INTRODUCTION

The accounting system of the U.S. Government evolved from the experiences of fiscal accountability under the Continental Congresses and the Articles of Confederation. The Standing Committee of the Treasury (later known as the Board of Treasury) was appointed on February 17, 1776, to examine accounts and to superintend the general finances of the Government and of officers engaged in handling public moneys. Six auditors were among the officials appointed to assist the Board of Treasury.

An act of September 11, 1781, abolished these positions and replaced them with a Treasurer, Comptroller, Register, Auditors, and clerks. The act of September 2, 1789 (1 Stat. 65), which established the Treasury Department under the Constitution of the United States, provided specifically for three accounting officers: a Register, a Comptroller, an Auditor. The Register kept the central fiscal records (including ledgers and journals), filed all settled accounts and claims, and prepared annual reports for Congress summarizing receipts and expenditures of the Government as reflected by the official balances. The Auditor settled all accounts and claims, subject to the approval of the Comptroller. The Comptroller examined the settled accounts and claims, certified their balances, and sent them back to the Register. The 1789 act also provided for a Treasurer, who was responsible for the receipt and disbursement of public funds. In addition to the duties described here briefly, these officers also performed various other functions related to the accounting for public funds.

From 1792 to 1816, three additional offices were established to assist the original accounting officers. On May 8, 1792, the Office of the Accountant for the War Department (predecessor of the Second Auditor) was established (1 Stat. 279). The Office of the Accountant for the Navy Department (predecessor of the Fourth Auditor) was created on July 16, 1798 (1 Stat. 610), and the Office of the Additional Accountant for the War Department was created on April 29, 1816 (3 Stat. 322).

On March 3, 1817, a major reorganization of the accounting officers took place (3 Stat. 366). The Comptroller of the Treasury was designated the First Comptroller and became responsible for civil expenditures only; the Second Comptroller was established to perform similar functions for military expenditures. The Auditor was designated the First Auditor and was made responsible for settling most civil accounts and claims. The Accountant for the War Department, the Additional Accountant for the War Department, and the Accountant for the Navy Department were designated the Second, Third, and Fourth Auditors, respectively. The Second Auditor settled accounts for pay and contingent expenses of the Army, the Third Auditor settled all other accounts of the War Department, and the Fourth Auditor settled accounts of the Navy Department. A Fifth Auditor was also established at this time to settle accounts of the State Department and of the Post Office Department and accounts of Indian affairs.

At various times between 1817 and 1894, changes were made in the specific areas of responsibility of the accounting officers. These changes are noted in this preliminary inventory in the introductory remarks for Office. Two additional offices were also created. The Sixth Auditor was established by an act of July 2, 1836 (5 Stat. 80), to relieve the Fifth Auditor of responsibility for settling accounts of the Post Office Department. Finally, the Office of the Commissioner of Customs was created by an act of March 3, 1849 (9 Stat. 396), and assumed the duties that the First Comptroller had performed for accounts and claims related directly to customs receipts and expenditures. The Commissioner of Customs became, in effect, a "third comptroller."

In 1894 the accounting offices were reorganized primarily as a result of the recommendations of the Dockery-Cockrell Commission, which had been established in 1893 to investigate and report to Congress on the organization and operations of the executive departments. The changes in the Treasury Department were incorporated in the Dockery Act of July 31, 1894 (28 Stat. 205). The Dockery Act abolished the Offices of First Comptroller, Second Comptroller, and Commissioner of Customs and simultaneously created the Office of Comptroller of the Treasury, to which the functions of the three former Offices were transferred. The auditors were renamed the Auditor for the Treasury Department, Auditor for the War Department, Auditor for the Interior Department, Auditor for the Navy Department, Auditor for the State and other Departments, and Auditor for the Post Office Department. The functions of the auditors were, as necessary, shifted to conform to the areas of responsibility indicated by their new titles. Most of the functions previously performed by the Register were transferred to the newly established Division of Bookkeeping and Warrants in the Office of the Secretary of the Treasury.

In 1921 the accounting offices were abolished. The Budget and Accounting Act of 1921 transferred the responsibility for fiscal accountability of Government funds from the Treasury Department to the newly created U.S. General Accounting Office (GAO). The GAO, headed by the Comptroller General of the United States, is part of the legislative branch of the Government.

The records described in this inventory consist of records of the accounting offices of the Treasury Department, 1789-1921, in the custody of the National Archives and Records Administration (NARA) as of December 31, 1979. They also include some pre-Federal records created under the Continental Congresses and Articles of Confederation as well as some records of the GAO that are direct continuations of series begun under the Treasury Department. These records are part of the body of records designated Records of the U.S. General Accounting Office, Record Group (RG) 217, and total approximately 23,000 cubic feet.

Some records that originated in the accounting offices but document functions subsequently transferred to other administrative units of the Treasury Department in or before 1921 are not included in this inventory. A primary example is the appropriation ledgers were transferred from the Office of the Register to the Division of Bookkeeping and Warrants in 1894 and are now part of Records of the Bureau of Accounts (Treasury), RG 39. The records of the Sixth Auditor (Auditor for the Post Office Department) are in Records of the U.S. Postal Service, RG 28. Although nominally an official of the Treasury Department, the Sixth Auditor reported directly to the Postmaster General.

Records closely related to those described in this inventory are found in other record groups in the custody of NARA. Registers and indexes for warrants and the original surety bonds of accountable officers are in RG 39. Many records of the Office of the Register relating to the public debt are in Records of the Bureau of the Public Debt, RG 53. Case files of the Southern Claims Commission claims rejected by Congress are in Records of the U.S. House of Representatives, RG 233. Most records relating to expenses of the District of Columbia are in Records of the Government of the District of Columbia, RG 351.

Other closely related records may be found in Records of the U.S. Customs Service, RG 36; Records of the Treasurer of the United States, RG 50; General Records of the Department of the Treasury, RG 56; Records of the Internal Revenue Service, RG 58; and Records of the Bureau of the Mint, RG 104. Related records for the pre-Federal period are in Records of the Continental and Confederation Congresses and the Constitutional Convention, RG 360. Related accounting records are often found also among the records of individual government agencies.

The inventory is divided into nine parts, one for each of the major accounting offices of the Treasury Department. Within each office, the records are described, in so far as possible, by the divisions that originated the records or that were responsible, as of 1894, for the functions to which the records relate.

Several series of records described in this inventory have been microfilmed by NARA. If the series is available on microfilm, that fact is noted in the series description. For further information on NARA microfilm publications, see the current *Catalog of National Archives Microfilm Publications* or write to the Publications Services Branch (NEPS), National Archives and Records Administration (NARA), Washington, DC 20408, stating the microfilm publication number or the subject of the microfilm desired.

This inventory was compiled by William F. Sherman. He has benefited from previous descriptions of the records covered by this inventory that were prepared by present and former NARA staff members Philip R. Ward, Sr., Albert U. Blair, William H. Hernandez, Joyce Davis Ciarrochi, and Frederick W. Pernell. Additions have been made by John Vandereedt.

OFFICE OF THE REGISTER OF THE TREASURY

The Office of the Register of the Treasury originated under the government of the Second Continental Congress. It was authorized for continuation under the Constitution of the United States by an act of September 2, 1789 (1 Stat. 65), which established the Treasury Department. The Register's duties were to keep an official record of all receipts and expenditures of the Government and maintain appropriate ledgers and journals; record all debts of, or payable to, the United States; preserve all settled accounts approved by the Comptroller; record all warrants for receipt or expenditure of public funds; and certify balances of settled accounts to the Secretary of the Treasury. An act of March 3, 1817 (3 Stat. 366), transferred the functions of filing military accounts and claims and recording military warrants to the Second, Third, and Fourth Auditors.

Responsibility for preparing statements of foreign commerce and navigation, based on returns received quarterly from collectors of customs, was made a function of the Register's Office by an act of February 10, 1820 (3 Stat. 541). This function was transferred to the Bureau of Statistics when the Bureau was created in the Treasury Department by an act of July 28, 1866 (14 Stat. 331). The bookkeeping functions of the Register were transferred to the Division of Bookkeeping and Warrants in the Office of the Secretary of the Treasury by an act of July 31, 1894 (28 Stat. 205), but the function of keeping personal accountability ledgers restored to the Register in 1921, when the U.S. General Accounting Office was established.

The only Divisions of the Register's Office for which records are described in this inventory are the Receipts and Expenditures Division and the Note, Coupon, Currency, and Files Division. The functions of these Divisions are described later in more detail. The most significant records of the Register's Office described in this inventory are the ledgers, journals, and daybooks, 1789-1894. Appropriation ledgers and most other records that once were a part of the records of the Registers Office are now a part of Records of the Bureau of Accounts (Treasury), RG 39, and Records of the Bureau of the Public Debt, RG 53. A list of Registers names and dates of service appears in Appendix 1.

RECEIPTS AND EXPENDITURES DIVISION

The Receipts and Expenditures Division is first mentioned as a Division in a report on Register's Office activities for the fiscal year starting July 1, 1861; its functions had been referred to in earlier reports as being performed by "desks." The main function of the Division was to maintain the general ledgers of the Treasury Department, appropriation ledgers, and personal accountability ledgers for the Treasury and other civil disbursing officers. The Division also certified balances of disbursing officers' accounts and certified amounts of advances to them, amounts of repayments by them, and amounts of their indebtedness to the Government, if any. Additionally, the Division prepared an annual report to Congress on the receipts and expenditures of the Government until this function was discontinued in 1894.

Ledgers

1.   INDEX TO GENERAL LEDGERS (ALPHABET BOOKS, OLD GOVERNMENT). Sept. 2, 1777-June 30, 1796. 5 cm, 2 in. 5 vol.

Arranged alphabetically by initial letter of title of account. Index to the general ledgers designated as ledgers A-D and described in entry 2. Index shows ledger designation, title of account (frequently the name of an accountable officer or claimant), page number, and whether the account was payable in new emissions, old emissions, or specie. (The terms "old emissions" and "new emissions" refer to two issues of Continental currency in use before and during the Revolutionary War and in the early Federal period; the term "specie" refers to gold.) Ledgers A-D were maintained by the Board of the Treasury under the Second Continental Congress. This volume is reproduced on roll 22 of National Archives and Records Administration (NARA) Microfilm Publication M1014, Central Treasury Records of the Continental and Confederation Governments, 1775-1789.

2.   GENERAL TREASURY LEDGERS. Apr. 1776-June 1907. 8.8 m, 29 ft. 103 vols.

Accounts are arranged randomly by type and thereunder chronologically. Appropriation accounts are arranged alphabetically by the keyword of the title of the appropriation. Accountable officers accounts are arranged alphabetically by initial letter of each officer's surname. The volumes are designated A-D, 1-8 (a consolidated volume), and 9-113. Ledgers A-D are for the pre-Federal period; volume 1 begins with the First Federal Congress. Only volumes A-D, 1-10, 80-104, and 106-113 are indexed; each of these volumes contains an index arranged by initial letter of the keyword of the title of the account (the complete title is given). An additional index to ledgers A-D is described in entry 1. Volumes 107-113 are entitled "Treasury Personal Ledgers." These volumes have various spine titles: "Ledger;" "General Treasury Ledger;" "Treasury Ledger;" "Treasury Personal Ledger." Spine numbers are from 11 to 113.

Ledgers contain entries that show, by account, the revenues of the U.S. Government and the use of funds appropriated by Congress. The ledgers include three types of accounts: (1) control accounts, such as the "General Account of Moneys Advanced" and "Warrants on the Treasurer;" (2) accounts for moneys appropriated by Congress for specific purposes, such as "Mint Establishment;" and (3) accounts in the names of individuals who were either accountable officers or claimants to whom the Government owed money. The appropriation and personal name accounts are cross-referenced to the control accounts. Entries show debits from and credits to the account, date on which the transaction was posted, numbers and balances of settled accounts, and numbers and amounts of warrants.

Ledgers A-D, 1776-89, are reproduced on rolls 18-21 of NARA Microfilm Publication M1014, Central Treasury Records of the Continental and Confederation Governments, 1775-1789.

3.   GENERAL AUXILIARY LEDGERS (TREASURY AUXILIARY LEDGERS). May 1812-Oct. 1907. 30 cm, 1 ft. 4 vols.

Accounts are arranged chronologically and thereunder by name of accountable officer in no particular order. Accounts showing an outstanding balance when the general ledgers were closed for the accounting period were transferred to the auxiliary ledger. Only volumes 3 and 4 are indexed; each contains an index arranged by initial letter of the officer's surname (the complete surname is given).

Ledgers contain entries needed to close the accounts of former disbursing officers or other accountable officers, including diplomatic, consular, judicial, and Territorial officials and Treasury and other departmental disbursing agents. The entries show accountable officer's name, titles of appropriation accounts from which funds were disbursed by him, balances carried forward from ledger accounts (entry 2), previous balances, debits and credits needed to close the accounts, and, sometimes, auditor's settlement numbers for individual accounts. Most of the adjustments recorded in volume 1 are for accounts opened in the 1830s.

4.   COMMERCE AND LABOR PERSONAL LEDGERS. July 1903-June 1909. 18 cm, 7 in. 2 vols.

Arranged chronologically. Each volume is arranged by administrative level and thereunder alphabetically by initial letter of accountable officer's surname in the case of lighthouse district inspectors and engineers. Each volume is indexed by initial letter of officer's surname.

Ledgers contain entries of Department of Commerce and Labor disbursing clerks, lighthouse district engineers, and lighthouse district inspectors. Each ledger account shows name and title of accountable officer; titles of accounts from which officer disbursed funds; date and amount of his surety bond (before 1906); dates, numbers, and balances of settled accounts; and dates, numbers, types, and amounts of warrants charged or credited to the account.

5.   GENERAL CUSTOMS LEDGERS. July 1849-June 1896. 3.1 m, 10 ft. 39 vols.

Arranged chronologically. Each volume is arranged alphabetically by initial letter of accountable officer's surname. Only volumes 1 and 29-39 are indexed; each contains an index arranged by surname of accountable officer.

Ledgers contain entries of customs officials who served as disbursing agents for lighthouses, marine hospitals, and revenue cutters and of other disbursing officers of the Treasury Department for expenditures for public buildings. The entries show accountable officer's name and title, type of disbursement, cross-references to the control accounts (such as "General Account of Moneys Advanced") and to earlier and later ledgers in the series, number and balance of previous account, and debit and credit entries for moneys advanced and for disbursements from the advances. This series of volumes contains various spine titles: "Ledger" and "Customs Ledger."

6.   CUSTOMS AUXILIARY LEDGER. July 1874-Dec. 1908. 5 cm, 2 in. 1 vol.

Arranged generally chronologically and thereunder by name of accountable officer in no particular order. Accounts showing an outstanding balance when the general ledgers were closed for the accounting period were transferred to the auxiliary ledger.

Ledger contains entries needed to close the accounts of former customs officers who had served as disbursing agents for lighthouses, marine hospitals, and revenue cutters. The entries show accountable officer's name and title, customs district where stationed, titles of appropriation accounts from which accountable officer disbursed funds, date of surety bond, balances carried forward from ledger accounts described in entries 2 and 5, numbers and balances of settled accounts, and debit and credit entries needed to close the account.

7.   CUSTOMS LEDGERS: RECEIPTS AND DISBURSEMENTS. Mar. 1825-June 1907. 3.7 m, 12 ft. 59 vols.

Arranged chronologically. Each volume is arranged geographically by customs district and thereunder by name of port. The first 11 ledgers (1825-36) are not numbered, the 12th ledger (1837) is numbered 37, and thereafter the ledgers are numbered consecutively through volume 83. Only the volumes for the years 1825-30 and 1833-34 and the volumes numbered 37 64 and 66-83 are indexed; they are indexed by initial letter of accountable officer's surname.

Ledgers contain entries for accounts of customs officers for the collection of customs duties and related expenses. The entries show accountable officer's name and title, where stationed, cross-references to other ledgers (customs activities before 1825 are included in the ledgers described in entry 2), and source and amount of receipts and expenses.

8.   CUSTOMS AUXILIARY LEDGERS: RECEIPTS AND DISBURSEMENTS. ca. 1826-Mar. 1891. 15 cm, 6 in. 2 vols.

Arranged chronologically and thereunder by name of accountable officer in no particular order. Accounts showing an outstanding balance when the general ledgers were closed for the accounting period were transferred to the auxiliary ledger. Each volume is indexed by initial letter of accountable officer's surname.

Ledgers contain entries needed to close accounts of former customs officers for receipts and disbursements of customs revenues. The entries show accountable officer's name and title, date of surety bond, where formerly stationed, balance carried forward from ledger accounts described in entry 7, numbers of settled accounts, and debits and credits needed to close the account. Months in which the entries were made are rarely shown; usually only the year of the entry is indicated.

9.   CUSTOMS EMOLUMENT LEDGERS. Jan. 1841-June 1903. 61 cm, 2 ft. 8 vols.

Arranged chronologically. Each volume is arranged alphabetically by State and thereunder by customs district. Each volume is indexed by initial letter of accountable officer's surname.
Ledgers contain entries that show accountable officer's district and sometimes port where stationed; date of surety bond; number of settled account; period covered; debits for fees, commissions, salaries, and other revenues; credits for salaries of clerks, for stationery, for other office expenses, and for total compensation the accountable officer was allowed by law; and balance due the Government or the accountable officer.

10.   CUSTOMS LEDGERS: MISCELLANEOUS RECEIPTS. Mar. 1872-June 1907. 61 cm, 2 ft. 8 vols.

Arranged chronologically. Volumes 1-3 are arranged geographically by customs district and thereunder by port; volumes 4-8 are arranged alphabetically by State and thereunder by port. Each volume is indexed by initial letter of accountable officer's surname.
Ledgers contain entries for miscellaneous receipts, such as for the sale of old materials, fees for deceased passengers, collections for the immigrant and marine hospital funds, and receipts for fines, penalties, and forfeitures. The entries show accountable officer's name and title, port and district where stationed, date of surety bond, title of appropriation account, numbers of settled accounts, debits for receipts, and credits for warrants. This series has various spine titles: "Customs Auxiliary Ledger Receipts;" "Miscellaneous Ledger;" "Customs Miscellaneous Ledger Receipts."

11.   DIPLOMATIC LEDGERS. July 1862-June 1900. 2.7 m, 9 ft. 31 vols.

Arranged chronologically. Each volume is arranged alphabetically by initial letter of accountable officer's surname. Only volumes 7-31 are indexed; they are indexed by initial letter of officer's surname.
Ledgers contain entries for accounts of diplomatic and consular officials and of disbursing agents for the Department of State. The entries show accountable officer's name and title; duty station (if overseas); cross-references to other ledgers (diplomatic expenses before 1862 are included in the ledgers described in entry 2) and, sometimes, to auxiliary ledgers described in entry 12; numbers, dates, and balances of settled accounts; debits for moneys advanced; and credits for amounts of warrants and for balances due accountable officer from previous accounts. Spine titles on this series include "Diplomatic Ledger;" and "Diplomatic Personal Ledger."

12.   DIPLOMATIC AUXILIARY LEDGERS. ca. 1874-Nov. 1906. 28 cm, 11 in. 4 vols.

Arranged chronologically and thereunder by name of accountable officer in no particular order. Accounts showing an outstanding balance when the general ledgers were closed for the accounting period were transferred to the auxiliary ledger. Each volume is indexed by initial letter of accountable officer's surname.
Ledgers contain entries needed to close the accounts of former diplomatic and consular officers and disbursing agents for the State Department. The entries show accountable officer's

name and title, where stationed, type of account, balances carried forward from ledger accounts described in entry 11, numbers and balances of settled accounts, and debits and credits needed to close the account.

13.   PUBLIC DEBT LEDGER, DISTRICT OF COLUMBIA LEDGER. July 1902-Feb. 1908.
         5 cm, 2 in. 1 vol.

         Accounts are randomly arranged by type and thereunder chronologically. Indexed by initial letter of accountable officer's surname.
         Ledger contains entries showing status of accounts of disbursing officers for expenditures for the District of Columbia. Types of entries include those on accounts for interest on the sinking funds; redemption of District of Columbia bonds; expenses of Providence Hospital, Garfield Hospital, and the Fire Department; and expenses for improvements and repairs. The entries show accountable officer's name and title; titles of appropriation accounts from which officer disbursed funds; balances carried forward from ledgers described in entry 2; numbers, dates, and balances of settled accounts; warrant numbers; amounts debited from and credited to the officer's account; and remaining balance.

14.   INTERIOR LEDGER, INTERIOR CIVIL LEDGERS. July 1855-Nov. 1907. 2.4 m, 8 ft.
         31 vols.

         The volumes are arranged chronologically. The accounts in each volume are arranged alphabetically by initial letter of officer's surname. Volumes 1 and 24-30 are missing. Only volumes 8-23 and 31-38 are indexed; they are indexed by initial letter of officer's surname. The indexes for volumes 8 and 9 are bound separately. There are gaps in the date span of these records; the actual dates covered are: July 1855-June 1892; July 1899-Nov. 1907.
         Ledgers contain entries showing status of accounts of disbursing agents of the Interior Department, Land Office officials, the Commissioner of Public Buildings, and U.S. marshals (through June 1870); the ledgers also contain entries showing expenses for boundary surveys. The entries show accountable officer's name and title; where stationed; type of disbursement; date of surety bond; balance from the ledgers described in entry 2; numbers, dates, and balances of settled accounts; and other debits and credits.

15.   INTERIOR CIVIL AUXILIARY LEDGER. ca. 1874-Nov. 1908. 8 cm, 3 in. 1 vol.

         Arranged chronologically and thereunder by name of accountable officer in no particular order. Accounts showing an outstanding balance when the general ledgers were closed for the accounting period were transferred to the auxiliary ledger. Indexed by initial letter of officer's surname.
         Ledger contains entries needed to close the accounts of former Land Office officials. The entries show accountable officer's name and title, where stationed, titles of appropriation accounts from which officer disbursed funds, date of surety bond, balances carried forward from ledger accounts described in entry 14, numbers and balances of settled accounts, and debits and credits needed to close the account.

16.   INDEX TO INDIAN PERSONAL LEDGER NO. 7: FISCAL OFFICERS. Mar. 1909-Nov.
         1919. 1 cm, 1/2 in. 1 box.

         Arranged alphabetically by initial letter of surname of officer or bank.
         Index to volume 7 of the Interior (Indian) ledgers described in entry 17, showing names of banks or individual fiscal officers and page references. If the fiscal officer was a bank, the location of the bank is shown. If the fiscal officer was an individual, the date of his surety bond is included.

17. FISCAL OFFICERS INDIAN LEDGERS. Mar. 1908-Oct. 1923. 30 cm, 1 ft. 5 vols.

Arranged chronologically. Volumes are identified as ledgers 6-10. Ledgers 6 and 7 are arranged by type of officer and thereunder alphabetically by name of officer. Ledgers 8 and 9 are arranged alphabetically by initial letter of accountable officer's surname. Ledger 10 is arranged alphabetically by the name of the city in which the bank was located. Only ledger 7 is indexed; it is indexed by initial letter of officer's surname. This index is described in entry 16 and is bound separately.

Ledgers contain entries showing status of accounts of fiscal agents, including banks and Indian disbursing agents. The entries show accountable officer's name and title; date and amount of bond; where stationed; number and balance of previous account; dates, numbers, and amounts of warrants debited or credited; and final summary debits and credits on settlement of the account. Volume 7 includes accounts for banks that served as fiscal agents; volume 10 relates to accounts of banks in Oklahoma. The ledgers also include control accounts in the names of Indian tribes.

18. PUBLIC LAND LEDGERS: RECEIPTS. Mar. 1832-June 1909. 91 cm, 3 ft. 16 vols.

Arranged chronologically. Each volume is arranged by State. Only volumes A, B, D, E, I, and K-Q are indexed; they are indexed by initial letter of accountable officer's surname. There is no volume J.

Ledgers contain entries for proceeds of land sales and related expenses. The entries show accountable officer's name and title (usually, the accountable officer was a receiver of public moneys); location of Land Office; dates of surety bonds; cross-references to the control accounts; numbers and balances of previously settled accounts; and other debits and credits.

19. LAND AUXILIARY LEDGER. Nov. 1832-Dec. 1890. 5 cm, 2 in. 1 vol.

Arranged chronologically and thereunder by name of accountable officer in no particular order. Accounts showing an outstanding balance when the general ledgers were closed for the accounting period were transferred to the auxiliary ledger. Indexed by initial letter of accountable officer's surname.

Ledger contains entries needed to close the accounts of former Land Office officials. The entries show accountable officer's name and title (usually, the accountable officer was a receiver of public moneys); location of Land Office; date of surety bond; dates, numbers, and amounts of warrants charged to him; numbers and balances of settled accounts; and debits and credits needed to close the account.

20. INTERNAL REVENUE LEDGERS: FISCAL OFFICERS. July 1865-Apr. 1902. 1.5 m, 5 ft. 21 vols.

Arranged chronologically. Volumes 1-14 are arranged by type of account or alphabetically by initial letter of accountable officer's surname. Volumes 15-21 are arranged alphabetically by State. Only volumes 4-21 are indexed; they are indexed by initial letter of accountable officer's surname. The index to volume 4 is bound separately. Volumes 6 and 8 have separately bound indexes in addition to the indexes within these two volumes.

Ledgers contain entries showing status of accounts of Internal Revenue collectors and of other disbursing agents for the Internal Revenue Service. The entries show accountable officer's name and title, where stationed, date of surety bond, type of expenditure or title of appropriation account, cross-references to the control accounts, numbers and balances of settled accounts, and other debits and credits.

21.   INTERNAL REVENUE AUXILIARY LEDGERS: FISCAL OFFICERS. ca. 1871-June 1905. 8 cm, 3 in. 1 vol.

Arranged chronologically and thereunder by name of accountable officer in no particular order. Accounts showing an outstanding balance when the general ledgers were closed for the accounting period were transferred to the auxiliary ledger.

Ledger contains entries needed to close the accounts of former Internal Revenue collectors and disbursing agents. The entries show former accountable officer's name and title; date of surety bond; where stationed; titles of appropriation accounts from which accountable officer disbursed funds; balances carried forward from ledger accounts described in entry 20; dates, numbers, and balances of settled accounts; dates, numbers, and amounts of warrants charged to accountable officer; and debits and credits needed to close the account.

22.   INTERNAL REVENUE LEDGERS: RECEIPTS. July 1875-June 1905. 1.2 m, 4 ft. 18 vols.

Arranged chronologically. Volumes 1-15 are arranged by type of account and thereunder mainly geographically by district. Volumes 16-18 are arranged alphabetically by State. Beginning with volume 7, the ledgers include accounts of the Commissioner of Internal Revenue and other headquarters officers. Volume 1 has an index only to the accounts that are not in geographical order; volumes 3-18 are each indexed by initial letter of accountable officer's surname. Volume 2 is not indexed.

Ledgers contain entries showing status of accounts of collectors and other officials for moneys received and related expenditures. The entries show accountable officer's name and district; date of surety bond; number and period of account; debits for assessments and stamps; credits for deposits, taxes abated, and discounts on stamps; and balance carried to next account.

23.   INTERNAL REVENUE AUXILIARY LEDGER: RECEIPTS. ca. 1866-June 1903. 5 cm, 2 in. 1 vol.

Arranged chronologically and thereunder by name of accountable officer in no particular order. Accounts showing an outstanding balance when the general ledgers were closed for the accounting period were transferred to the auxiliary ledger.

Ledger contains entries needed to close accounts of former Internal Revenue collectors. The entries show accountable officer's name and title, district where he was stationed, date of surety bond, balance from Internal Revenue ledgers; receipts (entry 22); numbers and balances of settled accounts, and debits and credits needed to close the account.

24.   JUDICIARY LEDGERS. July 1870-June 1907. 2.1 m, 7 ft. 30 vols.

Arranged chronologically. Entries in each volume are arranged by type of account and thereunder by initial letter of accountable officer's surname in volume 1, and alphabetically by State in volumes 2-30. Volumes 2-30 are each indexed by initial letter of officer's surname.

Ledgers contain entries of accounts of disbursing officers of the Justice Department and of accounts of accountable officers in States and Territories. The entries show accountable officer's name and title; where stationed; date of surety bond; type of expense; balance carried forward from Interior civil ledgers (entry 14, judicial expenses before July 1870 were included in that series of ledgers); cross-references to the control accounts (for volumes 1-17); numbers and balances of previously settled accounts; dates, numbers, and amounts of warrants; and debits and credits.

25.   JUDICIARY AUXILIARY LEDGERS: FISCAL OFFICERS. ca. 1874-Apr. 1909. 13 cm, 5 in. 2 vols.

Arranged chronologically and thereunder by name of accountable officer in no particular order. Accounts showing an outstanding balance when the general ledgers were closed for the accounting period were transferred to the auxiliary ledgers.

Ledgers contain entries needed to close the accounts of former judicial officers. The entries show accountable officer's name and title; where he had been stationed; date of surety bond; title of appropriation accounts from which funds were disbursed by him; balances carried forward from Interior civil ledgers (entry 14) or judiciary ledgers (entry 24): numbers, dates, and balances of accounts; and debits and credits needed to close the account.

26.   JUDICIARY EMOLUMENT LEDGERS. Dec. 1842-Dec. 1907. 30 cm, 1 ft. 5 vols.

Arranged chronologically. Each volume is arranged by type of official and thereunder alphabetically by State. Each volume in indexed by initial letter of accountable officer's surname.

Ledgers contain entries showing status of accounts for moneys due marshals, attorneys, and clerks for their services. The entries show accountable officer's name, title, and judicial district; debits and credits, including numbers and balances of settled accounts and warrant numbers and balances; and remaining balances carried to subsequent accounts. The debit entries were usually for fees, gross amount of emoluments, and balances owed from previous accounts; the credit entries were usually for maximum allowable compensation, disbursements, commissions, and credit balances from previous accounts.

27.   JUDICIARY AUXILIARY LEDGERS: COMMISSIONERS AND CLERKS. Mar. 1898-June 1901. 8 cm, 3 in. 1 vol.

Arranged chronologically and thereunder by name of accountable officer in no particular order. Accounts showing an outstanding balance when the general ledgers were closed for the accounting period were transferred to the auxiliary ledger.

Ledger contains entries needed to close the accounts of former commissioners of courts and clerks of courts. The entries show accountable officer's name and title, where stationed, title of appropriation account from which funds were disbursed by him, account numbers and balances debited, warrant numbers and amounts credited, and other entries needed to close the account.

28.   PUBLIC DEBT LEDGERS: FISCAL OFFICERS. July 1870-Jan. 1923. 61 cm, 2 ft. 9 vols.

Arranged chronologically. Each volume is arranged alphabetically by initial letter of disbursing officer's surname and thereunder by type of account. Volumes 5-7 and 10 are indexed by initial letter of officer's surname. The other volumes are not indexed.

Ledgers contain entries showing status of accounts of disbursing officers (usually the U.S. Treasurer or an Assistant Treasurer at a major city) for paying interest on the public debt or redemption of the debt. The entries also show officer's name and title, description of the securities and types of transactions, numbers of settled accounts, dates and amounts of warrants debited or credited, and balances carried forward to subsequent accounts.

29.   MISCELLANEOUS LEDGERS: RECEIPTS. ca. 1882-June 1907. 30 cm, 1 ft. 5 vols.

Arranged by year and thereunder by accountable officer's name. Each volume is indexed by initial letter of accountable officer's surname.

Ledgers contain entries showing miscellaneous receipts paid into the U.S. Treasury by accountable officers. The entries show accountable officer's name and title; where stationed; date of surety bond; title of appropriation account to be credited; dates, amounts, and sources of receipts; numbers of settled accounts in which reported; and dates, numbers, and amounts of warrants by which the moneys were covered into the Treasury. Accountable officers included customs officials, custodians of public buildings, U.S. Shipping Commissioners, collectors of taxes in the District of Columbia and Superintendents of U.S. mints and assay offices. Sources of receipts include sale and rental of Government property and fees collected for various purposes. This series has the following spine titles: "Miscellaneous Ledger;" "Miscellaneous Receipts Ledger;" "Miscellaneous Ledger Receipts;" "Miscellaneous Ledger Receipts Unclassified."

30.   MISCELLANEOUS AUXILIARY LEDGERS: RECEIPTS. Jan. 1840-June 1900. 13 cm, 5 in. 2 vols.

Arranged chronologically and thereunder by name of accountable officer in no particular order. Accounts showing an outstanding balance when the general ledgers were closed for the accounting period were transferred to the auxiliary ledger.

Ledgers contain entries needed to close the accounts of former disbursing officers. The entries show the former accountable officer's name, title, duty station, and date of surety bond; type of account; balance carried forward from customs emolument ledgers (entry 9), miscellaneous receipt ledgers (entry 29), and captured and abandoned property ledgers; numbers, dates, and balances of settled accounts; and debits and credits needed to close the account. Most of the accountable officers were marshals, attorneys, receivers of public moneys, and customs officials.

Journals and Related Records

31.   WASTE BOOKS. Apr. 16, 1776-Dec. 31, 1786. 30 cm, 1 ft. 4 vols. and 2 boxes.

Arranged chronologically and identified as volumes A-F.

Waste books, blotters (entry 32), and daybooks (entry 33) were widely used in the early accounting system of the Government for preliminary posting of financial transactions.

Entries in the waste books were normally posted in the general Treasury ledgers (entry 2) and the journals (entry 34). The entries show dates and explanations of the transactions, names of persons or titles of appropriations, and amounts. Typical transactions included payments to contractors; reimbursements to the Paymaster of the Board of Ordnance for disbursements for ordnance stores; payments of warrants drawn on the Treasurer of the United States; and issues and redemptions of bills of exchange. These volumes are reproduced on rolls 1-3 of NARA Microfilm Publication M1014, Central Treasury Records of the Continental and Confederation Governments, 1776-1789. Waste Book F, which is in box 2, is contained in the same volume as part of Journal D (Entry 34). Waste Book A is on the Pre-Federal List as item 2; Waste Book F is item 7; Journal D (Part) is item 11.

32.   BLOTTERS. Jan. 15, 1782-Sept. 4, 1810. 61 cm, 2 ft. 17 vols.

Arranged chronologically and numbered 1-17. There are gaps in the date span of these records; the actual dates covered are: Jan. 15-Oct. 30, 1782; Dec. 10, 1782-Nov. 19, 1802; Dec. 10, 1805-Sept. 4, 1810.

Blotters, waste books (entry 31), and daybooks (entry 33) were widely used in the early accounting system of the Government for preliminary posting of financial transactions. Entries in the blotters were made daily and normally posted in the general Treasury ledgers (entry 2) and the L journals (entry 34). The entries show dates and explanations of the transactions, names of persons or titles of appropriations, and amounts.

Typical transactions included payment to French merchants for furnishing medicines and clothing; payment of warrants drawn on the Treasurer of the United States; payment of salaries and expenses of Commissioners for settling accounts between the United States and individual States; and issue of bills of exchange.

These volumes are reproduced on rolls 4-11 of NARA Microfilm Publication M1014, Central Treasury Records of the Continental and Confederation Governments, 1776-1789.

33.   DAYBOOKS. Sept. 13, 1789-Sept. 29, 1894. 9.1 m, 30 ft. 110 vols.

Arranged chronologically and numbered 1-114. Volumes 98-104 are each bound in two parts, and volumes 78-107 are identified as "Treasury Journals." There are gaps in the date span of these records; the actual dates covered are: Sept. 13, 1789-Oct. 18, 1792; Mar. 5, 1793-Sept. 29, 1894. The following volumes are missing: 4, 14, 16, 33.

Daybooks, waste books (entry 31), and blotters (entry 32) were widely used in the early accounting system of the Government for preliminary posting of financial transactions. Unlike the former two, the use of daybooks continued until modern times.

Entries in the daybooks were made daily and normally posted in the general Treasury ledgers (entry 2) and the journals (entry 34). The entries show dates and explanations of transactions, names of persons or titles of appropriations, and amounts. Warrant numbers are also frequently shown. Typical transactions included payment of salaries to Government officials, payments to the U.S. Treasurer for amounts of warrants drawn in his favor on collectors of revenue, payments for Treasury notes redeemed, repayments for land erroneously sold, and payments of expenses of marshals, diplomatic and consular officials, and collectors of customs acting as disbursing agents for lighthouses.

Some volumes are reproduced on NARA Microfilm Publication T964, Day Book of the Register's Office of the Treasury, 1789-91.

34.   JOURNALS. Apr. 16, 1776-May 3, 1799. 61 cm, 2 ft. 5 vols. and 2 boxes.

Arranged chronologically and identified as volumes A-D, I, and K. The pages of the journals are numbered consecutively throughout the series. Parts of journal D are bound with journal C and with waste book F.

Daily records of transactions involving the Treasury Department, frequently compiled from waste books (entry 31) and blotters (entry 32) and usually posted in general Treasury ledgers (entry 2). The entries show dates and explanations of transactions, names of persons or titles of appropriations, and amounts. Typical transactions included payments of warrants drawn on the Treasurer, payments to contractors, and payments to military officers. The part of Journal D that is in box 2 is contained in the same volume as Waste Book F (Entry 31). Journal D is on the Pre-Federal List as item 11.

35.   CUSTOMS JOURNALS. July 6, 1849-Aug. 25, 1896. 4.3 m, 14 ft. 43 vols.

Arranged chronologically and identified as volumes 1-39. The last two volumes are again identified as volumes 1 and 2, respectively. Volumes 35 and 36 are each bound in two parts.

Journals contain entries showing dates and explanations of transactions, ledger references (entry 5), names of persons or titles of appropriations, warrant numbers, account numbers (entry 347), and amounts. Typical transactions included warrants and advances to collectors of customs as disbursing agents for lighthouses and marine hospitals; compensation of collectors; refund of duties erroneously exacted; compensation for expenses of collecting the revenue from customs; and warrants in favor of the Treasurer drawn on collectors of customs.

For earlier transactions, see daybooks (entry 33).

36.   DIPLOMATIC JOURNALS. July 1, 1862-Mar. 12, 1894. 4.0 m, 13 ft. 37 vols.

Arranged chronologically and identified as volumes 1-26. Volumes 16-26 are each bound in two parts.

Journals contain entries showing dates and explanations of transactions, diplomatic ledger references (entry 11), names of persons or titles of accounts, warrant numbers, and amounts. Typically transactions included payment of fees and salaries of diplomatic and consular officers and fees for relief of destitute seamen.

For earlier transactions, see daybooks (entry 33).

37.   INTERIOR CIVIL JOURNALS. Sept. 14, 1849-Sept. 29, 1894.2.1 m, 7 ft. 25 vols.

Arranged chronologically.

Journals contain entries showing dates and explanations of transactions, ledger references (entry 14), names of persons or titles of appropriations concerned, warrant numbers, account numbers (entries 115 and 347), and amounts. Typical transactions included advances to Receivers of Public Moneys and to disbursing clerks for the Department of Interior; warrants for salaries and contingent expenses of land offices; and expenses of charitable institutions in the District of Columbia.

For earlier transactions, see daybooks (entry 33).

38.   INTERNAL REVENUE JOURNALS. July 3, 1865-Sept. 29, 1894. 2.1 m, 7 ft. 23 vols.

Arranged chronologically and numbered 1-22. Volume 21 is bound in two parts.

Journals contain entries showing dates and explanations of transactions; names, titles, duty stations, and dates of surety bonds of accountable officers; Internal Revenue ledger references (entry 20); titles of appropriations; warrant numbers; and account numbers and amounts.

Typical transactions included payments for salaries and expenses, redemption of revenue stamps, and payment of drawbacks. For earlier transactions, see daybooks (entry 33).

39.   JUDICIARY JOURNALS. July 2, 1870-Sept. 29, 1894. 1.5 m, 5 ft. 17 vols.

Arranged chronologically.

Journals contain entries showing dates and explanations of transactions; names, titles, duty stations, and dates of bond of accountable officers; judiciary ledger references (entry 24); titles of appropriations; account numbers; warrant numbers; and amounts. Typical transactions included payments to marshals and clerks for fees and expenses, advances to disbursing clerks of the Department of Justice for expenditures, and warrant on the Treasurer for moneys due judicial officials in settlement of their accounts.

For earlier transactions, see daybooks (entry 33).

40.   PUBLIC DEBT JOURNALS. July 6, 1870-Sept. 29, 1894. 25 cm, 10 in. 3 vols.

Arranged chronologically.

Journals contain entries showing dates and explanations of transactions, Public Debt ledger references (entry 28), names and titles of accountable officers, and duty stations (if Assistant Treasurers), account numbers (entry 347), and amounts. Typical transactions included payment of interest on bonds, redemption of bonds, redemption of refund certificates, redemption of Oregon War Debt, and interest on Central Pacific and other railroad stock.

For earlier transactions, see daybooks (entry 33).

Other Records

41.   ABSTRACT OF RECEIPTS AND EXPENDITURES OF THE UNITED STATES, 1789-1883. n.d. 5 cm, 2 in. 1 vol.

In two major sections: (1) Receipts, 1789-1849 and 1850-74, showing source of funds, total received from each source for each year, and aggregate receipts for the year. Included is a recapitulation of "unavailable" funds in banks for the years 1832, 1837, 1839, 1840, 1842, 1845, and 1847. (2) Expenditures of the United States on account of the Civil List, arranged by

Department or type of expenditure and thereunder by title of appropriation account, 1789-1848, showing the year, object of disbursement, and total amount disbursed for the year for that purpose. The dates vary from those shown above for the following headings: expenditures on account of intercourse with foreign nations, 1789-1850; expenditures under direction of the War Department, 1789-1849; expenditures under the War Department—Indian Department, 1789-1883; and expenditures under the Navy Department, 1801-48. The years 1789-91 are in all cases grouped together as one entry.

42.   REPORTS MADE BY THE REGISTER (RECEIPTS AND STATEMENTS). June 16, 1829-Apr. 2, 1860. 8 cm, 3 in. 1 vol.

Arranged chronologically. Pages 438-446, identified as an "index," contain a listing of the page numbers on which reports appear and the subjects of the reports.

Fair copies of reports by the Register, some made at the request of the Secretary of the Treasury or Members of Congress, on such subjects as the import and export of gold and silver bullion and specie; receipts from duties on imports, from tonnage tax on vessels, and from moneys collected for the marine hospitals; general reports on activities of the Register's Office; balances of Treasury notes outstanding at specified times; and summaries of appropriations and expenditures for various purposes.

43.   INDEX TO ABSTRACTS OF EXPENDITURES OF THE UNITED STATES, 1791-1889. n.d. 15 cm, 6 in. 3 vols.

Arranged alphabetically by keyword of appropriation title.

Index to abstracts of expenditures in entry 44 showing appropriation title and page number. Volume 1 indexes abstracts of expenditures for the Treasury Department; volume 2 indexes abstracts of expenditures for the War and Navy Departments; and volume 3 indexes abstracts of miscellaneous expenditures.

44.   ABSTRACTS OF EXPENDITURES OF THE UNITED STATES, 1791-1889. n.d. 30 cm, 1 ft. 6 vols.

Arranged generally by Department and thereunder by appropriation title. Each volume contains an index arranged by type of expenditure.

Abstracts of expenditures showing appropriation title, total expenditures from each appropriation by year, and repayments to the appropriation. Volumes 1 and 2 are for expenditures for the Treasury Department; volumes 3 and 4 are for expenditures for the War and Navy Departments; and two volumes (each identified as "Volume 5") are for miscellaneous expenditures. The dates vary with the particular appropriation title concerned.

For a keyword index, see entry 43.

45.   QUARTERLY REPORTS ON COMMERCE AND NAVIGATION. Dec. 31, 1852-Jan. 1, 1853. 5 cm, 2 in. 1 box.

Arranged alphabetically by customs district and thereunder by type of information.

Quarterly reports on commerce and navigation, submitted to the Register of the Treasury by collectors of customs as required by section 13 of an act of February 10, 1820 (3 Stat. 541). This particular group of reports was submitted by the collectors of customs in the Districts of Buffalo Creek, Champlain, Cuyahoga, Oswego, Presque Isle, Sacketts Harbor, and Sandusky. The reports illustrate the type of information submitted to enable the Register to make annual reports to Congress on the commerce and navigation of the United States. Many of the 1852 reports include summary information on trade with Canadian ports.

NOTE, COUPON, CURRENCY, AND FILES DIVISION

The Note, Coupon, Currency, and Files Division was established in July 1884 by the consolidation of the Note and Coupon Division (established June 30, 1864) with the Note and Fractional Currency Division (established in July 1866). Even though the word "files" was not added to the title until 1893, the Division had custody of the files and archives of the Register's Office from July 1884. The Division's functions included examining and filing paid interest checks and coupons; canceling and destroying currency; receiving and filing settled accounts, warrants, and revenue stampbooks; and copying and certifying delinquent accounts for suit.

Records Relating to Destruction of Securities

46.   REGISTERS OF SECURITIES REDEEMED AND DESTROYED. Sept. 20, 1873-Feb. 12, 1886. 15 cm, 6 in. 4 vols.

Arranged by type of security.

Registers contain entries that show account number, type of security, value, and date redeemed or destroyed. The major types of securities included in these volumes are silver certificates, July 16, 1878- July 25, 1881; legal tender notes, October 9, 1873-February 12, 1886; and demand notes, September 20, 1873-February 8, 1886. One register in the series is for miscellaneous obligations, such as coil coupons, interest checks, and stocks redeemed, ca. 1880-85.

Warrants

A warrant is an authorization for the disbursement of moneys from the U.S. Treasury or for paying moneys into the Treasury. Warrants were signed by the Secretary of the Treasury and countersigned by the Register, the Comptroller, or a Department head (such as the Secretary of War). Four main categories of warrants are described in this inventory; settlement warrants (also known as pay warrants), accountable warrants, repay warrants, and covering warrants. The first two types are instructions to authorize the Treasurer to disburse funds from the Treasury for specified purposes; the other two types are orders to the persons on whom they are drawn to deposit funds to the credit of the U.S. Treasurer.

47.   REGISTER'S STATEMENTS OF WARRANTS ON THE TREASURER. Jan. 1, 1797-Jan. 30, 1798. 1 cm, 1/2 in. 1 vol.

Arranged chronologically.

Quarterly abstract showing for each quarter the warrant number, to whom payable, title of appropriation to be charged, and amount of the warrant. A recapitulation at the end of each 3-month period shows the total value of warrants recorded for the quarter for each appropriation.

48.   WARRANTS. Mar. 1801-Dec. 1921. 256.0 m, 840 ft. 276 boxes.

Arranged by year, thereunder by Department, thereunder by type of warrant, and thereunder by warrant number.

These warrants are subdivided into three chronological periods: (1) for the period 1801-52, the series consists of all warrants regardless of type; (2) for the period 1853-94, the series consists of all warrants except pay warrants and accountable warrants of the following classes: customs, internal revenue, judiciary, Navy, States (taxes), pensions, public debt, quarterly salaries, and war; (3) for the period 1895-1921, the series consists only of warrants relating to Indians and of a small group of warrants selected for their historical interest.

48A.   WARRANTS. 1801-1921. 2,404.75 ft. 4 vols. and 4820 boxes.

This series consists of one group of volumes numbered 1-4 and four groups of boxes numbered 1-507, 1-2, 1-1388, and 1-2923. The first group has boxes numbered 46A & 136A. The fourth group has 14 alpha boxes: 2A, 4A, 4B, 243A, 273A, 274A, 286A, 379A, 1721A, 2328A, 2314A, 2470A, 2549A, and 2856A.

OFFICE OF THE FIRST COMPTROLLER

The Office of the First Comptroller was created by an act of September 2, 1789 (1 Stat. 65), which established the Treasury Department. The First Comptroller's main functions were to superintend the adjustment of all accounts and claims, examine the accounts and claims settled by the Auditor, certify the balances to the Register, countersign warrants drawn by the Secretary of the Treasury, and establish regulations for the accountability of public moneys and the forms in which accounts were to be presented. The First Comptroller was also responsible for directing the filing of suits against delinquent officers.

The duties of the First Comptroller were changed by an act of March 3, 1817 (2 Stat, 366), which created the office of the Second Comptroller to relieve the First Comptroller of the responsibility for settling military accounts and claims. The duties of the First Comptroller were further modified by an act of March 3, 1849 (9 Stat. 366), which transferred functions relating to receipts and expenditures for collecting customs revenues to the Office of the Commissioner of Customs. An act of July 1, 1894 (28 Stat. 205), abolished the offices of the Second Comptroller and Commissioner of Customs and returned their functions to the First Comptroller, who was then renamed Comptroller of the Treasury.

Very little information is available about the internal organization of the First Comptroller's Office. A divisional structure within the Office was authorized by Congress in an appropriation act of August 15, 1876 (19 Stat. 149), which provided funds specifically, for the first time, for "four chiefs of divisions." An 1880 history of the Treasury Department mentions the existence of 14 branches to perform the functions of the Office. The units for which records are described in this inventory, termed "divisions" for consistency of reference, are the Customs Division, the District of Columbia Division, the Division of Foreign Intercourse, the Division of Internal Revenue Accounts, the Division of Judiciary Accounts, the Public Debt Division, the Division of Public Lands, the Division of Territorial Accounts, the Division of Miscellaneous Accounts, and the Division of Bonds, Contracts, and Powers of Attorney.

The most significant records of the Comptroller's Office are letters sent, 1791-1895, and letters received, 1789-1894 (many now described as records of the Commissioner of Customs, where they were transferred in 1849) and contracts and related registers, 1803-1926. Military contracts before 1894 are described with records of the Second Comptroller.

A list of names of First Comptrollers and dates of service appears in Appendix 2.

GENERAL RECORDS

Correspondence

49.   REGISTERS OF OFFICIAL AND MISCELLANEOUS LETTERS RECEIVED. July 1, 1850-Dec. 29, 1915. 3.4 m, 11 ft. 41 vols.

Arranged chronologically. Entries in each volume are arranged alphabetically by initial letter of writer's surname or title and thereunder chronologically.

Registers contain entries that show writer's name or title, date received, date of letter, and subject. Most letters relate to accounts, claims, or personnel actions. Many of the letters received by the First Comptroller from other Government officials are entered in these registers. The letters are described in entries, 52-58, 78-80, 82, 83, 95-97, 105, and 128.

50.   REGISTER OF LETTERS AND ACCOUNTS RECEIVED. Jan. 2, 1866-Sept. 6, 1868. 1 cm, 1/2 in. 1 vol.

Arranged chronologically.

Register contains entries that show date received, writer's name or title, and subject of letter or number of account. Most letters were from the Secretary of the Treasury; most accounts were received from the First Auditor and are among customs accounts and claims (entry 294) and miscellaneous customs accounts (entry 347).

51.   LETTERS RECEIVED FROM MEMBERS OF CONGRESS. Feb. 15, 1804-May 12, 1838. 15 cm, 6 in. 2 vols.

Arranged chronologically. An index in each volume is arranged alphabetically by initial letter of writer's surname.

Letters transmitting requests from constituents for information or requesting data for use by congressional committees.

52.   LETTERS RECEIVED FROM THE SECRETARY OF THE TREASURY. Feb. 2, 1801- Nov. 7, 1856. 61 cm, 2 ft. 7 vols.

Arranged chronologically. Each of the first five volumes (1801-40) has an index arranged alphabetically by subject or writer's surname. The last two volumes are not indexed.

Letters, some with enclosures, requesting information on accounts and claims or on the interpretation of customs regulations. Copies of the Comptroller's replies are filed with some of the letters. Some of these letters are entered in the registers described in entry 49.

53.   LETTERS RECEIVED FROM THE SECRETARIES OF WAR AND NAVY. July 17, 1834 - July 14, 1856. 5 cm, 2 in. 1 vol.

Arranged by office of origin and thereunder chronologically.

Letters from the Secretary of War, July 17, 1834-July 14, 1856, and from the Secretary of the Navy, July 31, 1834-June 23, 1853, relating primarily to balances of funds available for transfer to the surplus fund.

Included is a draft of a supplemental regulation, approved July 17, 1834, for carrying the Chickasaw Treaty into effect. Some of these letters are entered in the registers described in entry 49.

54.   LETTERS RECEIVED FROM THE POSTMASTER GENERAL. Sept. 9, 1825-Apr. 7, 1856. 4 cm, 1 in. 1 vol.

Arranged chronologically.

Letters relating chiefly to the need for additional funds for operating expenses and transmitting proposals for supplies and services needed by the Post Office Department. Accounts for contingent expenses of the Department were settled by the Fifth Auditor and are among his miscellaneous accounts and claims (entry 831). Some of these letters are entered in the registers described in entry 49.

55.   LETTERS RECEIVED FROM THE REGISTER AND THE COMMISSIONER OF CUSTOMS. Sept. 12, 1833-Dec. 22, 1856. 5 cm, 2 in. 1 vol.

Arranged by office of origin and thereunder chronologically.

Letters from the Register of the Treasury, September 12, 1833 - December 13, 1856, and from the Commissioner of Customs, November 2, 1853 - December 22, 1856. Letters from the Register typically transmit copies of documents or information requested by the Comptroller or request decisions on procedural matters, such as computation of interest on the public debt.

Most letters from the Commissioner of Customs are requests for copies of surety bonds of former customs officers. Some of these letters are entered in the registers described in entry 49.

56.   LETTERS RECEIVED FROM OTHER GOVERNMENT OFFICIALS. Apr. 28, 1834 - Dec. 26, 1856. 5 cm, 2 in. 1 vol.

Arranged by office of origin in the order listed below and thereunder chronologically.

Letters from the Commissioner of Patents, November 30, 1850 - December 26, 1856; from the Treasurer, April 20, 1837-December 18, 1856; from the Commissioner of the General Land Office, March 22, 1831-October 30, 1856; from the Commissioner of Indian Affairs, January 28, 1851-February 28, 1853; and from the Second Comptroller, April 28, 1834-April 25, 1853. Most letters relate to the settlement of accounts and claims and are typically routine inquiries. Some of these letters are entered in the registers described in entry 49.

57.   LETTERS RECEIVED FROM THE AUDITORS AND FROM THE ACCOUNTANT FOR THE WAR DEPARTMENT. May 11, 1801-Dec. 30, 1856. 30 cm, 1 ft. 5 vols.

Arranged by office of origin and thereunder chronologically. The volume of letters from the Accountant for the War Department is indexed alphabetically by name of person concerned in the letter.

Letters from the First Auditor, October 17, 1801-December 29, 1856; from the Accountant for the War Department, May 11, 1801-December 29, 1871; from the Second Auditor, October 14, 1834-December 30, 1856; from the Third Auditor, May 26, 1817-March 4, 1856; from the Fourth Auditor, April 4, 1834-October 16, 1855; from the Fifth Auditor, October 1, 1832-April 15, 1856; and from the Sixth Auditor, June 14, 1836-May 5, 1856. The letters chiefly concern preparation of lists of delinquent officials, administrative problems, and settlements of claims and appeals. Some of these letters are entered in the registers described in entry 49. The titles vary on each volume.

58.   MISCELLANEOUS LETTERS RECEIVED. July 21, 1810-June 28, 1912. 38.7 m, 127 ft. 37 vols. and 109 boxes.

Arranged in three subseries as follows: (1) letters received March 21 1839-January 25, 1858 (26 vols.), arranged by initial letter of writer's surname and thereunder chronologically; (2) letters received, June 21, 1878-December 30, 1892 (11 vols.), arranged chronologically; (3) unbound letters received, July 21, 1810-June 28, 1912, arranged chronologically.

The first two volumes of subseries 1 and each volume of subseries 2 have an index arranged alphabetically by initial letter of writer's surname or title. The records in subseries 3 are not indexed.

Letters from claimants, Government officials, and accountable officers (many including petitions and other enclosures of earlier date), typically concerning settlement of accounts and claims, pay of witnesses in legal cases, use of appropriated funds, and other matters relating to the functions of the Comptroller. Some of these letters are entered in the registers described in entry 49. Replies to some of these letters are among miscellaneous letters sent (entry 61).

59.   REGISTERS OF LETTERS SENT. Aug. 20, 1850-Dec. 18, 1880. 61 cm, 2 ft. 10 vols.

Arranged chronologically. Entries in each volume are arranged alphabetically by initial letter of title or surname of addressee and thereunder chronologically.

Registers contain entries that show to whom addressed, date of letter, and subject of letter or type and number of account. Some entries are under the general heading "disbursing agent" and cross-referenced to the names of the individual disbursing agents addressed. The letters and accounts relate chiefly to diplomatic, judicial, and public building expenses. Some of the letters entered in these registers are among letters sent to accountable officers (entry 60) and miscellaneous letters sent (entry 61). Some of the accounts are among the First Auditor's miscellaneous Treasury accounts (entry 347).

60.   LETTERS SENT TO ACCOUNTABLE OFFICERS. Oct. 16, 1839-June 30, 1871. 61 cm, 2 ft.
       8 vols.

            Arranged chronologically. Volumes 1 (Oct. 16, 1839-Apr. 14, 1841), 3 (Jan. 2-May 31,
       1869), and 6-8 (Jan. 3, 1870-June 30, 1871) have an index arranged by initial letter of surname or
       title of addressee. There are gaps in the date span of these records; the actual dates covered
       are: Oct. 16, 1839-Apr. 14, 1841; Sept. 13-Nov. 15, 1867; Jan. 2, 1869-June 30, 1871.
            Fair copies of letters to customs, diplomatic, and judicial officers; to cashiers of deposit
       banks; and to treasurers of branch mints relating mainly to settlement of their accounts. Some of
       these letters are entered in the registers described in entry 59. Some of the accounts are among
       the First Auditor's miscellaneous Treasury accounts (entry 347) and among the Fifth Auditor's
       miscellaneous accounts (entry 833).

60A.   LETTERS SENT, Aug. 16, 1878-June 1921. 92 vols.

            Vols. numbered 1-14, 1-58, 59A-B, 60A-C, 61-75. Volumes 39-75 read "Press Copies of
       Letters Sent."

61.   MISCELLANEOUS LETTERS SENT. Mar. 19, 1802-June 30, 1868. 5.5 m, 24 ft. 95 vols.

            Arranged chronologically. Each volume has an index arranged alphabetically by
       initial letter of surname or title of addressee.
            Fair copies of letters to auditors, claimants, accountable officers, and other Government
       officials chiefly in response to the letters received by the First Comptroller and the
       Commissioner of Customs described in entries 58 and 264. The letters relate to the settlement of
       accounts and claims, and many are cited in the index to decisions relating to accounts (entry 65).
       Some of these letters are entered in the registers described f in entry 59.

62.   MISCELLANEOUS LETTERS SENT. June 1, 1868-Jan. 10, 1895. 7.3 m, 24 ft. 77 boxes.

            Arranged chronologically. Each volume, except the volume for September and October
       1893, has an indexed arranged alphabetically by initial letter of surname of addressee.
            Press copies of letters to auditors and other Government officials, accountable officers,
       and claimants relating to the final settlement of a variety of accounts and claims, most of
       which had been previously adjusted by the auditors. Some of these letters are entered in the
       registers described in entry 59.
            For earlier letters in this series, see entry 61.

62A.   LETTERS SENT BY THE DEPUTY COMPTROLLER, Mar. 27, 1882-Dec. 1894. 3 vols.

                        Records Relating to Reports, Decisions, and Rulings

63.   INDEX TO THE FIRST COMPTROLLER'S REPORTS. Oct. 17, 1849-Aug. 18, 1852. 1 cm,
       1/2 in. 1 vol.

            Arranged alphabetically by initial letter of keyword of subject.
            Index to volume 1 of the First Comptroller's reports described in entry 64. The index
       contains entries showing subject of report and a citation to the text of the report. Some of the
       subjects included are advances, appropriations, Mexican indemnity claims, and judicial and
       Territorial expenses.

64.   REPORTS BY THE FIRST COMPTROLLER. Oct. 17, 1849-Nov. 14, 1867. 30 cm, 1 ft.
       5 vols.

       Arranged chronologically. An index to volume 1 is described in entry 63. Each of the
other volumes has an index arranged alphabetically by initial letter of keyword of subject.
       Fair copies of reports to the Secretary of the Treasury, furnishing data requested for use
by congressional committees; copies of documents submitted as supplemental information; and
copies of annual reports, 1863-67, for use by the Secretary in preparing his Annual Report on the
State of the Finances.

65.   ABSTRACTS OF DECISIONS RELATING TO JUDICIAL AND MISCELLANEOUS
       ACCOUNTS. ca. 1832-1850. 3 cm, 1 in. 1 vol.

       Arranged alphabetically by initial letter of keyword of subject.
       The abstracts show the subject and a citation to the text of the decision. Some citations
are to volumes and pages in the miscellaneous letters sent (entry 61); others provide only a date
or a date and volume number of an unidentified record series.

66.   ABSTRACTS OF DECISIONS RELATING TO REVENUE ACCOUNTS. Apr. 21, 1819 -
       Apr. 5, 1834. 5 cm, 2 in. 1 vol.

       Arranged alphabetically by initial letter of keyword of subject.
       The abstracts show subject and a citation to the text of each decision as it appeared in
volumes 31-48 of letters sent to customs officers (entry 74). The rest of the volume consists of
abstracts of decisions of the Secretary of the Treasury on restricted commercial intercourse,
April 19, 1861-April 13, 1864, as recorded in volumes 1-6 of the letters sent relating to restricted
commercial intercourse (BE series), which is in General Records of the Department of the
Treasury, RG 56.

67.   MISCELLANEOUS DECISIONS. June 4, 1849-Mar. 17, 1868. 28 cm, 11 in. 5 vols.

       Arranged chronologically. Volumes 2-5 (Feb. 21, 1851-Mar. 17, 1868) have indexes
arranged alphabetically by initial letter of keyword of subject. Volume 1 is not indexed.
       Fair copies of reports on decisions on miscellaneous matters, such as interpretation of
laws and regulations on such subjects as fees allowed in legal cases; Territorial printing; extra
pay for employees; and Mexican War claims.

67A.   DRAFTS OF DECISION & DECISIONS, June 1, 1869-May 6, 1880. 1 vol.

68.   ABSTRACTS OF DECISIONS ON MILITARY AND INDIAN CLAIMS. 1874-1900.
       10 cm, 4 in. 3 vols.

       Arranged   alphabetically   by   subject.   Each   volume   has   an   index   arranged
alphabetically by initial letter of keyword of subject.
       The abstracts concern decisions by the First Comptroller on military pay and other
matters, April 1893-December 1900, and by the Second Comptroller on Indian claims, 1874-98.
The abstracts show subject, summary of the decision, and citation of sources. Some citations are
to decisions on back pay, bounty, and property loss, 1894-1904, described in entry 69.

68A.   INDEX TO DECISIONS, April 1904-June 30,1921. 15 boxes.

68B.   DECISIONS, FIRST COMPTROLLER BOWLER, Aug. 1893-Sept. 1894; DECISIONS,
       COMPTROLLER BOWLER, Oct. - Dec. 1894. 1 vol.

68C.   DECISIONS, Jan. 1,1895-June 30,1921. 98 vols. (There are 2 parts for vol. 45).

69.   DECISIONS ON CLAIMS FOR BACK PAY, BOUNTY, AND PROPERTY LOSS (LETTERS AND DECISIONS: BACK PAY, BOUNTY, ETC.). Apr. 2, 1895 - May 31, 1904. 1.2 m, 4 ft. 14 vols.

Arranged chronologically. Each volume, except for the period December 27, 1900-June 14, 1902, has an index arranged alphabetically by initial letter of surname of claimant and major subject.

Press copies of reports on decisions on back pay, bounty, and related matters usually sent to the Comptroller for decision as a result of disputes between claimants and the Second Auditor. Many of the letters concern whether a case should be reheard or an account or a claim reopened on the basis of additional evidence. Earlier letters on similar subjects are among the records of the Second Comptroller's Army Paymasters Division (entry 196). Some decisions are cited in the abstracts of decisions described in entry 68.

70.   DOCKET BOOK ON APPEALS. Jan. 4, 1895-Aug. 31, 1919. 13 cm, 5 in. 2 vols.

Arranged chronologically by date of appeal. Each volume has an index arranged alphabetically by initial letter of appellant's surname.

There are gaps in the date span of these records; the actual dates covered are: Jan. 4, 1895-Nov. 5, 1896; Jan 20, 1902-Aug. 31, 1919.

The docket books contain entries showing actions taken on appeals relating to civil matters, January 4, 1895-November 5, 1896, and relating to Indian and military matters, January 20, 1902-August 31, 1909. The entries show appellant's name, date of appeal, subject or account number, and record of action taken. Copies of reports on decisions on some of these military appeals are among reports on decisions on claims for back pay, bounty, and property loss (entry 69).

Other Records

71.   REGISTER OF CASES REPORTED FOR SUIT. Sept. 5, 1821-Nov. 25, 1874. 5 cm, 2 in. 1 vol.

Arranged chronologically. This volume has a partial index arranged alphabetically by initial letter of surname of debtor.

Register contains entries that show date reported, name of debtor, explanation, names of sureties (if any), amount due, and status of case.

Debtors included contractors for the Cumberland Road; diplomatic and consular officials; customs, Land Office, and judicial officers; depositories of public moneys; and superintendents of branch mints. The entries sometimes refer to letters sent to the Solicitor of the Treasury by the Comptroller relating to a case.

72.   REGISTER OF LETTERS AND CONTRACTS RECEIVED. 1872-90. 2 cm, 1 in. 1 box.

The register of letters is arranged chronologically; the register of contracts is arranged by Department and thereunder by type of article.

There are gaps in the date span of these records; the actual dates covered are: Jan. 12, 1872-Oct. 1882; 1887-90.

Register contains entries that show (for letters) date received, date of letter, writer's name and address, and subject and (for contracts) whether the articles were purchased for the State Department or the Post Office Department, type of article, name of contractor, explanation, and price. The letters relate primarily to consular, judicial, and Internal Revenue accounts, and the contracts are primarily for stationery and office supplies.

CUSTOMS DIVISION

The dates of establishment and discontinuance of the Customs Division have not been determined. The First Comptroller's Office approved customs accounts and claims audited by the First Auditor and heard appeals on the accounts and claims from 1789 until the establishment of the Office of Commissioner of Customs in 1849. These functions were returned to the Comptroller in October 1894 when the Office of the Commissioner of Customs was abolished.

Correspondence

73.   LETTERS RECEIVED FROM COLLECTORS OF CUSTOMS. Apr. 3, 1833-Aug. 10, 1840. 61 cm, 2 ft. 11 vols.

Arranged geographically by State and thereunder by customs district.

Letters transmitting accounts, requesting more money, and enclosing original documents containing oaths of office and lists of employees.

The dates of the letters vary with the particular customs district.

For similar earlier and later letters received, see letters received by the First Comptroller and Commissioner of Customs, entry 264; for replies to some of the letters, see miscellaneous letters sent to customs officers, entry 75.

74.   LETTERS SENT TO CUSTOMS OFFICERS (REVENUE LETTERS). Jan. 26, 1791-Dec. 26, 1846. 4.0 m, 13 ft. 64 vols.

Arranged chronologically. Each volume has an index arranged alphabetically by initial letter of surname of addressee.

Fair copies of letters to customs officers concerning settlement of accounts, regulations relating to importation of goods, and collection of duties. Some of the letters are to merchants or importers.

For related incoming letters, see letters received by the First Comptroller and the Commissioner of Customs, entry 265. Some letters are cited in the abstracts of decisions relating to revenue accounts, entry 66.

75.   MISCELLANEOUS LETTERS SENT TO CUSTOMS OFFICERS (REVENUE LETTERS ON ACCOUNTS). Apr. 28, 1818-May 30, 1849. 1.5 m, 5 ft. 28 vols.

Arranged chronologically. Each volume has an index arranged alphabetically by initial letter of surname of addressee.

Fair copies of letters to customs officers relating to their activities as superintendents and disbursing officers for lighthouses, marine hospitals, and revenue cutters. Some of these accounts are among the First Auditor's customs accounts and claims (entry 294) and miscellaneous Treasury accounts (entry 347). Some of these letters are replies to letters received from collectors of customs (entry 73).

For related letters, see miscellaneous letters sent (entry 61).

Other Records

76.   APPOINTMENT LETTERS. Oct. 3, 1829-June 26, 1841. 6 cm, 2 in. 1 vol.

Arranged chronologically. Indexed alphabetically by initial letter of appointed official's surname.

Fair copies of letters notifying customs officers of their appointment or reappointment and furnishing instructions on filing surety bonds and on settling their accounts and those of their predecessors.

77.　　　REGISTER OF CUSTOMS APPOINTMENTS. Jan. 1, 1842-Nov. 17, 1860. 3 1 in. 1 vol.

Arranged chronologically by date of commission.
Registers contains entries that show dates of commission and appointment; accountable officers name, title, and duty station; name of predecessor; amount of bond; and dates of bond and oath.

DISTRICT OF COLUMBIA DIVISION

The administrative history of the District of Columbia Division has not been determined. In the 1880s the division was one of four branches within the Foreign Intercourse Division and apparently became an independent Division sometime between July 1885 and June 1893. Accounts for expenses of the District of Columbia were settled in part by the First Auditor and in part by the Fifth Auditor. Final approval of the accounts was the main responsibility of the District of Columbia Division.

Correspondence

78.　　　LETTERS RECEIVED FROM COMMISSIONERS FOR THE DISTRICT OF COLUMBIA. Sept. 5, 1878-May 31, 1895. 30 cm, 1 ft.

Arranged chronologically.
Letters enclosing accounts and contracts, explaining the Commissioners estimates of funds needed for the expenses of the District, and requesting opinions on legal matters or enclosing copies of opinions of the District's Attorney General. Some letters are entered in the registers described in entry 49. Replies to these letters are in entries 79 and 80. Contracts and related registers are described in entries 144 and 145. Some of the accounts are among the First Auditor's miscellaneous Treasury accounts (entry 347).

79.　　　LETTERS SENT TO COMMISSIONERS FOR THE DISTRICT OF COLUMBIA. July 17, 1878-Jan. 31, 1883. 10 cm, 4 in. 2 vols.

Arranged chronologically.
Fair copies of letters to the Commissioners relating to the settlement of accounts for the District of Columbia, the interpretation of laws and regulations, and the filing of surety bonds by the Commissioner. Accounts and contracts for the District of Columbia are described in entries 347 and 145, respectively. Some letters are entered in the registers described in entries 49 and 59.
For additional letters sent, see entry 80; for letters from the Commissioners, see entry 78.

80.　　　LETTERS SENT TO COMMISSIONERS FOR THE DISTRICT OF COLUMBIA. July 17, 1878-Oct. 15, 1894. 91 cm, 3 ft. 12 vols.

Arranged chronologically. Each volume has an index arranged alphabetically by initial letter of surname of addressee.
Press copies of letters relating primarily to the settlement of accounts and claims for expenditures by the District of Columbia and for goods and services furnished for the District by contractors and others. Accounts and contracts for the District are described in entries 347 and 145, respectively. Some letters are entered in the registers described in entries 49 and 59.
For additional letters sent, see entry 79; for letters from the Commissioners, see entry 8.

DIVISION OF FOREIGN INTERCOURSE

Although not specifically named in the law, the Division of Foreign Intercourse apparently was one of the four divisions established in the Office of the First Comptroller by the appropriation act of August 15, 1876 (19 Stat. 149). The main functions of the Division, known at various times as the Diplomatic and Consular Division, were to review accounts for diplomatic and consular expenses that had been audited by the Fifth Auditor, to approve accounts arising from treaties and conventions with other countries, to file surety bonds of consular officials, to record requisitions for diplomatic and consular expenses, and to correspond with the accountable officers and the Secretary of State about the status of accounts.

Correspondence

81.   REGISTERS OF CONSULAR LETTERS RECEIVED. Jan. 3, 1872-June 24, 1895. 8 cm, 3 in. 3 vols.

The earlier volume is arranged alphabetically by initial letter of writer's surname and thereunder chronologically; the other volumes are arranged chronologically by date received. There are gaps in the date span of these records; the actual dates covered are: Jan. 3, 1872-Aug. 20, 1877; Dec. 2, 1885-June 24, 1895.

Registers contain entries that show writer's name and title, date of letter, date received, subject, and disposition. Most of the letters were referred to the Fifth Auditor or the Secretary of the Treasury's Division of Public Moneys; relatively few were noted as "answered" and some of those so noted are among diplomatic and consular letters received (entry 83).

82.   LETTERS RECEIVED FROM THE SECRETARY OF STATE. Aug. 23, 1826-July 7, 1856. 8 cm, 3 in. 1 vol.

Arranged chronologically.

Letters from the Secretary of State, either directly or by transmittal through the Secretary of the Treasury, concerning such matters as tonnage taxes on foreign ships, regulations relating to the documentation of ships, and surety bonds of consular officers. Some letters are entered in the registers described in entry 49.

83.   DIPLOMATIC AND CONSULAR LETTERS RECEIVED. May 31, 1832-Dec. 29, 1892. 4.9 m, 16 ft. 55 vols.

Arranged chronologically. Each volume has an index arranged alphabetically by initial letter of writer's surname.

Letters received from diplomatic and consular officials, the State Department, and bankers. Letters relate to settling accounts, paying drafts and bills of exchange, and furnishing information requested by the Comptroller. Three volumes are identified as containing "supplemental" letters and cover the period December 16, 1861-June 30, 1886. Some letters are entered in the registers described in entries 49 and 81.

For replies to some of these letters, see entries 87 and 88.

84.   LETTERS RECEIVED RELATING TO PAYMENT OF JUDGMENTS AWARDED BY THE COMMISSIONERS FOR THE ALABAMA CLAIMS. Jan. 17, 1886-Dec. 6, 1886. 13 cm, 5 in. 1 vol.

Arranged chronologically. Indexed alphabetically by initial letter of claimant's or writer's surname.

Mainly letters from attorneys for the claimants, frequently accompanied by powers of attorney or other legal documents.

For additional information on these awards, see abstract of awards for the Alabama claims (entry 851) and copies of audit reports on these awards (entry 852).

85.   LETTERS RECEIVED RELATING TO VALUE OF FOREIGN COINAGE. Oct. 28 1857 - Sept. 30, 1861. 8 cm, 3 in. 1 vol.

Arranged chronologically. Indexed both alphabetically by name of reporting official and by location of consulate.

Letters received from consular officials at the request of the Comptroller relating to the value of foreign coins. Also included is a published synopsis of the value of these coins prepared by the U.S. Mint in Philadelphia. Related records are in Records of the Bureau of the Mint, RG 104.

86.   REPORTS ON OPERATIONS OF CONSULATES. Aug. 26, 1870-Dec. 31, 1872. 23 cm, 9 in. 3 vols.

Arranged chronologically. Volumes 1 and 2 have indexes arranged alphabetically by surname of agent making the investigation.

Letters reporting on investigations conducted under the direction of the Secretary of the Treasury as required by an act of July 11, 1870. The letters include an evaluation of the staffs and general operations of the consulates. The investigations of consulates took place during the period August 26, 1870-October 30, 1872; volume 3 consists of the final report of the investigation, December 31, 1872, and includes a copy of a proposed law resulting from the investigation.

87.   DIPLOMATIC AND CONSULAR LETTERS SENT. July 1, 1868-Oct. 21, 1879. 1.5 m, 5 ft. 26 vols.

Arranged chronologically. Each volume has an index arranged alphabetically by initial letter of surname of addressee. There are gaps in the date span of these records; the actual dates covered are: July 1, 1868-Jan. 23, 1878; July 1-Oct. 21, 1879.

Fair copies of letters to the State Department and to diplomatic and consular officials relating primarily to problems arising in the settlement of their accounts and requesting additional information. The incoming letters to which these letters reply are described in entry 83. Some letters are entered in the registers described in entry 59.

For a continuation of these letters, see entry 88.

88.   DIPLOMATIC AND CONSULAR LETTERS SENT. Nov. 1, 1877-July 31, 1895. 6.1 m, 20 ft. 94 vols.

Arranged chronologically. Each volume has an index arranged alphabetically by initial letter of name or title of addressee. There are gaps in the date span of these records; the actual dates covered are: Nov. 1, 1877-Sept. 29, 1886; Nov. 1, 1886-Sept. 30, 1891; Jan. 3, 1893-July 31, 1895.

Press copies of letters to the State Department and to diplomatic and consular officials relating to problems arising in the settlement of their accounts and requesting additional information. The incoming letters to which some of these letters reply are described in entry 83.

For copies of earlier letters, see entry 87.

Other Records

89. ABSTRACT OF CONSULAR ACCOUNTS (CONSULAR STATISTICS). Oct. 1, 1865 - June 30, 1887. 23 cm, 9 in. 4 vols.

Arranged by location of consulate but in no particular order. Each volume has an index arranged alphabetically by location of consulate.

Abstracts of consular accounts for fees, salaries, loss by exchange, contingent expenses, and relief of destitute seamen showing location of consulate, account number, name of accountable officer, period covered, fees, and expenditures.

For additional information, see copies of audit reports on accounts for consular salaries (entry 843), expenses for hiring clerks (entry 844), and relief of seamen (entry 845).

90. RECORD OF CONSULAR BILLS OF EXCHANGE. May 3, 1862-Jan. 23, 1864. 1 cm, 1/2 in. 1 vol.

Arranged chronologically by date of requisition.

The entries show dates of draft and requisition, number of the bill of exchange, to whom issued, location of consulate, explanation, and amount of draft. Some entries also show name of draft holder or the reason the decision on payment was referred to the Comptroller by the Fifth Auditor.

91. REGISTERS OF ACCOUNTS FOR MONEYS DUE ESTATES OF DECEASED AMERICAN CITIZENS. Mar. 19, 1865-Sept. 24, 1894. 8 cm, 3 in. 2 vols.

Arranged by account number. Each volume is indexed by location of consulate and name of deceased person.

Registers contain entries that show money due estates of American citizens who died in foreign countries, including account number, location of consulate, name of deceased person, assets, consular expenses deducted, net amount due estate, and to whom paid. Some entries also show date of death, date on which money was covered into the Treasury, or date of payment to the estate.

92. REGISTER OF CONSULAR ACCOUNTS FOR PASSAGE OF DESTITUTE SEAMEN. Nov. 16, 1888-Aug. 30, 1899. 5 cm, 2 in. 1 vol.

Arranged by location of consulate but in no particular order, and thereunder chronologically by date account was adjusted.

Register contains entries that show location of consulate, name of ship and master, names of seamen transported, and their destinations. The entries also show account numbers, date of certificate, date adjusted, amount paid, and to whom paid. The nationality of the ship is frequently shown.

For related information, see audit reports on accounts for passage of seamen (entry 846).

DIVISION OF INTERNAL REVENUE ACCOUNTS

The Division of Internal Revenue Accounts was established as an independent unit in late 1892 or early 1893. From about 1880 to 1892, the settlement of Internal Revenue accounts was a responsibility of the Internal Revenue and Miscellaneous Division. The Division of Internal Revenue Accounts was established to settle Internal Revenue accounts and claims audited by the First and Fifth Auditors, to approve accounts for deposits as a result of offers in compromise, to record and file surety bonds of revenue collectors and stamp agents, and to prepare suits against delinquent accountable officers.

Correspondence

93.   LETTERS SENT TO DIRECT TAX COLLECTORS (EXCISE LETTERS). Mar. 21, 1818 -
       Oct. 9, 1837. 13 cm, 5 in. 2 vols.

Arranged chronologically. Each volume has an index arranged alphabetically by
initial letter of name of addressee. There are gaps in the date span of these records; the actual
dates covered are: Mar. 21, 1818-Apr. 27, 1819; May 8, 1822-Oct. 9, 1837.
       Fair copies of letters to collectors of the direct tax, relating primarily to their surety
bonds or to the status of their accounts for collecting and depositing the tax.
       For related records, see abstracts of taxes deposited (entry 870) and records of taxes
collected (entry 871).

94.   LETTERS SENT TO INTERNAL REVENUE OFFICIALS. Jan. 13, 1864-Nov. 14, 1866.
       20 cm, 8 in. 4 vols.

Arranged chronologically. Each volume has an index arranged alphabetically by
initial letter of surname of addressee.
       Fair copies of letters to Internal Revenue collectors and other Internal Revenue officials
relating chiefly to problems arising in the settlement of their accounts for salaries and expenses
of collecting and assessing taxes.

DIVISION OF JUDICIARY ACCOUNTS

The Division of Judiciary Accounts apparently was one of the four original divisions
established in First Comptroller's Office in 1876. The Division was responsible for final
approval of accounts for judicial officers of circuit and district courts (including judges,
marshals, attorneys, and commissioners of courts) after review and audit of these accounts by
the Department of Justice and the First and Fifth Auditors; final approval of accounts for
payment of judgments awarded by the Court of Claims; and registered and filed surety bonds of
marshals.

Correspondence

95.   LETTERS RECEIVED FROM THE ATTORNEY GENERAL. Apr. 5, 1842-Dec. 30, 1884.
       28 cm, 11 in. 3 vols.

Arranged chronologically. There are gaps in the date span of these records; the actual
dates covered are: Apr. 5, 1842-Jan. 5, 1857; Mar. 25, 1871-Dec. 30, 1884.
       Letters from the Attorney General, either directly or by referral from other officials,
stating his opinion on legal matters or requesting the loan of judicial accounts for review. Some
of these letters are entered in the registers described in entry 49.

96.   LETTERS RECEIVED FROM THE SOLICITOR OF THE TREASURY. Mar. 21, 1831 -
       May 5, 1893. 1.2 m, 4 ft. 3 vols.

Arranged chronologically. Each of the first two volumes has an index arranged
alphabetically by initial letter of writer's surname.
       Bound letters, March 21, 1831-September 8, 1856, and unbound letters August 16, 1849-
May 5, 1893, relating to the results of legal cases and to the deposit of moneys collected as fines
and judgments; also requests for certified copies of transcripts of accounts of delinquent
accountable officers for use in preparing suits against them. Some of these letters are entered in
the registers described in entry 49. Three boxes of this series appear to be missing.

97.   LETTERS RECEIVED RELATING TO LEGAL CASES. Apr. 13, 1888-Jan. 22, 1917. 6.4 m, 21 ft. 21 boxes.

Arranged chronologically. There are gaps in the date span of this series; actual dates covered are April 13, 1888-June 20, 1894; January 23, 1900-January 22, 1917.

Letters, chiefly from Auditors, in reply to the Comptroller's request to furnish information needed by the Attorney General. Many of the letters include lists of judgments handed down by the U.S. Court of Claims. Relatively few letters are dated after 1909. Some of the letters are entered in the registers described in entry 49.

98.   LETTERS RECEIVED FROM MARSHALS, DISTRICT ATTORNEYS, AND OTHER JUDICIAL OFFICERS. Feb. 24, 1797-Oct. 25, 1830. 30 cm, 1 ft. 4 vols.

Arranged geographically by groups of States and thereunder chronologically. Each volume has an index arranged alphabetically by initial letter of writer's surname.

Letters relating to the settlement of accounts and claims for judicial expenses. The dates of the letters vary considerably from State to State. Some of the accounts mentioned are among the First Auditor's miscellaneous Treasury accounts (entry 347).

99.   LETTERS SENT RELATING TO DELINQUENT ACCOUNTS. May 1, 1820-Dec. 27, 1820. 5 cm, 2 in. 1 vol.

Arranged chronologically. Indexed alphabetically by initial letter of surname of addressee.

Fair copies of letters to district attorneys, Members of Congress, and persons who were sureties for accountable officers. The letters chiefly requested information about delinquent accountable officers or the filing of suits against them.

Other Records

100.   ABSTRACTS OF JUDGMENTS AND DECREES IN CUSTOMS CASES IN NEW ENGLAND STATES. Oct. 15, 1830-Dec. 20, 1838. 5 cm, 2 in. 1 vol.

Arranged geographically, thereunder by judicial district, and thereunder chronologically.

Abstracts showing designation of judicial district, date of decision or decree, against whom issued, description of merchandise involved, amount of judgment, and amount of cost awarded. The abstracts were prepared by clerks in district and circuit courts.

101.   ABSTRACTS OF FEES OF JUDICIAL OFFICERS. Jan. 1, 1851-June 30, 1891. 8 cm, 3 in. 2 vols.

Arranged alphabetically by name of State and thereunder by type of official in the following order: marshals, attorneys, clerks of district courts, and clerks of circuit courts.

Abstracts showing judicial district, name and title of officer, gross receipts for the 6 months ending on June 30 of the year concerned, office expenses, net receipts for the period, similar statistics for the 6 months ending on December 30 of the same year, and total net receipts for the year. These abstracts were prepared from the emolument returns of attorneys, clerks, and marshals (entry 316).

PUBLIC DEBT DIVISION

The Public Debt Division was established at an undetermined time, probably in the late 1880s in a consolidation of the functions of the Loan Division with the Division of Treasurers, Assistant Treasurers, and Public Printer's Accounts. Among the major types of accounts approved by this Division after auditing were those for interest on the public debt; Treasurer's accounts for general receipts and expenditures; accounts of outstanding liabilities; and accounts of the Public Printer for salaries, contingent expenses, paper, printing supplies, and related items. Records of personnel changes, time reports, and payrolls for the Office of the First Comptroller were maintained by this Division.

Correspondence

102.   LETTERS SENT TO COMMISSIONERS OF LOANS AND BANK OFFICIALS. Dec. 10, 1807-July 17, 1824. 15 cm, 6 in. 3 vols.

Arranged chronologically. Each volume has an index arranged alphabetically by initial letter of surname of addressee.

Fair copies of letters to Commissioners of Loans and officers of State banks and of branches of the Bank of the United States relating chiefly to settlement of accounts for paying interest on the public debt, transfer of ownership of stock, pension payments; deposits of public moneys in banks, redemption of the debt; and payment of the Commissioner's accounts for salaries and office expenses.

Other Records

103.   REGISTERS OF ACCOUNTS FOR UNPAID DIVIDENDS. Feb. 28, 1877-June 30, 1894. 13 cm, 5 in. 2 vols.

Arranged by loan and thereunder chronologically. There are gaps in the date span of these records; the actual dates covered are: Feb. 28, 1877-Feb. 28, 1881; Apr. 25-June 30, 1894.

One register is for unpaid dividends for the loan of 1891, and the other is for the loan of 1907. Registers contain entries that show loan, check number, name of payee, amount due, and number of account in which the dividend was finally paid. The records of unpaid dividends for the 1891 loan are for the period February 18, 1877-February 28, 1881; and those for the 1907 loan are for the period December 31, 1877-December 31, 1879, and April 25-June 30, 1894. Some accounts listed in these registers are among the First Auditor's miscellaneous Treasury accounts (entry 347).

104.   REGISTER OF PUBLIC DEBT ACCOUNTS. Jan. 3, 1851-June 5, 1866. 2 cm, 1 in. 1 vol.

Arranged numerically and thereunder by date approved.

Register contains entries that show account number, to whom payable, type and period of account, dates received and approved, and official balance. Accounts typically were for the redemption of certificates, purchase or sale of bills of exchange, interest on bounty land certificates, and commissions. Some of the accounts are among the public debt accounts (entry 330) and the miscellaneous Treasury accounts (entry 347)

DIVISION OF PUBLIC LANDS

The Division of Public Lands was established as an independent Division in the First Comptroller's Office about June 1885 to give final approval to accounts of Land Office officials and disbursing officers for the General Land Office after approval by the Commissioner of the General Land Office. The Division also settled claims for the refund of moneys for lands erroneously sold, handled accounts of States for their shares of the proceeds from the sale of public land, and recorded and filed surety bonds of Land Office officials and disbursing agents for the General Land Office.

In the period before June 1885, a single Division performed the preceding functions in addition to settling accounts of diplomats, the District of Columbia, and Territories.

Correspondence

105. LETTERS RECEIVED FROM THE SECRETARY OF THE INTERIOR. Nov. 8, 1849 - July 20, 1870. 30 cm, 1 ft. 4 vols.

Arranged chronologically. Each volume has an index arranged alphabetically by initial letter of writer's surname.

Letters relating chiefly to judicial accounts and the interpretation of laws and regulations relating to judicial expenses. Many of the accounts mentioned are among miscellaneous Treasury accounts (entry 347); some of the letters are entered in the registers described in entry 49.

106. LETTERS RECEIVED FROM THE COMMISSIONER OF THE GENERAL LAND OFFICE AND FROM LOCAL LAND OFFICE OFFICIALS. Dec. 12, 1815-Sept. 7, 1840. 18 cm, 7 in. 3 vols.

Arranged by office of origin and thereunder chronologically.

Letters from the Commissioner of the General Land Office, December 12, 1815-September 7, 1840 (2 vols.), and from registers and receivers of land offices, April 24, 1818-December 27, 1833 (1 vol.), relating chiefly to the settlement of accounts and claims, the filing of surety bonds and oaths of office, operating procedures to be followed by land offices, and problems resulting from the increase in land office business. The volume of letters from registers and receivers includes an extract from a letter dated March 8, 1805, from Albert Gallatin, Secretary of the Treasury, to the receiver of public moneys at Cincinnati relating to deposit of public funds.

For replies to some of these letters, see letters sent relating to public lands (entry 107).

One volume appears to be missing.

107. LETTERS SENT RELATING TO PUBLIC LANDS. Nov. 12, 1829-Dec. 28, 1874. 1.5 m, 5 ft. 24 vols.

Arranged chronologically. Volumes 1-19 (including letters dated Nov. 12, 1829-Oct. 31, 1870) have indexes arranged alphabetically by initial letter of surname of person addressed. An additional volume, covering the period April 12-September 12, 1868, includes letters not copied in volume 19.

Fair copies of letters from the Comptroller to the Commissioner of the General Land Office, to registers and receivers, and to the Solicitor of the Treasury relating chiefly to the settlement of accounts and to legal problems involved in the settlement.

For some of the incoming letters to which these letters are replies D see entry 106; for a continuation of the letters sent, see entry 108.

108. LETTERS SENT RELATING TO PUBLIC LANDS. Jan. 4, 1875-Nov. 6, 1894. 1.2 m, 4 ft. 17 vols.

Arranged chronologically. Each volume has an index arranged alphabetically by initial letter of surname of person addressed.

Press copies of letters to the Commissioner of the General Land Office and to registers and receivers relating to the settlement of accounts and problems arising in their adjustment. The last volume includes four letters dated March 9, 1895. The individual spine titles vary.

For earlier letters see entry 107.

Records Relating to Accounts

109.   INDEXES TO REGISTERS OF REPORTS ON ACCOUNTS OF RECEIVERS OF PUBLIC MONEYS. n.d. 3 cm, 1 in. 2 vols.

Arranged alphabetically by initial letter of receiver's surname Indexes to volumes 2 (dates unknown) and 7 (July 8, 1877-June 1, 1886) of the registers described in entry 110 showing officer's name, period covered, page reference, and sometimes an indication of the type of expense. Many of the persons named in the index identified as volume 2 were accountable officers during the period 1830-36. There are no indexes for register volumes 3-6, 8, or 9.

110.   REGISTERS OF REPORTS ON ACCOUNTS OF RECEIVERS OF PUBLIC MONEYS. Apr. 9, 1839-Oct. 26, 1894. 30 cm, 1 ft. 7 vols.

Arranged by account number and thereunder chronologically by date approved. The volumes are identified as volumes 4-9, with an overlapping, unnumbered volume partially duplicating volume 7.

Registers contain entries that show account number (entry 116), receiver's name and duty station, period covered, dates received and approved, and official balance. Some claims are included in these registers.

For an index to volume 7 (July 8, 1877-June 1, 1886), see entry 109.

111.   INDEXES TO REGISTERS OF REPORTS ON ACCOUNTS OF RECEIVERS AND DISBURSING AGENTS. July 13, 1885-Sept. 28, 1894. 8 cm, 3 in. 2 vols.

Arranged alphabetically by initial letter of accountable officer's surname. There are gaps in the date span of these records; the actual dates covered are: July 13, 1885-July 24, 1889; Apr. 3, 1893-Sept. 28, 1894.

Indexes to volumes 5 (July 13, 1885-July 24, 1889) and 7 (Apr. 3, 1893-Sept. 28, 1894) of the registers of reports on accounts of receivers and disbursing agents (entry 112) showing officer's name and page references. Register volume 6 has no index.

112.   REGISTERS OF REPORTS ON ACCOUNTS OF RECEIVERS AND DISBURSING AGENTS. July 13, 1885-Sept. 28, 1894. 18 cm, 7 in. 3 vols.

Arranged numerically and thereunder chronologically by date reported. Indexes to volumes identified as volume 5 (July 13, 1885-July 24, 1889) and 7 (Apr. 3, 1893-Sept. 28, 1894) are in entry 111. The additional volume is numbered 6.

Registers contain entries that show account number; officer's name and title; period covered; dates received, reported, and approved; and official balance.

For more detailed information, see abstracts of accounts of receivers, entry 113, and of disbursing agents, entry 114.

113.   ABSTRACTS OF ACCOUNTS OF RECEIVERS OF PUBLIC MONEYS. May 1801-Mar. 1917. 61 cm, 2 ft. 4 vols. and 9 boxes.

Arranged in three subseries as described below. The abstracts for 1801-8 and 1843-91 (12 vols.) are indexed alphabetically by initial letter of receiver's surname. An overlapping volume, 1846-51, is indexed alphabetically by type of account. Two volumes, 1891-94 and

1913-17, are indexed alphabetically by name of State. There are gaps in the date span of these records; the actual dates covered are: May 1801-July 1808; Jan. 1843-Nov. 1894; Sept. 1913-Mar. 1917.

Abstracts showing receiver's name, duty station, and date of bond; numbers and balances of previous and current accounts (entries 116 and 719); date and number of account current; date approved; summary of debits and credits; explanation of differences; and adjusted balance. The volumes for 1801-8 and 1843-91 are arranged by name of receiver; a volume for 1846-51 is arranged by type of account; and the volumes for 1891-94 and 1913-17 are arranged alphabetically by name of State. The information in these last two volumes is presented in tabular form.

113A.   ABSTRACTS OF ACCOUNTS OF RECEIVERS OF PUBLIC MONEYS, 1801-1917. 2 vols.

114.   ABSTRACTS OF ACCOUNTS OF DISBURSING AGENTS. Oct. 1849-Mar. 1895. 61 cm, 2 ft. 10 vols.

Arranged by initial letter of disbursing agent's surname and thereunder chronologically. Each volume has an index arranged alphabetically by initial letter of agent's surname.

Abstracts showing agent's name, duty station, and date of bond; account number; disbursements reported; debits and credits; explanation of differences; and adjusted balance. Volumes 4, 5, and 7 are missing.

115.   REPORTS ON LAND ACCOUNTS. Sept. 1823-Sept. 1842. 30 cm, 1 ft. 6 boxes.

Arranged by name of accountable officer and thereunder chronologically by initial letter of officer's surname. Each volume is indexed by initial letter of officer's surname.

Reports showing accountable officer's name, title, and duty station; date on which account was audited; abstract of debits and credits; account number (entry 116); explanation of differences; and adjusted balance.

For similar information for 1843-94, see entry 113.

116.   SETTLED ACCOUNTS OF RECEIVERS OF PUBLIC MONEYS. June 1811-Sept. 1894. 274.6 m, 901 ft. 984 boxes.

Arranged by account number and thereunder chronologically by date approved.

Accounts usually include some or all of the following types of documents: (1) statement of account; (2) abstract of land sales and of other receipts and disbursements (sometimes accompanied by vouchers and other supporting documents); and (3) report by the Commissioner of the General Land Office approving the account.

For registers and abstracts of some of these accounts, see entries 110 and 111; for later accounts, see miscellaneous land accounts (entry 719) and accounts for sale of Indian lands (entry 720).

Alpha boxes: 4A, 5A, 56A, 63A, 976A; missing box 822.

117.   AUDIT REPORTS ON ACCOUNTS OF RECEIVERS OF PUBLIC MONEYS (RECORD OF REPORTS UPON LAND ACCOUNTS). Mar. 3, 1837-July 9, 1839. 20 cm, 8 in. 3 vols.

Arranged by location of Land Office, thereunder by account number, and thereunder chronologically by date audited.

Copies of audit reports prepared by the Commissioner of the General Land Office showing account number, date audited, receiver's name and duty station, summary of debits and credits, and adjusted balance. The Land Offices for which these volumes include copies of reports were in the following States: Alabama, Illinois, Iowa, Michigan, Mississippi, Missouri, and Wisconsin. Some of the original reports copied in these volumes are included in the accounts of receivers of public moneys (entry 116).

118.   SETTLED ACCOUNTS OF SURVEYORS AND DEPUTY SURVEYORS OF PUBLIC LANDS. Oct. 1831-Sept. 1894. 145.7 m, 478 ft. 521 boxes.

Arranged by account number and thereunder chronologically by date reported.
Accounts of surveyors and deputy surveyors of public lands, usually employed under contract (see entry 126). Each account usually includes a statement of the account, abstracts of disbursements with vouchers and other supporting documents, and a report from the Commissioner of the General Land Office approving the account. Some of these accounts are entered in the registers of miscellaneous land accounts (entry 121).
Alpha boxes include: 15A, 224A, 328A, and 338A.

119A.   REGISTERS OF ACCOUNTS REPORTED ON BY THE COMMISSIONER OF THE GENERAL LAND OFFICE. Feb. 1, 1850-June 14, 1879. 61 cm, 2 ft. 7 vols.

Appears to be missing.
Arranged alphabetically by initial letter of officer's or claimant's surname and thereunder chronologically by date received.
Registers contain entries that show account number, officer's or claimant's name, and the dates on which the account was received, reported, and approved.

120.   INDEX TO REGISTERS OF MISCELLANEOUS LAND ACCOUNTS. Apr. 17, 1879 Nov. 1, 1886. 1 cm, 1/2 in. 1 box.

Arranged alphabetically by initial letter of officer's or claimant's surname.
Index to volume 6 of registers of miscellaneous land accounts (entry 121) showing officer's or claimant's name and page reference.

121.   REGISTERS OF MISCELLANEOUS LAND ACCOUNTS. Aug. 7, 1832-Oct. 29, 1894. 28 cm, 11 in. 5 vols.

Arranged chronologically by date reported and thereunder numerically by account number. Volumes 1-5 have been rebound into two consolidated volumes, identified as volumes 1-3 and 4/5 respectively.
Registers contain entries that show account number; officer's or claimant's name; type of account; dates on which account was received, reported, and approved; and adjusted balance. Accounts and claims recorded include those for salaries and transportation expenses of registers, receivers, and surveyors; repayments of moneys for lands erroneously sold; and moneys deposited to cover expenses of land surveys.
For an index to volume 6, see entry 120.

122.   AUDIT REPORTS ON ACCOUNTS AND CLAIMS FOR MISCELLANEOUS EXPENSES OF LAND OFFICES. July 7, 1868-Mar. 25, 1870. 5 cm, 2 in. 1 vol.

Arranged chronologically by date reported. Indexed alphabetically by initial letter of officer's or claimant's surname.
Copies of reports prepared by the Commissioner of the General Land Office on examination of accounts and claims for such expenses as printing stationery; office supplies and equipment and salaries and expenses for hiring clerks; arranging and inventorying records of Land Offices; renting rooms; and purchasing furniture and firewood. Each report shows account

number, name of claimant or official, date reported, balance due from the United States, explanation, title of appropriation to be charged, and payment instructions.

123.   REGISTER OF BALANCES OF ACCOUNTS OF TIMBER AGENTS. Mar. 1872-Apr. 1894. 3 cm, 1 in. 1 box.

Arranged chronologically. Indexed alphabetically by initial letter of agent's surname.
Register contains entries that show account number, dates received and approved, agent's name and duty station, and balance of account.

Other Records

124.   REGISTERS OF SURETY BONDS OF LAND OFFICE OFFICIALS. Nov. 1805-July 1913. 23 cm, 9 in. 6 vols.

Arranged by title of official and thereunder alphabetically by name of State in which Land Office was located. The two volumes relating to bonds of disbursing officers, registers, and receivers, 1805-1913, are indexed alphabetically by name of State. The other four volumes are not indexed.
Registers contain entries that show surety bonds of surveyors general, special disbursing agents, registers, and receivers. Entries show city and State in which Land Office was located, official's name and title, date of bond, and sometimes additional remarks on his duties or on consolidation of Land Offices within a State. The volumes do not all record the names of each type of official.

125.   REGISTER OF BONDS OF DEPUTY SURVEYORS. Sept. 23, 1822-Feb. 15, 1890. 5 cm, 2 in. 1 vol.

Arranged in three chronological segments; within each segment arranged alphabetically by initial letter of deputy surveyor's surname.
Register contains entries that show official's name and duty station, date and amount of bond, and frequently the number of the contract (see entry 126) by which his duties were assigned. Accounts numbers (entry 118) sometimes also are shown.

126.   CONTRACTS AND BONDS OF DEPUTY SURVEYORS. Aug. 1860-June 1906. 11.6 m, 38 ft. 41 boxes.

Arranged alphabetically by name of State or Territory and thereunder chronologically by date of contract. Also included at the end of the series is a small group of contracts signed by the Commissioner of the General Land Office, April 1863-June 1906.
Contracts between surveyors general and deputy surveyors for surveys of public lands in States and Territories, showing names of parties involved, area to be surveyed, and amount to be paid. Frequently, the bond of the deputy surveyor is a part of the contract form; but where they were separate they are filed at the end of the contracts for a particular State or Territory. Some of these bonds and contracts are entered in the register described in entry 125. The States and Territories for which contracts are included in this series are:

Arizona	Jan. 1871-Feb. 1894
California	Sept. 1860-May 1900
Colorado	Aug. 1861-July 1904
Florida	Oct. 1869-May 1892
Idaho	May 1867-Mar. 1903
Iowa	Apr. 1863-Sept. 1864
Kansas	Aug. 1860-Dec. 1875

Louisiana	Dec. 1870-Dec. 1893
Minnesota	July 1860-Aug. 1894
Montana	Aug. 1867-June 1894
Nebraska	July 1867-Sept. 1882
Nevada	July 1861-Jan. 1896
New Mexico	Oct. 1866-Feb. 1895
North Dakota (Territory)	Aug. 1860-Aug. 1882
Oregon	Sept. 1860-Apr. 1894
South Dakota	July 1883-May 1894
Utah	May 1869-June 1894
Washington	Feb. 1860-May 1894
Wisconsin	July-Aug. 1860
Wyoming	June 1870-Feb. 1884

127.   REGISTER OF SUITS FILED AGAINST DELINQUENT LAND OFFICE OFFICIALS. May 24, 1879-June 18, 1881. 3 cm, 1 in. 1 vol.

Arranged alphabetically by name of delinquent official and thereunder chronologically by date of suit. Indexed both alphabetically by initial letter of State name and by initial letter of debtor's surname.

Register contains entries that show debtor's name, duty station, and title; date of bond; delinquent balance; date on which the suit was ordered; and a synopsis of subsequent action.

DIVISION OF TERRITORIAL ACCOUNTS

The Division of Territorial Accounts was established as a separate Division in the First Comptroller's Office in June 1885.

In addition to giving approval to accounts for salaries and expenses of Territorial officials (Governors, Secretaries, legislators, and judges), the Division also was assigned at an undetermined time the function of approving salary accounts for the U.S. Supreme Court, the U.S. Court of Appeals, U.S. marshals and district attorneys and the salaries and expenses of local and supervising inspectors of steamships. Judicial accounts other than those relating to salaries were settled by the Division of Judiciary Accounts.

Correspondence

128.   LETTERS RECEIVED FROM TERRITORIAL OFFICIALS. Jan. 6, 1835-Dec. 19, 1891. 1.5 m, 5 ft. 21 vols.

Arranged chronologically by date received. Volumes 15-21 (Jan. 6, 1879-Dec. 19, 1891) have indexes arranged both alphabetically by initial letter of name of Territory and by initial letter of writer's surname; volumes 1-14 are not indexed.

Letters from Governors, Secretaries, and other Territorial officials relating chiefly to accounts for salaries and administrative or legislative expenses or explaining items that had been suspended or disallowed by the Auditor. Some of these accounts are among the First Auditor's miscellaneous Treasury accounts (entry 347) and the Fifth Auditor's Territorial judicial accounts (entry 901). Some of the letters are entered in the registers described in entry 49. Few of the letters are dated before 1850.

For replies to some of the letters, see entries 129 and 130.

129. LETTERS SENT RELATING TO TERRITORIAL EXPENSES. Dec. 4, 1854-June 30, 1880. 61 cm, 2 ft. 12 vols.

Arranged chronologically. Each volume except the last one has an index arranged alphabetically by initial letter of surname of addressee.

Fair copies of letters to Territorial officials and to Members of Congress relating primarily to the settlement of accounts for legislative and administrative expenses of Territorial governments. Some of the accounts concerned are among the First Auditor's miscellaneous Treasury accounts (entry 347); others are among the Fifth Auditor's Territorial judicial accounts (entry 901).

For later letters, see entry 130; for the incoming letters to which some of these letters reply, see entry 128.

130. LETTERS SENT RELATING TO TERRITORIAL EXPENSES. July 3, 1880-Sept. 24, 1894. 30 cm, 1 ft. 7 vols.

Arranged chronologically. Each volume has an index arranged alphabetically by initial letter of surname of addressee.

Press copies of letters to Territorial officials and Members of Congress relating primarily to settlement of accounts for legislative and administrative expenses of Territorial governments. Some of the accounts are among the First Auditor's miscellaneous Treasury accounts (entry 347); others are among the Fifth Auditor's Territorial judicial accounts (entry 901).

For earlier letters to Territorial officials, see entry 129; for incoming letters to which some of these letters reply, see entry 128.

Records Relating to Accounts

131. REGISTERS OF ACCOUNTS FOR SALARIES AND EXPENSES OF TERRITORIAL OFFICIALS. July 5, 1861-Sept. 24, 1894. 8 cm, 3 in. 2 vols.

Arranged by name of Territory. Volume 2 has an index arranged both alphabetically by name of Territory and by initial letter of official's surname. Volume 1 has no index.

Registers contain entries that show accounts of Governors, Territorial Secretaries, election officials, and judicial officers. Entries show each official's name and title, account number, type of account, date approved, balance, and payment instructions. The dates of the entries vary considerably from one Territory to another. Some of the accounts registered are among the First Auditor's miscellaneous Treasury accounts (entry 347).

Volume 2 includes a few miscellaneous entries, such as for accounts of the U.S. Civil Service Commission and for accounts of charitable organizations in the Territories.

For related correspondence, see entries 128-130.

DIVISION OF MISCELLANEOUS ACCOUNTS

The origin and history of the Division of Miscellaneous Accounts are not known, but the Division is mentioned in an 1880 report on the history of the Treasury Department as being responsible for the final adjustment of all accounts audited by the First and Fifth Auditors not assigned to other Divisions of the First Comptroller's Office for review.

Public buildings accounts and accounts for contingent expenses of the U.S.

House of Representatives and the U.S. Senate were included among accounts reviewed by this Division.

Correspondence

132.   LETTERS SENT RELATING TO THE PHILADELPHIA CENTENNIAL EXPOSITION.
       Nov. 9, 1874-Sept. 20, 1877. 1 cm, 1/2 in. 1 vol.

Arranged chronologically. Indexed alphabetically by initial letter of surname or title
of addressee.

Press copies of letters to the Treasury Department representative on the Board of
Governors of the Philadelphia Exposition relating to such matters as availability of funds for
Government exhibits, payment of bills, transportation expenses of agency representatives, and
judging of Government exhibits. Related records are in General Records of the Department of
the Treasury, RG 56.

133.   LETTERS SENT RELATING TO THE WORLD'S COLUMBIAN EXPOSITION. Mar. 12,
       1894-Aug. 8, 1894. 1 cm, 1/2 in. 1 vol.

Arranged chronologically.

Press copies of letters chiefly to disbursing agents for Government departments that had
exhibits at the exposition in Chicago and to officials of railroad companies who had claims for
transportation expenses in relation to the Government exhibits. Many of the accounts mentioned
in these letters are among the First Auditor's miscellaneous Treasury accounts (entry 347).

Related records are in General Records of the Department of the Treasury, RG 56.

Records Relating to Accounts and Claims

134.   ABSTRACT OF BOUNTY CLAIMS FOR CAPTURE OF SLAVE SHIPS. June 11, 1859 -
       Sept. 18, 1871. 5 cm, 2 in. 1 vol.

Arranged alphabetically by initial letter of claimant's surname and thereunder by
account number.

Abstract showing account number, claimant's name and rank, names of the capturing and
captured ships, amount due, and to whom payable.

Many of these accounts are among the First Auditor's miscellaneous Treasury accounts
(entry 347). Two pages at the front of the volume are used to record information on captured
ships libeled between March 8, 1856, and June 20, 1861, showing name of captured ship, dates
libeled and condemned, port brought to after seizure, amount paid into the Treasury, and date
and number of certificate of deposit or date of distribution of proceeds to officers and men on the
capturing ship.

135.   REGISTER OF MISCELLANEOUS ACCOUNTS (CONGRESSIONAL ACCOUNTS).
       Sept. 24, 1884-Jan. 15, 1886. 5 cm, 2 in. 1 vol.

Arranged by account number and thereunder chronologically by date approved.

Register contains entries that show account number, officer's or claimant's name, type of
account or claim, period covered, dates received and approved, number of vouchers submitted
with the account or claim, total disbursements, and adjusted balance. The accounts and claims,
many of which are among the First Auditor's miscellaneous Treasury accounts (entry 347)
typically include contingent expenses of the U.S. House of Representatives and the U.S. Senate,
payment of outstanding liabilities, payment to the sinking fund, payment for Pacific Railroad
bonds, payment for interest on the public debt, and miscellaneous expenses of the Department of
Agriculture.

Other Records

136. COMPTROLLER'S DECISION ON SETTLEMENT OF THE CLAIM OF THE BANK OF THE UNITED STATES AGAINST THE UNITED STATES. Nov. 26, 1847. 3 cm, 1 in. 1 box.

The Bank of the United States signed an agreement with the Secretary of the Treasury in 1833 to act as a fiscal agent for the United States in transferring $900,000 from France to the United States by purchasing a bill for that amount drawn against the French Government for credit to the U.S. Government. When the bill was not paid by France, the Bank of the United States filed a claim against the Treasury for the amount of the bill, expenses, damages, and interest and withheld payment of part of the dividend due the United States on its ownership of bank stock as a setoff against an unfavorable court decision against the bank. The 1847 decision of the Comptroller advised that final settlement of the claim be made in line with an agreement reached between the two parties after a court decision in New Orleans in 1846. A settlement was reached in 1848. Copies of correspondence of the Solicitor of the United States, transcripts of hearings, and copies of reports of the First Auditor are included in the records on this decision.

DIVISION OF BONDS, CONTRACTS, AND POWERS OF ATTORNEY

The organization and history of the Division of Bonds, Contracts, and Powers of Attorney are not known, but the Division is mentioned in an 1880 publication on the history of the Treasury Department as responsible for receiving, registering, and filing all civil contracts except those for the survey of public lands; recording and filing all bonds not filed in other divisions of the Comptroller's Office; and recording and filing all powers of attorney relating to claims and accounts. Indian and military contracts were filed with the Second Comptroller until 1894, when they were transferred to the First Comptroller. The function of filing contracts was eventually transferred to the offices of the Auditors concerned with the subject matter of the contracts.

General Registers of and Indexes to Bonds, Contracts, and Proposals

137. GENERAL REGISTER OF BONDS AND CONTRACTS. Feb. 28, 1798-Dec. 18, 1887. 3 cm, 1 in. 1 vol.

Arranged by type of bond or contract. The volume includes two indexes: one is arranged by type of contract and thereunder by contract number; the other is arranged alphabetically by initial letter of contractor's or bonded official's surname.

Register contains entries that show names of contractors or bonded officials and the date and purpose of the bond or contract. The bonds recorded are chiefly those for diplomatic and consular officials; disbursing agents for Government departments and agencies and for the U.S. House of Representatives and U.S. Senate; Treasurers and Assistant Treasurers of the United States; and judicial, mint, and Territorial officials. The contracts recorded are primarily for construction and supplies for the U.S. Customs Service, Revenue-Cutter Service, and Marine Hospital Service; some of the contracts are described in entries 143, 158, and 155, respectively.

138. REGISTERS OF BONDS, CONTRACTS, AND PROPOSALS. Jan. 4, 1860-Sept. 10, 1909. 91 cm, 3 ft. 13 vols.

Arranged in two subseries: registers of civil contracts, January 4, 1860-September 10, 1909 (9 vols.), and registers of military contracts, October 10, 1894-September 12, 1907 (4 vols.). The registers of civil contracts are arranged chronologically, although three volumes dated after 1900 are also partly arranged by initial letter of contractor's surname; the registers of military contracts are arranged alphabetically by initial letter of contractor's surname. The registers of civil contracts that are identified as volumes 2-7 have indexes arranged alphabetically by initial letter of contractor's surname. The other volumes are not indexed.

Registers contain entries that show, for civil contracts, contractor's name, contract date and number, and item to be furnished and, for military contracts, names of parties involved, item to be furnished, and record of payments to the contractor. Entries relating to bonds show name and title of bonded official and date and amount of bond.

Many of the civil contracts and proposals registered in these volumes are among contracts and accepted proposals described in entry 159. Registers of military contracts dated before 1894 are among the general registers of bonds, contracts, and leases described in entry 212.

139.   INDEX TO CIVIL AND MILITARY CONTRACTS. 1922-26. 9.1 m, 30 ft. 36 boxes.

Arranged in three chronological segments and thereunder alphabetically by initial letter of contractor's surname.

Card index showing contractor's name, contract number, department or agency with which the contract was made, and type of goods or services to be supplied. Among the entries are those for contracts for magazine subscriptions; beef; electricity, ice, water, and towels for public buildings; drayage; coal; leasing of wharves; road construction; and hats and shoes for the Home for Disabled Volunteer Soldiers. The first segment of the index (1922-23) relates only to contracts for civil departments and independent agencies.

For some of the original contracts entered in this index, see entry 161.

Civil Contracts

140.   CONTRACTS AND LEASES FOR THE DEPARTMENT OF AGRICULTURE. Apr. 1920 - June 1926. 1.5 m, 5 ft. 13 boxes.

Arranged in two subgroups and thereunder numerically.

Contracts and leases show date, names of parties to the lease or contract, terms, and amount. The contracts are chiefly for water, electricity, and cooperative work on spraying trees or conducting experiments. The leases are typically for grazing rights. Agreements made under the Weeks Forestry Act are filed as a separate subseries. Other Agriculture Department contracts are among contracts and accepted proposals described in entry 159 and contracts for civil departments and independent agencies described in entry 161.

141.   CONTRACTS WITH BANKS. Jan. 14, 1803-May 16, 1839. 20 cm, 8 in. 1 box.

Arranged in two subseries and thereunder chronologically.

There are gaps in the date span of these records; the actual dates covered are: Jan. 14, 1803-Feb. 4, 1805; Dec. 13, 1809-Feb. 11, 1816; July 7, 1836-May 16, 1839.

Contracts made by the Treasury Department with banks agreeing to serve as fiscal agents for placing loans in foreign banking centers, January 14, 1803-February 4, 1805, and December 13, 1809-February 11, 1816, and with banks agreeing to serve as depositories of public moneys under regulations specified by Congress, July 7, 1836-May 16, 1839. Both groups of contracts include dates, names of parties to the agreement, and services to be performed.

142.   CONTRACTS FOR THE DEPARTMENT OF COMMERCE. Aug. 1919-Jan. 1923. 91 cm, 3 ft. 7 boxes.

Arranged alphabetically by initial letter of contractor's surname.

Contracts, chiefly for construction and supplies for the Department's Bureau of Lighthouses, showing date, names of parties, terms of the agreement, and amount. The contracts are frequently accompanied by blueprints, particularly contracts for the construction and repair of ships.

Other contracts for the Department of Commerce are among contracts and accepted proposals (entry 159), contracts for the Lighthouse Service (entry 153), and contracts for civil departments and independent agencies (entry 161). Additional lighthouse contracts are in Records of the U.S. Coast Guard, RG 26.

143.   CONTRACTS FOR THE U.S. CUSTOMS SERVICE. Jan. 13, 1819-Oct. 8, 1890. 18 cm, 7 in. Unbound records.

This series appears to be missing.

Arranged chronologically by date of contract.

Contracts, chiefly for cartage, building materials, and lighting fixtures, showing date of contract, names of parties, terms, and amount. These contracts are for the following years: 1819-20, 1829, 1834-43, 1848, 1852, 1855, 1859, 1876, 1878, 1880-81, and 1884-90. Additional U.S. Customs Service contracts are among contracts and accepted proposals described in entry 159. Some of these contracts are entered in the register described in entry 137.

144.   REGISTER OF CONTRACTS FOR THE DISTRICT OF COLUMBIA. Sept. 5, 1874 - Oct. 3, 1898. 5 cm, 2 in. 1 vol.

Arranged numerically. Indexed alphabetically by initial letter of contractor's surname.

Register contains entries that show contractor's name, contract number, file number, and date and type of contract. Many of the contracts are for supplies needed for the District of Columbia government; the original contracts are described in entry 145.

145A.   CONTRACTS FOR THE DISTRICT OF COLUMBIA. Jan. 5, 1878-June 1923. 8.8 m, 29 ft. 26 boxes.

Arranged numerically by file number.

Contracts, January 5, 1878-September 27, 1894, for school construction and supplies, repair of streets, rental of rooms and buildings, purchase of horses and wagons for use in garbage disposal, and supplies needed by the Commissioners for the District of Columbia; contracts, July 1919-June 1923, with hospitals and training schools. The contracts show date, names of parties, services to be furnished, and price.

Some of the contracts are entered in the register described in entry 142 and in the indexes to contracts for civil departments and independent agencies (entry I61) and the index to civil and military contracts (entry 139).

145B.   CIVIL DEPARTMENTS AND AGENCIES, DISTRICT OF COLUMBIA, 1920-23. 1 box.

146.   INDEXES TO INDIAN CONTRACTS. Apr. 1895-June 1922. 91 cm, 3 ft. 11 boxes.

Arranged by chronological periods and thereunder alphabetically by initial letter of contractor's surname. Boxes are numbered 149, 214, 223, 242, 259, 289, 290, 317, 351 and 387.

Indexes to contracts, usually for furnishing supplies or transportation for the Indian Service, showing contractor's name, date, article or service to be provided, place of delivery, and contract number.

For earlier indexes, see entry 225; for a register of contracts, see entry 147. The original contracts are described in entries 148 and 227.

147.   REGISTER OF INDIAN CONTRACTS. May 18, 1894-Oct. 31, 1899. 5 cm, 2 in. 1 vol.

Arranged alphabetically by initial letter of contractor's surname.

Register contains entries that show date contract was received, contractor's name, supplies or services to be furnished, place of delivery, record of extensions, and contract number (entry 148). Earlier contracts are described in entry 227; related indexes are described in entries 146 and 225.

148.   INDIAN CONTRACTS. May 1894-Mar. 1922. 76.2 m, 250 ft. 249 boxes.

Arranged in chronological segments and thereunder by contract number.

Contracts for axes, cattle, window glass, food, and other supplies needed for support of Indian tribes; also contracts for transportation of supplies, showing date, names of parties to the contract, supplies or services to be furnished, and amount. Some of these contracts are entered in the indexes and the register described in entries 146 and 147, respectively. Series does not include boxes 149, 182, 214, 223, 242, 259, 289, 290, 317, 351, and 387 which form entry 146, Index to Indian Contracts. Earlier contracts and related indexes are described in entries 225 and 227.

149.   CONTRACTS FOR THE INLAND AND COASTAL WATERWAYS SYSTEM. June 1922-Oct. 1922. 5 cm, 2 in. 1 box.

Arranged chronologically.

Two contracts with the firm of Reed and Lowe, of Birmingham, Ala., and one with the firm of Kaucher, Hodge, and Co., of Memphis, Tenn., for various phases of construction of river and rail facilities at Vicksburg, Miss. The contracts show date, names of parties, terms of the contract, and amount.

150.   INDEX TO INTERIOR DEPARTMENT CONTRACTS. 1886-1911. 2.4 m, 8 ft. 9 boxes.

Arranged alphabetically by initial letter of contractor's surname.

Card index showing contractor's name and address, date, and after 1895, a number. Some cards have the notation "not enrolled" or "disbarred." The contracts to which this index relates have not been identified.

151.   CONTRACTS FOR THE INTERIOR DEPARTMENT. May 1922-Mar. 1923. 91 cm, 3 ft. 7 boxes.

Arranged in two subgroups and thereunder by contract number.

Civil contracts, May 1922-March 1923, primarily for water and grazing rights, timber sales, and use of research facilities; also Indian contracts, June 1922-January 1923, primarily for use of lands for agricultural and grazing purposes. Earlier Interior Department contracts are among the contracts and accepted proposals described in entry 159.

152.   REGISTER OF JUDICIAL CONTRACTS. May 28, 1897-May 24, 1905. 3 cm, 1 in. 1 vol.

Arranged numerically and thereunder by date of contract. Indexed alphabetically by initial letter of contractor's surname.

Register contains entries that show contracts for construction and repair of buildings or for the purchase of furniture or equipment, showing contract number, date received, contractor's name, type of contract, expiration date, and record of extensions or renewals of the contract.

153.   CONTRACTS FOR THE LIGHTHOUSE SERVICE. June 4, 1800-Mar. 17, 1903. 4.3 m, 14 ft. 24 boxes.

Arranged in two subseries and thereunder chronologically.

There are gaps in the date span of these records; the actual dates covered are: June 4, 1800-May 2, 1853; Aug. 6, 1887-Nov. 23, 1897; July 23, 1900-Mar. 17, 1903.

Contracts for construction and repair of lighthouses, June 4, 1800- May 2, 1853, arranged by location of lighthouse; also construction, repair, and supply contracts, August 6, 1887-November 23, 1897, and July 23, 1900- March 17, 1903. Many of the contracts include specifications and blueprints. Later lighthouse contracts are among contracts for the Department of Commerce (entry 142); additional contracts for the Service are among the Records of the U.S. Coast Guard, RG 26.

154.   CONTRACTS FOR THE LIFE-SAVING SERVICE. Sept. 11, 1878-Sept. 1, 1905, with gaps. 30 cm, 1 ft. Unbound records.

Arranged chronologically.

Annual supply contracts for the Life-Saving Service for the years 1878, 1891, 1893-94, 1901, and 1905, showing date, names of parties involved, articles to be furnished, and price. Construction contracts for the Life-Saving Service are frequently filed with the miscellaneous customs accounts (entry 311) by which the contractor was paid.

155.   CONTRACTS FOR THE MARINE HOSPITAL SERVICE. Oct. 1, 1825-Aug. 10, 1911. 1.8 m, 6 ft. 6 boxes.

Arranged chronologically.

There are gaps in the date span on these records; the actual dates covered are: Oct. 1, 1855-Feb. 18, 1901, May 19-Aug. 10, 1911.

Contracts for medical and surgical supplies, drugs, medicines, food, forage, ice, and other supplies needed by marine hospitals, showing date of contract, names of parties involved, terms, and prices. The contracts are for 1825, 1828-29, 1833, 1839-53, 1859, 1861, 1863-69, 1883-94, 1897-98, 1900-1901, and 1911. Some of these contracts are entered in the register described in entry 137.

156.   CONTRACTS FOR PUBLIC PRINTING AND BINDING. June 21, 1882-June 30, 1897. 91 cm, 3 ft. 6 boxes.

Arranged chronologically.

Bound volumes of contracts, June 21, 1882, and June 17, 1886-June 30, 1897, for printing and binding materials, paints, oils, dry goods, stereotype materials, and miscellaneous supplies; also unbound contracts, June 21, 1882-July 3, 1894, for paper and for engraving and lithographing illustrations for congressional and other Government documents and reports.

157.   CONTRACTS FOR THE U.S. RAILROAD ADMINISTRATION. Oct. 1918-Feb. 1920. 23 cm, 9 in. 2 boxes.

Arranged alphabetically by name of railroad.

Agreements to compensate railroad companies for operation of railroads and related facilities during the wartime emergency, showing date, names of parties involved, terms, and amount.

158.   CONTRACTS FOR THE REVENUE-CUTTER SERVICE. Jan. 1, 1839-July 2, 1894, with gaps. 91 cm, 3 ft. Unbound records.

Arranged chronologically.
Construction, repair, and supply contracts, January 1, 1839-April 5, 1867, and August 22, 1884-July 2, 1894, with a few for other dates. The construction and repair contracts usually include specifications and blueprints. Some of these contracts are entered in the register described in entry 137.

159.   CONTRACTS AND ACCEPTED PROPOSALS. June 24, 1852-July 22, 1901. 59.4 m, 195 ft. 1 vol. and 179 boxes.

Arranged in two subseries: alphabetically by (1) initial letter of contractor's bidder's surname (1865-94) and (2) department, agency, or type of contract.
Contracts and proposals of the following general types: (1) construction, repair, and building materials for such Government buildings as the Library of Congress, U.S. Capitol, customhouses, courthouses, and post offices; (2) general supply contracts for such material as stationery and office supplies for several departments; (3) specialized supply contracts for such material as paper and chemicals for the Bureau of Engraving and Printing; and (4) technical services (i.e., engraving illustrations). Proposals are usually accompanied by a letter of acceptance. A new series of contract numbers was begun in 1894. Many of these contracts are entered in the registers described in entry 138. The buildings and departments for which contracts are included in the second subseries are:

Department of Agriculture	Aug. 1867-Oct. 1894
Architect of the Capitol	Apr. 1871-Feb. 1894
Assay Offices	Oct. 1870-May 1879
Coast and Geodetic Survey	Dec. 1867-Dec. 1893
Department of Commerce and Labor	June 1888-July 1892
Fish Commission	Aug. 1879-Oct. 1894
Freedmen's Hospital	July 1883-Oct. 1892
Geological Survey	June 1880-Aug. 1894
Government Hospital for the Insane (Saint Elizabeth's)	July 1884-Sept. 1894
Department of the Interior	Aug. 1852-Sept. 1894
Library of Congress	June 1852-May 1894
Patent Office	May 1879-Oct. 1880
U.S. Mint in Philadelphia	Oct. 1900-July 1901
Post Office Department	Feb. 1868-Nov. 1893
Office of Public Printing	Feb. 1858-Feb. 1876
Department of Treasury	May 1885-Apr. 1892
Smithsonian Institution	Mar. 1879-Mar. 1894
Department of State	July 1883-Aug. 1894
State, War, and Navy Building	July 1883-Aug. 1894

160.   INDEX TO CONTRACTS FOR CIVIL DEPARTMENTS AND AGENCIES. 1900-12. 3.1 m, 10 ft. 12 boxes.

Arranged in three chronological segments and thereunder by initial letter of contractor's surname.
Card index showing contract number, contractor's name, department or agency concerned, date of contract, place of delivery, and article or service to be furnished. Beginning with fiscal year 1908, the reverse side of the card shows a record of payments to the contractor.
For a later index, see entry 139.

161.   CONTRACTS FOR CIVIL DEPARTMENTS AND AGENCIES. Dec. 1918-Aug. 1927.
        6.4 m, 21 ft. 51 boxes.

Arranged numerically by contract number.
Contracts for constructing and repairing vessels for the Coast Guard and Bureau of Lighthouses, leasing agricultural lands, furnishing X-ray equipment for marine hospitals, and furnishing supplies for the Public Health Service; also miscellaneous contracts. Some of the contracts are entered in the index described in entry 139.
For other contracts of a similar type for some of the same agencies, see especially entries 140, 142, and 159.

162.   CONTRACTS FOR MISCELLANEOUS AGENCIES. Nov. 1913-Oct. 1922. 13 cm, 5 in.
        2 boxes.

Arranged by agency in the order listed below and thereunder chronologically.
Contracts by the U.S. Shipping Board for repairing and modifying ships; by the Architect of the Capitol for purchasing boilers, pipes, flue vents, and railings for the Senate gallery and for constructing a greenhouse for the Botanical Gardens; and by the Government Printing Office for tunnels, electrical conduits, vault equipment, folding machines, and book presses.

163.   CONTRACTS FOR BATTLEFIELDS AND MILITARY PARKS. Aug. 1894-Sept. 1924.
        1.8 m, 6 ft. 6 boxes.

Arranged by location and thereunder chronologically.
Contracts for providing goods and services for parks, including photographic supplies; removing timber; constructing buildings, bridges, and roads; furnishing tools, padlocks, windmills, and water-storage tanks; making relief models; painting observation towers; and marking graves of Confederate soldiers. Contracts involving construction work are accompanied by blueprints. Many contracts are also accompanied by records of payments to contractors.

164.   CONTRACTS FOR MEMORIALS. June 1913-Apr. 1923. 9 cm, 3 in. 1 box.

Arranged by name of memorial.
Contracts and related correspondence concerning the following memorials and monuments: Arlington Cemetery Memorial Amphitheater, October 1914-April 1923; Lincoln Memorial, June 1913-July 1922; Monument to Women in the Civil War, March 1914-June 1917; and Monument to John Ericsson, May 1921-September 1922.

165.   BLUEPRINTS OF FREEDMEN'S HOSPITAL, HOWARD UNIVERSITY, AND U.S.
        PENSION OFFICE BUILDING. Oct. 1, 1909-July 16, 1910. 81 items.

This series appears to be missing.
Arranged by building and thereunder chronologically by date of drawing.
Floor plans, elevations, and utility system drawings for Freedmen's Hospital and other buildings on the Howard University campus (63 items), accompanied by the contract, specifications, and correspondence relating to the work for which the drawings were made; also drawings of the heating system for the U.S. Pension Office Building (18 items).

166.   RECORD OF COMPLETED CONTRACTS FOR THE PANAMA CANAL. 1904-21.
        30 cm, 1 ft. 3 boxes.

        Arranged alphabetically by initial letter of contractor's surname.
        Card record of payments on completed contracts for the Panama Canal (entry 167),
showing number of contract and work order, authorization for the work, names of parties
involved, article or service to be provided, amount, and record of payments.

167.   PANAMA CANAL CONTRACTS. Oct. 1904-Mar. 1922. 12.5 m, 41 ft. 33 boxes.

        Arranged numerically.
        Contracts between the Isthmian Canal Commission and various contractors for goods
and services, such as construction of cranes, other heavy machinery, dynamite, copper, brass,
rope, electrical transformers, switchboard equipment, and other articles needed for construction
and operation of the Canal. Contracts show date, names of the parties involved, articles to be
furnished, and price. Blueprints related to these contracts are filed in part with the contracts
themselves and in part at the end of the series. The record of payments on completed contracts
(entry 166) can be used as an index to this series.

Military Contracts

168A.   GENERAL CONTACTS FOR THE WAR DEPARTMENT. 1894-1926; CONTRACTS OF
        THE GENERAL FILE. 18.0 m, 59 ft. 66 boxes.

        Two boxes are labeled: "Miscellaneous 1923-26."

168B.   GENERAL CONTACTS FOR THE WAR DEPARTMENT. July 1902-June 1926. 4 boxes.

        Arranged numerically by contract number.
        Contracts between the War Department and various contractors for purchasing and
repairing airplanes, propellers, and other spare parts; furnishing airships; repairing
transports; repairing and tuning radios; and constructing oil barges. Most of the contracts are
accompanied by blueprints and specifications.
        Additional Army Air Corps and Army Signal Corps contracts are described in entries
169 and 180. Some of these contracts are entered in the index to civil and military contracts
described in entry 139 and the index to Army Signal Corps contracts described in entry 179.
Earlier general contracts for the War Department are described in entry 214.

169.   ARMY AIR CORPS CONTRACTS. July 1922-Dec. 1924. 2.1 m, 7 ft. 18 boxes.

        Arranged numerically by contract number.
        Contracts by disbursing officers of the Army Air Corps, primarily for purchase of
airplane parts, parachutes, hangars, bomb racks, varnish, and miscellaneous items needed by
the corps.
        For similar contracts, see entry 168. Some of the contracts are entered in index described
in entry 139.

170.   INDEX TO FRENCH CONTRACTS AND LEASES. 1917-19. 2.1 m, 7 ft. 7 boxes.

        Arranged alphabetically by initial letter of contractor's or lessor's surname.
        Card index to contracts and leases between the American Expeditionary Forces in France
and various French companies and citizens, chiefly for food and lodging for soldiers and the use
of buildings for hospitals and other military purposes. The cards show names of parties to the
contract or lease, terms, date filed, and expiration date.

For a record of payments under the contracts, see entry 171; the contracts are described in entry 172.

171.   RECORD OF PAYMENTS ON COMPLETED FRENCH CONTRACTS AND LEASES. Oct. 1917 - Apr. 1919. 91 cm, 3 ft. 3 boxes.

Arranged geographically by location of rest area.
Card record of payments to French hotels under contract to furnish food and lodging for U.S. soldiers in rest areas, showing name of hotel, name and address of owner, date and number of contract or lease, period covered, and record of payments. Some of the contracts and leases to which these cards refer are described in entry 172.

172.   FRENCH CONTRACTS AND LEASES. Oct. 1917-Apr. 1919. 16.2 m, 53 ft. 42 boxes.

Arranged numerically by contract or lease.
Contracts and leases for furnishing rooms and lodging for U.S. soldiers stationed in France and for using lands and buildings for military purposes. The prices stated in the leases and contracts are usually expressed in both U.S. dollars and French francs and are usually accompanied by signed forms releasing the United States from damage claims. Some of these contracts and leases are entered in the index described in entry 170.
For a record of payments under these contracts and leases, see entry 171.

173.   NATIONAL DEFENSE CONTRACTS. Feb. 1898-Feb. 1899. 61 cm, 2 ft. 2 boxes.

Arranged alphabetically by initial letter of contractor's surname.
Contracts entered into by the Chief of Ordnance, primarily for gun and mortar carriages, gun forgings, ammunition, projectiles, and telescopic sights.
For similar contracts, see entries 178 and 233.

174.   INDEX TO NAVY CONTRACTS. 1904-1925. 10.7 m, 35 ft. 42 boxes.

Arranged in three chronological segments and thereunder alphabetically by initial letter of contractor's surname.
Card index to contracts for miscellaneous supplies needed by the Navy Department, such as coal, fuel, meat, vegetables, dairy products, lumber, envelopes, forage, and machinery. Some of the contracts entered on these cards are described in entry 176 and are also entered in the registers described in entry 175.
For Navy contracts dated before 1894 and related registers, see entries 230 and 231.

175.   REGISTERS OF NAVY CONTRACTS. Jan. 4, 1895-Dec. 31, 1903. 23 cm, 9 in. 4 vols.

Arranged alphabetically by initial letter of contractor's surname and thereunder chronologically by date of contract.
Registers contain entries of contracts, typically for food, hardware, varnish, brass, steel, copper, coal, wood, and construction of buildings. Entries show names of the parties involved, contract number, place and date of contract, terms, and price.
Some of the contracts entered in these registers are described in entry 176. For a related index, see entry 174; for earlier Navy contracts and related registers, see entries 230 and 231.

176.   NAVY CONTRACTS. July 1894-Apr. 1924. 7.6 m, 25 ft. 46 boxes.

Arranged in four subseries by type of contract and thereunder in part chronologically and in part by initial letter of contractor's surname.

The four subseries are: (1) contracts entered into chiefly by the Chief of Ordnance or the Secretary of the Navy for supplies, provisions, brass, guns, steel, copper, projectiles, gun forgings, and gunsights; (2) contracts for constructing and repairing ships; (3) contracts for publishing recruiting advertisements in newspapers and magazines during 1919; and (4) permits allowing the Navy to use certain patented processes. Some of these contracts are entered in the indexes and registers described in entries 174 and 175. For earlier Navy contracts and related registers, see entries 230 and 231.

177. INDEX TO ORDNANCE CONTRACTS. 1907-21. 6.1 m, 20 ft. 17 boxes.

Arranged by year, thereunder by place of delivery, and thereunder alphabetically by initial letter of contractor's surname.

Card index to contracts for providing steel discs, brass tubing, ordnance supplies, boring mills, iron castings, machinery, lumber, steel, and cartridge belts, to be delivered to the U.S. Powder Depot, Dover, N.J., and to the arsenals at Augusta, Ga.; Benicia, Calif.; Frankford, Pa.; Manila, Philippines; Pickatinny, N.J.; Rock Island, Ill.; Sandy Hook, N.J.; Springfield and Watertown, Mass.; and Watervliet, N.Y. The index cards for the 1907-12 period show, on the reverse side, a record of payments made under the contracts. Some of the contracts entered in this index are described in entry 178. For earlier ordnance contracts, see entry 233.

178. ORDNANCE CONTRACTS. Oct. 1894-Dec. 1924. 13.4 m, 44 ft. 82 boxes.

Arranged by year and thereunder by place of delivery.

Contracts entered into by the Chief of Ordnance for supplies needed by the headquarters of the Ordnance Department of the Army and by arsenals and other departmental field units. The contracts were typically for iron casting, lumber, machinery, steel, supplies, and brass. Many of these contracts were eventually the subject of litigation and are accompanied by correspondence, court rulings, documents amending the original terms of the contracts, and records of payments to the contractors. Some of these contracts are entered in the index described in entry 177.

For earlier contracts and related registers, see entries 233 and 212. Alpha boxes: 132A

179. INDEX TO ARMY SIGNAL CORPS CONTRACTS. 1908-22. 61 cm, 2 ft. 2 boxes.

Arranged alphabetically by initial letter of contractor's surname.

Card index to contracts for materials such as spare parts for airplanes, radio control boxes, and compasses; contracts for remodeling airplanes and installing submarine signal apparatus; and contracts with educational institutions for providing technical instruction. Some of the contracts indexed in this series are described in entries 168 and 180.

For earlier Signal Corps contracts, see entry 239.

180. ARMY SIGNAL CORPS CONTRACTS. Mar. 1923-Sept. 1924. 30 cm, 1 ft. 4 boxes.

Arranged numerically by contract number.

Contracts for items needed by the Signal Corps, including radio tuners, amplifiers, transmitters, and meteorological balloons. Similar contracts are included in those described in entry 168. For earlier Signal corps contracts, see entry 239.

ASSISTANT COMPTROLLER, PARIS, FRANCE, 1918-20

180A. CORRESPONDENCE WITH THE PARIS BUREAU, OFFICE OF THE ASSISTANT COMPTROLLER OF THE TREASURY. 1918-20. 39 cm, 1 ft. 3 boxes.

Arranged alphabetically by subject.

Consists of correspondence, memorandums, cablegrams, vouchers, and other documents relating to the operations of the Paris Bureau during and after World War I. Included are the correspondence files of Lurtin Ginn, the Assistant Comptroller of the Treasury in Paris, which deal with policy matters of the office. Also included are files on subjects such as applications for appointments, statements of conditions of the office, disbursements of funds, transportation, use of foreign currency, decisions of the Comptroller and the Solicitor of the Treasury and personnel matters.

180B. DECISIONS OF THE ASSISTANT COMPTROLLER IN PARIS, FRANCE, Jan. 1918-Sept. 9, 1918. 1 box.

OFFICE OF THE SECOND COMPTROLLER

The Office of the Second Comptroller was established by an act of March 3, 1817 (2 Stat. 366), to improve accountability for public moneys. This act gave the Second Comptroller the duties formerly exercised by the First Comptroller with respect to reviewing and approving accounts and claims relating to military activities, countersigning warrants issued by the Secretaries of the War and Navy Departments, and regulating the preparation of accounts of a military nature. For more detailed information on the functions of the several auditors, see the introductions to the sections of this inventory describing the records of the auditors.

The Office of the Second Comptroller was abolished on October 1, 1894, under provisions of an act of July 1, 1894 (28 Stat. 205), which transferred the functions of the Second Comptroller to the newly established Office of the Comptroller of the Treasury. Little is known about the internal organization of the Second Comptroller's Office, but he described the Office in 1885 as consisting of seven divisions: the Army Back Pay and Bounty Division, Army Paymasters Division, Army Pension Division, Quartermaster Division, Navy Division, Indian Division, and Miscellaneous Claims Division. The functions of these units are described below, just before the descriptions of their records.

The most significant records of the Second Comptroller's Office include letters received, 1817-94; letters and decisions sent, 1875-94; abstracts of accounts and claims audited by the Second, Third, and Fourth Auditors, 1817-94; and contracts, ca. 1800-94, with related registers and indexes dating from about 1850. Contracts dated after 1894 are described with the records of the First Comptroller.

A list of names of Second Comptroller and their dates of service appear in Appendix 3.

GENERAL RECORDS

Correspondence

181.   REGISTERS OF LETTERS AND PAPERS RECEIVED. Jan. 4, 1847-Jan. 19, 1895. 61 cm, 2 ft. 9 vols.

Only 8 volumes have been found.

Arranged alphabetically by initial letter of writer's or interested party's surname or title and thereunder chronologically by date received.

There are gaps in the date span of these records; the actual dates covered are: Jan. 4, 1847-June 3, 1853; Mar. 14, 1863-Jan. 14, 1876; Jan. 3, 1879-June 30, 1889; June 1, 1892-Jan. 19, 1895.

Registers contain entries that show, in general, writer's name and title, date received, subject (frequently names of claimants) and action taken. The two registers for the period January 1847-June 1853 show the number assigned to the incoming letter. Volumes after 1853 are chiefly for letters referred to other offices for reply or for documents filed with accounts and to which no reply was made. Some of the letters registered in these volumes are described in entry 182.

182.   GENERAL LETTERS RECEIVED. Aug. 16, 1817-Sept. 30, 1894. 12.2 m, 40 ft. 184 vols. and 1 box.

Arranged chronologically by date received. The letters received during 1829 are bound in two volumes, with a joint index to both volumes in the first of the volumes. Each of the other volumes has its own index, except for the volumes for October 1891-June 1892 (three vols.) and January 1893-September 1894 (seven vols.), which are not indexed. The indexes are arranged by initial letter of writer's surname or title or by subject of letter. There are no volumes numbered 93 or 122. The spine titles vary.

Bound volumes of letters received, August 16, 1817-September 30, 1894, and a few unbound, received, October 23, 1876-April 14, 1894, that were overlooked when the other letters were bound. The letters are from claimants, accountable military officers, Auditors, and other Government officials concerning such matters as settlement of accounts and claims, requests for decisions, appeals of rulings, and personnel matters. Some letters relating to personnel matters (identified as "office letters") and some relating to delinquent accounts (identified as "delinquent officer's letters") were bound in separate volumes and are described in entries 183 and 184. Some of the letters are entered in the registers of letters received described in entry 181.

For copies of replies to some of these letters, see entries 255-257.

183. LETTERS RECEIVED RELATING TO PERSONNEL MATTERS. Jan. 6, 1864-Dec. 30, 1887. 30 cm, 1 ft. 7 vols.

Arranged chronologically by date received. Each volume is indexed by name of employee. Volume 3 is bound with volume 94 of entry 182. Volume 4 is bound with volume 104; volume 5 is bound with volume 113; volume 6 is bound with volume 120.

There are gaps in the date span of these records; the actual dates covered are: Jan. 6, 1864-June 8, 1865; Jan. 11, 1866-Dec. 17, 1867; Jan. 21, 1869-Dec. 17, 1870; Jan. 13-Dec. 30, 1887.

Letters relating chiefly to appointments, leaves of absence, punctuality of employees, and routine personnel matters. Oaths of office are also frequently included in these volumes. Additional letters relating to personnel matters are among letters described in entry 182.

184. LETTERS RECEIVED RELATING TO DELINQUENT ACCOUNTS. May 8, 1822-Dec. 29, 1876. 91 cm, 3 ft. 12 vols.

Eleven of these volumes appear to be missing. It appears that this series is scattered in several other series.

Arranged chronologically by date received. Each volume except the one for 1876 is indexed by initial letter of surname of writer.

There are gaps in the date span of these records; the actual dates covered are: May 8, 1822-Oct. 14, 1833; Oct. 9, 1863-Dec. 28, 1865; Jan. 8-Sept. 30, 1867; Jan. 14-Dec. 29, 1876.

Chiefly letters received from military officers explaining the reasons for the delay in filing their accounts or denying the delinquency. Some letters were from the Adjutant General's Office, listing names of officers who had satisfactorily explained their delinquency. Additional letters relating to delinquent officers are among the letters described in entry 182.

185. LETTERS OF APPLICATION AND RECOMMENDATION RECEIVED. Feb. 18, 1813 - Oct. 18, 1824. 5 cm, 2 in. 1 vol.

This series appears to be missing.

Arranged chronologically. Indexed alphabetically by initial letter of writer's surname.

Letters received by Richard Cutts, purveyor of military supplies and, later, Comptroller, on behalf of persons wishing to be appointed to positions in his office or to obtain other Government appointments. Many relate to the educational or work-related background of the applicant, and some are accompanied by letters and petitions dated as early as 1811. A few letters bound at the end of the volume do not show the year the letter was written.

186. CIRCULARS AND DECISIONS. Sept. 20, 1861-Oct. 26, 1891. 18 cm, 7 in. 3 vols.

Arranged chronologically. One volume, consisting chiefly of published circulars, dated December 29, 1885-September 8, 1888, is indexed alphabetically by subject. The other volumes are not indexed.

There are gaps in the date span of these records; the actual dates covered are: Sept. 20, 1861-Apr. 14, 1863; Nov. 20, 1877-Oct. 26, 1891.

Circulars and decisions relating to a variety of subjects, including purchase of arms, ammunition, and other military supplies during the Civil War; pay, bounty, and pension reimbursement claims; rates to be paid for postage and telegrams; and settlement of accounts.

For copies of other decisions on many of these same subjects, see entries 69, 192, and 204.

187.   ADMINISTRATIVE LETTERS SENT. July 23, 1887-July 6, 1894. 4 cm, 1 in. 2 vols.

Arranged chronologically. Each volume has an index arranged alphabetically by subject or initial letter of surname of addressee.

Press copies of letters relating to personnel actions, duties performed in the Second Comptroller's Office, and comments on proposed legislation affecting the settlement of accounts and claims.

187A.   DECISIONS, Jan. - Mar. 1892. 1 box.

Records Relating to Accounts and Suits

188.   REGISTERS OF TRANSCRIPTS OF ACCOUNTS REPORTED FOR SUIT. Oct. 1809 - May 4, 1887. 28 cm, 11 in. 6 vols.

Arranged alphabetically by initial letter of debtor's surname.

Composite series of registers containing entries that show, in general, debtor's name, capacity in which he was delinquent (e.g., "contractor," "pension agent," or "Indian agent"), when and by which Auditor the delinquency was reported, amount due, and, sometimes, remarks on the status of the case. One volume concerns contractors who were delinquent in fulfilling the work under their contracts, and another volume is used largely as a register of certificates of settled claims, January 1861-February 1864 (entry 242). A related docket book is described in entry 210.

189.   REGISTER OF SETTLED ACCOUNTS. Apr. 1, 1837-Apr. 30, 1850. 2 cm, 1 in. 1 vol.

Arranged chronologically by date settled.

Register contains entries that show officer's name and rank, capacity in which he disbursed funds, period covered, dates received and reported, and official balance. Part of this volume is used as a register of payments to contractors, 1852-54 (entry 245).

ARMY BACK PAY AND BOUNTY DIVISION

The Army Back Pay and Bounty Division was first mentioned as a Division of the Second Comptroller's Office in July 1885. Its primary function was the final adjustment and approval of accounts audited by the Second Auditor for back pay and bounty due Army officers and soldiers.

Correspondence

190.   LETTERS AND ENDORSEMENTS SENT BY THE BACK PAY AND BOUNTY DIVISION. Dec. 10, 1872-Dec. 8, 1879. 5 cm, 2 in. 2 vols.

Arranged chronologically. The first volume, dated December 10, 1872-November 27, 1878, is indexed alphabetically by subject, by name of claimant, and by name of addressee. The second volume is not indexed.

Fair copies of letters and endorsements relating to appeals in pay and bounty cases, along with copies of letters and memorandums considered by the Second Comptroller in reaching his decision. For other letters on pay and bounty claims, see entries 191 and 192.

191.   LETTERS SENT BY THE BACK PAY AND BOUNTY DIVISION. July 25, 1879 - Mar. 9, 1895. 91 cm, 3 ft. 31 vols.

Arranged chronologically. Volumes 4-12, 14-18, and 30 have indexes arranged alphabetically by initial letter of title or surname of addressee, or claimant. The index to volume 4 is bound in the back of the volume. The other volumes are not indexed.

There are gaps in the date span of these records; the actual dates covered are: July 25, 1879-Mar. 10, 1889; June 9, 1889-Mar. 9, 1895.

Press copies of letters and endorsements, chiefly to the Second Auditor, but some are to claimants or their representatives, relating to pay and bounty claims appealed to the Second Comptroller. Volume 30 contains copies of decisions, July 1, 1892-June 10, 1894.

For copies of other letters and endorsements on pay and bounty claims, see entries 190 and 192.

192.   LETTERS, ENDORSEMENTS, AND DECISIONS SENT RELATING TO PAY AND BOUNTY CLAIMS. Feb. 6, 1886-Feb. 27, 1893. 30 cm, 1 ft. 5 vols.

Arranged chronologically within each volume, with considerable overlapping of date coverage among the volumes. Each volume has an index arranged alphabetically by initial letter of surname of party in interest, and the first and last volumes also have separate indexes arranged alphabetically by subject.

Press copies of letters, endorsements, and decisions prepared in the Comptroller's Office for the guidance of Auditors responsible for settlement of pay and bounty claims.

For other letters and endorsements on these subjects, see entries 190 and 191.

193.   DECISIONS ON PAY AND BOUNTY CLAIMS. Oct. 19, 1889-July 19, 1892. 3 cm, 1 in. 1 vol.

Arranged chronologically.

Press copies of decisions showing date, subject, points involved, basic ruling, and usually a citation to the source in which the full text of the decision appears. Many of the citations are to letters sent by the Army Paymasters Division (entry 196).

For related abstracts and letters prepared by the First Comptroller, see entries 68 and 69.

Records Relating to Accounts and Claims

194.   REGISTERS OF ACCOUNTS AND CLAIMS. Nov. 1, 1885-Sept. 29, 1894. 91 cm, 3 ft. 8 vols.

Arranged alphabetically by first three letters of officer's or claimant's surname.

Registers contain entries that show number assigned to account or claim, name and identity of officer or claimant, type of claim (usually for back pay, bounty, or transportation), dates received and acted upon, and record of action taken. If a claim was approved, the title of the appropriation from which it was to be paid is shown.

ARMY PAYMASTERS DIVISION

The Army Paymasters Division was established in the Second Comptroller's Office on November 1, 1885, to take over the functions formerly performed by the Army Back Pay and Bounty Division with respect to paymasters accounts. The Division also reviewed accounts audited in the Second Auditor's Paymasters Division relating to expenditures for the National Home for Disabled Volunteer Soldiers; accounts of disbursing officers for the medical, ordnance, and recruiting services; and accounts for contingent expenses of the Army.

Correspondence

195.   LETTERS SENT RELATING TO PAY (PAY DECISIONS). Sept. 22, 1860-July 31, 1863. 3 cm, 1 in. 1 vol.

Arranged by subject, thereunder by type of document (letters, opinions, and decisions), and thereunder chronologically.

Fair copies of letters, opinions, and decisions of the Paymaster General, Adjutant General, and Second Comptroller, setting forth basic policy statements with respect to various questions arising relating to pay of troops. Documents relating to a specific subject are usually grouped together. A section at the back of the book specifies the legal basis for pay and emoluments of various ranks of military officers and furnishes instructions for the use of the Army Paymasters Division in settling accounts and claims.

For other letters relating to pay, see entries 69 and 196.

196.   LETTERS SENT BY THE ARMY PAYMASTERS DIVISION. Nov. 4, 1885-Nov. 28, 1894. 18 cm, 7 in. 7 vols.

Arranged chronologically. Each volume, except volume 2, has an index arranged alphabetically by initial letter of subject, surname or title of addressee, or surname of the party involved.

Press copies of letters and endorsements sent chiefly to Auditors, paymasters, and other War Department officials, relating to settlement of pay and recruiting accounts; contingent expenses of the Army; disbursements for the Soldiers Home, the National Home for Disabled Volunteer Soldiers, and the ordnance and medical services; and miscellaneous claims. Also included are copies of decisions on appeals.

For later decisions on these and similar subjects, see entry 69.

Records Relating to Accounts and Claims

197.   REGISTERS OF ACCOUNTS AND CLAIMS REPORTED ON BY THE SECOND AUDITOR (SECOND AUDITOR'S REPORTS). Mar. 15, 1817-July 30, 1894. 5.2 m, 17 ft. 69 vols.

Arranged by settlement number and thereunder chronologically by date of Comptroller's approval. Beginning with the volume for May 1, 1829, each volume has an index arranged alphabetically by initial letter of officer's or claimant's surname. The other volumes are not indexed.

There are gaps in the date span of these records; the actual dates covered are: March 15, 1817-Jan. 7, 1822; Mar. 20, 1824-July 30, 1894.

Registers contain entries that show date reported, settlement number, name of officer or claimant, debits and credits, date approved, balance, and titles of appropriations to be charged or credited. The account numbering system began again with number 1 approximately every 10,000 accounts, beginning with March 1836.

For a separate series of registers of paymasters accounts reported on by the Second Auditor after 1863, see entry 198. Some of the original accounts and claims entered in these two series of registers are among records described in entries 516, 517, 519, and 523.

198.   REGISTERS OF ARMY PAYMASTERS ACCOUNTS REPORTED ON BY THE SECOND AUDITOR (PAYMASTERS ACCOUNTS). Jan. 5, 1864-Nov. 28, 1894. 1.8 m, 6 ft. 21 vols.

Arranged numerically by settlement number and thereunder chronologically by date of approval by the Second Comptroller. Each volume has an index arranged alphabetically by initial letter of paymaster's surname.

Registers contain entries that show settlement number, officer's name, period covered by account, debits and credits, dates audited and approved, titles of appropriations to be charged or credited, and balance. Paymasters accounts dated before 1864 are entered in the registers described in entry 197.

For muster rolls and payrolls selected from paymasters accounts, 1861-67, see entries 517 and 519.

199.   REGISTER OF REPORTS ON CLAIMS FOR PAY DUE DECEASED SOLDIERS. Feb. 24, 1854-Mar. 15, 1861. 3 cm, 1 in. 1 vol.

Arranged numerically by claim number and thereunder chronologically by date approved.

Register contains entries of Second Auditor's reports on reimbursement claims filed by the Treasurer of the Military Asylum, showing date reported, claim number, claimant's name, date approved, settlement number, and amount allowed. The settlements are entered in the register described in entry 200.

For other records relating to claims on behalf of deceased soldiers, see entries 200, 201, and 439.

200.   REGISTER OF SETTLED CLAIMS ON BEHALF OF DECEASED SOLDIERS. July 28, 1862-Aug. 26, 1863. 8 cm, 3 in. 1 vol.

Arranged alphabetically by initial letter of deceased soldier's surname and thereunder chronologically by date claim was approved.

Register contains entries that show soldier's name; certificate number; claimant's relationship to soldier; agent's or attorney's name; soldier's rank, military unit, and period of service; type of claim; and date approved. Most claims were for pay and bounty.

For other records relating to claims for deceased soldiers, see entries 199, 201, and 439. This register is also used as a register of contracts for Army rendezvous described in entry 219.

201.   REGISTER OF PROCEEDS FROM SALE OF EFFECTS OF DECEASED SOLDIERS. July 16, 1863-Mar. 10, 1865. 5 cm, 2 in. 1 vol.

Arranged alphabetically by initial letter of soldier's surname and thereunder chronologically by date of payment.

Register contains entries that show deceased soldier's name, rank, and military unit; when and by whom proceeds for sale of effects were paid; and amount. Sometimes, a certificate number and date of the soldier's death are also shown.

For other records relating to claims on behalf of deceased soldiers see entries 199, 200, and 439.

ARMY PENSION DIVISION

The Army Pension Division was established in the Second Comptroller's Office about July 1885 to review and approve accounts audited by the Second and Third Auditors for disbursements by pension agents and for claims for reimbursement to heirs of deceased pensioners.

Correspondence

202.   LETTERS RECEIVED RELATING TO PENSIONS. June 4, 1819-Nov. 5, 1842. 3 cm, 1 in. 1 vol.

Arranged chronologically.
Letters from the War Department's Pension Office, relating chiefly to changes in pension rolls or in rates of pensions payable to specific pensioners, appointments of pension agents, and status of appropriations for the War and Navy Departments. Additional letters on some of these subjects are included among the letters described in entry 182.

203.   LAWS, REGULATIONS, AND DECISIONS RELATING TO PENSIONS. Jan. 1, 1854 - Dec. 4, 1882. 8 cm, 3 in. 1 vol.

Arranged chronologically. Indexed alphabetically by keyword of subject.
Compilation of laws, regulations, and decisions relating to the settlement of pension accounts and claims. Compiled under instructions of the Second Comptroller issued July 24, 1862. A copy of these instructions is included in the volume.
For other decisions relating to pension cases, see entries 186 and 204.

204.   LETTERS SENT ON DECISIONS RELATING TO PENSIONS. Jan. 13, 1880-Sept. 30, 1894. 13 cm, 5 in. 5 vols.

Arranged in two subseries and chronologically within each subseries. Each volume, except the one for 1894, has an index arranged alphabetically by initial letter of surname, title of addressee, or subject.
There is a gap in the date span of these records. Actual dates covered are: Jan. 13, 1880-Aug. 28, 1881; Nov. 17, 1887-Sept. 30, 1894.
Press copies of decisions in pension appeals, January 13, 1880-April 28, 1881, addressed chiefly to pension agents, Members of Congress, or the Attorney General; also press copies of letters sent to pension agents, pensioners, or their legal representatives, or to the Secretary of the Treasury relating chiefly to settlement of accounts of pension agents or settlement of pension reimbursement claims. Letters sent by the Third Auditor reflecting his initial action on these claims are described in entry 572. Most letters to the Secretary of the Treasury were time reports or work reports.
For other records relating to pension decisions, see entries 186 and 203.

Records Relating to Pensions

205.   REGISTERS OF PENSION ACCOUNTS AND CLAIMS REPORTED ON BY THE THIRD AUDITOR (PENSION REPORTS FROM THIRD AUDITOR). Jan. 3, 1882-Nov. 17, 1894. 1.8 m, 6 ft. 22 vols.

Arranged numerically by settlement number and thereunder chronologically by date of approval by the Second Comptroller. Each volume has an index arranged alphabetically by initial letter of pensioner's or officer's surname. The spine numbers are 89-111. No. 99 is missing.
There is a gap in the date span of these records. Actual dates covered are: Jan. 3, 1882-Dec. 5, 1888; May 13, 1889-Nov. 17, 1894.

Registers contain entries that show settlement number, pensioner's or pension agent's name, debits and credits, dates reported and approved, titles of appropriations to be charged and credited, and balance. The settlement numbers began again with number 1 in July 1887, December 1890, and May 1894. Reports on earlier pension claims are registered in the volumes described in entry 258.

For related correspondence, see entries 203 and 572.

206.   REGISTERS OF PENSION PAYMENTS. ca. 1811-68. 91 cm, 3 ft. 14 vols.

Arranged chronologically by date of pension act, thereunder geographically by location of pension agency, and thereunder alphabetically by initial letter of soldier's surname.

Registers contain entries of payments under pension acts of 1816, 1818, 1832, 1838, 1843, 1844, 1848, and 1862 showing location of pension agency, soldier's name and rank or pensioner's name and relationship to soldier, pension rate, and dates of payments. Dates of death, final payments, and transfers of pensioners from the rolls of one agency to another also are sometimes shown.

For related registers of pension payments, see entries 586 and 589.

QUARTERMASTER DIVISION

The Quartermaster Division is first mentioned as a Division in the Second Comptroller's Office in July 1885. Its chief functions were (1) review accounts and claims audited by the Third Auditor for expenses of the quartermaster, subsistence, engineer, and signal services of the Army and (2) recording and filing contracts. Contracts dated after 1894, with related registers and indexes, are described with records of the First Comptroller's Division of Bonds, Contracts, and Powers of Attorney.

Correspondence

207.   LETTERS SENT BY THE QUARTERMASTER DIVISION. Feb. 19, 1886-Nov. 19, 1894. 15 cm, 6 in. 6 vols.

Arranged chronologically. Each volume has an index arranged alphabetically by initial letter of surname of party in interest, title of official addressed, or subject.

Press copies of letters sent chiefly to Auditors and War Department officials, relating to the adjustment of quartermaster, engineer, and signal service accounts and claims and decisions on related appeals. Included are copies of work reports sent to the Secretary of the Treasury for use in preparing the Annual Report on the State of the Finances.

Records Relating to Accounts and Claims

208.   REGISTERS OF REPORTS ON ACCOUNTS AND CLAIMS FOR SUBSISTENCE, PENSIONS, AND BUREAU OF REFUGEES, FREEDMEN, AND ABANDONED LANDS (THIRD AUDITOR'S REPORTS, NEW SERIES). Aug. 1, 1865-Jan. 9, 1878. 1.8 m, 6 ft. 18 vols.

Arranged numerically by settlement number and thereunder chronologically by date of approval by the Second Comptroller. Each volume has an index arranged alphabetically by initial letter of officer's or claimant's surname.

Registers contain entries that show settlement number, name of accountable officer or claimant, debits and credits, dates reported and approved, titles of appropriations to be charged and credited, and balance. The account numbers began again with number 1 in July 1868 and September 1875. Other pension accounts and claims are entered in the registers described in entries 205 and 258; other subsistence accounts and claims are also included in entry 258.

209.   REGISTERS OF QUARTERMASTER ACCOUNTS AND MISCELLANEOUS CLAIMS
        REPORTED ON BY THE THIRD AUDITOR. Feb. 4, 1878-Dec. 18, 1894. 1.5 m, 5 ft.
        15 vols.

Arranged numerically by settlement number and thereunder chronologically by date of
approval by the Second Comptroller. Each volume has an index arranged alphabetically by
initial letter of officer's or claimant's surname.

Registers contain entries that show settlement number, name of accountable officer or
claimant, explanation of the account or claim, debits and credits, dates reported and approved,
titles of appropriations to be charged and credited, and balance. The settlement numbers began
again with number 1 in June 1883, March 1886, December 1887, and May 1890. Beginning in 1882,
a page and volume reference to docket books of miscellaneous claims is included instead of the
balance of the account, and, beginning in April 1885, the claim number is shown in addition to
the settlement number.

The accounts and claims registered in this series and related docket books are described
in entries 658 and 712.

210.   ABSTRACTS OF ACTION TAKEN ON ACCOUNTS AND CLAIMS (DOCKET NO. 1).
        Aug. 8, 1864-Jan. 25, 1870. 5 cm, 2 in. 1 vol.

Arranged chronologically. This volume has an index arranged alphabetically by
initial letter of officer's or claimant's surname.

Record of action on accounts, 1864-68, and on claims, 1869-70, showing name of
accountable officer or claimant, explanation of the account or claim, and dates and types of
action taken by the Third Auditor and the Second Comptroller. Entries for accounts usually
relate to efforts to collect from delinquent officers, and entries for claims relate primarily to
purchase of quartermaster stores or use of private vessels by the Government during the Civil
War for military purposes.

See also registers of accounts reported for suit, entry 188.

Index, Registers, and Abstracts

211.   GENERAL INDEX TO CONTRACTS. June 1862-Apr. 1889. 30 cm, 1 ft. 4 vols.

Arranged alphabetically by initial letter of surname of contracting official.

There is a gap in the date span of these records; actual dates covered are: June 1862-June
1867; Aug. 1887-Apr. 1889.

Index showing names of parties involved; type, date, and file number of contract; and
date received. Some of the more common types of contracts entered in these indexes are for
furnishing food, hay, clothing, lumber, hardware, transportation, and medical supplies and
services; improving rivers and harbors; dredging and other engineering services; renting,
repairing, and constructing buildings, and burying deceased soldiers. Many of these contracts are
also entered in the general registers of bonds, contracts, and leases, entry 212.

212.   GENERAL REGISTERS OF BONDS, CONTRACTS, AND LEASES. Nov. 1817-
        Nov. 1894. 61 cm, 2 ft. 10 vols.

Arranged alphabetically by initial letters of surnames of parties involved.

Registers contain entries that show names of parties involved, terms of contract or
lease, and price. Entries for bonds show bonded officer's name and title and date and amount of
bond. The contracts and leases entered in these registers are also frequently entered in the
general index to contracts (entry 211) and are for furnishing food, building materials, horses,
hay, straw, wood, clothing, and handguns; chartering ships; transportation; and constructing
roads and bridges. For later general registers of contracts, see entry 138.

213.   ABSTRACTS OF CONTRACTS AND LEASES. Dec. 20, 1877-June 24, 1885. 3 cm, 1 in. 1 vol.

Arranged chronologically. Indexed by initial letters of surnames of parties to contract or lease.

Abstracts show date, names of parties involved, and the terms.

The contracts were chiefly for medical services, and the leases were chiefly for use of Army rendezvous officials. Some of the original contracts are described in entries 216 and 229; they are also entered in the index described in entry 211.

Military Contracts and Leases

214.   GENERAL CONTRACTS FOR THE WAR DEPARTMENT. July 1878-Aug. 1893. 61 cm, 2 ft. 2 boxes.

Arranged by year and thereunder alphabetically by initial letter of contractor's surname.

Contracts, chiefly for stationery and office supplies for use by the War Department, showing names of parties involved, date, terms, and price. Some of these contracts are entered in the register described in entry 212.

For later general contracts for the War Department, see entry 168.

215.   REGISTER OF CONTRACTS FOR THE ADJUTANT GENERAL'S OFFICE. Sept. 1861 - Feb. 1876. 8 cm, 3 in. 1 vol.

Arranged alphabetically by initial letter of contractor's surname.

Register contains entries that show names of parties involved, dates signed and received for filing, terms, and cost. Most of the contracts were for furnishing rooms for administrative use of rendezvous or recruiting officers or lodging for recruits. Some of these contracts are described in entry 216.

For additional contracts for the Adjutant General's Office (AGO), see entries 212 and 219.

216.   CONTRACTS FOR THE ADJUTANT GENERAL'S OFFICE. July 1861-Oct. 1893. 3.4 m, 11 ft. 11 boxes.

Arranged by year and thereunder alphabetically by initial letter of contractor's surname.

Contracts show names of parties involved, date, terms, and price.

Contracts made by the AGO during the Civil War are chiefly for use of rooms for administrative and medical purposes by Army rendezvous officers and for furnishing lodgings for recruits. Later contracts are for furnishing coal, fuel, and lumber for military posts; furnishing fresh beef for military prisons; constructing monuments in military parks (frequently accompanied by blueprints); and furnishing stationery and office supplies. Later contracts relating to military parks are described in entry 163. Contracts for the AGO are entered in the registers described in entries 212, 215, and 219.

217.   ABSTRACT OF CONTRACTS FOR FURNISHING RATIONS FOR THE ARMY. Nov. 1811 - Mar. 1813. 1 cm, 1/2 in. Unbound records.

Arranged chronologically.

Abstract of contracts shows contractor's name, date of contract and period covered, place of delivery, prices of component parts of the ration, and total price.

218.   ARMY CONTRACTS. May 1794-July 1861. 10.4 m, 34 ft. 1 box.

Arranged by year and thereunder alphabetically by initial letter of contractor's surname.

There are gaps in the date span of these records; the actual dates covered are: May 1794 - Dec. 1817, with gaps; Jan. 1837-July 1861.

Contracts show date, names of parties involved, terms, and cost. Much of the same information is abstracted on the cover sheet of each contract. Contracts for 1794-1817 are fragmentary and are chiefly for furnishing rations. Later contracts include the furnishing of weapons, subsistence, medical supplies and services, and transportation and engineering services. Some of these contracts are entered in the registers described in entry 212.

Alpha boxes: 1A

219.   REGISTER OF CONTRACTS FOR ARMY RENDEZVOUS. Sept. 1861-Aug. 1865. 8 cm, 3 in. 1 vol.

This series is missing.

Arranged alphabetically by initial letter of surname of parties involved.

Register contains entries that show date, names of parties involved, location of the rendezvous, and cost per month. Entries giving the names of contractors are on one side of the page; entries giving the names of contracting officers are on facing pages. Many of these entries duplicate those in the register described in entry 215. Some of the contracts are described in entries 216 and 234. Part of this volume is used as a register of claims on behalf of deceased soldiers (entry 200).

220.   REGISTERS OF COMMISSARY CONTRACTS. Jan. 1862-Oct. 1887. 20 cm, 8 in. 3 vols.

Arranged alphabetically by initial letter of contractor's surname. Spine titles vary.

Registers contain entries that show date, names of parties involved, terms, and price. Most contracts were for furnishing clothing, food, fuel, and hay. Original contracts are described in entries 218 and 221; some of these contracts are also entered in the indexes and registers described in entries 211 and 212, respectively.

221.   COMMISSARY CONTRACTS. Nov. 1817-Nov. 1893. 32.0 m, 105 ft. 105 boxes.

Arranged by year and thereunder alphabetically by initial letter of contractor's surname.

There are gaps in the date span of these records; the actual dates covered are: Nov. 1817-Apr. 1836; Jan. 1861-Nov. 1893.

Contracts show date, names of parties involved, terms, and price.

The contracts are chiefly for furnishing rations, live cattle, hay, coffee, flour, soap, and candles. Some commissary contracts for the 1837-60 period are among those described in entry 218. Many of these contracts are entered in the index described in entry 211 and in the registers described in entries 212 and 220.

222.   REGISTER OF ENGINEER CONTRACTS. Sept. 1879-Oct. 1887. 5 cm, 2 in. 1 vol.

Arranged by initial letter of contractor's surname.

Register contains entries that show date of contract, names of parties involved, terms, unit price, amounts withheld, amounts actually paid, and titles of appropriations from which the payments were made. Many of these contracts were for supplies needed for improving rivers and harbors, dredging, and removing wrecks. Some of the contracts registered in this volume are described in entries 218 and 223, and some are entered in the index and registers described in entries 211 and 212.

223.   ENGINEER CONTRACTS. June 1817-Nov. 1893. 24.7 m, 81 ft. 81 boxes.

Arranged by year and thereunder partly by construction project and partly by initial letter of contractor's surname.
There are gaps in the date span of these records. Actual dates covered are: June 1817-Dec. 1836; Mar. 1860-Nov. 1864; June 1866-Nov. 1893.
Contracts show date, names of parties involved, terms, and price. The contracts for 1817-36 are chiefly for construction of the Cumberland Road and military roads and are arranged by project. The later contracts are for general construction or repair, constructing breakwaters, dredging rivers and harbors, and removing wrecks. Some contracts for the 1837-59 period are among those described in entry 218. These contracts are entered in the index described in entry 211 and in the registers described in entries 212 and 222.

224.   FREEDMEN'S BUREAU CONTRACTS. Mar. 1867-Aug. 1870. 10 cm, 4 in. 1 box.

Arranged chronologically.
Contracts show date, names of parties involved, terms, and cost. The contracts typically are for construction of schools in Florida, Kentucky, and South Carolina; construction of dormitories in the Washington, D.C., area; and supplies for Freedmen's Hospital. Some other Freedmen's Bureau contracts are entered in the registers described in entry 212.
For later supply contracts for this hospital, see entry 159.

225.   INDEXES TO INDIAN CONTRACTS. ca. July 1873-June 1894. 30 cm, 1 ft. 13 vols.

Arranged by initial letter of contractor's surname.
Index volumes show date, contractor's name, and, usually, contract number. Volumes after 1885 show the article or service to be furnished. Entries for transportation contracts show points of origin and delivery and length of time allowed. Two volumes, dated 1882-83 and 1883-84, also show the price to be paid and a record of deliveries actually made under the contract. The contracts registered in these indexes are among the records described in entry 227; they are also registered in the volumes described in entries 212 and 226. Boxes 110 and 126 also contain entry 277.
For later Indian contracts and related indexes, see entries 146 and 148.

226.   REGISTERS OF INDIAN CONTRACTS. 1874-94. 61 cm, 2 ft. 9 vols.

Arranged by initial letter of contractor's surname.
Registers contain entries that show date, names of parties involved terms, and price. Many of the contracts were for furnishing beef, food, clothing, coal, glue, hardware, or medical supplies, and transporting goods to Indian reservations. Some of these contracts are described in entry 227 and are entered in the indexes and registers described in entries 212 and 225.
For later Indian contracts and related indexes, see entries 146 and 148.

227.   INDIAN CONTRACTS. Nov. 1820-1894. 33.8 m, 111 ft. 138 boxes.

Arranged by year and thereunder partly by contract number and partly by initial letter of contractor's surname.
There are gaps in the date span of these records; the actual dates covered are: Nov. 1820-Nov. 1836; 1870-94.
Contracts show date, names of parties involved, terms, and price. The contracts were entered into by the Commissioner of Indian Affairs and other Government officials for such

items as bread, sugar, salt, window glass, axes, cattle, fresh beef, and transportation of supplies to Indian reservations. Some of these contracts are entered in the indexes described in entries 211 and 225 and in the registers described in entries 212 and 226. Later Indian contracts and related indexes and registers are described in entries 146-148. Boxes 110 and 126 contain parts of entry 225.

228.   CONTRACTS AND LEASES FOR THE MARINE CORPS. May 1888-Mar. 1892. 23 cm, 9 in. 1 box.

Arranged by type of contract and thereunder by year.

Contracts show date, names of parties involved, terms, and price. The leases are usually for rooms for use as office space for recruiting officers and assistant quartermasters. Contracts are grouped in the following categories: rations and fuel, clothing and contingencies, construction of barracks, building materials, forage, stationery, electricity, laundry service, military stores, and board and lodging. Not all of these types of contracts are available for each year.

229.   MEDICAL CONTRACTS. May 1821-Dec. 1893. 6.7 m, 22 ft. 23 boxes.

Arranged by year and thereunder by initial letter of contractor's surname.

There are gaps in the date span of these records; the actual dates covered are: May 1821-Oct. 1836; Nov. 1859-Dec. 1893.

Contracts show date, names of parties involved, terms, and price. Most contracts were for professional services, but some were for furnishing medicines and other necessary medical supplies. Some medical contracts, 1837-59, are among the Army contracts described in entry 218. Medical contracts are partially registered in the volumes described in entry 212, and some are abstracted in the volume described in entry 213.

230.   INDEX TO NAVY BONDS AND CONTRACTS. Nov. 1818-Oct. 1841. 5 cm, 2 in. 2 vols.

Arranged by initial letter of contractor's or official's surname.

Index shows names of bonded officers or contractors and the dates of their bonds or contracts, and, beginning with 1837, the type and terms of the contract. Some of these contracts are among those described in entry 232 and entered in the registers described in entries 212 and 231. Later Navy contracts and related indexes and registers are described in entries 174-176.

231.   REGISTERS OF NAVY CONTRACTS. Jan. 1841-Feb. 1895. 61 cm, 2 ft. 9 vols.

Arranged in part chronologically and in part by initial letter of surnames of parties involved. Three volumes, January 1, 1841-August 14, 1869, are arranged chronologically. Five volumes, July 1868-July 1889 and May 1875-December 1894, are arranged alphabetically by initial letter of contractor's surname. One volume, June 1888-February 1895, is arranged alphabetically by initial letter of contracting officer's surname. The three chronological volumes are each indexed by initial letter of contractor's surname.

Registers contain entries that show date, names of parties involved, and terms. The contracts are for such items as food, clothing, building materials, iron, fuel, oars, tools, and office supplies. The contracts registered in these volumes are described in entry 232, and some are entered in the indexes and registers described in entries 212 and 230.

For later Navy contracts, with related indexes and registers, see entries 174-176.

232.   NAVY CONTRACTS. May 1795-Oct. 1893. 52.4 m, 172 ft. Unbound records.

Arranged by year and thereunder by initial letter of contractor's surname.

Contracts show date, names of parties involved, terms, and price. Contracts are for construction, modification, and repair of vessels (particularly during the Civil War); armaments; gunpowder; wood; ship chandlery; food; and construction of diving bells. Plans and specifications are filed with many of these contracts. The contracts are entered in the indexes described in entries 211 and 230 and in the registers described in entries 212 and 231. There is a box 134A.

For later Navy contracts, with related indexes and registers, see entries 174-176.

233.   ORDNANCE CONTRACTS. Sept. 1798-Nov. 1893. 29.9 m, 98 ft. 99 boxes.

Arranged by year and thereunder by initial letter of contractor's surname.

There are gaps in the date span of these records; the actual dates covered are: Sept. 1798-Sept. 1836; June 1862-Nov. 1893.

Contracts show date, names of parties involved, terms, and price. Most of the contracts were for furnishing ammunition, coke, rivets, lumber, gun wads, extractor levers, cartridges, and articles needed for the care of weapons. Many of the contracts dated after the Civil War were for stationery and office supplies. Some Army ordnance contracts, 1837-61, are among the records described in entry 218. The contracts are entered in the registers described in entry 212.

For later ordnance contracts and related indexes, see entries 139, 177, and 178.

234.   PROVOST MARSHAL'S CONTRACTS. Dec. 1862-Apr. 1866. 91 cm, 3 ft. 2 boxes.

Arranged by initial letter of contractor's surname and thereunder by year.

Contracts show dates, names of parties involved, terms, and cost. Most of the contracts are accompanied by loyalty oaths and relate to furnishing rooms for use of recruiting officers and furnishing room and board for recruits. Similar contracts are described in entry 216. For a register of some of these contracts, see entry 219.

235.   REGISTERS OF QUARTERMASTER CONTRACTS. July 1876-Oct. 1887. 25 cm, 10 in. 4 vols.

Arranged by initial letter of contractor's surname.

Registers contain entries that show date, names of parties involved, terms, and price. Most of the contracts registered in these volumes were for furnishing food, clothing, wood, fuel, tents, horses, hay, and mules; chartering vessels; and renting lands, buildings, and equipment. The contracts are described in entry 236. Quartermaster contracts are also entered in the indexes and registers described in entries 211 and 212.

236.   QUARTERMASTER CONTRACTS. Dec. 1818-Dec. 1893. 93.9 m, 308 ft. 311 boxes.

Arranged by year and thereunder by initial letter of contractor's surname .

There are gaps in the date span of these records; the actual dates covered are: December 1818-Dec. 1836; Apr. 1860-Dec. 1893.

Contracts show date, names of parties involved, terms, and price. Among the many types of contracts in this series are those for furnishing horses, hay, straw, fodder, food, clothing, canteens, and blankets; construction work at Army posts and cemeteries; furnishing wagons, ambulances, and spare parts for them; chartering vessels for transportation of troops and supplies; and renting rooms and buildings. Some of these contracts are accompanied by plans and specifications. Some quartermaster contracts for 1837-59 are among the records described in entry 218. The contracts are entered in the indexes and registers described in entries 211, 212, and 235. Alpha boxes: 1A, 1B, 1C, 1D, 21A, 25A, and 185A.

237.   INDEXES TO CONTRACTS FOR CHARTER OF VESSELS (INDEXES TO CHARTER
        PARTIES). Mar. 1862-Mar. 1867. 3 cm, 1 in. 2 vols.

        Arranged alphabetically by initial letter of vessel name. The cover title of volume 1 is:
"Alphabet of Charter Parties;" the cover title of volume 2 is: "Index to Charter Parties."
        Indexes to vessel leases listed in volumes 4 and 5 of the general registers of bonds,
contracts, and leases (entry 212), showing type and name of vessel and page reference (but not
volume references) to the registers. The contracts are described in entry 238.

238.   CONTRACTS FOR CHARTER OF VESSELS (CHARTER PARTIES). June 1860-Mar.
        1867. 3.1 m, 10 ft. 11 boxes.

        Arranged alphabetically by name of vessel.
        Contracts show names of parties involved, date, name of vessel, and terms of charter.
Most of the contracts are for vessels chartered by the Quartermaster Department of the Army
for transporting troops and supplies during the Civil War. The indexes described in entry 237
can be used as a finding aid to these contracts. Some of the contracts are, in addition, registered
in the volumes described in entry 212.

239.   CONTRACTS FOR THE U.S. ARMY SIGNAL CORPS. June 1879-May 1893. 2.1 m, 7 ft.
        7 boxes.

        Arranged by year and thereunder by initial letter of contractor's surname.
        Contracts show date, names of parties involved, terms, and price. Many of the contracts
are for purchasing supplies needed for telegraph maintenance, wood, stationery, and office
supplies; constructing houses and cisterns; chartering vessels for use of the Signal Corps; and
renting rooms and buildings for office space. The series includes one contract for May 1871 and
one contract for June 1893. Some of these contracts are entered in the registers described in
entry 212.
        For later contracts for the Signal Corps and a related index, see entries 179 and 180.

NAVY DIVISION

        The Navy Division is first mentioned as a Division in the Second Comptroller's Office
in July 1885. Its primary function was the settlement of accounts and claims audited by the
Fourth Auditor for paymasters and Navy agents, for disbursing officers for the Navy
Department, and for agents who paid Navy and Marine Corps pensions. The Division also
settled accounts for pay, bounty, prize money due officers and crews of Navy ships, and
miscellaneous accounts and claims relating to the Navy and Marine Corps.

Correspondence

240.   LETTERS SENT BY THE NAVY DIVISION. Sept. 20, 1888-Mar. 10, 1894. 20 cm, 8 in.
        7 vols.

        Arranged chronologically. Each volume is indexed by initial letter of subject, by name
of person, and by title of official. Volumes 1-7 and 14 are missing.
        There are gaps in the date span of these records; the actual dates covered are: Sept. 20,
1888-Nov. 29, 1891; Jan. 1, 1893-Mar. 10, 1894.
        Press copies of letters relating to the resolution of disputes over the settlement of
accounts and claims. Most of the letters were addressed to the Fourth Auditor or the Secretaries
of the Navy and Treasury Departments.

Records Relating to Accounts and Claims

241.   INDEX TO SETTLED CLAIMS. Jan. 1855-July 1899. 25 cm, 10 in. 4 vols.

Arranged alphabetically by initial letter of claimant's surname and thereunder by month and year of settlement.

Partial index to registers of certificates of settled claims (Certificate Settlements) (entry 242), showing month and year of settlement, claimant's name, type of claim, and a settlement number or volume and page reference to the registers. Beginning with September 1897, only the claimant's name and type of claim are shown.

242.   REGISTERS   OF   CERTIFICATES   OF   SETTLED   CLAIMS   (CERTIFICATE SETTLEMENTS). July 5, 1844-Sept. 28, 1894. 1.2 m, 4 ft. 20 vols.

Volume 1 appears to be missing.

Volumes 1-3 (July 5, 1844-June 7, 1865) are arranged chronologically and indexed by initial letter of claimant's surname. Volumes 4-12 are arranged by initial letter of claimant's surname and thereunder chronologically.

Registers contain entries that show claimant's name and rank, date, type of claim, amount due, and when and where payable. Most claims are for bounty and prize money. Volume 1 was originally intended for use as a register of requisitions. Part of volume 2 is used as a register of transcripts of accounts sent to the Solicitor for suit, 1813-22 (entry 188).

Volumes 4-12 are each bound in two parts, covering surnames beginning with the letters A-K and L-Z, respectively. The second part of volume 12 is missing. Copies of some of the certificates are described in entry 778.

For a partial index to these registers, see entry 241.

243.   REGISTERS OF ACCOUNTS FOR CLAIMS REPORTED BY THE FOURTH AUDITOR. Jan. 10, 1822-Sept. 28, 1894. 2.1 m, 7 ft. 25 vols.

Arranged by settlement number and thereunder chronologically by date of Comptroller's approval. Beginning with the third volume (May 1, 1829), each volume is indexed by initial letter of claimant's surname.

There are gaps in the date span of these records; the actual dates covered are: Jan. 10, 1822-Dec. 30, 1824; June 26, 1827-May 31, 1836; Jan. 2, 1852-Sept. 28,1894.

Registers contain entries that show date reported and approved, settlement number, claimant's name, explanation, adjusted balance, and titles of appropriations to be charged. Many of the accounts were for settlement of individual pension claims; others were accounts of pension agents and Navy paymasters. The original accounts and claims are described in entry 812.

For other registers of accounts of these two types of officials, see entry 244.

244.   REGISTERS OF ACCOUNTS FOR CLAIMS REPORTED BY THE FOURTH AUDITOR, "A" SERIES. Oct. 4, 1870-Oct. 6, 1894. 91 cm, 3 ft. 10 vols.

Arranged by settlement number and thereunder chronologically by date of Comptroller's approval. Each volume is indexed by initial letter of claimant's surname.

Register contains entries that show settlement number, dates reported and approved, claimant's name, balance of previous settled accounts, debit and credit entries, title of appropriations concerned, and adjusted balance. Many of the accounts were submitted by Navy paymasters or pension agents or by former accountable officers. Certificates of settlement of these accounts and claims are described in entry 777.

For registers of accounts of these officials before 1870, see entry 243.

245.   REGISTER OF ACCOUNTS FOR PAYMENT TO CONTRACTORS. Apr. 20, 1853-
        Dec. 4, 1854. 1 cm, 1/2 in. 1 vol.

Arranged chronologically by date contract was approved.

Register contains entries that show contractor's name, dates contract was executed and
approved, voucher number, amounts payable and withheld, title of appropriation to be
charged, name of officer making the payment, period covered by account in which payment was
made, and date amount withheld was paid. Appropriations charged include navy yards, navy
hospitals, construction of vessels, provisions, contingent expenses, clothing, and ordnance. Some
of these contracts, and related registers, are described in entries 212, 231, and 232. Part of this
volume is used as a register of settled accounts, 1837-50 (entry 189).

INDIAN DIVISION

The Indian Division was first mentioned as a separate unit in the Second Comptroller's
Office in July 1885. The main function of the Division was to settle all accounts and claims
relating to Indians that were audited by the Second and Third Auditors. In addition, fiscal
records relating to treaties with the Cherokee Indians were required by law to be separately
maintained; such records, therefore, are also described as a part of the records of the Indian
Division. This function was transferred to the Department of the Interior by an act of
July 27, 1868.

Correspondence

246.   LETTERS RECEIVED RELATING TO INDIAN AFFAIRS. Apr. 12, 1875-Aug. 30, 1882.
        20 cm, 8 in. 1 box.

Arranged chronologically.

Primarily letters from the Commissioner of Indian Affairs transmitting copies of
contracts for supplies for the Indian Service, for constructing buildings on Indian reservations,
and for running boarding schools for Indians. Also included are a few letters from Indian agents
relating to their accounts. Registers of Indian contracts are described in entry 226, and the
original contracts in entry 227.

247.   LETTERS SENT BY THE INDIAN DIVISION. Apr. 10, 1875-Feb. 25, 1895. 1.2 m, 4 ft.
        37 vols.

Arranged chronologically. Each volume is indexed by name of person, title of official,
name of party in interest, and subject.

There are gaps in the date span of these records; the actual dates covered are: Apr. 10,
1875-Apr. 16, 1879; Jan. 23, 1880-June 25, 1887; Jan. 19, 1888-Feb. 25, 1895.

Press copies of letters to Auditors, other Government officials, and Indian agents and
their sureties relating principally to settlement of accounts and claims and the resolution of
disputes arising with relation to payments to contractors. Some memorandums, time reports, and
work reports are included in these volumes and indexed under M, T, and W, respectively.
Volumes 9, 10, and 31 are missing.

Fiscal Records

248.   CHICKASAW LEDGER. 1834-68. 8 cm, 3 in. 1 vol.

Arranged by title of account and thereunder chronologically. Indexed by initial letter of
title of account.

Ledger of receipts and expenditures under the Chickasaw Treaties of October 20, 1832, and May 24, 1834. Accounts show title of appropriation, dates and amounts of requisitions and warrants (entry 251), and source of funds.

249.   REGISTER OF REQUISITIONS FOR WARRANTS PAYABLE UNDER THE CHICKASAW TREATY OF OCTOBER 20, 1832. 1833-68. 8 cm, 3 in. 1 vol.

Arranged chronologically.

Register contains entries that show date and number of requisition, accountable officer's name, explanation, title of appropriation to be charged, and amount. Most of the requisitions were for moneys payable to surveyors-general, Indian agents, and contractors. Sometimes the date on which money actually was drawn against the requisition also is shown.

For a related register of warrants, see entry 250.

250.   REGISTERS OF WARRANTS ISSUED UNDER THE CHICKASAW TREATIES OF OCTOBER 20, 1832, AND MAY 24, 1834. 1837-68. 5 cm, 2 in. 2 vols.

Arranged by type of warrant and thereunder chronologically.

Registers contain entries that show date issued, warrant number, requisition number (entry 249), explanation, on whom drawn or in whose favor issued, title of appropriation to be charged or credited, and amount. The warrants were usually warrants in favor of the Treasurer, refund warrants, and warrants in favor of accountable officers.

251.   REQUISITIONS AND WARRANTS ISSUED UNDER THE CHICKASAW TREATIES OF OCTOBER 20, 1832, AND MAY 24, 1834. 1836-49. 8 cm, 3 in. 3 vols.

Arranged chronologically.

Requisitions show date and number of requisition, amount, name and title of accountable officer in whose favor requisition was issued, title of appropriation to be charged, and explanation. The warrants credited the Chickasaw Fund with moneys collected for interest on investments or from the sale of lands, and deposited into the Treasury for that purpose. The requisitions and warrants are interfiled in these volumes. Some of them are recorded in the ledger described in entry 248.

252.   REGISTER OF REQUISITIONS FOR REFUND WARRANTS. 1823-28. 3 cm, 1 in. 1 vol.

Arranged by requisition number and thereunder chronologically.

Register contains entries that show date and number of requisition, on whom drawn, explanation, title of appropriation concerned, ledger reference, and amount. These refund warrants were a method of transferring accountability for funds from the books of the Second Auditor to those of the Third Auditor.

Records Relating to Accounts and Claims

253.   REGISTER OF ACCOUNTS AND CLAIMS UNDER THE CHICKASAW TREATY REPORTED BY THE SECOND AUDITOR. 1834-68. 5 cm, 2 in. 1 vol.

Arranged by settlement number and thereunder chronologically by date of Comptroller's approval.

Register contains entries that show settlement number, claimant's or official's name, dates reported and approved, adjusted balance, and titles of appropriation accounts to be charged and credited. The accounts and claims were submitted to the Second Auditor by the General Land Office.

254.   REGISTERS OF ACCOUNTS FOR INDIAN CLAIMS REPORTED BY THE SECOND AUDITOR. Jan. 1875-Nov. 1894. 3.7 m, 12 ft. 39 vols.

Arranged by settlement number and thereunder chronologically by date of Comptroller's approval. Each volume is indexed by initial letter of claimant's or officer's surname. Volume 3 is missing.

There are gaps in the date span of these records; the actual dates covered are: Jan. 1875-July 1876; Feb. 1877-Nov. 1894.

Registers contain entries that show settlement number, dates reported and approved, claimant's or officer's name, explanation, titles of appropriations to be charged and credited, and adjusted balance. The settled accounts and claims are described in entry 525; for a record of balances of accounts of some of these Indian agents, see entry 255.

255.   REGISTER OF BALANCES OF ACCOUNTS OF INDIAN AGENTS. 1875-94. 5 cm, 2 in. 1 vol.

Arranged by officer's surname. Indexed by initial letter of officer's surname.

Register contains entries that show accountable officer's name and title, date of surety bond, where stationed, date account received, period during which moneys were disbursed, volume and page reference to statements of differences, volume and page reference to registers of accounts (entry 254), and adjusted balance. The settled accounts are described in entry 525.

MISCELLANEOUS CLAIMS DIVISION

The Miscellaneous Claims Division is first mentioned as a unit in the Second Comptroller's Office in July 1885. Its main function was to settle accounts audited by the Second and Third Auditors for claims relating to quartermaster stores, property lost in the service of the United States, State claims arising out of the Civil War, transportation and telegraph accounts and claims, and miscellaneous claims. The Division also issued duplicate checks, recorded requisitions and bonds, and transmitted transcripts of accounts for suit.

Correspondence

256.   LETTERS SENT BY THE MISCELLANEOUS CLAIMS DIVISION. Mar. 22, 1817 - Aug. 12, 1885. 3.7 m, 12 ft. 51 vols.

Arranged chronologically. Each volume is indexed by title of official or surname of addressee or party in interest.

Fair copies of letters sent to officials of the Treasury and War Departments, and to claimants and their representatives, relating to such matters as Civil War damage claims; settlement of accounts of Indian agents, pension agents, and Navy agents; estimates of funds; availability of appropriations; and receipt and filing of contracts and bonds. Other letters relating to Civil War claims are described in entry 257; other letters about Indian and pension agents' accounts are described in entry 258.

For some of the incoming letters to which these letters are replies, see entry 182.

257.   LETTERS SENT BY THE MISCELLANEOUS CLAIMS DIVISION. Feb. 1, 1886 Dec. 24, 1894. 61 cm, 2 ft. 17 vols.

Arranged chronologically. Each volume is indexed by initial letter of title of official, name of addressee, and name of party in interest.

Press copies of letters relating chiefly to Civil War damage claims, loss of horses in military service of the United States, and delinquent accounts. The letters were sent chiefly to

Auditors, other Government officials, and claimants. Other letters on these subjects are described in entry 258.

For some of the letters received, to which these letters are replies, see entry 182.

258.   LETTERS SENT BY THE MISCELLANEOUS CLAIMS DIVISION. July 23, 1885 - June 15, 1889. 1.5 m, 5 ft. 13 vols.

Arranged chronologically. Each volume is indexed by initial letter of title of official, name of addressee, and name of party in interest.

Carbon copies of letters relating chiefly to settlement of accounts of Indian agents and pension agents and to receipt and filing of bonds and contracts. Other letters on these subjects are described in entry 256.

For some of the letters received to which these letters are replies, see entry 182.

Records Relating to Accounts and Claims

259.   REGISTERS OF QUARTERMASTER AND MISCELLANEOUS ACCOUNTS AND CLAIMS REPORTED BY THE THIRD AUDITOR. Mar. 11, 1817-Nov. 30, 1894. 12.2 m, 40 ft. 145 vols.

Volumes are arranged chronologically. Entries in each volume are arranged numerically by settlement number, and thereunder chronologically by date of Comptroller's approval. The numbering of the accounts began again with number 1 on March 10, 1836, and approximately every 10,000 accounts thereafter. The registers are numbered 1-9 (Mar. 11, 1817-Mar. 9, 1836) and 1-135 (Mar. 10, 1836-Dec. 30, 1893). The two volumes for 1894 are not numbered. Beginning with May 1, 1829 (vol. 7), each volume is indexed by surname of claimant or accountable officer.

There are gaps in the date span of these records; the actual dates covered: Mar. 11, 1817-Nov. 23, 1819; June 28, 1823-Nov. 30, 1894.

Registers contain entries that show settlement number, name of claimant or accountable officer, explanation, dates reported and approved, titles of appropriations to be debited and credited, and adjusted balance. Registers of other accounts and claims reported by the Third Auditor are described in entries 208 and 209. Some of the original settled accounts and claims recorded in these registers are described in entry 712.

260.   ABSTRACTS OF DIFFERENCES IN SETTLEMENT OF ACCOUNTS OF DISBURSING AGENTS FOR THE FREEDMEN'S BUREAU (FREEDMEN'S BUREAU DIFFERENCES). Nov. 1866-Apr. 1882. 8 cm, 3 in. 1 vol.

Arranged by name of officer and thereunder chronologically. Indexed by name of officer.

Abstracts show officer's name, adjusted balance of his accounts for disbursements for the Freedmen's Bureau, balance reported by officer, and explanation of differences.

261.   ABSTRACTS OF PAYMENTS TO COLORED TROOPS (DISBURSEMENTS OF FREEDMEN'S BUREAU ON TREASURY CERTIFICATES). ca. July 1867-Apr. 1874. 30 cm, 1 ft. 5 vols.

Arranged by military unit.

Abstracts show name of military unit, soldier's name, number and amount of Treasury certificate issued, fees paid, amount paid to soldier, and total paid. The dates indicated above are the approximate payment dates of the Treasury certificates issued as reflected by the numerical range of the volumes.

For registers of claims of colored troops, see entries 441 and 443; for numerical registers of Treasury certificates paid, see entry 456.

262.   MISCELLANEOUS RECORDS RELATING TO HORSE CLAIMS. ca. Jan. 7, 1886 Aug. 8,
        1892. 5 cm, 2 in. 1 box.

Arranged by type of record.
These records consist chiefly of decisions of the Comptroller in horse claim cases,
January 23, 1890-August 8, 1892; lists of horse claims recommended by the Third Auditor for
approval, January 7, 1886; and partial unidentified indexes to allowed and rejected horse
claims.
For docket books relating to horse claims, see entry 643; for copies of favorable reports
on horse claim awards and related correspondence, see entries 611 and 649.

OFFICE OF THE COMMISSIONER OF CUSTOMS

The Office of the Commissioner of Customs was established by an act of March 3, 1849
(9 Stat. 396). The Commissioner of Customs performed the duties formerly assigned to the First
Comptroller, with respect to accounts for customs receipts and disbursements and other
disbursements of customs officials. The accounts and claims audited by the First Auditor with
respect to these matters were given final examination and approval by the Office of the
Commissioner of Customs. This Office was abolished effective October 1, 1894, under the terms
of an act of July 1, 1894 (28 Stat. 205), which transferred the functions of the Commissioner of
Customs to the newly established Office of the Comptroller of the Treasury.
Little information is available on the divisional structure within the Office of the
Commissioner of Customs, but an 1881 history of the Treasury Department lists the Divisions as
the Bookkeeper Division, Customs Division, and Miscellaneous Division.
The most significant records of the Office of the Commissioner of Customs are
correspondence, 1789-1894; records relating to the settlement of accounts, 1789-1894; and oaths of
office and related registers, 1857-94.
Records dated before 1849 were created or received in the Office of the First
Comptroller and transferred to the Office of the Commissioner of Customs when that Office
was established. A list of names of Commissioners of Customs appear in Appendix 4.

BOOKKEEPERS DIVISION

The origin of the Bookkeepers Division is not known, but it is listed in an 1880 history of
the Treasury Department as the Division of the Office of the Commissioner of Customs that
was responsible for keeping ledgers for receipts and disbursements of customs officers and an
official record of balances of all accounts and claims approved in the Commissioner's Office.
The function of maintaining these ledgers was transferred to the Division of Bookkeeping and
Warrants in the Secretary of the Treasury's Office in 1894, and the ledgers are now in Records of
the Bureau of Accounts (Treasury), RG 39.

Records Relating to Accounts and Claims

263.   REGISTERS OF MISCELLANEOUS ACCOUNTS. Dec. 1, 1853-Sept. 29, 1894. 61 cm,
        2 ft. 10 vols.

Arranged chronologically. Each volume is arranged by initial letter of surname of
officer or claimant and thereunder by date of Auditor's report. Registers contain entries that
show account number, claimant's or officer's name, type of account or claim, period covered,
dates reported and approved, and adjusted balance. Types of accounts and claims include
accounts for construction of and supplies for lighthouses, marine hospitals, and lifesaving
stations and claims for adjustment or refund of duties.

Some of these accounts are also entered in the First Auditor's registers of audits (entry 345), and some of the original accounts and claims are among miscellaneous customs accounts (entry 311) and miscellaneous Treasury accounts (entry 347).

For abstracts of some of these accounts, see entries 264 and 269.

264.   ABSTRACTS OF CONSTRUCTION ACCOUNTS (COLLECTOR'S CONSTRUCTION ACCOUNTS). Aug. 1853-Aug. 1894. 28 cm, 11 in. 5 vols.

Arranged chronologically. Each volume is arranged by name of accountable officer and, except for the first one, is indexed by name of customs district.

Abstracts show officer's name, title, where stationed, date of surety bond, number of settled account, date reported, period covered, debits and credits, and adjusted balance. The accounts were usually of disbursing officers or collectors of customs and concerned expenditures for lighthouses and other aids to navigation, construction and repair of customhouses and marine hospitals, and purchase and repair of furniture; also proceeds from rental or sale of Government property. Some of these accounts are registered in the volumes described in entries 263 and 345; the original accounts are among those described in entries 311 and 347.

CUSTOMS DIVISION

The Customs Division is listed in an 1880 history of the Treasury Department as part of the Office of the Commissioner of Customs. The Division was responsible for reviewing all accounts and claims audited by the First Auditor for receipts and expenditures of customs revenue and for accounts of customs officials as disbursing agents for lighthouses, revenue cutters, marine hospitals, and lifesaving stations; accounts for suits filed for collection of duty bonds; fees of judicial officers in customs cases; and emoluments of customs officers.

Correspondence

265.   LETTERS SENT TO CUSTOMS OFFICERS. Apr. 28, 1849-Sept. 28, 1894. 10.7 m, 35 ft. 184 vols.

Arranged chronologically. Beginning January 2, 1869, the letters are subdivided into two groups: (1) ports and districts beginning with letters A-L (57 vols.) and (2) ports and districts beginning with letters M-Z (79 vols.). The date span of the letters in each group of volumes is identical: January 2, 1869-September 28, 1894. Each of the first 66 volumes (Apr. 28, 1849-Oct. 23, 1873) is indexed by surname of customs officer. Each of the other volumes is indexed by name of port or district. The spine titles run 1-48 and 1-79. In the second numbered run, volumes 1-57 are double volumes.

Fair copies of letters relating to settlement of accounts, decisions on claims and appeals, interpretation of customs laws and regulations, and personnel actions. Some of these letters are in reply to the letters received described in entry 278; similar letters sent by the First Comptroller before 1849 are described in entry 74.

266.   LETTERS SENT RELATING TO SMUGGLING (SMUGGLING LETTER BOOKS). July 29, 1865-June 28, 1869. 10 cm, 4 in. 2 vols.

Arranged chronologically. Each volume is indexed by surname of person addressed.

Fair copies of letters to the Secretary of the Treasury relating to (1) the need for additional personnel to prevent smuggling and (2) the effect of proposed boundary changes for customs districts. Included are letters to customs officers and special agents stationed near the Mexican and Canadian borders about methods to control smuggling in those areas. These two volumes have been reproduced as NARA Microfilm Publication M497, Letters Sent by the Commissioner of Customs Relating to Smuggling, 1865-1869.

267. LETTERS SENT TO SPECIAL AGENTS (MISCELLANEOUS LETTER BOOK, NO. 20). Dec. 1, 1868-Oct. 22, 1875. 8 cm, 3 in. 1 vol.

Arranged chronologically and indexed by surname or title of addressee.

Fair copies of letters to special agents relating to settlement of their accounts for proceeds of restricted commercial intercourse and the sale of and captured and abandoned property and furnishing an analysis of departmental regulations relating to such accounts. Some letters relating to accounts of special agents were addressed to the Secretary of the Treasury or the First Auditor. This volume has been reproduced as NARA Microfilm Publication M498, Letters Sent by the Commissioner of Customs Relating to Captured and Abandoned Property, 1868-1875. Accounts of special agents for proceeds from the sale of captured and abandoned property are among miscellaneous Treasury accounts (entry 347). Other related records are in General Records of the Department of the Treasury, RG 56, and Records of Civil War Special Agencies of the Treasury Department, RG 366.

Records Relating to Accounts

268. REGISTERS OF CUSTOMS ACCOUNTS. Dec. 15, 1846-Sept. 29, 1894. 91 cm, 3 ft. 13 vols.

Arranged chronologically. Volumes 2-13, December 1, 1853-September 29, 1894, are each arranged alphabetically by name of customs district and thereunder chronologically by date reported. The first volume has no number on its spine; volumes 2-13 care the spine numbers 1-12.

Registers contain entries that show customs districts; account numbers; officer's name; dates reported, received, and approved; type of account; period covered; and adjusted balance. The accounts are usually those of collectors, surveyors, and naval officers and concern expenses of collecting the revenue, duties and fees collected, and official emoluments.

The accounts themselves are among the First Auditor's customs accounts (entry 297). Additional information on many of the accounts registered in these volumes is included in the abstracts described in entries 270-272.

269. ABSTRACTS OF CUSTOMS ACCOUNTS. July 1794-June 1842. 61 cm, 2 ft. 11 vols.

Arranged chronologically. Each volume is arranged geographically by State and thereunder chronologically by date account was settled. Each volume is indexed by State and thereunder by district.

Abstracts show customs district, official's name and account number, period covered, date reported, statement of differences, and adjusted balance. These volumes, identified as volumes 4-12 (two are numbered 11), were kept in the Office of the First Comptroller and transferred to the Commissioner in 1849. A few entries in the last volume are dated as late as 1845.

270. ABSTRACTS OF ACCOUNTS FOR COASTWISE AND INTERNAL INTERCOURSE. Aug. 1, 1862-June 30, 1864. 5 cm, 2 in. 1 vol.

Arranged geographically by district and thereunder chronologically. Indexed by name of district.

Abstracts show name of customs district; title of reporting official; month covered by report; type, amount, and value of merchandise; rate of duty charged; permit number; receipts from fees, fines, penalties, and forfeitures; and disbursements for salaries and contingent expenses. The merchandise was normally cotton, tobacco, or general merchandise; reporting officials were usually surveyors of customs or local special agents. These accounts are described in entry 297 and are entered in the registers described in entry 268. Related records are in Records of Civil War Special Agencies, RG 366.

271.   ABSTRACTS OF ACCOUNTS FOR FEES FOR DECEASED PASSENGERS. July 2, 1855 - June 30, 1894. 5 cm, 2 in. 1 vol.

Arranged by name of customs district and thereunder chronologically. Indexed by name of customs district.

Entries show customs district; date of report; names of vessel and master; port from which vessel arrived; name, age, and sex of each deceased passenger required to be reported; amount collected; and date and place of deposit. Most entries date from June 1867 and state that there were no transactions. Names of deceased passengers are reported for the following districts at various times: Boston and Charlestown; Baltimore; Charleston; Frenchman's Bay; New Orleans; Norfolk and Portsmouth; New York; Portland and Falmouth; Philadelphia; Oregon; San Francisco; and Texas. An act of March 3, 1855, regulating steamboats (10 Stat. 715), imposed a fine of $10 on the master of a ship for every passenger over the age of 18 who died during the voyage, except cabin passengers. Some of the accounts abstracted in this volume are described in entry 297 and are entered in the registers described in entry 268.

272.   ABSTRACTS OF ACCOUNTS OF SPECIAL AGENTS. May 1864 - Mar. 1872. 8 cm, 3 in. 1 vol.

Arranged by name of accountable officer and thereunder chronologically. Indexed, in part, by name of accountable officer. The index pages for letters A-H are missing.

Abstracts show officer's name and title (usually a special agent), account number, date reported, type of account, debits and credits, statement of differences, and adjusted balance. The most frequent types of accounts abstracted in this volume are fees for coastwise and internal intercourse; captured and abandoned property; Confederate property recovered in foreign countries; and sequestered property. Some of these accounts are described in entries 297 and 347.

For related registers, see entry 268; for letters to special agents relating to their accounts, see entry 267.

273.   STATEMENTS OF OFFICIAL EMOLUMENTS AND EXPENSES OF CUSTOMS. Jan. 1814 - Dec. 1844. 10 cm, 4 in. 12 vols.

Arranged chronologically. Each volume is arranged geographically by customs district.

There are gaps in the date span of these records; the actual dates covered are: Jan. 1814-Dec. 1828; Jan. 1835 - Dec. 1844.

Statements prepared annually for presentation to Congress showing customs district; name, title, and duty station of reporting official; year or partial year covered by report; amounts received as salary, fees, commissions, fines, and penalties; expenses of salaries for clerks, stationery, office fuel, rent, and other expenses; and balance payable to the official or to be refunded to the United States. The reports for 1814-16 and 1819 also include an abstract of remarks prepared by the official in relation to his return. These reports were required by an act of March 2, 1799 (1 Stat. 704).

Other Records

274.   COPIES OF QUARTERLY REPORTS TO THE SOLICITOR OF THE TREASURY. May 1845-Sept. 1850. 5 cm, 2 in. 1 vol.

Arranged alphabetically by name of customs district, thereunder by type of report, and thereunder chronologically.

Commissioner's copies of four types of reports submitted quarterly to the Solicitor of the Treasury by customs officers. The records consist of: (1) reports of suits requested by the collector for violation of law, showing name of person involved or article seized, section of law violated, date suit was requested, and nature of the violation (frequently the carrying of excess passengers); (2) reports of customs bonds placed in suit, showing names of principal and sureties, the type, number, amount, and date of bond, the date due, and the date the suit was directed; (3) reports of payments received as a result of suits, showing name of person or type of goods concerned, section of law violated, and amount paid (sometimes also showing amount of related expenses and date of payment); and (4) abstract of accounts of warehouse bonds, showing numbers of manifest and bond, date of bond, names of principals and sureties, amount of duties due, date paid, and balance of bonds remaining unpaid.

275.   REGISTER OF CASES REPORTED FOR SUIT. Mar. 4, 1875–June 14, 1893. 3 cm, 1 in. 1 vol.

Arranged chronologically by date of suit. Indexed by name of debtor.

Register contains entries that show date of suit; debtor's name, title, and duty station; sureties' names and residences; balance due; explanation; and notation of efforts to collect the debt. Most debtors were collectors or surveyors of customs. Many of the accounts mentioned in this register are among customs accounts (entry 294).

276.   CONSULAR DESPATCHES. Mar. 10, 1863–July 28, 1864. 1 cm, 1/2 in. 1 vol.

Arranged chronologically.

Copies of despatches prepared by U.S. consular officers relating to warehouse and customs regulations in Belgium, Denmark, France, and Switzerland. These copies were transmitted by the Secretary of State through the Secretary of the Treasury for the information of the Commissioner of Customs.

277.   REGISTER OF RECEIPT AND DISPOSITION OF CERTIFICATES OF DEPOSIT. June 4, 1864–Aug. 30, 1865. 2 cm, 1 in. 1 vol.

Arranged chronologically by date received.

Register contains entries that show accountable officer's name and title, duty station, place of deposit, source of funds, amount deposited, date and number of the certificate of deposit, date received by Commissioner of Customs, and date referred. The sources of funds were usually emoluments, fees for coastwise and internal intercourse, and proceeds of captured and abandoned property.

For other records relating to these latter types of accounts, see entries 270 and 272.

MISCELLANEOUS DIVISION

The origin of the Miscellaneous Division is not known, but it is mentioned in an 1881 history of the Treasury Department as the Division in the Office of the Commissioner of Customs responsible for maintaining the general files of that Office. The Division also kept records of customs appointments and a file of oaths of office. Additionally, it settled claims against the public revenue and for refund of excess duties.

Correspondence

278.   OFFICIAL AND MISCELLANEOUS LETTERS RECEIVED. Oct. 1789 - June 1892. 21.0 m, 69 ft. 232 vols.

Arranged by source (primarily customs district) and thereunder chronologically.

Letters received from merchants, customs officers, and Cabinet-level Government officials, relating to such matters as interpretation of regulations; administrative problems; the refund of duties on merchandise; claims for damaged merchandise; and the filing of oaths, bonds, and contracts. The letters dated before 1849 were addressed to and answered by the First Comptroller, but the incoming letters were transferred to the Commissioner of Customs in 1849 for filing or appropriate action. The First Comptroller's replies to the letters are described in entries 61 and 74; replies by the Commissioner of Customs are described in entries 265 and 280.

279.   ABSTRACTS OF DECISIONS (INDEX TO DECISIONS). ca. 1790-1851. 3 cm, 1 in. 1 vol.

Arranged alphabetically by keyword of subject.
Abstracts show subject of decision, date of letter in which decision was announced, citation to its location, and abstract of the decision.
Many of the letters abstracted were written during the period October 1849-May 1851, and citations are to the letters sent described in entry 280. Subjects included drawbacks, transfers of public moneys, services of deputies acting for their superiors, and the prohibition of the use of slaves in the Navy. For some major subjects, such as fines, penalties, and forfeitures, a list of congressional acts relating to the subject is given in place of a citation to a decision; such lists are usually for the period 1790-1820.

280.   OFFICIAL AND MISCELLANEOUS LETTERS SENT. Apr. 16, 1849-Sept. 29, 1894. 4.3 m, 14 ft. 74 vols.

Arranged chronologically. Each volume is indexed by initial letter of title of official or surname of officer or claimant addressed. Most volumes contain the spine title: "Miscellaneous Letter Book."
Fair copies of letters to Government officials, accountable officers, merchants, and claimants relating to such matters as settlement of claims for duties, interpretation of regulations, accounts and claims relating to expenses for lighthouses and lifesaving stations, transmittal of moneys owed by the Government, and comments on proposed legislation. Some of these letters are abstracted in the letters described in entry 279.
Some were written in response to the official and miscellaneous letters received described in entry 278.

Other Records

281.   REGISTERS OF MISCELLANEOUS OATHS OF OFFICE. Jan. 2, 1865-Sept. 21, 1894. 28 cm, 11 in. 6 vols.

Arranged chronologically. Each volume is arranged by initial letter of official's surname and thereunder chronologically by date of oath. The numbers on the spines run 1-5, and 7. There are gaps in the date span of these records. Actual dates covered are: Jan. 2, 1865 - Dec. 31, 1887; Aug. 15, 1893 - Sept. 21, 1894.
Registers contain entries that show official's name, title, duty station, and date of oath of office. Most persons whose names appear in these registers were customs or lighthouse employees.
For some of the original oaths, see entry 282.

282.   OATHS OF OFFICE. Aug. 18, 1856-June 20, 1894. 2.1 m, 7 ft. 30 vols.

Arranged by type of position and thereunder chronologically. Spine titles vary. Many are: "Lighthouse Oaths."

Oaths of office for lighthouse, lifesaving station, marine hospital, and revenue-cutter service personnel. Each oath shows date, person's name, position to which appointed, and signature. The lighthouse oaths usually also show place of birth and State from which appointed.

For a register of some of these oaths, see entry 281.

283.   REGISTERS OF CLAIMS AGAINST THE REVENUE. May 20, 1847-Dec. 31, 1869. 10 cm, 4 in. 2 vols.

Arranged numerically by claim number and thereunder chronologically by date certified by collector. Indexed by claimant's name.

Registers contain entries that show claim number, claimant's name, date certified, explanation of claim, amounts claimed and allowed, and date on which payment was ordered. Most of the claims were based on a decrease of duties because of damage to merchandise, depreciation of currency, or judgment in claimant's favor in legal cases. The account number by which these claims were settled can be located by using the First Auditor's registers of audits (entry 345). Many of the original accounts and claims are among the miscellaneous Treasury accounts (entry 347).

OFFICE OF THE FIRST AUDITOR

The original Office of the Auditor was authorized by an act of September 2, 1789 (1 Stat. 65), in which the Treasury Department was established. The Auditor was responsible for receiving and settling all public accounts and transmitting the accounts, with their vouchers and his certificates of settlement, to the Comptroller. The Auditor's settlement of military accounts and claims, however, ended with the establishment of the Office of the Accountant for the War Department by an act of May 8, 1792 (1 Stat. 279). An act of March 3, 1817 (3 Stat. 366), created the Offices of four additional Auditors and an additional Comptroller and gave the original Auditor the title of First Auditor with responsibility for all accounts accruing in the Treasury Department. However, the acts of March 3, 1863 (12 Stat. 725), and June 30, 1864 (13 Stat. 223), specifically assigned the settlement of Internal Revenue accounts and claims to the Fifth Auditor.

The First Auditor also had jurisdiction over two classes of accounts not specifically related to the Treasury Department. An act of March 3, 1849 (9 Stat. 395), "continued" his jurisdiction over settlement of judicial accounts, and an act of July 20, 1868 (15 Stat. 106), gave him responsibility for settling accounts of the Department of Agriculture.

An act of July 31, 1894 (28 Stat. 206), changed the titles of the several Auditors and revised their jurisdictions. The First Auditor became the Auditor for the Treasury Department, with responsibility for settling: (1) accounts for salaries and contingent expenses of the Office of the Secretary of Treasury and all offices and bureaus under the Secretary's direction and (2) all other accounts within the jurisdiction of the Department of the Treasury. The Auditor, by this act, obtained jurisdiction over the Internal Revenue accounts and lost jurisdiction over the accounts of the Departments of Agriculture and Justice. The Auditor's Office was abolished effective July 1, 1921, under provisions of the Budget and Accounting Act of June 10, 1921 (42 Stat. 25).

The main divisions of the First Auditor's Office were the Customs Division, Judiciary Division, Miscellaneous Division, and Public Debt Division. Records not attributable to the functions of a single division are described under the heading "general records." The most significant records of the Office include correspondence, January 1801-March 1911; settled accounts and claims, September 1790 - September 1894, with related registers; and Auditor's reports on accounts and claims, January 1801 - June 1888.

A list of names of First Auditors and the dates of their service appear in Appendix 5.

GENERAL RECORDS

Correspondence and Decisions

284.   REGISTERS OF LETTERS AND ACCOUNTS RECEIVED. Dec. 28, 1842-Dec. 30, 1904. 2.4 m, 8 ft. 39 vols.

Arranged chronologically. Within each volume entries are arranged by initial letter of writer's surname and thereunder chronologically.

There are gaps in the date span of these records; the actual dates covered are: Dec. 28, 1842-Jan. 11, 1851; Aug. 1, 1853-Sept. 30, 1896; Apr. 1, 1899-Dec. 30, 1904.

Registers contain entries that show date received, writer's name and address or title, and subject of letter or type of account. Most accounts and letters were from customs, judicial, or Territorial officials. Some of these letters are among those described in entry 288.

285.   REGISTERS OF LETTERS AND ACCOUNTS REFERRED TO THE AUDITOR BY OTHER GOVERNMENT OFFICIALS. Mar. 1, 1887-Mar. 6, 1912. 1.5 m, 5 ft. 23 vols.

Arranged chronologically. Within each volume, entries are arranged by initial letter of writer's surname and thereunder chronologically. The numbers on the volume spines vary considerably from the volume numbers on the tabs. The spine titles are: "Register of Letters and Accounts Received; and "Register of Letters Received."

Registers contain entries that show date received, writer's name and address or title, title of official referring the letter or account, and subject of letter or type of account. Most letters and accounts were from customs, judicial, and Territorial officials and were referred to the Auditor by the Commissioner of Immigration, the Commissioner of Internal Revenue, and the Assistant Secretary of the Treasury. Some of these letters are described in entry 288.

286.   REGISTERS OF LETTERS REFERRED TO OTHER OFFICERS FOR REPLY. July 6, 1888 - Dec. 22, 1911. 8 cm, 3 in. 3 vols.

Arranged chronologically. Each volume is arranged by initial letter of writer's surname and thereunder chronologically.

There are gaps in the date span of these records; the actual dates covered are: July 6, 1888 - Oct. 31, 1894; Feb. 2, 1904 - Dec. 22, 1911.

Registers contain entries that show date of letter, writer's name and address, subject, and office to which referred. Letters typically relate to explanations of suspended or disallowed items in accounts, transportation claims, and authorities to endorse interest checks.

287.   COPIES OF DECISIONS. July 11, 1895 - June 11, 1903. 5 cm, 2 in. 2 vols.

Arranged chronologically. Only the second volume is indexed (by subject and name of addressee).

There are gaps in the date span of these records; the actual dates covered are: July 11, 1895-Feb. 1, 1896; May 21, 1901-June 11, 1903.

Press copies of letters, primarily to the First Comptroller, stating the reason for his decisions in cases appealed to the Comptroller. Among the topics are refund of duties paid under protest, refund of income taxes, claims against Internal Revenue officials, bounty on sugar produced from beets, shortage in the bullion account at the Carson City Mint, and compensation and expenses of Chinese inspectors.

CUSTOMS DIVISION

The Customs Division was first specifically referred to in a report on the activities of the Office of the First Auditor for the fiscal year beginning July 1, 1868, but published sources listed it as a bureau within the Office in 1847. The Division audited the customs-related receipt and disbursement accounts of collectors and other ranking customs officers at the various ports and the accounts of these same officers as disbursing agents for lighthouses, marine hospitals, and revenue cutters. Other accounts and claims audited by the Division related to warehouse and bond accounts, official emoluments of customs officers, fines collected for violation of customs laws, refund of duties, and proceeds of sales of surplus Government property. Records relating to the U.S. operation of the customs service in Puerto Rico are also described with the records of this Division.

Correspondence

288.   LETTERS RECEIVED RELATING TO ENTRIES OF MERCHANDISE (LIQUIDATION OF ENTRIES). July 1, 1895-Feb. 19, 1909. 8.5 m, 28 ft. 67 vols.

Arranged chronologically. The letters in volumes 1-23 (July 1, 1895 - Dec. 29, 1897) are arranged alphabetically by district and thereunder chronologically. The letters in volumes 24-67 (Jan. 3, 1898 - Feb. 19, 1909) are arranged numerically. Volumes 1-23 are indexed by district; volumes 24-67 include registers of letters. There are no volumes numbered 2, 4, or 6.

Letters from customs officers, merchants, claimants, and the Secretary of the Treasury, relating primarily to correction of errors in accounts for entries of merchandise. Drafts of replies are frequently bound with these letters. Additional replies are described in entry 292.

Some of these letters are registered in entries 284 and 285.

289.   LETTERS AND REPORTS ON CUSTOMHOUSE BONDS. Aug. 15, 1823-Apr. 30, 1837. 5 cm, 2 in. 1 vol.

This series appears to be missing.

Arranged chronologically.

Fair copies of letters and reports prepared in reply to congressional inquiries on the status of duty bonds in New York and other major ports. Some of the reports include information on accounting procedures used in the settlement of bond accounts.

290.   LETTERS SENT BY THE CUSTOMS DIVISION (LETTER BOOKS ON CUSTOMS). Apr. 8, 1830-May 3, 1888. 1.8 m, 6 ft. 34 vols.

Arranged chronologically. Each volume except the last one (June 25, 1887-May 3, 1888) is indexed by surname of addressee.

Fair copies of letters sent to collectors and other customs officers concerning settlement of their accounts for customs receipts and expenditures and for disbursement accounts for lighthouses and marine hospitals. Many of the accounts concerned are among customs accounts described in entry 297 and miscellaneous customs accounts described in entry 311.

For additional letters, see entry 291.

291.   LETTERS SENT BY THE CUSTOMS DIVISION. Apr. 7, 1888-Sept. 16, 1910. 4.6 m, 15 ft. 10 vols. and 27 boxes.

Arranged chronologically. Each volume, except the one for December 1891-April 1892, is indexed by name of customs district, title of officer, or surname of addressee. The boxes are numbered 1-27 and the volumes are numbered 21-28 and 98-99.

There are gaps in the date span of these records; the actual dates covered are: Apr. 7, 1888-Mar. 16, 1903; July 26-Sept. 16, 1910.

Press copies of letters to collectors, other customs officers, and claimants relating to settlement of customs accounts, notification of the disallowance of items in accounts, and settlement of claims for refund of duties. Many of these accounts and claims dated before 1894 are among customs accounts described in entry 297 and miscellaneous customs accounts described in entry 311.

For other letters on customs accounts, see entry 290.

292.   LETTERS SENT RELATING TO ENTRIES OF MERCHANDISE. July 1, 1895 - June 30, 1906. 2.4 m, 8 ft. 20 vols.

Arranged chronologically. Each volume is indexed by name of customs district, title of officer, or surname of addressee.

Press copies of letters to customs officers and claimants relating chiefly to problems arising in the settlement of accounts for entries of merchandise. Many of the letters furnished instructions for the guidance of customs officers or returned invoices for correction. Drafts of many of these letters are bound with the incoming letters described in entry 288.

Records Relating to Customs Accounts and Claims

293.   ABSTRACTS OF CUSTOMS ACCOUNTS. May 25, 1825-Dec. 28, 1837.5 cm, 2 in. 2 vols.

Arranged chronologically by date of Auditor's report.
Abstracts show date reported, account number, officer's name, customs district, period covered, balance due, and amounts of cash and duty bonds for which the officer remained accountable. Some of the original accounts before 1838 are described in entry 297.
For copies of audit reports on some of these accounts, see entries 296 and 298.

294.   ABSTRACTS OF ACCOUNTS CURRENT. Jan. 1, 1814-Dec. 30, 1830. 5 cm, 2 in. 2 vols.

Arranged chronologically by 3-month periods and thereunder geographically by customs district.
Abstracts show period covered, names of customs district and reporting officer, date account received, previous balance, summary of receipts and disbursements, and adjusted balance of current account.

295.   REGISTERS OF AUDIT REPORTS ON CUSTOMS ACCOUNTS AND CLAIMS. May 11, 1837-Nov. 12, 1894. 30 cm, 1 ft. 7 vols.

Arranged chronologically. Entries in volumes 1-5 and 7 are arranged by number of Auditor's report and thereunder by date approved.
The entries in volume 6 are arranged by initial letter of officer's or claimant's surname and thereunder by date approved.
Registers contain entries that show account number, date approved, name of officer or claimant, and type of account or claim. Volumes 1-5, May 11, 1837-November 12, 1894, are for accounts of customs officers for expenses of collecting the revenue. These accounts are described in entry 297. An additional register of these accounts is described in entry 270. Volumes 6 and 7, July 8, 1872-September 27, 1894, are for accounts and claims relating to disbursements for revenue cutters and lifesaving stations, refunds of duties, and miscellaneous supplies. These accounts and claims are described in entry 311.
For an additional register of these accounts and claims, see entry 263.

296.   AUDIT REPORTS ON CUSTOMS ACCOUNTS AND CLAIMS. May 9, 1837 - May 31, 1850. 91 cm, 3 ft. 13 vols.

Arranged chronologically. Each volume is indexed by surname of officer or claimant.
Fair copies of reports showing report number, date prepared, name of officer or claimant, explanation of account or claim, adjusted balance, and explanation of differences. The accounts described in entry 297 usually include the originals of the reports copied in these volumes.

297.   SETTLED CUSTOMS ACCOUNTS AND CLAIMS. May 9, 1837 - Sept. 26, 1894. 1,043.6 m, 3,424 ft. 2753 boxes.

Arranged numerically.
Accounts and claims for expenses of collecting the revenue from customs (and, until 1852, claims for refund of duties), consisting generally of the Auditor's report; statement by the Register relating to outstanding warrants; officer's statement of his account; abstract of disbursements; and supporting documents, such as payrolls, receipts, and bills. Claim files usually consist only of the Auditor's report. Some of these accounts and claims are registered in the volumes described in entries 263, 270, and 295. Alpha boxes: 14A, 819A, 906A, 969A, 1156A, 1199A, 1209A, 1222A, 1248A, 1271A, 1316A, 1329A, 1329A, 1333, 1347A-B, 1351A, 1379A, 1385A,

1411A, 1427A, 1474A, 1565A, 1569A, 1640A-B, 1787A, 1801A-B, 1819A-B, 1902A, 1936A, 1996A, 2084A, 2090A, 2105A-B.
For copies of related audit reports, see entry 296.

298.   AUDIT REPORTS ON CLAIMS FOR REFUND OF DUTIES. Apr. 2, 1833-Mar. 28, 1836. 30 cm, 1 ft. 8 vols.

Arranged numerically. Each volume is indexed by claimant's name.
Fair copies of reports showing date prepared, report number, name of importer or his agent or assignee, amount of refund due, customs district into which the merchandise had been imported, and year imported.
One report is dated October 16, 1845. Each report number has the suffix "B." Some of these accounts are described in entry 299. The numbers were assigned at the time the Auditor's report was prepared.

299.   SETTLED CLAIMS FOR REFUND OF DUTIES. May 2, 1833 - Apr. 7, 1834. 20 cm, 8 in. 2 boxes.

Arranged numerically.
Accounts and claims for refund of duties, usually consisting only of the Auditor's report. The numbers were assigned at the time the Auditor's report was prepared, and each report in series was assigned the suffix "B." These claims were at one time a part of the series of miscellaneous Treasury accounts described in entry 347.

300.   AUDIT REPORTS ON CLAIMS FOR REFUND OF DUTIES ON WINES. Mar. 8, 1834 - Apr. 8, 1836. 8 cm, 3 in. 2 vols.

Arranged numerically. Each volume is indexed by claimant's name.
Fair copies of reports showing date prepared, report number, name of importer or his agent or assignee, amount of refund due, customs district into which the wine had been imported, and year imported. The numbers were assigned at the time the Auditor's report was prepared, and each report was assigned the suffix "C." Only six reports are dated after December 1834.
The claims files are no longer extant.

301.   REGISTERS OF CUSTOMHOUSE BONDS. Apr. 1821 - Jan. 1843. 3.1 m, 10 ft. 41 vols.

Arranged geographically by customs district as follows: Maine, Connecticut, Rhode Island, and Massachusetts (2 vols.); Boston (6 vols.); New York (18 vols.); small ports north of Philadelphia (1 vol.); Philadelphia (6 vols.); small ports south of Philadelphia (1 vol.); Baltimore (3 vols.); Virginia, North Carolina, and Georgia (1 vol.); Charleston (1 vol.); and Mississippi (2 vols.). The entries within each volume are arranged by port and thereunder chronologically. Volumes that include more than one district are indexed by district. The other volumes are not indexed.
Registers contain entries that show name of customs district, date and number of duty bond, names of principals and sureties, amount of bond, date due, and date paid or put in suit. The dates of the bonds vary considerably from one district to another.
For additional information on duty bonds in suit, see entry 302; for related memorandums and reports, see entry 289.

302.   REGISTERS OF DUTY BONDS PUT IN SUIT. Apr. 1796 - Sept. 1842. 28 cm, 11 in. 4 vols.

Arranged geographically as follows: districts north of New York; New York; New York to Baltimore; and south of Baltimore. Within each volume, entries are arranged by district and thereunder chronologically.

Each volume is indexed by district.

Registers contain entries that show name of customs district; date, number, and amount of duty bond; names of principals and sureties; due date; and date paid. The dates vary considerably from one district to another.

For other registers of duty bonds, see entry 301; for related memorandums and reports, see entry 289.

303.   REGISTERS OF SEIZURES, FINES, PENALTIES, AND FORFEITURES. July 1880 - Mar. 1918. 1.2 m, 4 ft. 21 vols.

Arranged chronologically. Entries within each volume are arranged alphabetically by customs district and thereunder chronologically.

Volumes 5-17 are each indexed by name of district. The other volumes are not indexed.

Registers contain entries that show name of customs district, date seized, name of vessel, name of person fined or from whom merchandise was seized, section of law violated, name of informer, value of merchandise, amount realized, and disposition of the case (usually date on which moneys were turned over to the Treasury Department). The fines were usually equal only to the amount of duty due on the merchandise seized.

Records Relating to Customs Activities in Puerto Rico.

304.   RECORDS OF RECEIPTS AND DISBURSEMENTS IN THE CUSTOMS DISTRICT OF PUERTO RICO. Aug. 1, 1898 - July 14, 1900. 5 cm, 2 in. 2 vols.

Arranged by name of port in the order listed below and thereunder chronologically.

Records show port, source and amount of receipts, amounts disbursed, and amounts deposited. The first volume includes entries for San Juan, Ponce, Mayaguez, Arecibo, Aguadilla, Arroyo, Jumaico, Fajado, and Vieques. A recapitulation in the volume shows, for each of these ports, a summary of the receipts and disbursements during U.S. occupation of the port. The second volume is only for Mayaguez and includes adjusted balances of the accounts of the collector at that port.

305.   ABSTRACTS OF CUSTOMS RECEIPTS AND DISBURSEMENTS. Oct. 1, 1898 - Jan. 31, 1899. 3 cm, 1 in. 1 vol.

Arranged by port in the order listed below and thereunder chronologically.

Abstracts show name of port, month or other period covered by report, amounts of receipts and disbursements, and amounts deposited with the banking firm of De Ford and Co. The volume is for the ports of Mayaguez, Ponce, San Juan, Vieques, and Arecibo.

306.   REGISTER OF ACCOUNTS RECEIVED. June 30, 1899 - Feb. 13, 1900. 3 cm, 1 in. 1 vol.

Arranged chronologically.

Register contains entries that show date on which account was received, name and title of accountable officer, port at which stationed, type of account, period covered, to whom referred, and when certified.

Part of this volume is used as a record of unclaimed merchandise in general order stores (entry 309).

307.   REGISTER OF VESSEL ARRIVALS. Apr. 8 - Aug. 27, 1900. 3 cm, 1 in. 1 vol.

Arranged alphabetically by name of vessel.
Register contains entries that show month of entry; manifest number; name of vessel; place and date of arrival; home port; and fees paid for tonnage, light money, entrances, clearances, and passengers. Part of this volume is used for a register of entries of merchandise (entry 308).

308.   REGISTER OF ENTRIES OF MERCHANDISE. May 7 - Dec. 10, 1900. 3 cm, 1 in. 1 vol.

Arranged by name of port in the order listed below and thereunder numerically by entry number.
Register contains entries that show name of port, month, voucher number, entry number, name of vessel, date of arrival, date entry was liquidated, amounts of estimated and actual duties, amounts due or to be refunded, charges, and amount of difference between the account as submitted and the account as audited. The volume is for the ports of San Juan, Ponce, Mayaguez, Fajado, Arecibo, Arroyo, Humacao, and Aguadilla. Part of the volume is used as a register of vessel arrivals (entry 307).

309.   RECORD OF UNCLAIMED MERCHANDISE IN GENERAL ORDER STORES. Apr. 10, 1899 - Apr. 22, 1904. 5 cm, 2 in. 1 vol.

Arranged chronologically. Within each volume, entries are arranged by name of port and thereunder chronologically.
Record shows port of arrival, description of merchandise (including marks and numbers on packages), date imported, name of ship on which it arrived, weight of shipment, date merchandise sold or duties paid, and declaration number. Part of the first volume is used as a register of accounts received, June 30, 1899-February 12, 1900 (entry 306).

Records Relating to Other Accounts and Claims

310.   REGISTER OF ACCOUNTS FOR EXPENSES OF THE LIFE-SAVING SERVICE. Dec. 9, 1873 - May 2, 1900. 10 cm, 4 in. 2 vols.

Arranged chronologically. Entries in each volume are arranged by name of officer or claimant and thereunder by date approved. Each volume is indexed by name of officer or claimant.
Registers contain entries that show officer's name and title or claimant's name and address, title of appropriation from which funds were disbursed or explanation of the claim, account number, dates received and reported, total disbursements or amount due, and remaining balance, if any.
The accounts registered include those for disability claims, construction and repair of stations, purchase of supplies and equipment, and salaries and expenses of district superintendents. These accounts are a part of the miscellaneous customs accounts described in entry 311. When an account involved payment of a contract, the number of the account with which the contract was filed is shown.

311.   SETTLED MISCELLANEOUS CUSTOMS ACCOUNTS AND CLAIMS. June 29, 1872 - Sept. 27, 1894. 192.0 m, 630 ft. 539 boxes.

Arranged numerically.
Settled accounts of customs officers for disbursements for lifesaving stations, revenue cutters, and marine hospitals; claims of contractors for construction, repair, and supplies for these installations; and claims for refund of duties. An account or claim usually includes several of the following types of documents: a statement of the account or claim, account current, report

by the Auditor on his examination of the account or claim, report by the Register on warrants charged or credited to the officer presenting the account, abstract of disbursements, and bills or other supporting documents serving as vouchers. Accounts for expenses of revenue cutters frequently include copies of payrolls for the cutter; accounts for lifesaving stations frequently include the original contract for its construction or repair, with plans and specifications. The account numbers were assigned at the time Auditor's report was prepared. Many of these accounts and claims are registered in the volumes described in entries 263 and 295. Other settled claims are included among the records described in entries 295 and 347.

312.   REGISTERS OF AUDIT REPORTS ON LIGHTHOUSE, JUDICIARY, AND MARINE HOSPITAL ACCOUNTS. July 20, 1853 - Mar. 20, 1895. 61 cm, 2 ft. 9 vols.

Arranged chronologically. Entries in the first five volumes (July 20, 1853 - July 2, 1879) are arranged by initial letter of officer's surname and thereunder by account number; entries in the remaining four volumes (July 2, 1879 - March 20, 1895) are arranged numerically by account number and thereunder chronologically by date of Comptroller's approval.

Registers contain entries that show account number, officer's name, date approved, type of account, and period covered. Most of the entries after 1880 relate to judiciary accounts.

For copies of audit reports on some of these accounts, see entry 313.

313.   AUDIT REPORTS ON LIGHTHOUSE, JUDICIARY, AND MARINE HOSPITAL ACCOUNTS. July 11, 1853 - June 30, 1888. 6.1 m, 20 ft. 100 vols.

Arranged chronologically by date of Auditor's report. Each volume is indexed by name of officer.

Fair copies of audit reports, showing date and number of report, name and title of officer, type of account, previous balance, debits and credits, and adjusted balance. Lighthouse and marine hospital accounts were reviewed by the Commissioner of Customs after auditing; judiciary accounts were sent to the First Comptroller for review.

For registers of these reports, see entry 312.

JUDICIARY DIVISION

The Judiciary Division was first referred to as a Division in the First Auditor's Office in a report on activities of the Office beginning July 1, 1868. This Division audited the accounts for salaries and expenses of marshals and other judicial officers, rent of courtrooms, and other expenses. These accounts were sent to the First Comptroller for review after auditing, and decisions of the Auditor could be appealed to the Comptroller. The Division was abolished in September 1894, when the function of auditing judicial accounts was transferred to the Office of the Fifth Auditor by an act of July 31, 1894 (28 Stat. 208).

Correspondence

314.   LETTERS SENT BY THE JUDICIARY DIVISION. Apr. 3, 1893 - Sept. 29, 1894. 13 cm, 5 in. 4 vols.

Arranged chronologically. Each volume is indexed by name of person addressed.

Press copies of letters to judicial officers, disbursing clerks for the Department of Justice, and claimants relating primarily to the settlement of accounts and claims. Other letters concerning judicial accounts and claims are included with letters sent by the Miscellaneous Division (entries 331 and 332) and letters sent by the Fifth Auditor's Judiciary Division (entry 897).

Records Relating to Accounts

315.   ACCOUNTS FOR EXPENDITURES FOR PRISONERS IN THE WAR OF 1812. Aug. 26, 1812-June 1, 1816. 5 cm, 2 in. 1 vol.

Arranged by marshal's name in the order given below and thereunder by type of document.

Fair copies of accounts current and abstracts of disbursements. The accounts current show marshal's name, period covered by account, amounts of disbursements and commissions, amount paid to marshal, and remaining balance. The abstracts of disbursements show date, name of person paid, explanation, and amount paid. Types of disbursements typically included salaries of guards, parole officers, and pilots of ships; purchase of provisions; transportation and support of prisoners; and purchase of coffins. The marshals for whom records are included are James Prince, T. Melvill, S. P. Allin, Joseph H. Dill, W. P. Smith, Alexander Steward, E. K. Dexter, John Eppinger, and T. G. Thornton.

316.   EMOLUMENT RETURNS FOR DISTRICT ATTORNEYS, CLERKS OF COURTS, AND MARSHALS. July 1842 - Mar. 1907. 66.8 m, 219 ft. 185 boxes.

Arranged alphabetically by name of State and thereunder by type of official. The first run of boxes is numbered 1-124 and carries the title "Emolument Returns - Clerks and Attorneys, 1842-1906." The next run of boxes is numbered 1-61 and carries the title "Emolument Returns - Marshals, 1842-1906."

Returns consist of abstracts approved by the Attorney General showing source and amount of funds received by the official, services he performed, approved mileage charges, and miscellaneous expenses for which he was entitled to compensation. Vouchers usually are included with the abstracts. The abstracts for marshals also show the names of deputy marshals and the amounts to which they were entitled as fees, salaries, and expenses. After September 1894, the emolument returns were transmitted to the newly created office of the Auditor for the State and other Departments (formerly called the Fifth Auditor) for settlement.

317.   REGISTER OF ACCOUNTS FOR RENTAL OF COURTROOMS. Oct. 1, 1892 - Sept. 18, 1894. 5 cm, 2 in. 1 vol.

Arranged alphabetically by name of State or Territory, thereunder by city, and thereunder chronologically.

Register contains entries that show date and number of account, name of city in which courtrooms were located, name of property owner, period for which rent was paid, and amount allowed.

PUBLIC DEBT DIVISION

The Public Debt Division was first referred to as a Division in the First Auditor's Office in a report on activities for the fiscal year beginning July 1, 1878, which commented on the increase in the business of the Division "over the past two years." The main functions of the Division were auditing accounts for (1) paying interest on the public debt (including bonds of the District of Columbia and other special bond issues); (2) redeeming bonds, currency, certificates payable in coin, old notes, and bounty scrip; and (3) destroying notes and fractional currency. Most of the accounts were those of the U.S. Treasurer or of Assistant U.S. Treasurers in major cities. The audited accounts were sent to the First Comptroller for review. Related records are in Records of the Treasurer of the United States, RG 50, and Records of the Bureau of Public Debt, RG 53.

Correspondence

318.   REGISTERS OF LETTERS SENT AND ACCOUNTS AND PAPERS RECEIVED.
        June 1, 1880 - June 30, 1910. 91 cm, 3 ft. 13 vols.

Arranged chronologically. Entries within each volume are arranged by type of
document and thereunder chronologically.

There are gaps in the date span of these records; the actual dates covered are: June 1,
1880-Apr. 19, 1902; Jan. 2, 1904-June 30, 1910.

Entries for accounts received show date received, number of accounts, type of security,
and amount of principal and interest involved. Entries for letters sent show date of letter, to
whom sent, and subject. Some of the letters entered in these registers are described in entries 320
and 321. Entries for papers received show date received; name, title, and address of writer; and
type of document received (usually authority to receipt for checks).

319.   LETTERS SENT RELATING TO ACCOUNTS. Mar. 19, 1830 - May 30, 1836. 5 cm, 2 in.
        1 vol.

Arranged chronologically. Indexed by name of addressee.

Fair copies of letters to officials of branches of the Bank of the United States (successors
to Commissioners of Loan Offices), relating to their accounts for interest paid on stock and for
cancellation of stock certificates.

320.   MEMORANDUMS   AND   REPORTS   (MEMORANDA   ON   TREASURER'S
        ACCOUNTS). May 22, 1794 - June 4, 1850. 10 cm, 4 in. 2 vols.

Arranged chronologically. Within each volume, the memorandums and reports are
grouped by subjects and thereunder chronologically.

Copies of miscellaneous reports and memorandums, including (1) a report to Congress,
dated May 22, 1794, on the condition of the Treasury Department; (2) statements of differences
in the settlement of the accounts of the Treasurer, November 26, 1829-September 16, 1830,
explaining the differences between the accounts as submitted and as audited; (3) a report on
Treasury notes received by collectors of customs in payment of customs duties, January 6, 1838-
January 14, 1850, accompanied by explanation of the methods used in settlement of the
collector's accounts for Treasury notes received (some of these accounts are among public debt
accounts described in entry 330 and miscellaneous Treasury accounts described in entry 347); and
(4) an undated abstract of interest paid on U.S. funds deposited with the Agricultural Bank of
Mississippi and the Bank of Michigan at Detroit.

321.   LETTERS SENT BY THE PUBLIC DEBT DIVISION. Sept. 29, 1887-June 30, 1893. 1.5 m,
        5 ft. 29 vols.

Arranged chronologically. The volumes for September-November 1887 (vol. A) and June
1888-January 1890 (vols. C-M, 1, and 2) are each indexed by name of addressee. The other
volumes are not indexed.

Fair copies of letters to Assistant U.S. Treasurers, banking officials, other persons, and
organizations. Most of the letters concern receipt of authorizations to endorse checks and collect
moneys due from the Government. Many of these letters are entered in the registers described in
entry 318.

For a continuation of the letters, see entry 322.

322.   LETTERS SENT BY THE PUBLIC DEBT DIVISION. July 5, 1893-June 2, 1906. 1.2 m, 4 ft.
          29 vols.

          Arranged chronologically. The volumes for July 1, 1896-December 30, 1898, and February
21, 1899-June 2, 1906, are each indexed by name and title of addressee. The other volumes are not
indexed.
          There are gaps in the date span of these records; the actual dates covered are: July 5,
1893-Nov. 20, 1899; Apr. 22-May 19, 1902; Sept. 3-Oct. 19, 1903; July 10-Sept. 5, 1905; Apr. 4-June
2, 1906.
          Press copies of letters to Assistant U.S. Treasurers, banking officials, and the Register of
the Treasury relating chiefly to receipt of authority to endorse checks and collect moneys due
from the Government and to settlement of accounts for redemption of securities and payment of
interest. Some of these letters are entered in the registers described in entry 318; other letters on
similar subjects are described in entry 321.

Records Relating to Accounts

323.   RECORD OF SECURITIES SOLD. Apr. 19, 1866 - Aug. 7, 1871. 3 cm, 1 in. 1 vol.

          Arranged by type of information in the order listed and thereunder chronologically.
          This volume includes (1) a report on 5/20 bonds sold for the Government by the banking
firm of Jay Cooke and Co., April 19-August 29, 1866, and by H. H. Van Dyke, Assistant U.S.
Treasurer at New York, May 1-September 1, 1866, showing for both the date of sale, name of
purchaser, value of securities, rate and amount of premium, and total paid; (2) a report on the
purchase of compound interest notes, January 5, 1867-August 7, 1871, showing date of purchase,
name of purchaser (usually the Assistant U.S. Treasurer at New York), principal amount of
notes, rate and amount of premium, and amount of interest payable; and (3) a register of
commissions paid to the Assistant U.S. Treasurer at New York, March 5-June 29, 1867, showing
date and amount of drafts in favor of the Assistant Treasurer, date commission was paid, name
of purchaser, value of securities', rate of commission, and amount of commission paid.

324.   REGISTERS OF AUDITS ON PUBLIC DEBT ACCOUNTS. July 16, 1864 - Apr. 15, 1887.
          15 cm, 6 in. 2 vols.

          Arranged chronologically. Entries in the first volume, July 16, 1864-April 15, 1883, are
arranged alphabetically by name of claimant or title of official; entries in the second volume,
April 16, 1883-April 15, 1887, are arranged numerically.
          Registers contain entries that show account number, name of claimant or title of official,
type of account (usually paying interest on the public debt or the redemption of securities), and
date approved.

325.   REGISTER OF ACCOUNTS ADJUSTED. July 2, 1866 - Aug. 9, 1894. 8 cm, 3 in. 1 vol.

          Arranged by account number.
          Register contains entries that show account number, name of official, type of account,
number of vouchers, amount payable, and date adjusted. Entries for accounts for Assistant
Treasurers show the names of the cities in which they were located. Amount of principal,
interest payable in coin and currency, and premium payable are sometimes shown. Some of the
accounts registered in this volume are among miscellaneous Treasury accounts described in
entry 347.

326.   ABSTRACTS OF PUBLIC DEBT ACCOUNTS. July 20, 1866 - Sept. 12, 1885. .5 cm, 2 in. 1 vol.

Arranged chronologically by date approved.

Abstracts show account number, name of official or claimant, type of account, period covered, dates received and approved, adjusted balance, and whether due to or from the United States. Accounts are usually those of the Treasurer or Assistant Treasurers for payment of interest, commission on sales, coupons paid or canceled, interest due from railroads, salaries, and contingent expenses. Some of the accounts abstracted in this volume are among public debt accounts described in entry 330.

327.   AUDIT REPORTS ON PUBLIC DEBT CERTIFICATES CANCELED. Dec. 14, 1789 - May 25, 1793. 28 cm, 11 in. 6 vols.

Arranged numerically.

Copies of reports showing number of report, date prepared, name of owner of surrendered certificate, number of certificates surrendered, by whom issued, value in old emissions, specie value, amount to be credited to owner, and date from which interest was to begin. Related records are in Records of the Bureau of Public Debt, RG 53.

328.   AUDIT REPORTS ON ACCOUNTS FOR THE FUNDED DEBT. Oct. 5, 1790 - June 12, 1799. 1.2 m, 4 ft. 25 vols.

Volume 25 appears to be missing.

Arranged numerically.

Copies of reports showing number of report, date prepared, name of owner of surrendered certificate, number of certificate surrendered, by whom issued, specie value, interest due, and value of funded debt certificates to be issued in exchange for the surrendered certificates. Related records are in RG 53.

329.   AUDIT REPORTS ON THE REGISTERED DEBT. Jan. 1, 1799 - Feb. 1, 1837. 3 cm, 1 in. 1 vol.

Arranged numerically. Indexed by name of owner.

Copies of reports showing date prepared, report number, name of owner of surrendered certificate, number of certificates surrendered, principal and interest payable in specie, additional interest payable, amount to be paid in specie, and amount to be paid interest-bearing public debt certificates. The interest rate on these funded debt certificates was 3 percent. Related records are in RG 53.

330.   SETTLED PUBLIC DEBT ACCOUNTS. Nov. 15, 1812 - Jan. 6, 1891. 7.3 m, 24 ft. 40 boxes.

Arranged numerically.

These accounts are chiefly of the following types: (1) accounts of collectors of customs for notes received in payment of customs duties, (2) accounts of the Treasurer of the United States for interest payments, (3) accounts of Assistant Treasurers for payment of certificates of deposit, and (4) accounts for destruction of currency and securities. The accounts consist of a report by the Auditor and supporting documents pertinent to the type of account. The account number was assigned when the Auditor's report was prepared. Some of these accounts are entered in the registers described in entry 326. Accounts of the Treasurer and Assistant Treasurers for payment of interest on the public debt are among miscellaneous Treasury accounts described in entry 347 and are entered in the registers described in entry 345.

MISCELLANEOUS DIVISION

The Miscellaneous Division was first referred to as a Division in a report on activities of the First Auditor's Office for the fiscal year beginning July 1, 1885, and apparently resulted from consolidation of the functions of several "miscellaneous desks" in the Auditor's Office that date from the late 1860's. Among the numerous auditing responsibilities of the Miscellaneous Division were accounts of the U.S. Senate, U.S. House of Representatives, and Library of Congress; accounts of disbursing agents for numerous departments and agencies; accounts of the Treasurer and Assistant Treasurers; accounts for construction and repair of lifesaving stations, marine hospitals, mints, assay offices, and other public buildings; accounts for public printing and binding; and accounts for paying moneys awarded by the U.S. Court of Claims. Some of these functions were performed, from time to time, by the Customs and Public Debt Divisions of the First Auditor's Office.

Correspondence

331.   LETTERS SENT BY THE MISCELLANEOUS DIVISION. Jan. 31, 1801 - Apr. 19, 1888. 3.1 m, 10 ft. 56 vols.

Arranged chronologically. Each volume, except the last one, May 23, 1887-April 19, 1888, is indexed by name and title of addressee.

Fair copies of letters to disbursing officers, other Government officials, and claimants relating to diverse topics. Included are letters relating to cancellation of Treasury notes; payments of interest on Treasury notes; powers of attorney; authority to collect moneys owed by the Treasury Department; expenses of Territorial legislatures; and settlement of judicial, diplomatic, and salary accounts.

For a continuation of these letters, see entry 332. Additional letters relating to judicial accounts are described in entry 314.

332.   LETTERS SENT BY THE MISCELLANEOUS DIVISION. Mar. 17, 1888 - Mar. 28, 1911. 3.7 m, 12 ft. 96 vols.

Arranged chronologically. Each volume is indexed by name and title of addressee.

There are gaps in the date span of these records; the actual dates covered are: Mar. 17, 1888-Jan. 27, 1897; Mar. 18, 1897-Mar. 15, 1900; Apr. 12, 1900-Dec. 29, 1902; Mar. 15-28, 1911.

Press copies of letters to disbursing agents, other Government officials, and claimants on a wide variety of topics. Included are letters relating to accounts for salaries of officials; accounts for lighthouses, lifesaving stations, marine hospitals, and mints; accounts for expenses of the District of Columbia and Territorial governments; accounts of disbursing officers for the Treasury Department; claims for transportation furnished the Government; and claims for injuries suffered while employed in the Life-Saving Service. For other letters in this series, see entry 331.

Records Relating to Accounts and Claims

333.   REGISTER OF ACCOUNTS FOR PAYMENTS TO CHARITABLE INSTITUTIONS IN THE DISTRICT OF COLUMBIA. Oct. 27, 1873 - Sept. 25, 1894. 5 cm, 2 in. 1 vol.

Arranged randomly by name of person representing the institution.
Indexed by name of person and name of institution.
Register contains entries that show name and title of person submitting account, name and location of the institution, account number (see entry 347), dates received and stated, total disbursements, adjusted balance, and in whose favor. Some of the institutions included are St. Ann's Infant Asylum, Government Hospital for the Insane, Children's Hospital, and

Columbia Institution for the Deaf and Dumb. Most accounts were submitted by treasurers of the institutions concerned.

334.   REGISTERS OF ACCOUNTS FOR CONTINGENT EXPENSES. Apr. 12, 1847 - Apr. 11, 1904. 23 cm, 9 in. 4 vols.

Arranged chronologically. Entries within each volume are arranged by name of disbursing agent and thereunder by title of appropriation. Each volume is indexed by name of agent.

There are gaps in the date span of these records. Actual dates covered are: Apr. 12, 1847-Mar. 24, 1862; Oct. 16, 1877-Apr. 11, 1904.

Registers contain entries that show name of departmental disbursing agent, title of appropriation from which funds were disbursed, account number (see entry 347), dates received and reported, period covered by account, adjusted balance, and in whose favor. Appropriations included contingent expenses of the U.S. House of Representatives, the U.S. Senate, and the Treasury Department; detection of frauds against the revenue; and salaries and expenses of the Bureau of Animal Industry.

335.   REGISTER OF MINT, TRANSPORTATION, AND TERRITORIAL ACCOUNTS. Sept. 1, 1891 - June 30, 1899. 8 cm, 3 in. 1 vol.

Arranged alphabetically by initial letter of officer's or claimant's surname and thereunder chronologically.

Register contains entries that show account number, officer's or claimant's name, type of account or claim, period covered, dates received and audited, adjusted balance, and in whose favor. The accounts and claims dated through September 1894 are also entered in the register described in entry 345. The original accounts and claims for that period are among the miscellaneous Treasury accounts described in entry 347.

336.   REGISTER OF FURNITURE PURCHASED FOR THE TREASURY BUILDING EXTENSION. May 11, 1864 - Aug. 16, 1871. 3 cm, 1 in. 1 vol.

Arranged randomly by requesting office and thereunder chronologically.

Register contains entries that show date and number of requisition, item requested, date furnished, and cost. Entries for May 11, 1864-March 15, 1866, are for requests for furniture for specified offices in the buildings; entries for March 15, 1866-August 16, 1871, are for articles supplied on requisition of the general superintendent of the building or the chief clerk. Entries included such items as desks, chairs, hardware, bookcases, lighting fixtures, locks, footstools, and hatracks.

337.   REGISTERS OF ACCOUNTS FOR PUBLIC BUILDINGS. Apr. 5, 1870 - Nov. 29, 1911. 30 cm, 1 ft. 6 vols.

Volumes are arranged chronologically. Within each volume, entries are arranged by name of disbursing agent in no particular order and thereunder by type and location of building. Each volume is indexed by name of agent.

Registers contain entries that show name of disbursing agent, type and location of building, account number, date received and reported, period covered, total disbursements, and adjusted balance. Entries usually relate to site selection, construction, repair, and contingent expenses. Within the listings for a building there are sometimes separate lists containing the names of contractors or claimants whose accounts and claims pertained to the building. Many of the accounts dated through September 1894 are among the miscellaneous Treasury accounts described in entry 347.

338.   REGISTER OF PAYMENTS ON CONTRACTS FOR PUBLIC BUILDINGS. Oct. 14, 1890 - June 30, 1894. 3 cm, 1 in. 1 vol.

Arranged randomly by type and location of building and thereunder chronologically. Indexed by name of contractor.

Register contains entries that show contractor's name, type and location of building, date of contract, amount of contract, account numbers for payments, and dates and amounts of payments. These accounts are among the miscellaneous Treasury accounts described in entry 347.

339.   REGISTERS OF SALARY ACCOUNTS. Jan. 1, 1868 - Sept. 30, 1894. 61 cm, 2 ft. 7 vols.

Volumes are arranged chronologically. Within each volume the entries are arranged by type of official and thereunder chronologically. Each volume is indexed by name of official.

Registers contain entries that show official's name and title, account number, period covered, dates received and approved, amount due, and where payable. The salaries were chiefly those of the President and Vice President, members of the Supreme Court and of district and circuit courts, and Territorial Governors. The reports through 1882 registered in these volumes are filed with the miscellaneous Treasury accounts described in entry 347.

For additional copies of the reports, see entry 341.

340.   REGISTER OF DISBURSING AGENTS' ACCOUNTS FOR PAYING SALARIES. July 19, 1893 - Feb. 2, 1904. 5 cm, 2 in. 1 vol.

Arranged randomly by name of disbursing agent and thereunder chronologically. Indexed by name of agent.

Register contains entries that show disbursing agent's name, office for which he paid salaries, account number, date approved, period covered, amount disbursed, and balance. Some of these accounts are among the miscellaneous Treasury accounts described in entry 347.

341.   AUDIT REPORTS ON SALARY ACCOUNTS (SALARY CERTIFICATES). June 22, 1882 - May 9, 1893. 91 cm, 3 ft. 15 vols.

Arranged chronologically. Volumes 2-5 (May 29, 1883-Sept. 29, 1886) and 12 (Mar. 17-Dec. 11, 1890) are each indexed by name of official. The other volumes are not indexed. Copies of reports for salary payments to the President and Vice President, Supreme Court justices, Federal judges, and Territorial Governors, showing date prepared, account number, official's name and title, salary due, and for what period. These reports are entered in the registers described in entry 339. Salary accounts through December 1882 are entered in the registers described in entry 345 and are filed as a part of the miscellaneous Treasury accounts described in entry 347.

342.   REGISTER OF SPECIAL ACCOUNTS. June 15, 1875 - Sept. 14, 1894. 5 cm, 2 in. 1 vol.

Arranged by initial letter of officer's surname and thereunder chronologically by date audited.

Register contains entries that show date audited, account number, officer's name and title, type of account, for what period, and adjusted balance. Accounts typically are for proceeds from sale of old material or surplus property, rental of Government-owned buildings, and sale of obsolete revenue cutters and lighthouse vessels. The accounts are among the miscellaneous customs accounts described in entry 311 and the miscellaneous Treasury accounts described in entry 347.

343.   REGISTER OF MISCELLANEOUS ACCOUNTS. Aug. 9, 1864 - Jan. 25, 1866. 3 cm, 1 in.
        1 vol.

Arranged chronologically and thereunder by surname of disbursing agent in no
particular order.

Register contains entries that show disbursing agent's name, title of appropriation from
which he disbursed funds, account number, dates received and audited, total disbursements
reflected in the account, and adjusted balance. Many of the accounts registered are for
construction and repair of customhouses and marine hospitals or expenses of the public printer or
are accounts of Land Office officials acting as Government timber agents. Except for the latter
category, these accounts are among the miscellaneous Treasury accounts described in entry 347.

344.   REGISTER OF MISCELLANEOUS CLAIMS. June 19, 1851 - May 16, 1853. 5 cm, 2 in.
        1 vol.

Arranged by account number. Indexed by name of claimant.

Register contains entries that show account number, claimant's name, type of claim,
authority for payment, where and to whom paid, and amount paid. Most settled claims were
for cash bounties in lieu of land or compensation for horses and other property lost in the
military service of the United States. The accounts listed in the volume were paid by the First
Auditor during the period June 19, 1851-May 16, 1853, and include certificates from the Third
Auditor authorizing the payment. Only a few pages of this volumes were used.

Some of these claims are among miscellaneous Treasury accounts, described in entry 347.

345.   REGISTERS OF AUDIT REPORTS ON ACCOUNTS AND CLAIMS. Mar. 15, 1790 -
        Sept. 29, 1894. 1.5 m, 5 ft. 19 vols. and 7 boxes.

Arranged chronologically. The entries in volumes 1-3 (Mar. 15, 1790-Nov. 19, 1838) and
volumes 17-19 (Jan. 10, 1881-Sept. 29, 1894) are arranged numerically; the entries in volumes 4-
16 (Nov. 20, 1838-Jan. 9, 1881) are arranged by initial letter of officer's or claimant's surname
and thereunder numerically.

Registers contain entries that show account number, date approved, name of officer or
claimant, type of account or claim, and period covered. These accounts and claims covered
nearly all types of civil expenditures of the U.S. Government.

The first volume of this series, March 15, 1790-March 3, 1814, has been reproduced as
NARA Microfilm Publication T899, Register of Audits of "Miscellaneous Treasury Accounts"
(First Auditor's Office).

For audit reports on these accounts and claims, see entry 346; for the original accounts
and claims, see entry 347.

346.   AUDIT REPORTS ON ACCOUNTS AND CLAIMS. Jan. 29, 1801 - June 30, 1888. 9.1 m,
        30 ft. 137 vols.

Arranged numerically. Each volume is indexed by initial letter of surname of officer or
claimant.

There are gaps in the date span of these records; the actual dates covered are: Jan. 29,
1801-Oct. 7, 1837; Jan. 31-June 27, 1842; Oct. 31, 1867-June 30, 1888.

Reports show number, date prepared, name of officer or claimant, type of account or
claim, summary of debits and credits, and adjusted balance. Accounts for approved claims show
the basis of the claim and amount due claimant. These reports cover nearly all types of civil
expenditures of the U.S. Government, except for customs receipts and disbursements (described in
entry 297) and diplomatic, Internal Revenue, and Post Office accounts, which were settled by
the Fifth Auditor.

For a register of these reports, see entry 345; the original reports are filed with the accounts and claims described in entry 347.

347.   SETTLED MISCELLANEOUS TREASURY ACCOUNTS. Sept. 6, 1790 - Sept. 29, 1894. 2,529.8 m, 8,300 ft. 1654 vols. and 7271 boxes.

Arranged numerically. The boxes are in 4 separate groups: 1-1884 (include alpha boxes: 115A, 1714A-C; 1-4750 (alpha boxes: 110A, 452A, 1417A, 1679A, 2758A); 1-883 (alpha boxes: 156A, 177A, 184A, 241A, 325A, 407A, 766A, 798A), there is no box 722; 1-22. Boxes 1-1189 of the first set of boxes have been microfilmed. There are alpha volumes: 168A and 1697A-H

Settled accounts and claims for most civil activities of the Federal Government, including construction and repair of Government buildings; salaries and contingent expenses of Government officials and Cabinet-level departments and agencies; expenses of the U.S. Senate, the U.S. House of Representatives, and Territorial governments; expenses of the U.S. Mint at Philadelphia, branch mints, and assay offices, including the purchase and coinage of gold and silver; disbursements for lighthouses and other aids to navigation; sale of cotton and other property seized from the Confederate States during the Civil War; and approved claims of persons and companies for articles provided to or services performed for the Government or allowed by special acts of Congress. Account numbers were assigned when the Auditor's report was prepared. Accounts of Indian agents and pension agents have been removed from this series and are described separately with records of the Second and Third Auditors, respectively.

The bound volumes are primarily oversize documents that formed part of the account or claim and are chiefly for mint and Treasurer accounts.

These accounts and claims are entered in the registers described in entry 345. Copies of audit reports on the accounts and claims are described in entry 346. The accounts and claims through July 15, 1840, have been reproduced as NARA Microfilm Publication M235, Miscellaneous Treasury Accounts of the First Auditor (Formerly the Auditor) of the Treasury Department, September 6, 1790-July 15, 1840.

347A.   INDEX OF DECISIONS OF THE COMPTROLLERS, Jan. 1, 1884 - Dec. 31, 1914. 1 box.

OFFICE OF THE SECOND AUDITOR

The Office of the Second Auditor had its origins in an act of May 8, 1792 (1 Stat. 279), which authorized the appointment of an Accountant for the War Department. The duties of the Accountant were settlement of accounts for pay of the Army, subsistence of officers, bounty, expenses of recruiting, and incidental and contingent expenses of the War Department; settlement of claims for personal services; and settlement of military claims formerly filed with the Paymaster General and the Commissioner of the Army accounts (both offices created under the Continental Congress) to the extent that they were not barred by limitations of other acts of Congress. The Accountant reported the balances of accounts and claims for inspection and revision by the Comptroller of the Treasury. Responsibility for settlement of Navy and Marine Corps accounts and claims was transferred to the Accountant for the Navy by an act of July 16, 1798 (1 Stat. 610).

The Office of the Accountant was abolished by an act of March 3, 1817 (3 Stat. 366), which authorized establishment of the Office of the Second Auditor. The Second Auditor was responsible for settlement of accounts for pay and clothing of the Army, subsistence of officers, bounties and premiums due soldiers, military and hospital stores, and contingent expenses of the War Department. The Office also filed the accounts and claims after approval by the Second Comptroller, kept a record of receipts and disbursements of public moneys as they related to the functions of the office, and recorded warrants drawn by the Secretary of War.

An appropriation act of July 31, 1894 (28 Stat. 206), changed the name of the Office to the Auditor for the War Department and assigned to his jurisdiction the settlement of all accounts and claims relating to that Department. All other functions formerly exercised by the Second Auditor were transferred to the jurisdiction of the Auditor for the Interior Department (formerly the Third Auditor). The Office was abolished effective July 1, 1921, under provisions of the Budget and Accounting Act of June 10, 1921 (42 Stat. 25).

The operating divisions of the Second Auditor's Office in June 1893 were the Bookkeepers Division; the Paymasters Division; the Ordnance, Medical and Miscellaneous Division; the Indian Division; the Pay and Bounty Division; the Division for the Investigation of Fraud; the Property Division; the Division of Inquiries and Replies; the Mail Division; and the Archives Division. In October 1894, further changes were made in the internal structure of the Office. The records described below reflect the major changes in organizational name and function as of October 1894.

A list of names of Second Auditors and dates of their service appear in Appendix 6.

GENERAL RECORDS

Records Relating to Personnel

348.   REGISTER OF EMPLOYEES. Mar. 4, 1817 - Aug. 1, 1900.3 cm, 1 in. 1 vol.

Arranged alphabetically by initial letter of employee's surname and thereunder by year of appointment.

Register contains entries that show name of employee, State where born and from which appointed, length of military service (if any), dates of appointment and of later personnel actions, and date and cause of termination of service.

BOOKKEEPERS DIVISION

The Bookkeepers Division was first referred to as a separate Division in the Office of the Second Auditor in that official's report to the Secretary of the Treasury regarding operations during the fiscal year ending June 30, 1869. The Division kept appropriation and personal accountability ledgers and journals for all claims other than for arrears of pay and bounty, recorded warrants and requisitions, and issued certificates of indebtedness or nonindebtedness with respect to claimants. The Division also kept a record of the valuable effects of deceased soldiers and furnished information on the status of suits. The functions relating to appropriations were transferred to the Secretary of the Treasury's Division of Bookkeeping and Warrants by an appropriation act of July 31, 1894 (28 Stat. 208).

Ledgers

349.   LEDGER OF MILITARY EXPENDITURES: ALBANY, N.Y. (LEDGER OF SUNDRY ARMY ACCOUNTS). Apr. 1775 - Sept. 1780. 3 cm, 1 in. 1 vol.

This series appears to be missing.
Arranged randomly by title of account.
Ledger contains entries of military expenditures under the Continental Congress showing title of account (usually the Paymaster General, or names of Government officials, or military officers, or the titles of specific appropriations); dates; and debits and credits. Most debit or credit entries are for warrants issued by the Paymaster General or cash disbursed by him and generally show names of persons paid and a brief explanation of the reason for the payment.

350.   LEDGERS OF MILITARY EXPENDITURES (REVOLUTIONARY WAR LEDGER BOOKS). July 1779 - Dec. 1781. 5 cm, 2 in. 2 vols.

This series appears to be missing.
Arranged by title of account in the order listed. Volume 1 consists chiefly of accounts of the Continental Treasurer, the treasurers of New York and Rhode Island, and the Commissary of Purchases; volume 2 consists chiefly of accounts of paymasters and military officers and accounts in the names of militia units. Ledgers contain entries of military expenditures under the Continental Congress, showing title of account and debits and credits.

Debits are frequently for pay of troops or for the value of clothing and equipment issued; credits normally show amounts of settlements of accounts.

351.   MISCELLANEOUS INDEX. ca. 1795 - 1805. 3 cm, 1 in. 1 vol.

This series appears to be missing.
Arranged alphabetically by initial letter of officer or claimant or by type of expenditure.
Miscellaneous index, on pages originally intended to be indexes to a ledger, showing soldiers' names and ranks, names and other identifying information for nonmilitary claimants, general subjects (such as Hospital Department), and page references. The purpose of the index is not known. Correspondence with the accountable officers mentioned and with some of the contractors and other claimants (see entries 493 and 496) is usually for the period 1795-1805.

352.   INDEX TO LEDGERS OF THE ACCOUNTANT FOR THE WAR DEPARTMENT (SET 1). May 1792 - Mar. 1809. 5 cm, 2 in. 1 vol.

Arranged alphabetically by title of account.
Index to volumes A-D of the ledgers of the Accountant for the War Department (set 1), entry 353, showing title of account (usually the name of accountable officer or claimant) and page references to the ledgers.

353.   LEDGERS OF THE ACCOUNTANT FOR THE WAR DEPARTMENT (SET 1). May 1792 - Mar. 1809. 30 cm, 1 ft. 4 vols.

Arranged by title of account.

Ledgers contain entries showing title of account (usually general appropriation accounts or accounts in the names of military units, individual officers, or other persons); rank, title, or other identifying information, in the case of an account in a personal name; and debits and credits. Entries usually include dates, numbers and amounts of warrants, and explanations of sources of other funds received and disbursed. References to pertinent pages in the journal described in entry 366 are also included.

For an index, see entry 352.

354.   INDEX TO LEDGERS OF THE ACCOUNTANT FOR THE WAR DEPARTMENT (SET 2). Mar. 1809 - Mar. 1817. 5 cm, 2 in. 1 vol.

Arranged alphabetically by initial letter of surname of officer or claimant.

Index to ledgers of the Accountant for the War Department (set 2), entry 355, showing title of account (usually the name of an accountable officer or claimant), title of appropriation concerned, and page references.

When this volume was repaired, some of the pages were bound out of order.

355.   LEDGERS OF THE ACCOUNTANT FOR THE WAR DEPARTMENT (SET 2). Mar. 1809 - Mar. 1817. 61 cm, 2 ft. 6 vols.

Arranged by title of account.

Ledgers contain entries showing title of account (usually a military officer, contractor, Indian agent, or paymaster), title of appropriations concerned, debits, and credits. Entries include dates, numbers, and amounts of requisitions and warrants charged or credited to the person. Journal references (entry 366) are also included.

For an index, see entry 354.

356.   GENERAL INDEX TO LEDGERS (INDEX TO FISCAL OFFICERS' LEDGERS). May 1816 - Mar. 1912. 23 cm, 9 in. 2 vols.

Arranged alphabetically by initial letter of surname of officer or claimant.

Index shows name of officer or claimant, rank or other identifying information, ledger series indexed, and pertinent folio numbers. The series indexed by these volumes are the general ledgers (old series), entry 357; miscellaneous ledgers (new series), entry 362; auxiliary ledgers, entry 359; paymasters' ledgers, entry 358; and Indian ledgers, entry 361.

357.   GENERAL LEDGERS (OLD SERIES). May 1816 - July 1868. 1.5 m, 5 ft. 16 vols.

Arranged by title of account.

Ledgers contain entries showing title of account (usually an accountable officer or claimant), title of appropriation concerned, debits and credits, and dates and numbers of warrants. Titles of appropriations include bounty pay, recruiting expenses, forage, subsistence, and pay of the Indian Department.

For an index, see entry 356.

358.   PAYMASTERS' LEDGERS. Jan. 1864 - June 1908. 1.2 m, 4 ft. 15 vols.

Arranged by title of account.

Ledgers contain entries showing name of paymaster or assistant paymaster, date of bond, titles of appropriations concerned, debits and credits, and usually also dates and numbers of requisitions and warrants and names of persons to whom funds were disbursed or from whom funds were received. Appropriations concerned included pay of the Army, subsistence of officers, bounty, and pay of volunteers.

For an index, see entry 356; for related journals, see entry 369.

359.   AUXILIARY LEDGERS. Sept. 1855 - Mar. 1912. 20 cm, 8 in. 3 vols.

Arranged by title of account in no particular order. Accounts showing an outstanding balance when the general ledgers were closed for the accounting period were transferred to the auxiliary ledger.

Ledgers contain entries of accounts of former paymasters and other former disbursing agents showing name and rank of officer, date and cause of termination of service, titles of appropriations concerned, and debits and credits required to close the account.

360.   INDEX TO FISCAL OFFICERS' LEDGERS (INDIAN LEDGERS). July 1, 1867 - Apr. 26, 1907. 5 cm, 2 in. 1 vol.

Arranged alphabetically by initial letter of surname of officer or claimant.

Index to the ledgers described in entry 361 showing name of officer or claimant, rank or other identifying information, and page numbers in the ledgers. Claimants are specifically identified as such in the index.

361.   FISCAL OFFICERS' LEDGERS (INDIAN LEDGERS). July 1, 1867 - Apr. 26, 1907. 1.8 m, 6 ft. 21 vols.

Arranged by title of account.

Ledgers contain entries showing title of account (usually a disbursing agent or a claimant), title of appropriation concerned, and debits, and credits. Entries usually include account numbers (entry 525) and warrant numbers.

For an index, see entry 360.

362.   MISCELLANEOUS LEDGERS (NEW SERIES). July 1868 - Sept. 1895. 1.5 m, 5 ft. 18 vols.

Arranged by title of account.

Ledgers contain entries showing the status of accounts of officers other than paymasters, with name and rank of accountable officer, name of military unit, titles of appropriations concerned, and debits and credits.

The entries show dates and numbers of accounts and requisitions and names of persons from whom funds were received or to whom funds were disbursed.

For an index, see entry 356; for related journals, see entry 371.

363.   LEDGER OF INDIAN REQUISITIONS (INDIAN LEDGER, VOL. 23). Aug. 1888 - June 1894. 8 cm, 3 in. 1 vol.

Arranged by title of account.

Ledger contains entries that show title of account, summary of debit and credit requisitions affecting the account, monthly summary of amounts of requisitions to be debited or credited, and balance carried forward.

364.   ABSTRACTS OF SETTLED ACCOUNTS (LEDGER OF EXPENDITURES). Sept. 1821 - Dec. 30, 1824. 13 cm, 5 in. 2 vols.

Arranged chronologically.

There are gaps in the date span of these records; the actual dates covered are: Sept. 1821-June 1822; Jan. 2-Dec. 30, 1824.

Abstracts show date and number of settlement (entry 523); accountable officer's name, rank, and title; titles of appropriations from which he disbursed funds; and amounts disbursed from each. Appropriations were typically for pay of the Army, subsistence, clothing, recruiting expenses, ordnance, pensions, and road and canal surveys.

Journals

365.   JOURNALS OF MILITARY EXPENDITURES. June 25, 1776 - Aug. 24, 1786. 23 cm, 9 in.
4 vols.

This series appears to be missing.
Arranged by location in the order listed and thereunder chronologically.
Journals created at the Philadelphia Pay Office, June 25, 1776-November 27, 1784; at
Albany, N.Y., December 2, 1776-September 13, 1780; at the Central Treasury in Philadelphia,
January 7, 1780-September 13, 1781; and at the New York Pay Office, November 21, 1785-August
24, 1786.
Entries show date, type of expense, names of persons to whom payments were made, and
amount paid. The journals of expense at Albany were concerned chiefly with funds disbursed in
Canada and disallowances in the accounts of officers; the other journals relate primarily to pay
of militia, subsistence and mileage for officers, and recruiting expenses.

366.   JOURNALS OF THE ACCOUNTANT FOR THE WAR DEPARTMENT. May 15, 1792 -
Mar. 3, 1817. 1.5 m, 5 ft. 22 vols.

Arranged chronologically. Journals A-Q, 1-6, and one additional account book make up
22 volumes; journals I and J are missing. Volume Q overlaps volumes 1-6 in date span, but there is
no duplication of content. The final volume is for the transfer of accounts to the books of the
Additional Accountant for the War Department on March 3, 1817. Entries show title of
appropriation concerned, warrant and requisition numbers, name of payee, explanation, amount,
and ledger reference (entry 355).

367.   JOURNAL OF THE ACCOUNTANT FOR THE WAR DEPARTMENT. May 15, 1792 -
Mar. 30, 1793. 5 cm, 2 in. 1 vol.

Arranged chronologically.
Entries show date posted, titles of accounts, persons to be charged and credited, and
explanation. Most of the entries in this journal relate to pay of military officers and units,
reimbursement of persons for moneys advanced, and expenses relating to Indians. Sometimes
warrant numbers are shown. Some of the entries in this journal are repeated in the series of
journals described in entry 366, but much of the information is not duplicated in that series.

368.   SECOND AUDITOR'S JOURNALS (OLD SERIES). May 10, 1816 - June 30, 1868. 1.2 m,
4 ft. 20 vols.

Arranged chronologically.
Entries show date transaction was recorded, ledger reference (entry 358), warrant
number, appropriation title, name of accountable officer or claimant, settlement number,
explanation, and amount paid. Expenditures were military-related and Indian-related.

369.   PAYMASTERS' JOURNALS (NEW SERIES). Jan. 1, 1864 - Jan. 27, 1908. 91 cm, 3 ft.
17 vols.

Arranged chronologically.
Entries show date recorded, ledger reference (entry 358), name of paymaster, name of
person to whom payment was made, titles of appropriations concerned, and amount paid. Some
of the entries also show the numbers, dates, and amounts of requisitions drawn and names of
persons in whose favor they were issued.

370.   INDIAN JOURNALS (NEW SERIES). July 5, 1867 - Sept. 29, 1894. 1.8 m, 6 ft. 29 vols.

Arranged chronologically.

Entries show date recorded, settlement number (entry 525), ledger reference (entry 361), name of claimant or accountable officer, explanation and amount of claim, and title of appropriation to be charged. Included periodically are summaries of the numbers and amounts of requisitions charged and credited to the several appropriations.

For a continuation of this series, see Indian Agents' Journals (entry 549).

371.   MISCELLANEOUS JOURNALS (NEW SERIES). July 1, 1868 - Feb. 3, 1906. 91 cm, 3 ft. 15 vols.

Arranged chronologically. There are two volumes numbered 8 and two numbered 9; volumes 10 and 11 are not present.

Entries show date and number of settlement (entry 525), ledger reference (entry 362), name and title of accountable officer to be debited, explanation, amount to be debited, and title of appropriation to be credited. Many of the entries are for correction of errors in accounts of officers.

372.   CLAIMS JOURNALS (NEW SERIES). Jan. 3, 1866 - June 29, 1874. 10 cm, 4 in. 2 vols.

Arranged chronologically.

Entries show date confirmed, claim number, name of claimant, basis of claim, amount claimed, date settled, requisition number, in whose favor, title of appropriation to be charged, and amount paid. Entries relate to Indian claims, such as fulfilling treaty obligations and to military claims, such as payment of medical expenses. At the end of the entries for June 1872, June 1873, and June 1874 is a recapitulation of the account numbers of settled Indian claims and settled military claims listed by the appropriations from which they were paid.

Records Relating to Warrants and Requisitions

373.   INDEXES TO REGISTERS OF WARRANTS (ALPHABET TO WARRANT BOOKS). Jan. 1, 1800-Nov. 8, 1813. 10 cm, 4 in. 5 vols.

Arranged alphabetically by initial letter of payee's surname.

There are gaps in the date span of these records; the actual dates covered are: Jan. 1, 1800-Dec. 31, 1802; June 18, 1810-Feb. 10, 1812; Jan. 1-Nov. 8, 1813.

Indexes to volumes 4, 6, 7, 9, and 11 of registers of warrants (entry 374) showing payee's name, rank or other identifying information, and warrant number.

374.   REGISTERS OF WARRANTS. Oct. 2, 1795-Dec. 31, 1821. 61 cm, 2 ft. 10 vols.

Arranged chronologically and identified as volumes 3-5 and 8-14; the latest volume is identified as volume 1. Volumes 1, 2, 6, and 7 have not been located.

There are gaps in the date span of these records; the actual dates covered are: Oct. 2, 1795-Dec. 31, 1805; Mar. 6, 1809-Dec. 20, 1815; May 9, 1816-Dec. 31, 1821.

Registers contain entries that show warrants recorded by the Accountant for the War Department, including warrant date and number, title of appropriation to be charged, to whom issued, explanation, and amount.

Appropriations include Army pay, fortifications, subsistence, and camp equipment. The 1817-21 volume was created by the Second Auditor, who was the successor to the Accountant for the War Department.

For a partial index, see entry 373.

375.   REGISTERS OF WARRANTS ISSUED IN SETTLEMENT OF REVOLUTIONARY WAR
        CLAIMS UNDER AN ACT OF MAY 15, 1828. May 31, 1828-May 6, 1835. 5 cm, 2 in.
        2 vols.

Arranged chronologically and thereunder numerically.
Registers contain entries that show date and number of warrant, to whom issued, period
for which pay was due, and amount.

376.   INDEX TO REGISTERS OF INDIAN REQUISITIONS. Mar. 8, 1849-Sept. 30, 1894.
        23 cm, 9 in. 4 vols.

Arranged alphabetically by initial letter of payee's surname.
Index to registers of requisitions (entry 377) showing payee's name, rank or other
identifying information, year, and requisition numbers.

377.   REGISTERS OF INDIAN REQUISITIONS (DEBIT REQUISITIONS: INDIANS). Mar.
        8, 1849-Sept. 29, 1894. 1.8 m, 6 ft. 44 vols.

Arranged by requisition number.
Registers contain entries that show requisition number, ledger reference, name of
accountable officer, settlement number (entry 525), title of appropriations to be charged, and
amount.
For an index, see entry 376.

378.   REGISTER OF CREDIT REQUISITIONS. July 2, 1890-Sept. 29, 1894. 5 cm, 2 in. 1 vol.

Arranged chronologically.
Register contains entries that show credit requisitions, chiefly for Indian agents,
including requisition number, warrant number, name and title of accountable officer, date of
surety bond, title of appropriation, amount of credit requisition, number of transfer requisition,
and settlement number (entry 525).

PAYMASTER, ORDNANCE, AND MEDICAL DIVISION

The Paymaster, Ordnance, and Medical Division was established in the Second
Auditor's Office on October 14, 1893, as a result of the consolidation of the Paymasters Division
(established during the fiscal year ending June 30, 1867) with the Ordnance, Medical, and
Miscellaneous Division (established during the fiscal year ending June 30, 1891). The combined
Division was responsible for settling all Army disbursing accounts, military accounts of the
disbursing clerk for the War Department, claims presented under special acts of Congress, and
claims for the refund of bounty money. It also kept book records of payments to Regular and
Volunteer Army officers, adjusted accounts for the National Home for Disabled Volunteer
Soldiers, and computed the longevity status of officers.

Records Relating to Paymaster's Accounts

379.   ABSTRACT OF OFFICERS' ACCOUNTS OPENED ON THE BOOKS OF THE
        PAYMASTER GENERAL. Dec. 9, 1788. 3 cm, 1 in. Part of 1 vol.

This series appears to be missing.
Arranged by type of payment and thereunder chronologically.
Abstract prepared by Joseph Nourse, Register of the Treasury, on December 9, 1788,
compiling information on the books of the Paymaster General relating to debits and credits in
the accounts of paymasters and military officers. Separate sections of the volume concern

balances payable in old emissions, new emissions, specie, and bills of exchange and show date, name of officer, explanation, and amounts debited or credited. The dates of the entries are for the period November 23, 1781-May 16, 1788 (approx.). Part of the volume is used for a register of warrants described in entry 381.

380.   LIST OF ACCOUNTS SETTLED BY THE ACCOUNTANT FOR THE WAR DEPARTMENT BEFORE MARCH 3, 1817, AND FILED IN THE THIRD AUDITOR'S OFFICE. 1833. 1/4 in. 1 vol.

Arranged alphabetically by initial letter of surname of accountable officer.

List of accounts, prepared "immediately after the burning of the Treasury Building in 1833" showing name of accountable officer, settlement number, and date of settlement. The accounts were settled during the period June 14, 1805-March 3, 1817.

381.   REGISTER OF WARRANTS ISSUED AND REDEEMED. Feb. 27, 1796-June 30, 1815. 3 cm, 1 in. Part of 1 vol.

This series appears to be missing.

Arranged chronologically.

Register contains entries that show date warrant was received, warrant number, on whom drawn, amount, date discharged, and date sent to the Auditor. Part of this volume is used as a record of officers' accounts opened on the books of the Paymaster General (entry 379).

382.   REGISTERS OF PAYMASTERS' ACCOUNTS. Sept. 1, 1865-Jan. 10, 1911. 5 cm, 2 in. 2 vols.

Arranged chronologically.

Registers contain entries that show date received, name of paymaster, account number, and period covered by account.

383.   RECORD OF PAYMASTERS' SETTLEMENTS. Nov. 2, 1861-Apr. 17, 1883. 2 cm, 1 in. 1 vol.

Arranged numerically. Indexed by name of paymaster.

Record shows settlement number, name of paymaster, room and box in which account was filed, latest period covered by settlement, and date confirmed.

384.   PAYMASTERS' ABSTRACTS. Aug. 21, 1861-Feb. 13, 1882. 1.8 m, 6 ft. 57 vols.

Arranged alphabetically by name of paymaster and thereunder chronologically.

Bimonthly abstracts submitted by paymasters as part of their accounts typically showing voucher number, date of payment, soldier's name and military unit, certificate numbers, and purpose and amount of payment.

Most entries were for bounty paid under various acts. The following are the names of paymasters whose abstracts are included in this series, dates covered by each paymaster's abstract and number of volumes.

Dyer, George W.	May 26, 1867-Nov. 30, 1868	4 vols.
Gardner, Thomas H.	June 30, 1864-June 30, 1868	4 vols.
Hodge, J. Ledyard	Aug. 21, 1861-Sept. 7, 1871	12 vols.
Holmes, Oliver	June 1-Nov. 30, 1862	1 vol.

Moore, Edwin L.	May 12, 1866-Nov. 30, 1868	7 vols.
Robinson, Albert D.	Jan. 29, 1863-Nov. 30, 1868	7 vols.
Rochester, William B.	Jan. 2-Dec. 31, 1863, and Apr. 1, 1867-Feb. 13, 1882	5 vols.
Taylor, David	Dec. 8, 1866-Nov. 30, 1868	5 vols.
Truesdell, George	Dec. 22, 1866-Nov. 30, 1868	5 vols.
Tucker, Nathaniel A.	July 29, 1864-Nov. 30, 1868	5 vols.
Vrooman, Wellington	June 23-Nov. 30, 1868	2 vols.

385.   REGISTER OF SETTLED ACCOUNTS OF DISBURSING OFFICERS. Apr. 1868-Aug. 1885. 5 cm, 2 in. 1 vol.

Arranged alphabetically by initial letter of officer's surname.

Register contains entries that show name and rank of disbursing officer, his military unit, period covered, date account received, volume and page references to settlement books 1-5, date confirmed, and settlement number. These accounts were registered in the registers of accounts and claims reported on by the Second Auditor (entry 197). A majority of the accounts were payable from appropriations for Army pay.

Records Relating to Pay of Army Units

386.   REGISTERS OF PAY OF MILITARY UNITS. Jan. 1, 1813-Dec. 31, 1896. 91 cm, 3 ft. 15 vols.

Arranged by designation of military unit and thereunder chronologically. Volumes 1, 2, 8-13, and 15 are each indexed by name of military unit or of its commanding officer. The other volumes are not indexed.

Registers contain entries that show name of unit, name of its commanding officer, period for which paid, name of paymaster, and date of settlement. Volumes 1 and 2 also show voucher number and account number, and volumes 7-15 generally also show file number, voucher number, and account number. Beginning with volume 7, the information is shown for each 2-month period, instead of the longer periods typical of the earlier volumes.

387.   ROSTER OF OFFICERS AND REGULAR ARMY UNITS SERVING IN THE MEXICAN WAR. Jan. 1845-Jan. 1850. 2 cm, 1 in. 1 vol.

Arranged by type of information.

Entries show, for officers, the officer's name, rank, military unit, and career history (e.g., dropped, declined commissions, or resigned) and, for military units, the unit's identity; name of commanding officer; organization, strength, and history of the unit; date the unit was paid; name of paymaster; voucher number; and settlement number.

388.   REGISTERS OF PAYMENTS TO REGULAR AND VOLUNTEER UNITS. Jan. 1, 1861 - Dec. 31, 1870. 13 cm, 5 in. 2 vols.

Arranged by unit designation and thereunder chronologically. Indexed by unit designation.

Registers contain entries that show name of major unit (e.g. 1st Cavalry); designations of companies, detachments, and other subsidiary units; name of paymaster for each 2-month period; and settlement number. Voucher numbers and account numbers also are sometimes shown. These volumes partially overlap one another in content and partially duplicate the information in volumes 7 and 18 of the registers described in entry 386.

389.   REGISTER OF PAYMENTS TO MISCELLANEOUS UNITS (POST BOOK). May 1861-Aug. 1867. 8 cm, 3 in. 1 vol.

Arranged by type of unit and thereunder geographically by location. Indexed alphabetically by location of unit.

Register contains entries that show payments to arsenals, barracks, camps, hospitals, and recruiting parties showing identity of the unit, period for which paid, paymaster's name, and pertinent account, settlement, and voucher numbers.

390.   REGISTER OF PAYMASTERS' SETTLEMENTS FOR ARMY POSTS. 1861-74. 5 cm, 2 in. 1 vol.

Arranged chronologically.

Register contains entries that show month and year of payment, location of unit, name of paymaster, and settlement number. Most of these units appear to have been camps or forts.

391.   REGISTER OF PAYMENTS TO INDIAN SCOUTS AND INDIAN HOME GUARDS. May 1862-Feb. 1882. 3 cm, 1 in. 1 vol.

Arranged alphabetically by designation of unit. The volume is indexed by location of unit.

Register contains entries that show identity and location of unit, period for which paid, name of paymaster, settlement number, and account number. If a unit consisted of more than one company, the payments to each company are listed separately. Most of these special Indian units were attached to military forts and camps in Western States. The volume is partially duplicated by the register of payments to volunteer and special units (entry 530).

392.   MISCELLANEOUS RECORDS OF PAY AND ALLOTMENTS. ca. 1893-1904. 5 cm, 2 in. 1 vol.

Arranged by type of information.

Records include undated lists of officers; lists of hospital personnel, 1893-94, and the paymasters by whom they were paid; records of allotments from pay of volunteer infantry units, 1899-1902; records of pay of units of the 6th and 7th Artillery, March 1898-May 1901, including names of paymasters and account and settlement numbers; and records of pay of detachments of the Signal Corps, July 1, 1898-December 31, 1904, including location of detachment, name of paymaster, and account and settlement numbers.

Records Relating to Pay for Military Service

393.   RECORDS OF BOUNTY DUE RECRUITS. Feb. 24, 1795-Apr. 18, 1796. 1/4 in. 1 vol.

This series appears to be missing.

Arranged chronologically by date of enlistment.

Entries show soldier's name, by whom recruited, date of enlistment, bounty to which he was entitled, amount paid, by whom paid, bounty to be withheld until soldier joined his assigned military unit, and by whom remaining bounty would be paid.

394.   REGISTER OF ARMY PAY FOR WHICH RECEIPTS WERE NOT SIGNED. Mar. 1,
       1800 - Dec. 31, 1808. 5 cm, 2 in. 1 vol.

       Arranged numerically.
       Register contains entries that show moneys received, an unidentified number, soldier's
name and rank, his military unit, name of paymaster, period for which paid, amount paid, and
remarks on soldier's status (e.g. discharged, deceased, deserted, or transferred).

395.   ABSTRACTS OF PAYMENTS TO OFFICERS. Jan. 17, 1817-Jan. 24, 1820. 1 cm, 1/2 in.
       1 vol.

       Arranged chronologically.
       Entries show officer's name and rank, name of paymaster, and period for which officer
had been paid. The dates shown above are the approximate dates of settlement of the accounts
from which the abstracts were complied.
       In a few cases, the periods for which officers were paid are dated as early as 1812.

396.   REGISTERS OF PAYMENTS TO DISCHARGED SOLDIERS. May 1817-June 1865. 30 cm,
       1 ft. 7 vols.

       Arranged alphabetically by initial letter of soldier's surname.
       Registers contain entries that show soldier's name and rank, sometimes his military
unit, paymaster's name, and month and year of settlement. Some of the volumes partly
duplicate one another, particularly for the period 1817-50.

397.   REGISTERS OF PAYMENTS TO COLORED TROOPS (PAYMENTS TO DISCHARGED
       SOLDIERS: U.S. COLORED TROOPS). May 1863-June 1868. 61 cm, 2 ft. 5 vols.

       Arranged by initial letter of soldier's surname and thereunder chronologically.
       Registers contain entries that show soldier's name, rank, and military unit; period for
which he was paid; amount paid; name of paymaster; account number; and date paid.
Variations in pay are explained and are generally for travel pay, bounty, or pay stoppages.
Some entries are claims for pay in arrears and were settled as late as 1889.

398.   INDEX TO REGISTERS OF PAYMENTS TO OFFICERS. 1862-65. 8 cm, 3 in. 4 vols.

       Arranged by rank officer and thereunder by initial letter and initial vowel of surname
of officer. The volumes are lettered A-D.
       Index to the registers of payments to officers (entry 399) showing volume and page
reference and name and rank of officer. Sometimes a military unit is designated (e.g., 13 Ind. or
24 Ohio). Volume A lists assistant quartermaster, quartermasters, commissaries, and surgeons;
volumes B and C each list assistant adjutant generals, aides de camp, inspectors, and judge
advocates; volume D lists generals, paymasters, and ordnance and signal officers.

399.   REGISTERS OF PAYMENTS TO OFFICERS. 1862-65. 20 cm, 8 in. 4 vols.

       Arranged by rank of officer and thereunder by initial letter of officer's surname and
designated as volumes A to D. An index is in entry 398.
       Registers contain entries that show officer's name, rank, military unit; month and year
of payment; amount paid; and settlement number.

400.   RECORD OF PAY STOPPAGE AGAINST PRISONERS OF WAR (LEDGER A: KNOXVILLE). Nov. 1861-Aug. 1864. 3 cm, 1 in. 1 vol.

Arranged alphabetically by initial letter of soldier's surname.

Record shows date of stoppage; voucher number; soldier's name, rank, and military unit; period during which he was a prisoner; and amount. If this amount was later paid, the name of the person who received it is also shown.

401.   RECORD OF PAYMENTS TO PAROLED AND EXCHANGED PRISONERS (PAY ACCOUNTS). Jan. 1863-Apr. 1865. 15 cm, 6 in. 4 vols.

Arranged by month and thereunder by name of State. Indexed alphabetically by name of State.

Record shows period covered; soldier's name, rank, and military unit; and amount. The name of the paymaster is also sometimes included.

Volume 4 is a consolidation of the other three volumes.

402.   RECORD OF PAYMENTS TO PRISONERS OF WAR. Sept. 15, 1863-Apr. 25, 1865. 5 cm, 2 in. 1 vol.

Arranged by initial letter of prisoner's surname and thereunder by date of payment.

Record shows date paid; soldier's name, rank, and military unit; period for which paid; and amount. Sometimes name of paymaster and name of person to whom payment was made are also shown.

403.   REGISTER OF MONEYS DUE PRISONERS (MONEY REGISTER OF PRISONERS). May 1865-Feb. 1866. 5 cm, 2 in. 1 vol.

Arranged by initial letter of soldier's surname.

Register contains entries that soldier's name and military unit, case number, amount turned over to Chief Paymaster and by whom, date and amount repaid, and to whom repaid. Most of the repayments were made to the National Military Asylum. If the amount was repaid in full, the entry also shows paymaster's name and the account number and voucher number in which repayment was reported.

404.   RECORD OF PAY OF CUBAN ARMY. May 1899-Sept. 1899. 3 cm, 1 in.

Arranged by initial letter of officer's surname.

Record shows officer's name, rank, and military unit: month for which paid; name of paymaster; and sheet, voucher, and account numbers. A special listing for escorts, guards, and inspectors is included.

405.   RECORD OF MILITIA OFFICERS' PAY AT CAMPS AND AT GARRISON SCHOOLS. Apr. 1911-July 1916. 3 cm, 1 in. 1 vol.

Arranged in part by camp location and in part by initial letter of officer's surname. Indexed alphabetically by initial letter of officer's surname.

Record shows voucher number; officer's name, rank, and military unit; duty station or points between which he was being paid to travel; name of paymaster; and date and amount paid. Some lists also show the location of the camp at which the officer was stationed. Part of this volume is used as a register of settled claims, 1871-88 (entry 462).

Records Relating to Deposits and Repayments

406.   INDEX TO REGISTERS OF DRAFT RENDEZVOUS ACCOUNTS. May 1864-Apr. 1865.
        3 cm, 1 in. 1 vol.

        Arranged by location of rendezvous and thereunder by initial letter of soldier's
surname. Indexed by location of rendezvous.
        Index shows location of rendezvous, soldier's name, and page reference to registers of
draft rendezvous accounts (entry 407).

407.   REGISTERS OF DRAFT RENDEZVOUS ACCOUNTS. May 1864-Apr. 1865. 15 cm, 6 in.
        2 vols.

        Arranged by location of rendezvous and thereunder by initial letter of soldier's
surname. Indexed by location of rendezvous. An index arranged by name of soldier is in entry 406.
        Registers contain entries that show location of rendezvous, names of commanding
officers and paymasters, soldier's name, unit to which he was assigned, date and amount
received from soldier, date and amount repaid, by whom and to whom repayment was made,
and account number and voucher number. If the repayment was made to the National Military
Asylum, the date of the soldier's death or desertion is shown by way of explanation. Each
volume also includes a copy of the regulations governing moneys received from soldiers at draft
rendezvous and instructions for preparing the register of rendezvous accounts.

408.   LEDGER OF MONEYS DEPOSITED AT CAMP CALDWALDER AND OTHER
        RENDEZVOUS (REGISTER OF BOUNTY MONEY FROM VOLUNTEERS AND
        SUBSTITUTES). 1864-65. 5 cm, 2 in. 1 vol.

        Arranged by title of account. Partially indexed by name of soldier.
        Ledger contains entries of moneys received from recruits at Camp Caldwalder and other
rendezvous by Capt. A. J. Cohen and deposited by him under provisions of Adjutant General's
Order 305 (Dec. 12, 1864). This order provided that recruits were required to turn over, at the
rendezvous, all money in excess of $20. The paymaster or other designated officer deposited the
funds with a bank or the Assistant U.S. Treasurer and issued the soldier a checkbook credited
with the amount deposited. On arrival at his duty station the soldier could require full
repayment of the deposit, or he could draw upon the funds as needed. The entries in this ledger
show the title of account (i.e., soldier's name, rank, and military unit) and debits and credits. If
the soldier was a substitute, this fact is also noted.

409.   LEDGER OF MONEYS DEPOSITED AT CAMP CHASE (LOCAL BOUNTY LEDGER).
        Jan. 6, 1865-Feb. 22, 1865. 5 cm, 2 in. 1 vol.

        Arranged by title of account. Indexed by surname of soldier.
        Ledger contains entries of deposits made at Camp Chase by Gen. W. P. Richardson under
provision of Adjutant General's Order 305 (see entry 408) showing title of account (i.e., soldier's
name), journal reference (entry 410), credits (including receipt numbers), and debits.

410.   JOURNAL OF CASH RECEIPTS AT CAMP CHASE. Jan. 12, 1865-Feb. 22, 1865. 5 cm,
        2 in. 1 vol.

        Arranged chronologically.
        Journal contains entries of moneys received at Camp Chase by General Richardson
showing date of deposit, soldier's name, ledger page reference (entry 409), receipt number, and
amount deposited. General Richardson turned these funds over to Charles C. Jones, Additional

Paymaster of the Army, during March 1865, under provisions of Adjutant General's Order 305 (see entry 408).

411.   LEDGER OF MONEYS DEPOSITED AT ELMIRA, N.Y. Feb. 1, 1865-Feb. 11, 1865. 3 cm, 1 in. 1 vol.

Arranged by title of account. Indexed by name of soldier.

Ledger contains entries of moneys deposited at the rendezvous at Elmira, N.Y., under provisions of Adjutant General's Order 305 (see entry 408) showing title of account (i.e., soldier's name and military unit), debits and credits.

412.   REGISTER OF LOCAL BOUNTY CERTIFICATES. Nov. 14, 1866-Mar. 20, 1879. 3 cm, 1 in. 1 vol.

Arranged numerically.

Register contains entries that show certificate number, date paid, in whose favor issued, name of paymaster, name and address of person actually paid, amount paid, and explanation. Most entries appear to relate to moneys deposited by soldiers with paymasters who accounted for them and later repaid the deposits to the soldiers or their heirs or legal representative.

413.   REGISTERS OF DEPOSITS BY SOLDIERS. Mar. 22, 1875-Dec. 17, 1880. 15 cm, 6 in. 2 vols.

Arranged by surname of paymaster in no particular order and thereunder chronologically by date of deposit. Indexed by surname of paymaster.

Registers contain entries that show paymaster's name; period covered by the record of deposits; specific dates of deposits; soldier's name, rank, and military unit; amount deposited; by whom repaid; and date repaid.

414.   REGISTERS OF RECEIPTS, DEPOSITS, AND EFFECTS. Jan. 1888-July 1907. 13 cm, 5 in. 3 vols.

Arranged alphabetically by initial letter of soldier's surname.

Registers contain entries that show soldier's name and military unit, explanation (i.e., 'D' if a deposit, 'R' if a receipt, and 'E' in the case of deceased's effects), amount, and date of action. The name of the depositing officer is shown for deposits, and the name of the person signing the receipt is shown for receipts. In the case of effects, the entries also show date of death, type or value of effects, and by whom received.

Records Relating to Hospitals

415.   HOSPITAL BLOTTER. Nov. 13, 1815-Mar. 3, 1817. 3 cm, 1 in. 1 vol.

Arranged chronologically.

Distribution of medical supplies to various installations for which doctors or others had furnished receipts and for which they were accountable and inventories of supplies on hand. The entries show name and title of accountable officer (usually a doctor, military storekeeper, hospital steward, or post surgeon), where stationed, quantity, and lists of articles furnished or on hand (such as lancets, mugs, and surgical needles). On most of the lists the articles are arranged in approximate alphabetical order.

416.   REGISTER OF PAYMENTS TO OFFICERS IN CHARGE OF HOSPITALS AND OTHER UNITS. July 1, 1855-Oct. 31, 1867. 5 cm, 2 in. 1 vol.

Arranged by type of unit and thereunder by surname of officer. Indexed by location of unit.

Register contains entries that show identity and location of unit, names and position of officers paid (e.g., surgeons), voucher number, period for which paid, name of paymaster, and date paid.

For a record of payments to the staffs of hospitals and other units, see registers of paymasters' settlement for hospitals and other units, entry 417.

417.   REGISTERS OF PAYMASTERS' SETTLEMENTS FOR HOSPITALS AND OTHER UNITS. May 1, 1861-June 30, 1904. 61 cm, 2 ft. 10 vols.

Arranged geographically by location of hospital or other unit. Each volume is indexed alphabetically by location of unit.

There are gaps in the date span of these records; the actual dates covered are: May 1, 1861-Dec. 31, 1894; Sept. 1, 1901-June 30, 1904.

Registers contains entries that show identity and location of unit, period for which paid, paymaster's name, and account and settlement numbers. Volume 4 appears to be a consolidation of the information in volumes 1 and 2.

For a record of payments to surgeons and other commanding officers at some of these units, see entry 416.

418.   REGISTER OF PAYMENTS TO SURGEONS AND ACTING ASSISTANT SURGEONS. May 1898-Aug. 1908. 8 cm, 3 in. 1 vol.

Arranged by initial letter of surname of surgeon or assistant surgeon.

Register contains entries that show name of surgeon or acting assistant surgeon, his residence, date of contract, amount payable monthly under the contract, name of paymaster, account and settlement numbers, date paid, period for which payment was made, and amount. Also included is a record of special payments, such as charges for transportation between military posts.

Records Relating to Civilian Pay

419.   REGISTER OF PAYMENTS TO CIVIL EMPLOYEES. Sept. 1, 1835-Dec. 31, 1841. 8 cm, 3 in. 1 vol.

Arranged alphabetically by initial letter of employee's surname.

Register contains entries that show employee's name; occupation (usually wagonmaster, express rider, teamster, carpenter, or laborer); monthly rate of pay; period employed; amounts due, actually paid, and remaining due; and by whom paid.

420.   REGISTER OF PAY OF OFFICERS IN MILITARY RECONSTRUCTION DISTRICTS (REGISTERS OF PAYMENTS OF CIVIL OFFICERS). Jan. 1867-Dec. 1869. 10 cm, 4 in. 2 vols.

Arranged by military reconstruction district. A sheet pasted to the front cover of each volume shows the boundaries of the respective districts, names of paymasters, and their settlement numbers.

Registers contain entries that show number of district, name of officer, period for which paid, amount, and settlement and voucher numbers.

Payments for transportation or mileage paid to the officer are recorded separately from normal monthly pay of the officer.

421.   RECORD OF PAYMENTS TO EMPLOYEES IN MILITARY RECONSTRUCTION DISTRICTS. Jan. 2, 1869-Feb. 20, 1871. 3 cm, 1 in. 1 vol.

Arranged chronologically.
Record of payments to employees, mainly in Alabama, Louisiana, and Texas showing receipt number, name of employee, type of expense (usually mileage, headquarters expense, or military trials), amount approved, check number, date issued, and amount.

422.   RECORD OF EXPENSES OF THE MILITARY DISTRICT OF TEXAS (CASHBOOK). July 6, 1867-Dec. 30, 1868. 5 cm, 2 in. 1 vol.

Arranged by administrative unit, with the headquarters district preceding the several registration districts. Indexed alphabetically by initial letter of employee's surname.
Record shows name and title of employee, type of duty or service performed (usually registrars, clerks, or supervisors), period of service, gross pay, taxes, net pay, date and number of check, when forwarded, by whom paid, on which Assistant U.S. Treasurer drawn, and amount. In the case of registration districts, the county which comprised the district is shown along with the name and mailing address of the employee.

423.   REGISTER OF PAYMENTS TO EMPLOYEES OF THE 5TH MILITARY DISTRICT (MILITARY DISTRICT OF TEXAS). Jan. 28, 1869-Apr. 6, 1871. 3 cm, 1 in. 1 vol.

Arranged chronologically.
Register contains entries that show receipt number, name of county in which employee served, his name, paymaster's name and duty station, explanation of services (usually as registrars, clerks, or deputy sheriffs), period of service, amount due, date and number of check, date received, and amount paid. Most checks were drawn on the Assistant U.S. Treasurer at New Orleans. Many of the entries include reference to letters received and sent. Some of the letters sent are described in entry 424.

424.   LETTERS SENT BY CHARLES E. MORSE. Aug. 1, 1870-Sept. 28, 1870. 5 cm, 2 in. 3 vols.

Arranged chronologically. Indexed by initial letter of addressee's surname or name of party involved.
Morse was Secretary for Civil Affairs in the headquarters of the Military Reconstruction District of Texas. The letters are primarily instructions to the Assistant U.S. Treasurer at New Orleans or to other disbursing agents to settle claims of civil employees for service as registrars, clerks of court, and deputy sheriffs. Reference to some of these letters is found in the register of payment to employees of the 5th Military District, entry 423.

425.   REGISTER OF PAYMENTS TO WITNESSES AND OTHERS. May 1893-July 1896. 5 cm, 2 in. 1 vol.

Arranged by initial letter of claimant's surname.
Register contains entries that show claimant's name, basis for claim (e.g., citizen witness or stenographer), time for which paid, when and by whom paid, amount paid, and account and voucher numbers. If a person was paid for services in more than one case, references are also included to location of information on additional payments.

PAY AND BOUNTY DIVISION

The Pay and Bounty Division was first established in the Office of the Second Auditor during the fiscal year ending June 30, 1867. The Division registered and reviewed claims of soldiers for back pay and bounty and claims of sutlers, laundresses, and others for personal services performed for soldiers; filed, approved, and rejected claims; and corresponded with claimants and Members of Congress about the status of claims.

The Third Auditor's Claims Division was transferred to the Auditor for the War Department (formerly Second Auditor) in 1894 and became responsible for settling all other types of claims.

Decisions

426.   DIGEST OF DECISIONS AFFECTING THE WORK OF THE PAY AND BOUNTY DIVISION. Nov. 1871-Aug. 1895. 8 cm, 3 in. 2 vols.

Arranged alphabetically by subject. Each volume is indexed by keyword of subject.

Digests show the primary subject, abstract of the decision, and citations of letters in which the decision was announced or of legal precedents on which the decision was based. The volumes contain copies of circular letters published in the 1880's and 1890's. The subjects include attorneys' claims, duplicate certificates, injuries, pay on assignment to duty, pay for use and risk of horses, reopening of accounts and claims, and veterans' bounty.

Records Relating to Pay and Bounty Claims

427.   ABSTRACTS OF SETTLEMENTS. Sept. 1816-July 1836. 8 cm, 3 in. 2 vols.

Arranged alphabetically by initial letter of soldier's surname.

Abstract shows soldier's name, rank, and military unit; name of paymaster; date of accounts showing a balance in favor of the soldier; explanation of balance; amount due; amount of deductions; when and to whom the balance was paid (frequently to the Soldier's Home); settlement number (entry 523); and amount paid.

428.   REGISTERS OF CLAIMS SETTLEMENTS (OLD, OLD SERIES). Aug. 1817-Dec. 1862. 91 cm, 3 ft. 24 vols.

Arranged alphabetically by initial letter of claimant's surname.

The covers of volume 1-6 and 8-14 indicate the military units represented by claims entered in the particular volume.

Registers contain entries that show claimant's name, rank, and military unit; by whom claim was presented; date presented; and date and type of action taken. Beginning with claims presented in 1838, the claim, settlement, or certificate number (see entry 429) is also shown for claims that were approved.

429.   RECORDS RELATING TO CLAIMS (OLD, OLD SERIES). Feb. 24, 1832-Aug. 5, 1862. 20.7 m, 68 ft.

Arranged numerically. Some of these claims are registered in the volumes described in entry 428.

Approved claims for pay, bounty, effects, and other moneys due soldiers or their estates for military service before the Civil War. The records are of two types: (1) cover or cross-reference sheets showing claim number, soldier's name, rank, and military organization; period of service on which claim was based; amount due; to whom payable; name of paymaster to whom claim was referred; and voucher number on which payment was recorded. (2) In addition to the cover sheet, some files include correspondence, reports on amounts due soldiers for various purposes, inventories of effects of deceased soldiers, and other related documents.

430.   REGISTERS OF SETTLED CLAIMS. Nov. 1829-May 1855. 8 cm, 3 in. 2 vols.

Arranged by initial letter of soldier's surname.
Register contains entries that show soldier's name, rank, and military unit; by whom claim was presented; date of claim; and record of action taken or such miscellaneous remarks as "not found on rolls" or "see letter." If a claim was for a pension, this fact is also noted.

431.   REGISTERS OF SETTLED CLAIMS FOR EXTRA PAY (EXTRA PAY, REGULARS). Aug. 1848-July 1850. 10 cm, 4 in. 2 vols.

Arranged alphabetically by initial letter of soldier's surname and thereunder chronologically.
Soldiers who served in the Mexican War were entitled, under an act of July 19, 1848 (9 Stat. 247), to 3 months' extra pay.
Registers of settled claims filed under the act by soldiers not receiving the extra pay at the time they were discharged. Shows date paid; name, rank, and military unit; name of paymaster; and to whom the extra money was paid. Some of the claims were settled by paymasters other than the ones to whom the claims had been referred for settlement, as explained by a note in the front of each volume.

432.   REGISTER OF SETTLED CLAIMS FOR 3 MONTHS' EXTRA PAY. Apr. 1849-Mar. 1852. 3 cm, 1 in. 1 vol.

Arranged alphabetically by initial letter of soldier's surname.
Register contains entries that show soldier's name, rank, military unit, voucher number, and date paid. The claims were paid by Paymaster David Hunter through October 1850 and thereafter by Paymaster St. Clair Denny. Some of these claims are listed in the register of claims for 3 months' extra pay (entry 433).

433.   REGISTER OF CLAIMS FOR 3 MONTHS' EXTRA PAY. July 1848-Jan. 1849. 5 cm, 2 in. 1 vol.

Arranged alphabetically by initial letter of soldier's surname.
Register contains entries that show date of claim, soldier's name, rank, and military unit, and amount. Voucher numbers and settlement numbers are also occasionally included.
For a record of payment of some of these claims, see register of settled claims for 3 months' extra pay (entry 436).

434.   RECORD OF ACTION TAKEN ON CLAIMS FOR 3 MONTHS' EXTRA PAY. Jan. 1849 - July 1850. 8 cm, 3 in. 1 vol.

This series appears to be missing.
Arranged geographically by name of State and thereunder by type of action. Indexed alphabetically by name of State.
Record shows claims paid by Paymaster Lloyd I. Beall, claims referred to other paymasters for settlement and rejected claims. Each category of action includes information on the name and military unit of the soldier and the name and address of the claimant, if other than the soldier.
For an additional record of the claims paid by Beall, see entry 435.

435.   ABSTRACT OF PAYMENTS FOR 3 MONTHS' EXTRA PAY. Nov. 10, 1848-June 30, 1849. 3 cm, 1 in. 1 vol.

Arranged by surname of paymaster and thereunder by military unit. Indexed by name of State furnishing troops.

Abstracts of payments by Paymasters Beall and Roger S. Dix, submitted as part of their respective accounts showing voucher number; date of payment; soldier's name, rank, and military unit; and amount. Other records of payments by Beall are included in the register of claims for 3 months' extra pay (entry 434).

436.   REGISTER OF SETTLED CLAIMS FOR 3 MONTHS' EXTRA PAY. July 1848-June 1892. 5 cm, 2 in. 2 vol.

Arranged by initial letter of soldier's surname. Numbers on spine are volume 2 and 3.

Register contains entries that show soldier's name, rank, and military unit; number of certificate of settlement; date claim was received; date paid; and amount paid. Some of these claims are also included in the register of claims for 3 months' extra pay (entry 433).

437.   CLAIMS OF VOLUNTEER UNITS IN THE MEXICAN WAR FOR 3 MONTHS' EXTRA PAY. ca. 1846-48. 3 cm, 1 in. 2 vols.

Arranged alphabetically by name of State and thereunder by military unit. Each volume is indexed alphabetically by name of State.

Record of claims of volunteer units showing name of State and military unit, name of paymaster, account number, voucher number, name and rank of the unit's commanding officer, and file location.

438.   REGISTER OF CLAIMS APPROVED BY THE HAWKINS-TAYLOR COMMISSION. May 1864-July 1871. 5 cm, 2 in. 1 vol.

Arranged alphabetically by initial letter of soldier's surname.

The Hawkins-Taylor Commission was created to settle pay claims of soldiers of the Missouri Home Guard for service during the Civil War. This register of approved claims shows soldier's name, rank, and military unit; period for which paid; amount; name of paymaster; account number; and date of payment.

439.   REGISTER OF SETTLED CLAIMS FOR BACK PAY (MILITARY ASYLUM). Sept. 1851-Oct. 1853. 5 cm, 2 in. 1 vol.

Arranged alphabetically by initial letter of soldier's surname.

Register contains entries of payments made to the Treasurer of the Military Asylum of moneys due deceased soldiers showing soldier's name, rank, and military unit; period for which back pay was due; name of paymaster; settlement and voucher numbers; amounts due for back pay, effects, and extra pay; total due; and date of settlement. Sometimes the date of the soldier's death is also shown.

For other records relating to pay due deceased soldiers, see entries 197-201.

440.   REGISTER OF SETTLED PAY AND BOUNTY CLAIMS. Dec. 1857-Dec. 1861. 5 cm, 2 in. 1 vol.

Arranged alphabetically by initial letter of soldier's surname.

Register contains entries of settled pay and bounty claims filed in behalf of deceased soldiers showing soldier's name, rank, and military unit; certificate number; to whom payable; amount due; explanation; and when and by whom passed.

441.   REGISTERS OF PAYMENTS TO U.S. COLORED TROOPS. Nov. 1867-Nov. 1885. 30 cm, 1 ft. 7 vols.

Arranged by military unit and thereunder chronologically.

Registers contain entries of payments under provisions of a joint resolution (15 Stat. 26), which established procedures for settlement of approved pay and bounty claims for members of the U.S. Colored Troops. The entries show soldier's name and military unit; date of claim; certificate of settlement number (entry 456); amounts due for pay, regular bounty, and special bounty; total due; amount paid claimant; and amount paid as attorney's fees.

For an additional register, see entry 443.

442.   REGISTER OF CLAIMS OF U.S. COLORED TROOPS. Aug. 1879-Nov. 1899. 5 cm, 2 in. 1 vol.

Arranged alphabetically by initial letter of surname of soldier.

Register contains entries that show name of soldier and military unit with which he served. Some entries are followed by the notation "return to claimant" or "Mr. Smith, Room 74," followed by a date.

443.   REGISTERS OF SETTLED CLAIMS. ca. 1861-1900. 9.1 m, 30 ft. 120 vols.

Arranged by name of State furnishing troops, and within each volume alphabetically by initial letter of soldier's surname.

Registers contain entries of settled claims filed under acts of July 22, 1861, and July 28, 1866, showing soldier's name, rank, and military unit; date claim was received; and number of certificate of settlement if the claim was approved. A numerical register of certificates of settlement issued and paid, with related information, is described in entry 456.

For Second Comptroller's abstracts of payments to colored troops see entry 261.

444.   DOCKET BOOK OF SETTLED CLAIMS (SUNDRY CLAIMS). Nov. 1865-May 1869. 5 cm, 2 in. 1 vol.

Arranged alphabetically by initial letter of claimant's surname.

Claim number and type of claim (usually for additional pay); claimant's name, rank, and military unit; when and by whom filed; and record of action taken on the claim, such as rejection or referral to a paymaster for settlement.

445.   REGISTERS OF BOUNTY CLAIMS. Nov. 18, 1865-Dec. 20, 1870. 13 cm, 5 in. 2 vols.

Arranged alphabetically by initial letter of claimant's surname and thereunder chronologically.

Register contains entries that show date of claim; claimant's name, rank, and military unit; attorney's name and residence; and sometimes a notation of action taken. Volume 1 includes surnames starting with the letters A-F and begins April 21, 1866. It includes a supplemental list of claims referred to the Second Auditor under the act of July 28, 1866.

Volume 2 includes surnames starting with the letters K-Z and begins November 18, 1865; it does not include the supplemental list.

446.   RECORD OF ACTION TAKEN ON CLAIMS. Sept. 1866-Feb. 1869. 8 cm, 3 in. 1 vol.

Arranged by initial letter of claimant's surname.

Record shows date claim was received; claimant's name, rank, and military unit; and when claim was rejected or when and to whom paid. If the claim was paid, the voucher number is also shown.

447. REGISTERS OF CLAIMS REFERRED TO PAYMASTERS. Apr. 1865-Feb. 1866. 13 cm, 5 in. 2 vols.

Arranged alphabetically by initial letter of claimant's surname.

Registers contain entries that show date referred; soldier's name, rank, and military unit; type of claim (pay, bounty, or both); and to whom claim was referred for action. Sometimes the date of settlement or rejection of the claim is also known.

For further information on some of these claims, see registers of referred claims settled by paymasters, entry 448.

448. REGISTERS OF REFERRED CLAIMS SETTLED BY PAYMASTERS. Nov. 1864 - Nov. 1868. 1.2 m, 4 ft. 21 vols.

Arranged by name of paymaster and within each volume alphabetically by initial letter of soldier's surname.

Registers contain entries that show, in general, date claim was received; soldier's name, rank, and military unit; name and address of claimant; date and amount paid; check number; and voucher number. If the claim was rejected, the date of rejection is indicated. Some paymasters also included a listing of the documents they received in connection with the claim and indicated what they did with the documents. The names of the paymasters, the dates they received claims for settlement, and the number of volumes are:

Allison, Thomas S.	Feb. 1866-Apr. 1867	1 vol.
Atwell, Joseph D.	Sept. 1866-Feb. 1867	1 vol.
Dyer, George W.	Aug. 1865-Feb. 1867	1 vol.
Ely, George B.	May 1865-July 1866	2 vols.
Gardner, Thomas H.	Dec. 1866-Nov. 1868	1 vol.
Holmes, Calvin	Nov. 1865-Mar. 1867	1 vol.
Jones, Charles S.	June 1865-May 1867	1 vol.
Lawyer, Joseph A.	Apr. 1865-May 1866	1 vol.
Moore, Edwin L.	Apr. 1866-Mar. 1867	3 vols.
Nicholls, James W.	Nov. 1865-Jan. 1867	1 vol.
Sabin, John A.	July 1865-Mar. 1866	1 vol.
Sallade, Jacob	May 1865-Feb. 1866	1 vol.
Sherman, William C. H.	Nov. 1864-Mar. 1865	1 vol.
Tucker, Nathaniel A.	Apr. 1866-June 1867	1 vol.
Vedder, Nicholas	Aug. 1865-Mar. 1867	2 vols.
Wilson, Thomas J.	July 1865-May 1866	2 vols.
(Unidentified)	Nov. 1866-Mar. 1867	1 vol.

449. DISALLOWED CLAIMS OF U.S. COLORED TROOPS. ca. 1864-93. 82.0 m, 269 ft. 207 boxes.

Arranged by military unit and thereunder alphabetically by soldier's surname.

Case files of disallowed claims for additional bounty or other moneys, consisting usually of the original petition of the soldier or his heirs, affidavits, correspondence between the Auditor and War Department Officials relating to possible basis for the claim, and a statement of the basis on which the claim was rejected. The claim cover sheet shows the soldier's name and military unit. Box 111 appears to be missing.

450.   DISALLOWED CLAIMS OF SUTLERS. ca. 1864-94. 1.8 m, 6 ft. Unbound records.

Arranged alphabetically by name of sutler.

Case files of disallowed claims of sutlers for services performed for soldiers (usually deceased soldiers or deserters) generally consisting of affidavits, correspondence, and other supporting documents. Most of the rejected claims were based on a lack of evidence of indebtedness of the soldier on the muster rolls or payrolls of his military unit.

451.   DISALLOWED CLAIMS OF LAUNDRESSES. ca. 1862-94. 61 cm, 2 ft. Unbound records.

Arranged alphabetically by name of laundress.

Case files of disallowed claims for laundresses for services performed by them for deceased soldiers or soldiers who deserted consisting chiefly of a statement of the basis for the claim and related correspondence. Rejection was based on a lack of evidence of indebtedness of the soldier on the muster rolls or payrolls of his military unit.

452.   REGISTERS OF SETTLED CLAIMS. Mar. 16, 1889-Jan. 20, 1898. 10 cm, 4 in. 3 vols.

Arranged chronologically.

Registers contain entries of claims, most of which were presented under provisions of an act of August 30, 1890, relating to payment to heirs of deceased soldiers who had been prisoners of war during the Civil War.

The entries show settlement number, soldier's or claimant's name, date received and mailed, by whom paid, military service on which claim was based, check number, date of check, and amounts paid to claimant and as attorney's fees.

453.   REGISTERS OF CLAIMS OF SOLDIERS FROM VOLUNTEER UNITS. Aug. 1898-Aug. 1899. 91 cm, 3 ft. 13 vols.

Arranged geographically (beginning with New England), thereunder by initial letter of soldier's surname, and thereunder by military unit.

Registers contain entries that show soldier's name, rank, and military unit; date claim was received; and sometimes the number of a certificate of settlement or a cross-reference, such as "Signal Corps" or "Hospital Corps."

Records Relating to Other Accounts and Claims

454.   REGISTER   OF   SETTLED   ACCOUNTS   (ALPHABETICAL   REGISTER   OF MISCELLANEOUS SETTLEMENTS). 1861-73. 5 cm, 2 in. 1 vol.

Arranged by initial letter of surname of accountable officer.

Register contains entries that show ledger reference (entry 362), name and rank of officer, military unit or capacity in which he was accountable, year account was settled, and settlement number. Most of the persons listed were military officers but some were soldiers, Indian agents, and military storekeepers. If the person died or was otherwise separated from the Army, the date and type of separation are shown.

455.   ALPHABETICAL REGISTERS OF TREASURY CERTIFICATES PAID. Aug. 1863-Dec. 1864. 20 cm, 8 in. 4 vols.

Arranged alphabetically by initial letter of claimant's surname.

Registers contain entries that show claimant's name, certificate number, amount, paymaster's name, month and year of payment, and name of person paid. Some of these certificates are also recorded in a numerical register of Treasury certificates paid (entry 456).

456.　NUMERICAL REGISTERS OF TREASURY CERTIFICATES PAID. July 16, 1862 - Aug. 30, 1899. 2.1 m, 7 ft. 41 vols.

Arranged numerically in three groups—numbers 1-729,999 (July 16, 1862-Apr. 24, 1885); numbers 1-9,999 (Jan. 12, 1882-Oct. 18, 1886); and numbers 110,000-169,999 (May 7, 1889-Aug. 30, 1899).

There are gaps in the date span of these records; the actual dates covered are: July 16, 1862-Oct. 18, 1886; May 7, 1889-Aug. 30, 1899.

Register entries show the certificate number, in whose favor, amount, name of paymaster, date paid, voucher number, check number, and name and address of person paid. Only a few entries are in the last two groups of numbers.

457.　REGISTER OF SETTLED ACCOUNTS AND CLAIMS. Apr. 1862-Oct. 1884. 3 cm, 1 in. 1 vol.

Arranged alphabetically by initial letter of officer's or claimant's surname.

Register contains entries that show officer's or claimant's name, amount claimed, explanation, dates received and confirmed, and settlement number. Entries include such diverse matters as approved horse claims, funeral expenses, claims for transportation of recruits, compensation for professional services, payments under acts for relief of specific persons, claims under the 8-hour law, and Internal Revenue taxes withheld from salaries and transferred to Internal Revenue funds. The 8-hour law was passed June 25, 1868 (15 Stat. 77), and the claims registered in this volume were authorized by act of May 18, 1872 (17 Stat. 134).

458.　REGISTERS OF MISCELLANEOUS SETTLEMENTS. Jan. 6, 1863-June 30, 1915. 61 cm, 2 ft. 13 vols.

Four volumes, January 1863-December 1896, are arranged alphabetically by initial letter of officer's or claimant's surname. Nine volumes, April 1, 1863-August 13, 1889, and July 1, 1897-June 30, 1915, are arranged chronologically and each has an index arranged alphabetically by initial letter of officer's or claimant's surname. The other volumes are not indexed.

Entries in the chronological volumes show number of accounts received, name and title of official or name of claimant, type of account or claim or title of appropriation concerned, period covered, dates reported and confirmed, settlement number, and adjusted balance.

Entries in the alphabetical volumes show officer's or claimant's name; rank and military unit if an officer; period covered or explanation of the account or claim; dates received and settled; and settlement number.

459.　REGISTERS OF PRIVATE MEDICAL CLAIMS. Jan. 1863-Aug. 1884. 30 cm, 1 ft. 4 vols.

Arranged by initial letter of claimant's surname.

Registers contain entries that show name of claimant, amount claimed, explanation, dates received and confirmed, and certificate number. Entries in the volume for 1866-84 sometimes show a settlement number instead of the certificate number. If a claim was rejected, that fact is noted. Claims were usually for the services of doctors or nurses, laundry, and medical supplies.

For copies of letters sent relating to medical claims, see entry 500; for copies of contracts for medical supplies and series, see entry 229.

460.   REGISTER OF ACCOUNTS AND CLAIMS RECEIVED (LOCAL BOUNTY ACCOUNTS AND CLAIMS). July 1864-Sept. 1888. 3 cm, 1 in. 1 vol.

Arranged alphabetically by initial letter of officer's or claimant's surname. Under each letter of the alphabet, entries are arranged in three categories: accounts, claims, and letters.

Register contains entries for accounts that show name of paymaster, whether the account was for moneys due deserters or minors, what time period, amount involved, dates reported and confirmed, and settlement number. The entries for claims show name of soldier or claimant; whether the claim was for deserter's money, minor's money, or refund of deposit; date reported; whether confirmed or rejected; amount claimed; and (if paid) settlement number or certificate number and to whom paid. A few entries are for letters received showing only the name and military unit of the writer.

461.   RECORD OF ACTION TAKEN ON ACCOUNTS AND CLAIMS. Oct. 26, 1865-June 30, 1887. 13 cm, 5 in. 2 vols.

Arranged chronologically. Each volume is indexed by initial letter of claimant's surname.

The entries show soldier's name, rank, military unit, explanation of the case (usually claims for pay and bounty due or for recovery of amounts overpaid on the settlement of accounts), and a notation of action taken to settle the account or claim.

462.   REGISTER OF SETTLED CLAIMS. July 7, 1871-Oct. 22, 1888. 3 cm, 1 in. 1 vol.

This series appears to be missing.

Arranged numerically. Indexed by initial letter of claimant's surname.

Register contains entries that show claim number; claimant's name, rank, or capacity in which he was claiming (e.g., citizen); explanation, dates reported and confirmed; settlement number; and amount. Most of the entries for citizens are for expenses relating to military reconstruction; the entries for military officers relate chiefly to stoppage of pay, commutation of quarters, longevity pay, and claims for additional rations. Part of the volume also concerns pay of militia officers, 1911-16 (entry 405).

463.   REGISTER OF SETTLED CLAIMS. July 1, 1872-Sept. 10, 1875. 5 cm, 2 in. 1 vol.

Arranged by name of paymaster in no particular order. Indexed by name of paymaster.

Register contains entries that show paymaster's name; date of claim; soldier's name, rank, and military unit; by whom paid; date paid; and amount.

464.   ABSTRACT OF SETTLED ACCOUNTS OF DISBURSING OFFICERS FOR THE FREEDMEN'S BUREAU. Feb. 1874-June 1882. 5 cm, 2 in. 1 vol.

Arranged by month of settlement. Indexed alphabetically by surname of disbursing officer.

Shows name and rank of disbursing officer, year and number of settlement, date of settlement, and debits and credits (including names of persons to whom moneys were advanced or from whom moneys were received, titles of appropriations concerned, and amounts), and dates accounts were reported and confirmed. Most appropriations concerned were for pay and bounty for volunteers and colored troops.

INDIAN DIVISION

The Indian Division was first established as a Division in the Second Auditor's Office during the fiscal year ending June 30, 1867. Its primary functions were the settlement of accounts of Indian agents and the settlement of related claims. The Division was abolished by an act of July 30, 1894 (28 Stat. 208), and its functions were transferred to the Office of the Auditor for the Interior Department (formerly Third Auditor).

Correspondence

465.   LETTERS RECEIVED FROM THE COMMISSIONER OF INDIAN AFFAIRS. Oct. 3, 1836 Mar. 24, 1883. 1.2 m, 4 ft.

Arranged chronologically.
Routine letters relating chiefly to inquiries about the status of accounts of Indian agents and other officials, deposit of funds, verification of names of Indians on annuity rolls, and payment of claims.

466.   LETTERS RECEIVED RELATING TO SURETY BONDS OF INDIAN AGENTS. Aug. 14, 1854 - Nov. 26, 1879. 10 cm, 4 in.

Arranged alphabetically by initial letter of agent's surname.
Letters from the Second Comptroller acknowledging receipt and filing of surety bonds of Indian agents. The letters show the agent's name and duty station, date and amount of bond, and names of sureties.
The bonds are in Records of the Bureau of Accounts (Treasury), (RG 39). These letters are only for agents whose surnames began with the letters A and F-K.
For a register of these bonds, see entry 471.

467.   LETTERS SENT RELATING TO EXPENDITURES UNDER THE CHICKASAW TREATY. May 9, 1836-Apr. 2, 1859. 5 cm, 2 in. 1 vol.

Arranged chronologically. Indexed by initial letter of addressee's surname.
Fair copies of letters primarily to disbursing agents relating to settlement of accounts for expenditures under the Treaties of 1832 and 1834 with the Chickasaw Indians, including requisition for funds to pay claims in favor of the Indians, payments to contractors and surveyors, and payments into the Chickasaw trust fund. Some of the letters were to Members of Congress, the Commissioner of Indian Affairs, and other Government officials. There are only a few letters after June 1853.
For the accounts themselves, see entry 524.

468.   LETTERS SENT BY THE INDIAN DIVISION. Aug. 6, 1846-Feb. 1, 1887. 1.5 m, 5 ft. 25 vols.

Arranged chronologically. Each volume is indexed by initial letter of claimant's or officer's surname.
Fair copies of letters primarily to Indian agents, contractors, private claimants, and other Government officials concerning settlement of accounts and claims for expenditures, such as the transportation of goods, the purchase of Indian supplies, and the taking of censuses of Indian tribes.
For a continuation of these letters, see entries 469 and 661.

469.   LETTERS SENT BY THE INDIAN DIVISION. Feb. 2, 1887-Sept. 11, 1893. 30 cm, 1 ft. 14 vols.

Arranged chronologically. Each volume is indexed by initial letter of surname of addressee, subject of letter, or title of official.

There are gaps in the date span of these records; the actual dates covered are: Feb. 2, 1887-July 30, 1892; Dec. 19, 1892-Sept. 11, 1893.

Press copies of letters to Indian agents, claimants, and Government officials concerning the settlement of accounts and claims related to expenditures for Indians, including property accounts, transportation claims, land titles, and timber sales.

For earlier letters sent by this Division, see entry 468; for later letters, see entry 661.

Records Relating to Indian Agents

470.   LISTS OF INDIAN AGENTS, AGENCIES, AND SCHOOLS. Feb. 1862-June 1896. 15 cm, 6 in. 4 vols.

Arranged by administrative unit. Volumes 1, 2, and 4 are indexed by location of agency or school. Volume 3 is not indexed.

Volumes contain lists that show name and location of the school or agency, name of official in charge, and dates of service. Dates of bonds are also sometimes shown.

471.   REGISTER OF BONDS OF INDIAN AGENTS AND DISBURSING OFFICERS. Mar. 27, 1843-June 12, 1890. 3 cm, 1 in. 1 vol.

Arranged alphabetically by initial letter of accountable officer's surname.

Register contains entries that show official's name and title, date and amount of bond, and names of sureties. Officials other than Indian agents are usually specifically identified as such.

For a register of earlier and later surety bonds of Indian agents and disbursing officers, see entry 662. The bonds themselves are in Records of the Bureau of Accounts (Treasury), RG 39.

Records Relating to Accounts and Claims

472.   REGISTER OF INDIAN AGENTS' ACCOUNTS RECEIVED AND SETTLED (OLD SERIES). May 1817-June 1899. 61 cm, 2 ft. 5 vols.

Arranged alphabetically by initial letter of accountable officer's surname.

Registers contain entries that show date received, officer's name, period covered, dates reported and approved, settlement number (entry 525), and adjusted balance. The last volume also shows dates of appointment, periods of service, and the names of predecessors and successors.

For a continuation of this series, see entry 664. Some of the accounts were settled by the Third Auditor and are filed with the accounts described in entry 717.

473.   REGISTER OF INDIAN AGENTS' ACCOUNTS RECEIVED AND SETTLED. Dec. 12, 1890-June 30, 1894. 8 cm, 3 in. 1 vol.

Arranged alphabetically by initial letter of accountable officer's surname and thereunder chronologically by date received.

Register contains entries that show date received, officer's name and title, number of account(s) included in settlement, dates reported and approved, period covered, settlement number (entry 525), adjusted balance, and date of officer's bond. A few entries are for accounts received and settled during the period February 19, 1873-September 12, 1876; a few items,

August 1-October 26, 1899, are for final settlement of accounts. Some of the accounts were settled by the Third Auditor and are filed with the accounts described in entry 717.

474.   REGISTERS OF INDIAN CLAIMS. Mar. 1819-July 1894. 91 cm, 3 ft. 15 vols.

Arranged alphabetically by initial letter of claimant's surname.
Registers contain entries that show date received, claimant's name, explanation, amount claimed, dates reported and allowed, settlement number (entry 525), and amount allowed. Typical claims were for supplies and services for Indians; awards in depredation claims; and mapping and surveying Indian lands. The two volumes for the period 1819-69 are identified as 'gold series" and the remaining volumes as "new series." For a continuation of these claim registers, see entry 675.

475.   REGISTERS OF ACCOUNTS OF INDIAN AGENTS AND OTHER ACCOUNTABLE OFFICERS. Mar. 1825-July 1894. 10 cm, 4 in. 4 vols.

Arranged alphabetically by initial letter of accountable officer's surname. Three volumes are indexed by officer's surname or location of agency. The fourth volume is not indexed. One volume appears to be missing.
Registers contain entries that show officer's name, title and duty station, period of service, account numbers (entry 525), dates reported and confirmed, and balances. Dates of surety bond and oath of office are also frequently shown. One of the volumes, March 1825-May 1885, includes only a few entries and concerns only agents whose surnames began with the letter A.

476.   LIST OF INDIAN SETTLEMENTS. Jan. 3, 1881-Sept. 18, 1885. 5 cm, 2 in. 1 vol.

Arranged chronologically.
The list shows date, settlement number (entry 525), officer's or claimant's name, and amount allowed. After February 2, 1885, the amounts allowed are not shown.

477.   RECORD OF BALANCES DUE THE UNITED STATES BY FORMER ACCOUNTABLE OFFICERS. 1820-98. 1 cm, 1/2 in. 1 vol.

Arranged alphabetically by initial letter of debtor's surname.
Register contains entries that show accountable officer's name, date of bond, folio references to Indian ledgers(entry 361), amount due, and date and number of last settlement (entry 525). Most delinquent officials had been Indian agents or subagents or Superintendents of Indian Schools.
Some of the entries are duplicated by the registers of suits against Indian agents (entries 478 and 678).

478.   REGISTER OF SUITS AGAINST INDIAN AGENTS. June 1875-Sept. 1894. 5 cm, 2 in. 1 vol.

Arranged alphabetically by initial letter of agent's surname.
Register contains entries that show agent's name; date of bond; dates transcripts of accounts were requested, received, and forwarded for suit; outstanding balance; and results of the suit. Some of these entries are duplicated in the register of balances due the United States (entry 477).
For a continuation of the register of suits, see entry 678.

Records Relating to Payments to Indian Tribes

479.   RECORD OF ANNUITY PAYMENTS TO INDIAN TRIBES. 1831-94. 3 cm, 1 in. 2 vols.

Arranged alphabetically by name of tribe.
There are gaps in the date span of these records; the actual dates covered are: 1831-55; 1884-94.
Record shows name of tribe, the location of file, settlement number (entry 524), by whom paid, for what year, how paid (cash, specie, or goods), date paid, and amount. The date paid is frequently omitted.
For a continuation of this series, see entry 679 and 680.

480.   ABSTRACT OF AWARDS UNDER THE CHEROKEE TREATY OF DECEMBER 1835. Aug. 1837-June 1848. 5 cm, 2 in. 3 vols.

Arranged by volume and page number in the registers of approved claims. Volume 3 is missing.
Abstract of awards approved by Commissioners William M. Carroll and John F. Schermerhorn, appointed to settle claims arising under the treaty of December 1835 with the Cherokee Nation. Shows volume and page reference to registers of approved claims (entry 481), name of claimant, valuation of property, amounts awarded for specific objects, and total amount awarded.

481.   REGISTERS OF AWARDS UNDER THE CHEROKEE TREATY OF DECEMBER 1835. Aug. 1837-June 1848. 15 cm, 6 in. 8 vols.

Arranged as described below.
Registers contain entries of awards paid under the treaty of December 1835 with the Cherokee Nation showing settlement number (entry 525), name of disbursing officer, date of settlement, volume and page reference to abstracts of awards (entry 480), number of certificate of approval granted by the Commissioners of Claims, to whom the certificate was issued, to whom moneys were paid, total paid, and amounts paid for specific objects. Four volumes, arranged by settlement number, are for payments to Indians agreeing to move under the terms of the treaty; two volumes, arranged by settlement number, are for payments to Indians who had already voluntarily moved before the treaty (old settlers). Two other volumes, identified as volumes 5 and 5 1/2, are copies of acts of Congress relating to the removal of the Cherokees and reports by the accounting officers on the implementation of the provisions of the treaties of 1835 and 1846.

482.   RECORD OF MISCELLANEOUS PAYMENTS UNDER THE CHEROKEE TREATIES. ca. 1836-85. 1 cm, 1/2 in. 1 vol.

Arranged by title of account. Partially indexed by accountable officer's surname.
Record of payments for expenses, such as education of Indian children, interest on securities used for the benefit of Indian schools, accounts of disbursing officers, and claims paid to specific persons. Many of the entries include references to ledgers (not identified) and were a result of the treaty of December 29, 1835, and a supplemental treaty of March 1, 1836.

483.   RECORD OF PAYMENTS TO CHEROKEE INDIANS. ca. 1835-85. 2 cm, 1 in. 1 vol.

Arranged in general by type of information.
Record of miscellaneous payments to Cherokees showing, in general, name of disbursing agent or name of payee, date of payment, type of expense, and amount paid.

Other Records

484.   ABSTRACT OF EXPENDITURES FOR THE INDIAN SERVICE. May 31, 1827-Sept. 30, 1832. 3 cm, 1 in. 1 vol.

Arranged chronologically by closing date of calendar quarter and thereunder by title appropriation.

Most of this volume of abstracts shows, for each quarter, titles of appropriations, disbursements from the appropriations, and total disbursements from all appropriations. Part of the volume was also used to record the Indian disbursements of specific individuals, such as Gen. William Clark and Lewis Cass. Expenditures include pay of Indian agents, interpreters, gunsmiths, and blacksmiths; presents and annuities for Indian tribes; and transportation of provisions.

485.   JOURNALS OF SUPPLIES FOR THE INDIAN SERVICE. July 7, 1884-July 30, 1894. 61 cm, 2 ft. 11 vols.

Arranged geographically by place of delivery. Each volume is indexed alphabetically by contractor's surname.

Journals contain entries showing contractor's name and address, date of contract, place of delivery, contract number (entry 227), settlement number (entry 525), shipment date, agency to which delivery was made, description of goods delivered (including identification and weights of various packages and quantity and type of goods delivered), and cost.

For later journals, see entry 687; for similar record arranged by agency, see entry 488.

486.   RECORD OF GOODS TRANSPORTED TO AGENCIES. July 1886-June 1887. 3 cm, 1 in. 1 vol.

Arranged alphabetically by agency. Indexed by name of agency.

Record shows agency's name, volume and page reference to the journals of supplies for the Indian Service (entry 485), date purchased, identification of packages, supplier's name, type and quantity of goods purchased, places of delivery and final destination, settlement numbers for purchase (entry 525) and for transportation accounts, amount of shrinkage (if any), and name of Indian agent responsible.

487.   REGISTERS OF CLAIMS FOR INDIAN SUPPLIES. July 1, 1887-June 30, 1894. 61 cm, 2 ft. 7 vols.

Arranged alphabetically by agency. Each volume is indexed by agency.

Registers contain entries that show agency name, page reference to journals of supplies for the Indian Service (entry 485), settlement number (entry 525); name of supplier, identification of packages, and type and quantity of items ordered and received. Typical items include washtubs, horse collars, nails, needles, hatchets, and shirting.

488.   REGISTERS OF GOODS TRANSPORTED TO INDIAN AGENCIES. Aug. 1888-June 1894. 30 cm, 1 ft. 6 vols.

Arranged alphabetically by agency. Each volume is indexed by agency.

Registers contain entries that show agency name, transportation contractor's name, settlement number (entry 525), page reference to journals of supplies for the Indian Service (entry 485), date received, identification of goods, contractor's name, points between which transportation was furnished, weight of shipment, date delivered, and by whom received.

489.   RECORD OF GOODS TRANSPORTED BY WAGON. July 1891-June 1892. 5 cm, 2 in.
        1 vol.

   Arranged by agency. Indexed alphabetically by agency.
   Record shows agency for which shipment was intended, place and date of delivery,
supplier's name, settlement number (entry 525), description of shipment, and a reference to the
account in which transportation charges were paid. For a continuation of this series, see
entry 688.

490.   TRANSPORTATION RECORD. July 1893-June 1894. 13 cm, 5 in. 2 vols.

   Arranged by package number.
   Record shows package number, contractor's name, settlement number (entry 525), weight
and contents of each package, reference to account in which transportation charges were paid,
and agency to which goods were sent. For a continuation of this series, see entry 689.

MAIL AND PROPERTY DIVISION

   The Mail and Property Division was established on October 13, 1893, by the
consolidation of the functions of the Property Division and the Inquiries and Replies Division
(both established during the fiscal year beginning July 1868) with the functions of the Mail
Division (established during the fiscal year beginning July 1886). The functions of the Division
included receiving, recording, briefing, and distributing letters, claims, and other papers to the
proper Divisions for reply; forwarding letters that were not pertinent to the Second Auditor's
functions; replying to inquiries from other Government officials; verifying signatures; furnishing
copies of records for official use; and filing clothing, camp, and garrison equipment accounts.
Some of the correspondence filed with this Division originated with the Third Auditor's
Claims Division, which was transferred to the Auditor for the War Department (formerly
Second Auditor) in 1894.

Correspondence

491.   REGISTERS OF LETTERS RECEIVED. Mar. 2, 1818-Oct. 30, 1899. 5.2 m, 17 ft. 68 vols.

   Two volumes, 1818-22, are arranged chronologically; the other volumes are arranged
alphabetically by initial letter of writer's surname, and thereunder chronologically.
   There are gaps in the date span of these records; the actual dates covered are: Mar. 2,
1818-Dec. 31, 1822; Mar. 1, 1839-Dec. 31, 1855; Oct. 1, 1862 - Oct. 30, 1899.
   Registers contain entries that show dates written and received, name of writer, subject,
and action taken. Letters from the Adjutant General usually transmitted special orders or
statements of final settlement of accounts. None of the letters registered in these volumes have
been located, but replies to some of them are among copies of miscellaneous letters sent (entry
496).

492.   LETTERS RECEIVED BY THE PAYMASTER GENERAL. June 17, 1778-July 6, 1785. 3 cm,
        1 in. Unbound records.

   This series appears to be missing.
   Arranged alphabetically by name of writer.
   Letters received chiefly relating to pay of troops and written by the Board of War, May
22-26, 1781; Joseph Carleton, November 1, 1778-July 6, 1785; Robert Harrison, June 17, 1778-
March 10, 1780; William Jackson, June 21-September 16, 1783; Henry Knox, May 16, 1785;
Benjamin Lincoln, July 11, 1782- October 30, 1783; William Livingston, November 20, 1784; James
Milligan, October 11, 1782; and George Washington, December 21, 1778-July 22, 1779.

493.   LETTERS RECEIVED BY THE ACCOUNTANT FOR THE WAR DEPARTMENT. Nov. 24, 1794-Dec. 23, 1817. 7.9 m, 26 ft. Unbound records.

Arranged alphabetically by initial letter of writer's surname, and thereunder chronologically.

Letters received from Government officials, current and former accountable officers, contractors, and Members of Congress concerning Indian relations, payment for provisions furnished under contract, settlement of paymaster and recruiting accounts, and similar subjects.

For replies to some of these letters, see entries 495 and 496.

494.   MISCELLANEOUS LETTERS RECEIVED RELATING TO CLAIMS. Oct. 1894-May 1898. 61 cm, 2 ft. Unbound records.

Arranged roughly by month.

Letters received concerning the status of claims, verification of military service, and authority of claims agents to act for claimants.

For earlier letters in this series, see entry 606.

495.   LETTERS SENT BY DAVID HENLEY, AGENT FOR THE WAR DEPARTMENT. May 1, 1799-May 7, 1800. 3 cm, 1 in. 1 vol.

Arranged chronologically.

Fair copies of letters to the Secretary of War while Henley was stationed in Knoxville. The letters concern pay of troops and other military expenditures, relations with Indian tribes, running boundary lines, the purchase and transportation of supplies, and related subjects. A few of these letters are to other Government officials and to private citizens.

496.   MISCELLANEOUS LETTERS SENT BY THE ACCOUNTANT FOR THE WAR DEPARTMENT AND THE SECOND AUDITOR. Apr. 14, 1795-May 5, 1886. 6.7 m, 22 ft.

Arranged chronologically. Each volume is indexed by initial letter of addressee's surname.

There are gaps in the date span of these records; the actual dates covered are: Apr. 14, 1795-Sept. 5, 1798; May 16, 1799-May 5, 1886.

Fair copies of letters to accountable officers, Government officials, contractors, and heirs or representatives of soldiers relating chiefly to settlement of paymaster, ordnance, and recruiting accounts; purchases of supplies and military equipment; and settlement of pay and bounty claims. Additional letters on these subjects are described in entries 497-500. Many of the letters dated before 1817 are in reply to the letters received described in entry 493; the letters received that are dated after 1817 have not been located but are included in the registers of letters received (entry 491).

497.   LETTERS SENT RELATING TO MILITARY SUPPLIES. Jan. 3, 1816-May 9, 1851. 91 cm, 3 ft. 12 vols.

Arranged chronologically. Each volume is indexed by initial letter of addressee's surname.

There are gaps in the date span of these records; the actual dates covered are: Jan. 3, 1816-July 21, 1837; Jan 1, 1842-June 29, 1849; June 4, 1850-May 9, 1851.

Fair copies of letters to military storekeepers, quartermasters, contractors, and Members of Congress relating to settlement of accounts and claims for arms, clothing, and equipment issued to soldiers. Additional letters on these subjects are among the miscellaneous letters sent (entry 496).

498.   LETTERS SENT BY THE ADDITIONAL ACCOUNTANT FOR THE WAR DEPARTMENT. May 8, 1816-Mar. 5, 1817. 13 cm, 5 in. 3 vols.

Arranged chronologically. Each volume is indexed by initial letter of addressee's surname.
Fair copies of letters by the Additional Accountant for the War Department (a temporary office established to consider claims for the War of 1812) relating chiefly to settlement of accounts of paymasters, quartermasters, and recruiting officers; claims for transportation of troops and equipment; and verification of service of soldiers in the War of 1812. Additional letters on these subjects are among letters sent relating to military supplies (entry 497) and letters sent relating to recruiting accounts (entry 499).

499.   LETTERS SENT RELATING TO RECRUITING ACCOUNTS. Mar. 11, 1864-Mar. 3, 1886. 20 cm, 8 in. 3 vols.

Arranged chronologically. Each volume is indexed by initial letter of addressee's surname.
Fair copies of form letters to recruiting officers and the Adjutant General's Office (AGO) acknowledging receipt and settlement of recruiting accounts. The forms were filled in to show the officer's name, rank, and military unit; period covered; adjusted balance; and amount of difference (if any between the officer's statement and the audited account. Other letters relating to accounts of recruiting officers are among miscellaneous letters sent (entry 496).

500.   LETTERS SENT RELATING TO CLAIMS. Feb. 5, 1848-Apr. 22, 1886. 1.8 m, 6 ft. 28 vols.

Arranged chronologically. Each volume is indexed by initial letter of addressee's surname.
There are gaps in the date span of these records; the actual dates covered are: Feb. 5, 1848-Oct. 6, 1854; May 1, 1858-Dec. 23, 1859; Dec. 2, 1861-Apr. 22, 1886.
Fair copies of letters to officers, claimants, and heirs of soldiers relating chiefly to the settlement or rejection of claims. Most of the letters through 1859 relate to claims based on service in the Mexican War and generally include the name, rank, and military unit of the soldier on whose service the claim was based. Later letters relate primarily to settlement of accounts and claims for furnishing medical supplies and services and for purchasing weapons. Additional letters on some of these subjects are among miscellaneous letters sent (entry 496).

501.   LETTERS SENT RELATING TO CIVIL WAR CLAIMS. Nov. 3, 1894-Oct. 2, 1895. 8 cm, 3 in. 2 vols.

Arranged chronologically. Each volume is indexed by initial letter of soldier's surname.
Press copies of letters relating to verification of service of soldiers in State units during the Civil War. Most letters were sent to the Commissioner of Pensions or the Chief of the Pay and Bounty Division in response to inquiries. These claims were under the jurisdiction of the Third Auditor until the reorganization of 1894.

502.   MISCELLANEOUS LETTERS SENT RELATING TO CLAIMS. Sept. 6, 1894-Aug. 31, 1899. 1.5 m, 5 ft. 46 vols.

Arranged chronologically. Each volume is indexed by initial letter of addressee's surname except the last one, which includes only letters dated August 31, 1899.
Press copies of letters to accountable officers, Government officials, and claimants relating to such matters as verification of Civil War service, horse claims, transportation claims, claims of States arising from services of their units during the Civil and

Spanish-American Wars, pension claims, and cases coming before the Southern Claims Commission and the U.S. Court of Claims. Many of these functions were the responsibility of the Third Auditor until the reorganization of 1894.

ARCHIVES DIVISION

The Archives Division was first established in the Office of the Second Auditor during the fiscal year beginning July 1, 1868. The chief functions of the Division were the filing of muster rolls, payrolls, and settled accounts and claims; repairing and copying damaged records and loaning records to other offices needing them; and keeping book records of payments' to officers and enlisted men from State units, hospitals, batteries, recruiting parties, and other miscellaneous units of the Regular Army.

Records Relating to Muster Rolls, Payrolls, Accounts, and Claims

503.   PAYMASTERS' ACCOUNTS. Mar. 17, 1777-Mar. 7, 1781. 3 cm, 1 in. 2 vols.

This series appears to be missing.
Arranged by name of paymaster and thereunder chronologically.
Accounts of Edward Crawford, Paymaster of the 1st Pennsylvania Regiment, March 1, 1779-March 7, 1781; and of James Johnston, Paymaster of the 2d Pennsylvania Regiment, March 17, 1777-August 11, 1779. Both accounts show the period for which the troops were paid; name of commanding officer; names of officers and soldiers; amount paid; amounts due for dead, discharged, or absentee soldiers; and amount due for prisoners. Crawford's account lists the names of the soldiers in these four special categories, but Johnston's account does not list the names.

504.   ACCOUNT BOOK FOR EXPENSES OF CAPT. AARON OGDEN'S COMPANY OF THE 1ST NEW JERSEY REGIMENT. Jan. 1-Oct. 31, 1782. 1 cm, 1/2 in. 1 vol.

This series appears to be missing.
Arranged by type of account. Indexed by surname of soldier.
Register of the names of the members of Ogden's company, with their place of birth, place of residence, physical description, and date of enlistment; reports of furloughs granted, desertions, court-martials, and dead and discharged soldiers; record of clothing, arms, ammunition, and camp equipment received for the use of the company; muster rolls; and a record of property issued to individual soldiers.

505.   INDEXES TO LETTERS AND SETTLED CLAIMS FOR REVOLUTIONARY WAR SERVICE. ca. 1828-May 28, 1835. 10 cm, 4 in. 2 vols.

Arranged in part chronologically and in part by initial letter of claimant's surname.
Indexes to letters and settled claims, in two subseries. The first volume, arranged by initial letter of claimant's surname and dated ca. 1828-35, shows claimant's name, file number of letters received and sent, page reference to registers of claims received, numbers of reports on approved claims for semiannual payments (entry 507), number of pay certificate, numbers of warrants for payments of moneys due, and sometimes cross-references to additional files relating to the claimant. The second volume, arranged chronologically and dated May 8, 1832-May 28, 1835, shows number assigned to each incoming letter, date received, writer's name, subject, and date and number assigned to the reply.

506.   REGISTER OF AUDITS FOR REVOLUTIONARY WAR CLAIMS. May 31, 1828-Apr. 22, 1835. 3 cm, 1 in. 1 vol.

Arranged chronologically. Indexed by initial letter of claimant's surname: Register contains entries that show audit reports on claims filed under an act of May 15, 1828, with date of report, report number (entry 507), veteran's name and rank, payment period, date approved, and amount paid.

507.   AUDIT REPORTS ON REVOLUTIONARY WAR CLAIMS. May 31, 1828-Apr. 28, 1835. 91 cm, 3 ft. 19 vols.

Arranged in two subseries and thereunder numerically within each.

Fair copies of reports on claims filed under an act of May 15, 1828 (4 Stat. 269), that provided full military pay for life, starting March 3, 1826, for commissioned officers who served during the Revolutionary War who had been entitled to half-pay under an act of October 21, 1780; and to noncommissioned officers, musicians, and privates who had served during the Revolutionary War and who had been entitled to an award of $80 for such service under a Continental Congress resolution in 1778. Pensions paid officers were to be deducted from amounts paid them under this act, and no persons on the pension rolls were entitled to benefit from the act.

Soldiers were to receive lump-sum payments for the period March 3, 1826-March 2, 1828 (retroactive pay), and thereafter benefits were to be paid semiannually. The audit reports are for (1st subseries) retroactive pay, May 31-September 3, 1828, and November 21, 1828-April 22, 1835 (6 vols.); and for (2d subseries) semiannual payments, September 12-October 6, 1828, and October 20, 1828-April 28, 1835 (13 vols.).

Each report shows number and date of report, name and address of claimant, amount of pay due (after deducting pensions in the case of officers), and rank and military unit with which the officer or soldier had served during the Revolutionary War.

For copies of the claims on which these payments were based, see entry 513.

508.   AUDITOR'S REPORTS ON REVOLUTIONARY WAR CLAIMS. Aug. 5, 1828-Feb. 17, 1835. 18 cm, 7 in. 2 boxes.

Arranged numerically.

Reports on settlement of claims filed under the act of May 15, 1828, showing date, report number, veteran's name and address, rank and military unit during the Revolutionary War, and amount. For bound copies of these reports, see entry 507.

509.   ABSTRACTS OF SETTLED REVOLUTIONARY WAR CLAIMS. Jan. 1831-Sept. 1833. 1 cm, 1/2 in. 1 box.

Arranged chronologically and thereunder numerically.

Abstracts of claims filed under the act of May 15, 1828, settled by Richard Smith, cashier of the Bank of the United States and an agent for paying claims under the act, showing period covered, voucher number, claimant's name, and amount. These abstracts, together with the audit reports described in entry 508 and the vouchers described in entry 511, were originally filed together as settled accounts of the agents for paying Revolutionary War claims. The accounts were submitted quarterly. The accounts were settled by the First Auditor and subsequently transferred to the Second Auditor's Office for filing.

510.   REGISTER OF VOUCHERS FOR SETTLED REVOLUTIONARY WAR CLAIMS. Mar. 3, 1831-Mar. 3, 1834. 5 cm, 2 in. 1 vol.

Arranged by initial letter of claimant's surname.

Register volume contains entries that show claimant's name and rank, amount of pay to which he was entitled, military unit, residence, and voucher numbers for semiannual payments received by him from claims agents (usually cashiers of the Bank of the United States) under provisions of an act of May 15, 1828. The veteran's date of death is also shown if pertinent. Some of the vouchers listed are among those described in entry 511. The settlement numbers for these claims are listed on the first page of the A's in this register but are not repeated elsewhere.

511.   VOUCHERS FOR PAYMENTS OF REVOLUTIONARY WAR CLAIMS. Sept. 1829-Mar. 1834. 4.6 m, 15 ft. 9 boxes.

Arranged alphabetically by initial letter of veteran's surname.

Vouchers for payments under the act of May 15, 1828, showing date of verification of veteran's entitlement, name and address, rank and military unit during the Revolutionary War, amount of pay to which he was entitled, and payment instructions. A receipt signed by the veteran is frequently attached to these vouchers. The vouchers, together with the abstracts (entry 509) and audit reports (entry 508), were originally filed as accounts of agents for paying Revolutionary War claims and were a part of the First Auditor's miscellaneous Treasury accounts (entry 347). The accounts were recorded in the First Auditor's registers of audits (entry 345).

512.   SETTLED ACCOUNTS FOR REVOLUTIONARY WAR CLAIMS. July 1828-Mar. 1831. 3.1 m, 10 ft. 12 boxes.

Arranged by initial letter of veteran's surname.

Accounts consisting of one or both of the following documents: (1) report from the Secretary of the Treasury to the Auditor certifying that the veteran was entitled to receive the pay claimed; and (2) report by the Auditor showing report number, date, veteran's name and address, rank and military unit during the Revolutionary War, and amount of pay to which he was entitled. If the account includes both types of documents, they have both been given the same number.

For additional copies of audit reports, see entries 507 and 508.

513.   CLAIMS FILED BY REVOLUTIONARY WAR VETERANS. Sept. 16, 1828-Aug. 3, 1835. 2.7 m, 9 ft. 53 vols.

Arranged in 14 subseries by due date of benefits and chronologically within each subseries.

Affidavits filed by veterans to receive the semiannual payments due them under an act of May 15, 1828 (discussed in entry 507). The affidavits show the veteran's name and address, his rank and military unit during the Revolution and where he wished the draft to be sent to him for payment.

Many of the affidavits for the first and second payments are accompanied by copies of the audit reports described in entry 507, and, in most cases, the two types of documents have a common file number. Beginning with the payment due September 3, 1829, a new system of verifying entitlement to benefits (known as pay certificates) came into use, and copies of the audit reports are rarely filed with affidavits after this time.

514.   REGISTERS OF PAY CERTIFICATES ISSUED IN SETTLEMENT OF REVOLUTIONARY WAR CLAIMS. Aug. 3, 1829-Aug. 7, 1835. 8 cm, 3 in. 2 vols.

Arranged numerically by pay certificate number and thereunder by payment period.
Registers contain entries that show certificate number, when and to who issued, claimant's residence, location of branch bank at which payment was to be made, veteran's rank and military unit during the Revolutionary War, amount due every 6 months, and date certified to receive each semiannual payment. Dates of death of the veterans are recorded when appropriate.
For a partial index, see entry 505.

515.   AUDIT REPORTS ON MILITARY ACCOUNTS AND CLAIMS. Apr. 14, 1795-Dec. 31, 1817. 61 cm, 2 ft. 9 vols.

Arranged numerically. Each volume is indexed by initial letter of accountable officer's or claimant's surname.
Fair copies of reports by the Accountant for the War Department showing date and number of report, name of accountable officer or claimant, amount due, explanation, appropriation to be charged, and payment instructions. Many of the reports are for military service or for goods furnished under contract.

516.   SETTLED ACCOUNTS OF ARMY PAYMASTERS. 1815-61. 627.9 m, 2,060 ft. 1736 boxes.

Arranged numerically. Alpha boxes: 375A and 576A.
Accounts for forage, pay, subsistence, bounty, and similar expenses of the Army. A typical account consists of a copy of the Second Auditor's report, statement of the account, abstract of disbursements, vouchers (frequently muster rolls and payrolls), correspondence, and other supporting evidence. The payrolls and muster rolls have been removed from these accounts and are described separately (see entries 517 and 519).
Paymasters' accounts after 1861 were not accessioned by NARA.
For registers of reports on the settlement of these accounts, see entry 197.

516A. SETTLED ACCOUNTS OF ARMY PAYMASTERS, 1863. 3 vols.

517.   MUSTER ROLLS AND PAYROLLS. 1815-66. 190.5 m, 625 ft. 385 boxes.

Arranged by military unit.
Muster rolls and payrolls of Regular Army and Volunteer units, each identifying the military unit and its commanding officer, names and ranks of officers and soldiers attached to the unit, amounts paid, and remarks on the service of the officer or soldier if he was not present for the entire period covered by the payroll. These muster rolls and payrolls were selected from settled accounts of Army Paymasters (entry 516). Some of the payrolls and muster rolls for the period 1815-21 have been interfiled with similar rolls from Records of the Adjutant General's Office, 1780s-1917, RG 94, to form a collection of payrolls of Regular Army units, 1784-1821.

518.   REGISTERS OF COPIED PAYROLLS (INDEX TO MUTILATED ORIGINAL VOUCHERS). 1861-67. 15 cm, 6 in. 4 vols.

Arranged by initial letter of paymaster's surname and thereunder by assigned number. Two volumes are indexed by name of paymaster. The other two are not indexed.
Registers contain entries that show paymaster's name, voucher number, and old and new settlement numbers. These records document the function of the Archives Division in copying muster rolls that were damaged by frequent use, and they serve as a partial index to selected original muster rolls and payrolls, 1861-67 (entry 519).

519.   SELECTED ORIGINAL MUSTER ROLLS AND PAYROLLS (COPIED ROLLS). 1861-67.
        95.4 m, 313 ft. 989 boxes.

        Arranged numerically. A partial register is in entry 518.
        Rolls identify military unit and its commanding officer, names and ranks of officers and
enlisted men in the unit, and amount paid. Each payroll or muster roll is in an envelope showing
the new settlement number, voucher number, identity of the military unit, name of its
commanding officer, paymaster's name and account number, and number of the box in which the
account was originally filed. These original muster rolls and payrolls were withdrawn from the
main series because of their deteriorating condition, and copies were made and substituted for
these originals in the main series (entry 517).

520.   ACCOUNTS CURRENT OF MAJ. EUGENE VAN NESS. Mar. 28, 1850-Feb. 28, 1852.
        3 cm, 1 in. 1 vol.

        Arranged chronologically.
        Accounts current of Major Van Ness, Paymaster of the U.S. Army for pay of officers and
cadets at the U.S. Military Academy showing amounts paid by Van Ness for the purposes
stated, balance carried forward to next account, moneys received from the U.S. Treasurer for the
payroll, and credits for moneys repaid by officers because of overpayments or erroneous charges.
Each account current is for a 2-month period. On February 16, 1852, Van Ness turned the money
remaining in his hands over to his successor.

521.   PAYROLLS OF THE ENROLLED MISSOURI MILITIA. 1861-65. 1.8 m, 6 ft. 37 vols.
        1 box.

        Arranged by unit and thereunder by roll number.
        The Enrolled Missouri Militia was a Volunteer organization in the service of the State
of Missouri during the Civil War. A typical payroll shows the unit's identity; name of
commanding officer; dates organized, ordered into service, and dismissed from service; period of
payroll; names and ranks of officers and enlisted men; days of service during the period covered
by payroll; days for which paid; rate of pay; amounts due for pay and allowances; amounts
deducted; amount actually paid; and soldier's signature. These payrolls were submitted by the
State of Missouri as evidence in support of a claim for reimbursement to the State for a part of
its Civil War expenses.

522.   VOUCHERS FOR ENLISTMENT BOUNTY PAID TO MEMBERS OF THE 125TH
        REGIMENT OF NEW YORK VOLUNTEERS. Aug. 27, 1862. 5 cm, 2 in. 1 box.

        Arranged by military unit and thereunder alphabetically by initial letter of soldier's
surname.
        Vouchers for bounty paid to members of Companies A, B, D, F, H, I, and K of the 125th
Regiment of New York Volunteers. These vouchers were a part of the recruiting account of the
unit's commanding officer and show date of payment, military unit, soldier's name, amount due
($2 per soldier), from whom received, signatures of the soldier and witness and place of
payment.

523.   SETTLED ACCOUNTS AND CLAIMS. Mar. 15, 1817-June 30, 1894. 563.9 m, 1,850 ft.
        1203 boxes.

        Arranged numerically. Registers for these accounts are in entry 197. There are gaps in
the date span of these records; actual dates covered are: Mar. 15, 1817-Mar. 24, 1853; Jan. 30,
1862-June 30, 1894. Alpha boxes: 164A.

Accounts and claims settled by the Second Auditor, primarily for contingent expenses of paymasters, quartermasters, recruiting officers, disbursing clerks for the War Department, and persons furnishing various goods and services for the Army. A typical account or claim includes a copy of the Auditor's report, abstract of disbursements, account current, statement of the account, vouchers, correspondence, and other evidence of the validity of the account or claim. Accounts after 1853 represent a sample selected by the NARA staff; the remaining accounts for 1853-98 have been disposed of. Includes M1678, Accounts and Claims Settled by the Second Auditor of the Treasury Department Relating to the Arsenal at Harper's Ferry, 1817-1851. 62 rolls

524.   CLAIMS SETTLED UNDER THE CHICKASAW TREATY. July 6, 1833-Apr. 7, 1871.
         4.6 m, 15 ft. 13 boxes.

Arranged numerically.
Case files of settled claims arising under the Chickasaw Treaty of October 20, 1832, relating chiefly to land sales, land surveys, expenses of Indian agents, and expenses of removal and subsistence of Indians. The files consist chiefly of a report by the Auditor on his examination of the claim and supporting documents filed by the claimant to substantiate the claim. There are few settled claims after 1851.

525.   SETTLED INDIAN ACCOUNTS AND CLAIMS. Jan. 1794-Feb. 1894. 1,097.3 m, 3,600 ft.
         4,687 boxes.

Arranged numerically. Alpha boxes: 3A, 3B, 146A, 148A, 149A, 184A, 204A, 244A-B, 249 A-B, 340A, 341A, 528A, 569A, 695A, 773A, 802A. The following boxes appear to be missing 309, 1106, 4081, 4199, 4299, 4243, 4278, 4421, 4379, 4469.
Accounts of Indian agents, other officials responsible for expenditures relating to Indians, and private claimants. An account or claim usually consists of a statement of the account or claim, documents submitted in its support, and a report by the Auditor on his examination of the documents submitted. The admitting of Indian accounts and claims was, at various times, under the jurisdiction of the First Auditor, the Accountant for the War Department, and the Fifth Auditor, as well as the Second Auditor. Records from these other offices are filed with this series and are registered in the series described in entries 345 and 830. Before January 1875, the accounts and claims were filed with those described in entry 523 but were withdrawn from that series later to form the present series. For a register of the accounts and claims settled by the Second Auditor, see entry 474.

526.   COTTON AND COTTONSEED CASE FILES. Aug. 1918-Sept. 1920. 5.2 m, 17 ft. 18
         boxes.

Arranged by contract number.
Files consisting chiefly of vouchers for settlement of contracts with companies for the storage of and insurance on these items for the War Department. The seeds were converted to cottonseed oil and used in the manufacture of explosives.

Records Relating to Pay of Volunteer Units

527.   RECORD OF VOLUNTEER UNITS PAID. 1846-48. 8 cm, 3 in. 2 vols.

Arranged by military unit. Each volume is indexed by name of Volunteer unit.
Record of pay of Volunteer units in the Mexican War, showing name of military unit, name of commanding officer, designation of company, name of paymaster, period for which unit was paid, voucher number, account number, and box number in which account was filed.

528. ROSTER OF FREMONT'S BATTALION OF CALIFORNIA VOLUNTEERS IN THE MEXICAN WAR. 1846-48. 2 cm, 1 in. 1 vol.

Arranged alphabetically by initial letter of soldier's surname.
Roster shows soldier's name and rank, number of muster roll and payroll on which his name appeared, and sometimes numbers of certificates of settlement or amount of extra pay received.

529. ROSTER OF MEMBERS OF TEXAS VOLUNTEERS IN THE MEXICAN WAR. 1846-48. 3 cm, 1 in. 1 vol.

Arranged alphabetically by initial letter of soldier's surname.
Roster shows soldier's name, rank, and number; name of company commander; and such miscellaneous remarks as date of soldier's death, transfer or resignation and whether he had been paid. Included in the front of the volume is an alphabetical list of captains commanding Texas Volunteer Units, June 2, 1846-December 16, 1848.

530. REGISTER OF PAYMENTS TO VOLUNTEER AND SPECIAL UNITS DURING THE CIVIL WAR. 1861-66. 1.2 m, 4 ft. 34 vols.

Arranged geographically by State or type of unit. Each volume is indexed by designation of military unit.
Registers contain entries that show identity of military unit and its commanding officer, period for which paid, name of paymaster, settlement number, account number, and voucher number. If a unit did not serve during the entire Civil War, its dates of establishment and dissolution are shown.
Included are two volumes for payments to U.S. Colored Troops; one volume for payments to the Veterans Reserve Corps; and two volumes (called Omnibus Books) for payments to headquarters and other miscellaneous units.

531. REGISTERS OF PAYMENTS TO MILITIA UNITS. Dec. 1861-Nov. 1871. 3.4 m, 11 ft. 36 vols.

Arranged geographically (beginning with New England) and thereunder by initial letter of soldier's surname.
Registers contain entries that show soldier's name and rank, period for which paid, date and amount paid, paymaster's name and account number, and identity of the soldier's military unit. These records were copied from a set in the Office of the Paymaster General.

532. REGISTERS OF ADVANCE BOUNTY PAID TO STATE VOLUNTEER UNITS IN THE CIVIL WAR. July 1862-Mar. 1865. 8 cm, 3 in. 3 vols.

Arranged alphabetically by name of State.
Registers contain entries that show settlement number, name and station of paymaster, designation of troops paid advance bounty in the settlement, and period for which payment was made. Attached to the inside cover of the first volume are handwritten copies of laws relating to payment of advance bounty and list of Volunteer units from New York and Pennsylvania that received bounty payments in 1862.

533. REGISTER OF SYNONYMS FOR VOLUNTEER UNITS IN THE CIVIL WAR. 1861-65. 1 cm, 1/2 in. 1 vol.

Arranged alphabetically by name of unit.

Register contains entries that show name of organization and name of unit of which it was part. Records of payments to most of the units are found in the registers of payments to volunteer and special units (entry 530).

534.   REGISTER OF TRANSFERS TO VETERANS RESERVE CORPS. May 1863-Nov. 1865. 5 cm, 2 in. 1 vol.

Arranged by initial letter of officer's or soldier's surname.

Register contains entries that show name of person, his rank (if an officer), former unit, and unit of the Veterans Reserve Corps to which he was transferred. A voucher number is also sometimes shown. The Veterans Reserve Corps was first established about May 1863 and disbanded in November 1865.

Records Relating to Pay of Volunteer Soldiers

535.   REGISTERS OF PAYMENTS TO OFFICERS AND ENLISTED MEN FROM VOLUNTEER UNITS. June 1836-Dec. 1861. 30 cm, 1 ft. 6 vols.

Arranged alphabetically by initial letter of soldier's surname.

Registers contain entries chiefly for service in the Mexican War and show soldier's name, rank, military unit, period of service, date paid, and name of paymaster. Many of the entries in the various volumes duplicate each other.

For a record of later payments, see entry 537.

536.   RECORD OF PAYMENTS TO OFFICERS FROM NEW YORK VOLUNTEER UNITS. 1861-65. 30 cm, 1 ft. 5 vols.

Arranged by military unit and thereunder alphabetically by initial letter of officer's surname.

Entries show name of unit, name and rank of officer, and for each year the voucher numbers, settlement numbers, and amounts paid. Additional information includes dates of promotions or termination of service, payment by a different paymaster, and explanation of variations in pay (e.g., from changes in rank during a reporting period).

537.   REGISTERS OF PAYMENTS TO OFFICERS AND ENLISTED MEN FROM VOLUNTEER UNITS. Dec. 1861-June 1873. 1.8 m, 6 ft. 23 vols.

Arranged geographically (beginning with Vermont) and thereunder by initial letter of soldier's surname.

Registers contain entries that show officer's name and rank, period for which paid, date and amount paid, paymaster's name, account number, and military unit with which the officer served. Amounts of pay stopped or of travel pay or extra pay included for a particular time period are also indicated where appropriate. The volumes for payments to troops from Western States also include special employees, such as contract surgeons and witnesses. One volume is for payments to the Veterans Reserve Corps. These records were copied from a set kept in the Office of the Payment General.

For records of earlier payments, see entry 535.

538.   INDEX TO OFFICERS OF VOLUNTEER UNITS. ca. 1861-65. 3 cm, 1 in. 1 vol.

Arranged by initial letter of officer's surname.

The index contains identity of the unit, name and rank of officer, and references to a "Volume 38," apparently nonexistent.

539.   SELECTED LIST OF PERSONNEL OF VOLUNTEER MILITARY UNITS. ca. 1863-65.
13 cm, 5 in. 4 vols.

Arranged by military unit and thereunder alphabetically by initial letter of soldier's
surname.
The list contains identity of the unit and names of persons. If a unit was also known by
another name or if it was merged with another unit or its personnel were transferred, the fact is
noted. The dates of changes, when indicated, are during the period 1863-65. The volumes are for
units from the following States: volume 1-Pennsylvania, Maryland, Virginia, Kentucky,
Tennessee, and Michigan; volume 2-Maine, New Hampshire, Vermont, Massachusetts, Rhode
Island, Connecticut, District of Columbia, Iowa, Arkansas, North Carolina, Nebraska, Georgia,
Florida, Mississippi, Alabama, Louisiana, and Texas; volume 3-Ohio, Indiana, Illinois,
Missouri, Kansas, and Minnesota; volume 4-New York, California, New Jersey, Delaware, and
Wisconsin. The list in volume 4 also includes U.S. Troops and U.S. Colored Troops.

OFFICE OF THE THIRD AUDITOR

The Office of the Third Auditor had its origins in the Office of the Additional Accountant for the War Department, which was authorized by an act of April 29, 1816 (3 Stat. 322), to settle all accounts relating to the War of 1812 that remained unsettled at that time. The Office of the Additional Accountant was abolished by an act of March 3, 1817 (3 Stat. 366), which established the Office of the Third Auditor to settle subsistence and quartermaster accounts and all other accounts of the War Department "not otherwise provided for." The Third Auditor certified balances of accounts to the Second Comptroller for his decision, kept records of receipts and disbursements of public moneys, and registered and recorded warrants.

An act of April 20, 1818 (3 Stat. 466), gave the Third Auditor responsibility for settling all unsettled accounts and claims relating to the War of 1812 that had not been acted upon by the Commissioner of Claims, a temporary position created by an act of April 9, 1816 (3 Stat. 261).

Claims for horses and other property lost while in the military service were settled by the Third Auditor under an act of March 3, 1849 (9 Stat. 415); for the loss of steamboats and other vessels in military service under an act of June 25, 1864 (13 Stat. 160); and for reimbursement of States for expenses of the Indian wars and the Civil War under an act of September 30, 1890 (26 Stat. 539), and other appropriation acts passed at various times.

An act of August 30, 1890 (26 Stat. 399), also made the Third Auditor responsible for settling Signal Corps accounts.

The Third Auditor was redesignated Auditor for the Interior Department by an act of July 31, 1894 (28 Stat. 296), with responsibility for settling all accounts of the Office of the Secretary of the Interior and of all divisions and bureaus under his direction: Pension, Public Lands, Indian, Geological Survey, and Architect of the Capitol. This act transferred the Indian functions of the Second Auditor and the pension functions of the Second and Fourth Auditors to the Auditor for the Interior Department. The Military Division and Claims Division were abolished and their functions transferred to the Office of the Auditor for the War Department (formerly Second Auditor).

The records of the Third Auditor are described as those of the Army Pension Division, the Bookkeepers Division, the Military Division, the Claims Division, the Indian Division, and the Land, Files, and Miscellaneous Division. Records relating to the functions of more than one Division are described as general records. The most significant records of the Third Auditor are settled accounts and claims, 1817-50 and 1878-97, with related registers, indexes, and docket books; pension accounts; letters sent, 1817-94; records of Special Claims Commissions; and records of claims of States for reimbursement of expenses relating to the Mexican War, suppression of Indian hostilities, and raising and supplying troops at the start of the Civil War.

A list of names of Third Auditors and dates of service appear in Appendix 7.

GENERAL RECORDS

Correspondence

540.   REGISTERS OF LETTERS AND CLAIMS RECEIVED AND REFERRED TO DIVISIONS FOR REPLY. Jan. 2, 1892-Dec. 28, 1908. 61 cm, 2 ft. 7 vols.

Arranged chronologically. Within each volume entries are arranged alphabetically by initial letter of writer's surname or title and thereunder by date received.

There are gaps in the date span of these records; the actual dates covered are: Jan. 2, 1892-June 30, 1897; July 3, 1900-Dec. 30, 1905; July 9-Dec. 28, 1908.

Registers contain entries that show writer's name, address or title, date received, date of letter, subject, Division to which referred, and sometimes date of reply. Most of the letters and papers concerned accounts and claims under the jurisdiction of the Law, Indian, Land, or

Pension Division and were referred to one of those Divisions for reply. Many of the entries in the volumes for 1908 are written in shorthand. One volume, September 16, 1904-December 30, 1905, relates primarily to letters and papers referred to the Indian Office.

540A.   REPORTS TO THE PRESIDENT BY THE COMMITTEE ON DEPARTMENT METHODS. 1 vol.

BOOKKEEPERS DIVISION

The Bookkeepers Division was first established in the Third Auditor's Office in April 1853. The Division maintained appropriation ledgers, personal accountability ledgers for quartermasters and pension officers, and general ledgers for other appropriations under the jurisdiction of the Third Auditor. The Division kept records of balances of accounts sent to the Second Comptroller for revision and records of balances of accounts sent to the War and Interior Departments for issuance of requisitions. The Division also kept a record of all requisitions and counter requisitions. The Division was abolished in the reorganization of 1894 and its functions were transferred to the Division of Bookkeeping and Warrants in the Office of the Secretary of the Treasury. Functions other than those relating to appropriations were returned to the General Accounting Office in 1921.

Ledgers

541.   PARTIAL INDEX TO GENERAL LEDGERS. Mar. 1817-Apr. 1862. 5 cm, 2 in. 1 vol.

Arranged alphabetically by name of official.
Index to volumes 1-33 of the general ledgers (entry 542) showing officer's name, title or rank, military unit, and page references to the ledgers.

542.   GENERAL LEDGERS. Mar. 1817-Dec. 1895. 9.1 m, 30 ft. 73 vols.

Arranged chronologically. Within each volume the entries are arranged by title of account and thereunder chronologically. The pages are numbered continuously throughout the series.
Folio pages 1239-1882, 22388-22738, and 11977-12728 are missing, but there are no significant gaps in the date coverage of the ledgers.
Ledgers contain entries showing title of account (usually an accountable officer or claimant but sometimes a general appropriation) and debits and credits, including, where appropriate, dates and numbers of requisitions and dates and numbers of settlements (entry 712). Also shown are references to the general journals (entry 547).
For an index to volumes 1-33 (Mar. 1817-Apr. 1862), see entry 541.

543.   COMMISSARY AND PENSION LEDGERS. July 1865-May 1896. 1.2 m, 4 ft. 17 vols.

Arranged chronologically. Within each volume the entries are arranged by title of account and thereunder chronologically. The pages are numbered consecutively.
Ledgers contain entries of disbursements for subsistence of the Army and for payment of pensions showing title of account (i.e., name, rank, and title of accountable officer), and debits and credits for disbursements and receipts. Many entries includes references to the journals (entry 548).
In the case of military officers, the ledgers frequently show date and cause of termination of service and sometimes show balances being carried to the "suspense ledger." For later commissary and pension ledgers, see entries 544 and 546, respectively.

544. COMMISSARY LEDGER. May 1904-Dec. 1907. 8 cm, 3 in. 1 vol.

Arranged by title of account and thereunder chronologically.

Ledger contains entries for disbursements of subsistence of the Army showing title of account (i.e., name and rank of accountable officer), journal references, and debits and credits for receipts, advances to other officers, and disbursements.

For earlier commissary ledgers, see entry 543.

545. INDEX TO PENSION LEDGER B. ca. 1864-86. 1 cm, 1/2 in. 1 vol.

Arranged alphabetically by name of pension agent or claimant.

Index shows names of individuals, identifying information (e.g., agent, Indian pensioner, or ex-surgeon), and page references. The ledger to which this index related has not been located.

546. PENSION LEDGERS. Aug. 1869-Oct. 1903. 23 cm, 9 in. 3 vols.

Arranged chronologically. Within each volume entries are arranged by title of account (usually name of pension agent) and thereunder chronologically.

There are gaps in the date span of these records; the actual dates covered are: Aug. 1869-Mar. 1871; July 1894-Oct. 1903.

Ledgers contain entries of accounts showing name of pension agent, date of bond, location of pension agency, debts for amounts payable under various pension acts and for repayments of pension, and credits for amounts paid for pensions and expenses of the pension agency. Part of the volume numbered 25 (1894-95) is used as an auxiliary ledger for pension agents accounts.

For other pension ledgers, see entry 543.

Journals

547. GENERAL JOURNALS. Mar. 4, 1817-Mar. 21, 1895. 6.1 m, 20 ft. 73 vols.

Arranged chronologically. The volumes are identified as 1-69 (Mar. 4, 1817-June 30, 1892) and 65-69 (June 13, 1892-Mar. 21, 1895). The pages in the volumes are numbered consecutively. There is no volume 2.

Journals contain entries showing date posted, date of transaction, settlement number (entry 712), ledger reference (entry 542), explanation, amount, and balance. Names of persons to whom moneys were advanced, and the detailed nature of expenditures are usually shown. Beginning July 1, 1876 (volume 56), the journals are identified as quartermaster and engineer journals.

548. COMMISSARY AND PENSION JOURNALS. July 1, 1865-Feb. 21, 1899. 1.2 m, 4 ft. 21 vols.

Arranged chronologically. Beginning with volume 20 (August 5, 1890), the volumes are identified as subsistence and pension journals. The pages are numbered consecutively.

There are gaps in the date span of these records; the actual dates covered are: July 1, 1865-June 30, 1866; July 1, 1867-June 30, 1868; July 2, 1869-Feb. 21, 1899.

Journals contain entries showing date posted, date of transaction, settlement number, ledger reference (entries 544 and 546), and explanations including names of accountable officers, names of persons to whom funds were advanced, and whether the account was balanced.

549. INDIAN AGENT'S JOURNALS. July 1, 1897-Mar. 19, 1908. 25 cm, 10 in. 4 vols.

Arranged chronologically and identified as volumes 30-33.

Journals contain entries showing date, settlement number (entry 717), ledger reference, name of accountable officer, date of bond, titles of appropriations concerned, explanation, and amount to be charged or credited to the appropriation.

For earlier volumes in this series, see Indian journals, new series, entry 370.

Records Relating to Requisitions and Warrants

550.   INDEX TO WARRANTS. Oct. 1816-Nov. 1817. 1 cm, 1/2 in. 1 vol.

Arranged alphabetically by name of payee.

Index maintained by the Additional Accountant for the War Department showing payee's name and identifying information and warrant number. This volume partially indexes the warrant blotter in entry 551.

551.   WARRANT BLOTTERS. Oct. 2, 1815-Dec. 15, 1817. 8 cm, 3 in. 1 vols.

Arranged chronologically and thereunder numerically. A partial index is in entry 550.

There are gaps in the date span of these records; the actual dates covered are: Oct. 2, 1815-Feb. 29, 1816; Oct. 28, 1816-Dec. 15, 1817.

The entries show number and date of warrant, name of payee, explanation, title of appropriation to be charged, and amount.

For a later record of warrants, see entry 552.

552.   REGISTERS OF WARRANTS. Mar. 11, 1817-June 27, 1822. 25 cm, 10 in. 5 vols.

Arranged chronologically. Volume 5, the only one indexed, is indexed by surname of payee.

Registers contain entries that show date and number of warrant, to whom issued, explanation, title of appropriation to be charged, and amount. Most of the warrants relate to quartermaster, subsistence, and pension disbursements.

For a record of earlier warrants, see entry 551.

553.   REGISTER OF REFUND WARRANTS. Mar. 15, 1817-Dec. 30, 1822. 2 cm, 1 in. 1 vol.

Arranged chronologically.

Register contains entries that show date and number of warrant, on whom drawn, explanation, title of appropriation to be credited, and amount.

These warrants were later known as repay warrants.

554.   REGISTERS OF INDIAN REQUISITIONS. July 1898-June 1903. 15 cm, 6 in. 2 vols.

Arranged chronologically. Within each volume entries are arranged by surname of accountable officer and thereunder by month. Each volume is indexed by surname of officer.

Registers contain entries that show officer's name and title, date and amount of bond, date and number of requisition, when approved, amount requested, and titles of appropriations to be charged.

555.   REGISTERS OF PENSION REQUISITIONS. Mar. 6, 1849-Sept. 25, 1894. 91 cm, 3 ft. 21 vols.

Arranged chronologically. Each volume is indexed by surname of pensioner or pension agent.

Registers contain entries that show date and number of requisition, to whom payable, address, appropriation or pension act involved, period covered, settlement number, and amount.

Many of the early entries relate to payment of claims filed by heirs of deceased pensioners under provision of an act of April 6, 1838 (5 Stat. 225), which transferred responsibility for paying unclaimed pensions from pension agencies to the U.S. Treasurer.

Records Relating to Settlement of Accounts

556.   GENERAL REGISTERS OF SETTLEMENTS. Dec. 2, 1857-Sept. 21, 1894. 1.2 m, 4 ft.
        15 vols.

Arranged chronologically. Within each volume the entries are arranged by initial letter of surname of accountable officer or claimant and thereunder by date reported. The spine designations begin with "A" and then run form volumes 1 to 14.

Registers contain entries that show date received, name of accountable officer or claimant, rank and title of officer, settlement number, type of account, period covered, and date reported. The adjusted balance of the account or claim is also frequently shown. Among the most common types of accounts and claims registered in these volumes are those of surgeons, military storekeepers, pensioners, pension agents, Indian War claims, and settlements authorized by private acts of Congress for the relief of the persons filing claims.

557.   ABSTRACTS OF ENGINEER ACCOUNTS. Mar. 1841-Apr. 1867. 8 cm, 3 in. 2 vols.

Arranged chronologically and identified as volumes 10 and 13. One volume appears to be missing.

Within each volume the entries are arranged by surname of accountable officer and thereunder chronologically. Volume 10 is indexed by surname of officer.

There are gaps in the date span of these records; the actual dates covered are: Mar. 1841-Oct. 1852; Mar. 1860-Apr. 1867.

Abstracts show officer's name, rank, and duty station; debits and credits; titles of appropriations concerned (usually fortifications, improvement of rivers and harbors, and expenses of the Military Academy at West Point); and usually the adjusted balance and settlement numbers. The loose pages, 1841-52, are part of two volumes, the rest of which have not been located.

558.   REGISTERS OF ENGINEER SETTLEMENTS. July 15, 1885-Aug. 5, 1886. 13 cm, 5 in.
        2 vols.

Arranged chronologically. Within each volume the entries are arranged alphabetically by surname of official and thereunder by date reported.

Registers contain entries that show officer's name, rank, and duty station; the period covered by account; dates received, reported, and approved; settlement number; and official balance.

559.   ABSTRACTS OF PENSION AGENTS ACCOUNTS. Sept. 1, 1818-Sept. 21, 1836. 25 cm,
        10 in. 4 vols.

Arranged chronologically. Within each volume the entries are arranged by location of pension agency. Each volume is indexed by surname of pension agent.

Abstracts show name and location of pension agent (usually an officer of a bank), previous balance, dates and amounts of receipts and disbursements, settlement numbers, and remaining balances.

560.   ABSTRACTS OF QUARTERMASTER ACCOUNTS. Mar. 1819-Apr. 1857. 61 cm, 2 ft.
         15 vols.

Arranged chronologically. Within each volume the entries are arranged by surname of
accountable officer. Each volume, except the earliest, is indexed by name of officer. One volume
appears to be missing.

There are gaps in the date span of these records; the actual dates covered are: Mar.
1819-Aug. 1823; Mar. 1832-Apr. 1857.

Abstracts show name and rank of accountable officer, duty station, and debits and
credits, disbursements, titles of appropriations concerned (usually Quartermaster Department,
transportation of officers, or transportation of the Army), adjusted balance of the account, and
sometimes settlement numbers.

561.   ABSTRACTS OF CONTRACTORS ACCOUNTS. Feb. 1819-Mar. 1860. 10 cm, 4 in.
         4 vols.

Arranged chronologically. Entries within each volume are arranged by contractor's
surname. The last three volumes are indexed alphabetically by contractor's surname.

There are gaps in the date span of these records; the actual dates covered are: Feb.
1819-June 1823; June 1830-Apr. 1835; Dec. 1850-Mar. 1860.

Abstracts show name of contractor; date of contract; type, quantity, and value of goods
furnished; amount due contractor; and date and number of settlement. The unbound papers are
numbered 25-83.

For related registers, see entry 563.

562.   ABSTRACTS OF SUBSISTENCE ACCOUNTS. Dec. 1824-Sept. 1864. 1.2 m, 4 ft.
         23 vols.

Arranged chronologically. Within each volume the entries are arranged by initial
letter of surname of accountable officer. Each volume, except the first, is indexed
alphabetically by officer's surname.

There are gaps in the date span of these records; the actual dates covered are: Dec.
1824-Aug. 1826; Aug. 1829-Feb. 1831; Mar. 1832-Sept. 1864.

Abstracts show officer's name, rank, and duty station; debits and credits (usually
including an explanation of the purpose of the expense); adjusted balance; and date and number
of settlement. For related registers, see entry 563.

563.   REGISTERS OF SUBSISTENCE SETTLEMENTS. Sept. 6, 1841-Aug. 7, 1886. 61 cm, 2 ft.
         13 vols.

Arranged chronologically. Within each volume the entries are arranged by initial
letter of surname of contractor or accountable officer and thereunder by date reported.

Registers contain entries that show name of contractor or name and rank of accountable
officer; period covered; dates received, reported, and approved; balance reported by officer or
contractor; settlement number; and adjusted balance. Related abstracts are in entries 561 and
562; related ledgers, journals, and contracts are described in entries 236, 544, and 548,
respectively. Some of the entries in these volumes are for letters of explanation received from
officers or for corrected vouchers returned for filing with earlier settlements.

For registers arranged by settlement number, see entry 564.

564. NUMERICAL REGISTERS OF SETTLED ACCOUNTS AND CLAIMS. Mar. 3, 1817-Sept. 29, 1894. 61 cm, 2 ft. 17 vols.

Arranged chronologically by month and year and thereunder by settlement number. Only 12 volumes have been found.

Registers contain entries that show settlement number, date of settlement, name of officer or claimant, and usually type of account or claim. Through November 17, 1841, the exact dates of settlement are shown.

Entries include quartermasters and engineer accounts (through Jan. 1878); subsistence and pension accounts (through July 1865); and miscellaneous claims.

For certificates of settlement of some of these accounts and claims before September 1851, see entry 715; for original accounts and claims for the same period, see entry 712. For abstracts of settlement, see entry 562.

For registers of settlements arranged by name of officer, see entry 563.

ARMY PENSION DIVISION

The Army Pension Division was first established in the Third Auditor's Office during the fiscal year beginning July 1, 1877, as the successor to the Pension Division (first established during the fiscal year beginning July 1, 1865). The name of the Division again became the Pension Division in 1894 when the settlement of Navy pension accounts and claims was transferred from the Fourth Auditor to the Third Auditor.

The Army Pension Division recorded and settled accounts of pensioners and pension agents, recorded changes in pension rolls, handled claims for reimbursement of funeral expenses of deceased pensioners, and recorded certificates of deposit for pension payments. The Division also registered and replied to letters relating to pensions. Settled pension accounts and other related records are described among the records of the Land, Files, and Miscellaneous Division.

Correspondence

565. CIRCULARS AND DECISIONS. May 7, 1877-July 18, 1912. 5 cm, 2 in. 1 vol.

Arranged chronologically. Indexed alphabetically by subject.

Published and manuscript copies of circulars and decisions relating to pension accounts and claims, including copies of decisions of the Comptroller in cases appealed to him by claimants. Also included are copies of circulars on various administrative matters. For copies of other decisions by the Comptroller relating to pension claims, see entry 203.

566. REGISTER OF LETTERS RECEIVED (MISCELLANEOUS PENSION LETTERS). July 2, 1866-Dec. 31, 1897. 61 cm, 2 ft. 12 vols.

Entries in the first two volumes (July 2, 1866-Dec. 30, 1873) are arranged chronologically; entries in the remaining volumes are arranged by initial letter of surname of writer or pensioner and thereunder chronologically.

Registers contain entries that show date of letter, name of pensioner or writer, title of writer (if a Government official), subject, date received, date answered, and action taken. Subjects include the transmittal of pension accounts and claims or inquiries about payments to specific pensioners.

567.   REGISTER OF PENSION LETTERS RECEIVED. Jan. 5, 1874-June 27, 1904. 30 cm, 1 ft.
        9 vols.

Arranged chronologically. Within each volume the entries are arranged
alphabetically by initial letter of surname of writer or pensioner and thereunder
chronologically.
There are gaps in the date span of these records; the actual dates covered are: Jan. 5,
1874-Feb. 12, 1884; Jan. 5, 1891-June 30, 190; May 9, 1902-June 27, 1904.
Registers contain entries that show date of letter, name of writer, name of pensioner,
pension certificate number, subject, date received, and date answered. Letters frequently concern
requests for certified copies of documents or requests for verification of pension payments.

568.   REGISTERS OF LETTERS RECEIVED RELATING TO DECEASED PENSIONERS.
        Sept. 4, 1882-May 16, 1903. 8 cm, 3 in. 2 vols.

Arranged chronologically. Within each volume the entries are arranged by initial
letter of surname of writer or pensioner and thereunder chronologically.
There are gaps in the date span of these records; the actual dates covered are: Sept. 4,
1882-Dec. 5, 1883; Jan. 3, 1898-May 16, 1903.
Registers contain entries that show date and subject of letter, name and address of
writer, dates received and answered, and action taken. Many of the letters registered were
claims for reimbursement of funeral expenses of deceased pensioners; in such cases the name of
the deceased pensioner and the number of the pension certificate are shown as the subject of the
letter.
For copies of replies to some of these letters, see entry 571.

569.   REGISTER OF PENSION LETTERS RECEIVED AND SENT. Nov. 22, 1876-Jan. 8, 1878.
        5 cm, 2 in. 1 vol.

Arranged by initial letter of pensioner's surname and thereunder chronologically.
Register contains entries that show dates letter was written and received, name of
pensioner, number of pension certificate, location of pension agency, subject of letter, abstract of
reply, and date of reply.
Most of the letters relate to reductions of individual pension payments, verification of
dates of final payments, and deletion of names of dropped pensioners.

570.   LETTERS SENT TO THE COMMISSIONER OF PENSIONS. Sept. 21, 1870-Mar. 7, 1885.
        61 cm, 2 ft. 8 vols.

Arranged chronologically. Indexed by initial letter of pensioner's name.
Fair copies of letters relating chiefly to changes in rolls of pension agencies, changes in
rates of pensions payable to specific persons and status of accounts of pension agents. Many of
the letters show the names of pensioners and numbers of their pension certificates.

571.   MISCELLANEOUS LETTERS SENT BY THE PENSION DIVISION. Nov. 24, 1838-
        Apr. 19, 1887. 3.4 m, 11 ft. 60 vols.

Arranged chronologically. Each volume is indexed by name of pensioner or addressee.
There are gaps in the date span of these records; the actual dates covered are: Nov. 24,
1838-July 27, 1876; Apr. 27, 1877-Apr. 19, 1887.
Fair copies of letters to pensioners, their heirs or legal representatives, and to pension
agents relating chiefly to the adjustment of accounts and claims, final payments to estates of
deceased pensioners, and authorization for payment of arrears of pensions.
For a continuation of these letters, see entry 572.

572.   MISCELLANEOUS LETTERS SENT BY THE PENSION DIVISION. Apr. 23, 1888 -
Jan. 2, 1900. 3.7 m, 12 ft. 1 volume and 38 boxes.

Arranged chronologically. Each volume is indexed by surname of pensioner or
addressee. For 1894-95 the letters are in two groups: (1) textual letters, January 27, 1894-January
2, 1900; (2) form letters, January 2-July 10, 1894, and November 19, 1894-November 19, 1895.
There are gaps in the date span of these records; the actual dates covered are: Apr. 23,
1888-Jan. 19, 1892; Aug. 11, 1892-Oct. 17, 1892; Nov. 18, 1892-Mar. 17, 1893; June 24, 1893-Jan. 2,
1900.
Press copies of letters to pensioners, their heirs or legal representatives, and pension
agents relating primarily to the settlement of accounts and claims, the correction of errors on
vouchers, the payment of fees owed attorneys by pensioners, and the verification of pension
payments.
For copies of earlier letters on these subjects, see entry 571.

Records Relating to Settlement of Pension Accounts and Claims

573.   REGISTER OF SURETY BONDS OF PENSION AGENTS. Jan. 1821-Oct. 1910. 3 cm, 1 in.
1 vol.

Arranged alphabetically by State and thereunder chronologically.
Register contains entries that show pension agent's name, location of agency, date and
amount of agent's bond, and the period of disbursements.
Most of the entries date from the early 1840s. Some entries show the period of
disbursements but no dates and amounts of surety bonds. Before 1840 most pension agents were
officers of State banks. A list in the front of the volume shows the names of pension agents,
1789-1818, whose accounts and vouchers had been destroyed during the War of 1812 or during
the Treasury Department fire of 1833. Many of the surety bonds recorded in this register are in
Records of the Bureau of Accounts (Treasury), RG 39. In 1900 many of the surety bonds were
transferred to the Appointment Division on the Office of the Secretary of the Treasury.

574.   REGISTERS OF PENSION AGENTS ACCOUNTS. Feb. 1, 1819-June 17, 1869. 13 cm, 5 in.
5 vols.

Arranged chronologically. Within the first two volumes (Feb. 1, 1819-Mar. 31, 1831),
the entries are arranged alphabetically by initial letter of agent's surname. Entries in the last
three volume are arranged alphabetically by initial letter of State name.
Registers contain entries that show name of agent, where stationed, period covered by
account, and dates received and settled. Amounts allowed the agents as commission are also
sometimes shown. In the case of banks acting as pension agents, the entries are in the name of
the president or cashier of the bank.

575.   REGISTERS OF SETTLED ACCOUNTS OF PENSION AGENTS. May 28, 1861-June 6,
1913. 10 cm, 4 in. 3 vols.

Arranged chronologically. Within each volume the entries are arranged by location of
pension agency. The first volume, 1861-66, is indexed by name of city in which pension agency
was located. The other volumes are not indexed.
Registers contain entries that show name of pension agent, where stationed, date of
bond, period covered by account, settlement number, dates settled and confirmed, and balance
due.

576.   NUMERICAL REGISTERS OF SETTLED ACCOUNTS AND CLAIMS. Feb. 7, 1878 - Nov. 30, 1896. 10 cm, 4 in. 3 vols.

Arranged chronologically and thereunder by settlement number.

Registers contain entries that show date reported, settlement number, name of claimant, and type of claim. The claims relate primarily to arrears of pensions, contingent expenses of pension agencies, and fees of doctors for examining disabled pensioners. The settlement numbers were assigned at the time the Auditor reported on the claim.

577.   REGISTER OF PENSION REIMBURSEMENT CLAIMS RECEIVED. Aug. 29, 1882 - Sept. 26, 1885. 5 cm, 2 in. 1 vol.

Arranged alphabetically by initial letter of deceased pensioner's surname and thereunder chronologically.

Register contains entries that show pensioner's name, certificate number, pension agency, claimant's name, type of documentation submitted, and dates received and reported. If the claim was reported for rejection, this fact is also noted.

578.   ABSTRACTS OF ACTION TAKEN ON PENSION REIMBURSEMENT CLAIMS (DOCKET BOOKS). Sept. 21, 1885-July 14, 1904. 5 cm, 2 in. 2 vols.

Arranged chronologically. Within each volume the entries are arranged by initial letter of pensioner's surname and thereunder by date reported.

Abstracts show certificate number, name of pensioner, amount of accrued pension, name and address of claimant, amount claimed, and summary of findings of the Third Auditor. Included are findings of the Secret Service Division in the Office of the Solicitor of the Treasury when the claim was referred to that Division for investigation. The amount recommended by Auditor, date reported, summary of Comptroller's action, amount approved, and settlement number are also shown.

579.   REGISTERS OF SETTLED CLAIMS FOR PENSION REIMBURSEMENTS. Oct. 6, 1882-Oct. 18, 1900. 61 cm, 2 ft. 9 vols.

This series appears to be missing.

Arranged chronologically. Within each volume the entries are arranged by initial letter of pensioner's surname and thereunder by date confirmed.

Registers contain entries that show name of deceased pensioner; pension certificate number; pension agency; dates received, reported, and confirmed; settlement number; when and to whom paid; and amount paid. Warrant numbers are also sometimes included. These claims were filed under an act of March 3, 1873 (17 Stat. 524), which provided that heirs of deceased pensioners could apply for payment of pensions due from date of last payment to date of death, and that the accrued pension could also be used to reimburse persons who had paid for the expenses of the illness and burial of the pensioner if the proceeds of the deceased person's estate had not been sufficient to cover the expenses.

580.   NUMERICAL REGISTERS OF PENSION REIMBURSEMENT SETTLEMENTS. Oct. 1, 1894 Sept. 11, 1913. 30 cm, 1 ft. 7 vols.

Arranged chronologically and thereunder by settlement number. One volume appears to be missing.

Registers contain entries that show settlement number, date of claim, names of claimant and pensioner, appropriation from which payable, amounts claimed and allowed, and (in most cases) date and number of warrant.

Settlement numbers were assigned in sequence on the date the account was reported by the Auditor.

581.   ABSTRACT OF SETTLEMENT OF ACCOUNTS FOR ACCRUED PENSIONS. Mar.
         1895 Sept. 1899. 3 cm, 1 in. 1 vol.

         Arranged by location of pension agency and thereunder chronologically by date voucher
was sent to pension agent.
         Abstract relating to accrued pensions due estate of deceased pensioners under an act of
March 2, 1895 (28 Stat. 965), showing location of pension agency, month and year covered by
account, the number of vouchers sent to pension agent, and dates sent and returned. Also included
are a copy of the act and a list of the names of agents at the various pension agencies indicating
the dates of their surety bonds and the dates they began their service as agents.

582.   REGISTER OF PENSION CLAIMS SETTLED (INDEX TO VIRGINIA CLAIMS FOR
         HALF-PAY). July 22, 1835-Apr. 10, 1855. 1 cm, 1/4 in. 1 vol.

         Arranged alphabetically by initial letter of claimant's surname and thereunder
chronologically by date paid.
         Register contains entries that show officer's name and rank, whether he was an Army
or Navy officer, rate of pay per year, pension payments, and settlement number and/or date of
payment. The volume contains two lists-(1) claims paid by the First and Third Auditors, July
22, 1835-April 10, 1855; (2) claims approved by the Commissioner of Pensions and paid through
the Third Auditor, July 29, 1835-February 22, 1853. Entries in the first list for settlements made
by the Third Auditor are usually repeated in the second list. The first list shows, in some cases,
that payments were made by the State of Virginia.

583.   REGISTERS OF PENSION CLAIMS SETTLED BY THE THIRD AUDITOR. Apr. 2, 1860
         Sept. 1, 1869. 5 cm, 2 in. 2 vols.

         Arranged chronologically. Within each volume, the entries are arranged by initial
letter of claimant's surname and thereunder by date reported. The second volume appears to be
missing.
         Registers contain entries that show names of pensioner and claimant, the act under
which the claim was filed, location of pension agency, rate of pension, dates reported and
returned, settlement number, and amount allowed.

584.   REGISTER OF MISCELLANEOUS CLAIMS. Jan. 6, 1905-Oct. 22, 1910. 1 cm, 1/2 in.
         1 vol.

         Arranged chronologically. Indexed by surname of claimant.
         Register contains entries that show date received, claim number, name of claimant,
explanation, and amount claimed. Entries typically are claims of railroads for transportation
furnished, claims of doctors for examining pension applicants, claims for office supplies
furnished to pension agencies, claims for replacement of lost checks, and claims for attorneys
fees.

585.   REGISTER OF REJECTED CLAIMS. June 1, 1886-May 8, 1889. 2 cm, 1 in. 1 vol.

         This series appears to be missing.
         Arranged by initial letter of pensioner's surname and thereunder by date of rejection.
         Register contains entries that show name of pensioner or presumed pensioner, claimant's
name, claim number or certificate number, dates received and rejected, date and type of action
by Comptroller, date claimant was notified, and file number assigned to the rejected claim. If
the Comptroller overruled the decision of the Auditor, the date, number, and amount of award
are shown.

Records Relating to Pension Payments

586.   REGISTER OF PENSION PAYMENTS. May 29, 1813-July 27, 1866. 3 cm, 1 in. 1 vol.

Arranged by name of deceased soldier and thereunder chronologically by date of payment. Indexed by surname of deceased soldier.

There are gaps in the date span of these records; the actual dates covered are: May 29, 1813-Apr. 30, 1817; Mar. 18, 1819; June 4, 1821-June 19, 1822; July 20, 1836-Mar. 30, 1853; July 22, 1856-July 27, 1866.

Register contains entries that show name and rank of deceased soldier, his military unit, date and cause of death, whether the soldier had left a widow and/or children, date of pension payment, to whom paid, period covered, and amount. Two special sections of the book, included in their proper chronological sequence, are payments to heirs of Cherokee warriors, March 18, 1819; and pension payments made by the Third Auditor, June 4, 1821-June 19, 1822. Except for these two sections, a separate page was used to record payments to the heirs of each veteran. The pensions recorded in this volume generally were payable over a period of 5 years; some were paid in full in advance by special order of the War Department.

587.   REGISTERS OF HALF-PAY PENSIONS PAID BY THE OFFICE OF THE PAYMASTER GENERAL TO WIDOWS AND ORPHANS OF WAR OF 1812 VETERANS. May 1813 - Dec. 1820. 61 cm, 2 ft. 24 vols.

Arranged by name of State in which veteran resided, thereunder by initial letter of veteran's surname, and thereunder chronologically by date of payment.

Registers contain entries that show date, soldier's name and rank, family relationship of person paid, date pension started, monthly rate, amount payable each 6 months, and date and amount of each payment. The names of the States are not legible on most of the volumes.

For a register of payments after December 1820, see entry 588. For settled accounts, see entry 726.

588.   REGISTER OF HALF-PAY PENSIONS PAID BY THE THIRD AUDITOR TO WIDOWS AND CHILDREN OF WAR OF 1812 VETERANS. Nov. 1811-June 1833. 3 cm, 1 in. 1 vol.

Arranged alphabetically by initial letter of veteran's surname and thereunder chronologically by date paid.

Register contains entries that show veteran's name, rank, and military unit, name and family relationship (if any) of claimant, period for which pension was paid, rate per month, total paid, and when and to whom paid. This function was transferred to the Third Auditor from the Paymaster General in May 1821. The period for which pension payments were due was approximately November 1811-June 1833; the dates of the Third Auditor's payments were approximately May 1821-July 1862. For registers of payments by the Paymaster General, see entry 587. For settled accounts, see entry 726.

589.   REGISTERS OF PENSION PAYMENTS. Mar. 1789-Mar. 1872. 1.2 m, 4 ft. 25 vols.

Arranged by date of pension act, thereunder by location of pension agency, thereunder by initial letter of veteran's or pensioner's surname, and thereunder chronologically by date paid. Indexed by location of pension agency.

Registers contain entries that show location of pension agency, name of veteran or pensioner, pension rate, and record of payments. Many of the entries also show the beginning date of the pension and the date of death of the soldier or date of termination of pension. The volumes record payments under various pension acts passed between 1789 and 1858.

For the accounts and vouchers to which these registers relate, see entries 721 and 722.

590.   QUARTERLY ABSTRACTS OF PENSION PAYMENTS (PENSION ROLLS). Mar. 4,
         1817 -Mar. 29, 1819. 8 cm, 3 in. 3 vols.

Arranged geographically by location of pension agency, thereunder alphabetically by
initial letter of deceased soldier's surname, and thereunder chronologically by date of
payment. The volumes cover the following areas: (1) Maine, New Hampshire, Vermont,
Massachusetts, Connecticut, New York, New Jersey, Pennsylvania, and Maryland; (2) Virginia,
North Carolina, South Carolina, Georgia, and Tennessee; and (3) Kentucky, Ohio, Illinois, and
Missouri.
        Quarterly abstracts submitted to the Paymaster General's Office showing payments to
persons entered on pension rolls under an act of April 16, 1816, and earlier acts. For each pension
agency is shown the period covered by abstract; deceased soldier's name and rank; whether
payment was made to widow, children, or both; date half-pay pension originally started;
period covered by settlement shown in the abstract; period of time covered by payment; rate of
pension; and amount paid. Sometimes dates of final payment are shown, if the person to whom
the pension was payable became ineligible to receive further payments because of death or
remarriage.

591.   PENSION REPORTS. Jan. 1818-Dec. 1869. 61 cm, 2 ft. 4 vols. and 4 boxes.

Arranged by State, thereunder by date of pension act, and thereunder by type and date
of change in pension rolls.
        There are gaps in the date span of these records, the actual dates covered are: Jan.-Dec.
1818; Aug. 1832-Dec. 1852; Jan.-Dec. 1869.
        Chiefly reports sent to the Third Auditor by the Pension Office showing changes in the
pension rolls of the several State pension agencies (such as persons added to the rolls, changes
in pension rates, and pensioners dropped from the rolls). Generally shown is the name of the
pensioner, the act under which he was entitled to a pension, and the beginning or ending dates
of the pension payments. Also included in these reports are copies of reports from pension
agencies listing changes in their pension rolls.

MILITARY DIVISION

The Military Division was established in the Third Auditor's Office on November 10,
1885, by the consolidation of the Quartermaster, Subsistence, and Engineer Divisions. These
three Divisions had been established in the Office in September 1854. The Military Division
was abolished on October 1, 1894, when its functions were transferred to the Office of the
Auditor for the War Department (formerly by Second Auditor).
        The Military Division was responsible for the settlement of money and property
accounts for quartermaster, subsistence, engineer, and signal service officers; also accounts of the
U.S. Military Academy, military prisons, and military parks and battlefields. The settled
accounts and returns (and related records) are among records of the Land, Files, and
Miscellaneous Division. Records of related claims are among records of the Claims Division.

Correspondence

592.   REGISTERS OF QUARTERMASTER, ENGINEER, SUBSISTENCE, AND PENSION
         LETTERS AND ACCOUNTS RECEIVED. June 1874-Dec. 1895. 30 cm, 1 ft. 5 vols.

Arranged chronologically. Entries within each volume are arranged by initial letter of
title or surname of writer.
        There are gaps in the date span of these records; the actual dates covered are: June 1874-
July 1876; Oct. 1879-Dec. 1882; Dec. 1889-Dec. 1895.

Registers contain entries that show date received, name or title of writer, name of the parties involved subject of letter or description of document received, and to whom assigned for reply. Many of the letters enclosed certificates of deposit for crediting to accounts of quartermasters.

593.   REGISTER OF LETTERS RECEIVED FROM THE QUARTERMASTER GENERAL. July 1, 1886-Sept. 29, 1894. 5 cm, 2 in. 1 vol.

Arranged chronologically.
Register contains entries that show date received, subject of letter (usually of the name of a claimant), and to whom referred for reply.

594.   REGISTER OF LETTERS RECEIVED FROM THE COMMISSARY GENERAL OF SUBSISTENCE AND THE CORPS OF ENGINEERS. Dec. 2, 1889-Sept. 29, 1894. 5 cm, 2 in. 1 vol.

Arranged by office and thereunder chronologically.
Register contains entries that show date received, title of writer, to whom referred, and subject of letter.

595.   LETTERS SENT BY THE QUARTERMASTER AND COLLECTION DIVISIONS. Jan. 1, 1854-June 2, 1885. 91 cm, 3 ft. 19 vols.

Arranged chronologically. The first eight volumes are indexed by initial letter of surname of addressee. The other volumes are not indexed.
Fair copies of letters to quartermasters or their representatives, chiefly of two types: (1) those written by the Quartermaster Division acknowledging the receipt and settlement of accounts; (2) those written by the Collection Division (absorbed into the Quartermaster Division) requiring former accountable officers to pay balances charged against them in their accounts. Two volumes, dated April 18, 1862-September 28, 1864, and January 2-July 29, 1880, overlap the date span of a majority of the volumes, and relate partly to claims; an additional volume, dated September 27, 1875-June 2, 1885, consists chiefly of letters to the Secretary of the Treasury.

596.   LETTERS SENT BY THE COLLECTION DIVISION. Mar. 15, 1883-Nov. 11, 1896. 1.5 m, 5 ft. 2 vols. and 13 boxes.

Arranged chronologically. Each volume is indexed by name of addressee and name of party involved.
There are gaps in the date span of these records; the actual dates covered are: Mar. 15-June 27, 1883; Sept. 22, 1885-Oct. 9, 1888; Nov. 20, 1888-Feb. 4, 1892; Mar. 7, 1892-Dec. 21, 1893; Jan. 13-June 16, 1894; Oct. 4, 1894-Nov. 11, 1896.
Press copies of letters reflecting the two major functions of the Collection Division before its merger into the Military Division: (1) collection of delinquent balances from former accountable officers; (2) verification, at the request of the Commissioner of Pensions, of service of soldiers in the War of 1812 and later wars.
For fair copies of letters sent by the Collection Division, see entry 595.

Records Relating to Quartermaster and Other Accounts

597. REGISTERS OF QUARTERMASTERS ACCOUNTS SETTLED. Feb. 1836-Dec. 1886. 61 cm, 2 ft. 15 vols.

Arranged chronologically. Entries within each volume are arranged by initial letter of soldier's surname and thereunder by date reported.

Beginning with 1865 there are separate volumes for alphabetical groupings within a given date span. For the period 1885-86, the volume includes only surnames beginning with the letters M-Z.

Registers contain entries that show quartermaster's name and rank, where stationed, period covered by disbursements, dates received and approved, settlement number, balance reported by quartermaster, and adjusted balance.

For some of the original settled accounts before 1851, see entry 712.

598. LIST OF OFFICERS OF THE QUARTERMASTER DEPARTMENT. June 1841-June 1861. 3 cm, 1 in. 1 vol.

Arranged by location of military unit and thereunder by name of quartermaster or other accountable officer. Indexed alphabetically by name of unit.

Names of accountable officers stationed at arsenals, barracks, camps, and forts showing name and type of unit, sometimes its location, and periods covered by their accounts.

For similar registers arranged by name of officer, see entry 597.

599. LIST OF PROPERTY OF THE QUARTERMASTER DEPARTMENT SEIZED BY THE CONFEDERATE STATES OF AMERICA. Jan. 1861-Sept. 1861. 3 cm, 1 in. 1 vol.

Arranged chronologically by quarter.

Record of property seized from quartermasters and other accountable officers by authorities in Alabama, Arkansas, Florida, Georgia, Louisiana, North Carolina, and Texas showing name and rank of accountable officer, where stationed, number of the abstract and voucher of the property account on which the seized property was listed, when and to whom surrendered, and quantity and type of property. Sometimes the condition of the property is also listed. The accountable officers were eventually indemnified for the loss of the property.

CLAIMS DIVISION

The Claims Division was first established in the Office of the Third Auditor in January 1855 to settle all claims coming before the Office. At various times it shared its duties with such special claims Divisions as the Bounty Land and Soldier's Claim Division (1859); State War Claims Division (1865); Horse Claims Division (1868); and the State and Horse Claims Division (1877). The Claims Division was also merged for a time with the Miscellaneous Division and from 1865-75 was known as the Miscellaneous Claims Division. Most of the records of the Claims Division consist of claims of States and individuals relating to the Revolutionary War, the War of 1812, Indian wars, and Civil War; and of records of Commissions established to settle claims arising from the War of 1812 and the Civil War. The duties of the Claims Division were transferred to the Office of the Auditor for the War Department (formerly the Second Auditor) in October 1894.

Correspondence

600. REGISTERS OF LETTERS RECEIVED. June 17, 1817-Dec. 30, 1841. 3 cm, 1 in. 1 vols.

Arranged chronologically.

There are gaps in the date span of these records; the actual dates covered are: June 17, 1817-Apr. 18, 1818; Dec. 18, 1819-Apr. 21, 1820; Dec. 1, 1823-Jan. 4, 1825; April 10, 1835-June 30, 1836; May 18-Dec. 30, 1841.

Registers contain entries for letters relating to claims showing date received, name of writer, and subject. Most entries relate to subsistence and engineer claims.

For some of the letters to which this register relates, see entry 601.

601.   MISCELLANEOUS LETTERS AND PAPERS RECEIVED. Aug. 20, 1810-Jan. 8, 1900. 22.0 m, 72 ft. 68 boxes.

Arranged chronologically. Registers of some of these letters are in entry 600.

The letters are chiefly about accounts and claims. Included are letters concerning transfers of pensioners from the rolls of one agency to the rolls of another; letters relating to the settlement of accounts and claims and documents submitted as additional evidence in the matter of accounts and claims in dispute; horse claim files; requests for addresses of soldiers; and property returns.

602.   REGISTERS OF LETTERS AND CLAIMS RECEIVED FROM MEMBERS OF CONGRESS. Nov. 23, 1816-July 11, 1838. 5 cm, 2 in. 1 box.

Arranged chronologically.

Registers contain entries that show name of person by whom the claim was presented, date received, name of claimant, type of claim, and action taken. These claims relate primarily to property damage during the War of 1812; to compensation for goods and services furnished during the War; and to pay and bounty. Some volumes overlap one another in date span and to some extent duplicate one another in content. The dates of the letters and claims correspond to periods when Congress was in session; there generally are no entries, therefore, for the period May-November each year.

603.   REGISTER OF LETTERS RECEIVED RELATING TO STATE CLAIMS. May 28, 1866-Sept. 26, 1885. 5 cm, 2 in. 1 vol.

Arranged alphabetically by name of State or title of official and thereunder chronologically by initial letter of writer's surname.

Register contains entries that show name of State or of Government official, name of writer, date received, subject, date of reply, and occasional references to fair copies of letters sent relating to State claims (entry 617). Some of the letters registered are among the letters received relating to State claims, entry 604.

604.   LETTERS RECEIVED RELATING TO STATE CLAIMS. Apr. 29, 1861-Mar. 30, 1887. 30 cm, 1 ft. 3 boxes.

Arranged by name of State, and thereunder chronologically. A partial register is in entry 603.

There are gaps in the date span of these records; the actual dates covered are: Apr. 29, 1861-Oct. 3, 1876; Sept. 26, 1885-Mar. 30, 1887.

Letters from officials of State governments, the War Department, and from Members of Congress relating chiefly to the status of claims of States for reimbursement of expenses in raising troops during the Civil War. Some letters relate to the use of State ordnance stores by Federal troops at the start of the war.

For replies to these letters, see entries 617 and 618; for approved claim files, see entry 759.

605.   REGISTERS OF LETTERS AND CLAIMS RECEIVED. Aug. 1876-Nov. 1899. 61 cm, 2 ft.
        9 vols.

        Arranged by initial letter of surname of writer.
        There are gaps in the date span of these records; the actual dates covered are: Aug.
        1876-Aug. 1879; July 1880-Dec. 1885; May 1887-Nov. 1889; Aug. 1894-Nov. 1899.
        Registers contain entries that show date received, name of writer, and subject
        (sometimes including the number of the claim). Many of the entries relate to horse claims, land
        claims, quartermaster stores, and the commutation of rations.

606.   MISCELLANEOUS LETTERS RECEIVED RELATING TO CLAIMS. Feb. 12, 1864-Sept.
        26, 1894. 10.7 m, 35 ft. 27 boxes.

        Arranged chronologically. A register is in entry 605.
        Verification of military service, claims for quartermaster stores and commutation of
        rations, requests from congressional committees, and inquiries about the authority of certain
        claims agents to represent claimants.
        For a continuation of the letters, October 1894-May 1898, see records of the Second
        Auditor's Mail and Property Division, entry 494.

607.   REGISTER OF LETTERS SENT. May 10, 1866-Apr. 12, 1871. 1 cm, 1/2 in. 1 vol.

        Arranged chronologically.
        Register contains entries that show name and address of recipient, subject, and date
        answered or title of official to whom letter was referred for reply.
        For some of the replies registered in this volume, see entry 613.

608.   LETTERS SENT TO MEMBERS OF CONGRESS. Dec. 13, 1832-Dec. 21, 1864. 91 cm, 3 ft.
        16 vols.

        Arranged chronologically. Each volume is indexed by initial letter of surname of
        Congressman and of party in interest.
        Fair copies of letters to individual Members of Congress and to the Committee on
        Claims relating primarily to verification of military service, settlement of horse claims and
        bounty claims, claims arising from contracts, and claims for reimbursement of expenses of Pacific
        Railroad surveys.
        For other letters to Members of Congress, see letters sent relating to accounts and claims,
        entry 613.

609.   LETTERS SENT RELATING TO THE SEMINOLE INDIAN WAR. May 27, 1822-Mar. 1,
        1827. 3 cm, 1 in. 1 vol.

        Arranged chronologically. Indexed by initial letter of surname of addressee.
        Fair copies of letters relating to the settlement of Seminole Indian War claims
        presented under provisions of an act of May 4, 1822 (3 Stat. 676). The letters were sent chiefly to
        Members of Congress and to claimants or their attorneys notifying them of action taken on their
        claims for loss of horses and other property. This volume includes, in addition to the letters, a
        copy of the act; a copy of the opinion of the Attorney General, dated May 22, 1822, interpreting
        the law; rules and regulations governing the settlement of the claims by accounting officers; and
        a notice to the public about the provisions of the law.

610.   LETTERS SENT RELATING TO HORSE CLAIMS. Jan. 24, 1837-June 30, 1880. 3.7 m, 12 ft. 65 vols.

Arranged chronologically. Each volume is indexed by surname of addressee and surname of party involved.

There are gaps in the date span of these records; the actual dates covered are: Jan. 24, 1837-Dec. 5, 1842; June 11, 1844-Jan. 29, 1875; Jan. 2-June 30, 1880.

Fair copies of letters to claimants, their representatives, or Members of Congress relating to the status of claims for property lost in the military service. These claims were filed under provision of laws of January 18, 1837 (5 Stat. 142), and March 3, 1849 (9 Stat. 414). The letters usually show the claim number, summary of evidence submitted in relation to the claim, and the Third Auditor's decision.

For a continuation of these letters, see entry 612.

611.   LETTERS SENT RELATING TO HORSE CLAIM AWARDS. July 25, 1865-Aug. 2, 1866. 13 cm, 5 in. 2 vols.

Arranged chronologically. Each volume is indexed by surname of claimant.

Fair copies of letters to claimants announcing favorable action on their claims for loss of horses and other property in the military service showing date and amount of award, description and circumstances of loss, and claimant's name and address.

For letters relating to the status of claims not yet settled, see entries 610 and 612; for copies of certificates of awards of horse claims, see entry 649.

612.   LETTERS SENT RELATING TO HORSE CLAIMS. Aug. 20, 1885-June 23, 1892. 30 cm, 1 ft. 4 boxes.

Arranged chronologically. Each volume is indexed by initial letter of surname of addressee and party involved.

There are gaps in the date span of these records; the actual dates covered are: Aug. 20-Dec. 5, 1885; Feb. 9-Nov. 24, 1886; Mar. 16-June 19, 1891; Apr. 14-June 23, 1892.

Press copies of letters relating to claims for horses and other property lost in the military service. These claims were presented under provisions of a law of March 3, 1849 (9 Stat. 414). The letters are usually to claimants or their attorneys indicating the status of the claim and showing the claim number and summary of the evidence presented.

For fair copies of letters relating to horse claims, see entry 610.

613.   LETTERS SENT RELATING TO ACCOUNTS AND CLAIMS. Mar. 7, 1817-May 19, 1873. 8.8 m, 29 ft. 163 vols.

Arranged chronologically. Each volume is indexed by initial letter of surname or title of addressee or party involved. Fair copies of letters to Members of Congress, Government officials (including the Secretary of the Treasury and the Attorney General), and to accountable officers and claimants. The letters relate chiefly to settlement of a variety of accounts and claims, verification of military service, and correction of errors in accounts.

For additional letters to Members of Congress, see entry 608.

614.   LETTERS SENT RELATING TO THE OREGON AND WASHINGTON INDIAN WARS. Mar. 26, 1861-Sept. 30, 1871. 30 cm, 1 ft. 6 vols.

Arranged chronologically. Each volume is indexed by initial letter of surname of addressee or party involved.

Fair copies of letters chiefly to claimants or their attorneys relating to the receipt and settlement of claims for the Oregon and Washington Indian Wars. Some of the letters requested additional information for use in settlement of the claims.

For approved claims files and related registers, see entry 750.

615.   LETTERS SENT RELATING TO STEAMBOAT AND OTHER CLAIMS. June 3, 1863-Sept. 17, 1871. 13 cm, 5 in. 2 vols.

Arranged chronologically. Each volume is indexed by name of claimant or ship.

Fair copies of letters relating to claims for loss of steamboats or other property in the military service. These claims were filed under provisions of an act of March 3, 1849 (9 Stat. 414). Most of the claims were filed by owners of steamboats; some were damage claims filed by railroads. Other records relating to steamboat claims include claims registers (entry 658), docket books (entry 651), and approved case files (entry 652).

For additional letters relating to steamboat claims (some of which duplicate the letters in these volumes), see entry 616.

616.   LETTERS SENT RELATING TO OREGON AND WASHINGTON INDIAN WAR CLAIMS AND TO STEAMBOAT CLAIMS. Jan. 12, 1867-May 6, 1892. 30 cm, 1 ft. 3 boxes.

Arranged chronologically. The volumes for the periods January 12, 1867-January 12, 1870; October 23, 1873-October 19, 1876; and November 1, 1883-June 23, 1888, are indexed by initial letter of surname of addressee and party involved.

Press copies of letters to claimants or their representatives relating to the status of claims. Copies of additional letters relating to these two types of claims are described in entries 614 and 615, respectively.

617.   LETTERS SENT RELATING TO STATE CLAIMS. July 30, 1861-July 20, 1877. 30 cm, 1 ft. 6 vols.

One volume appears to be missing.

Arranged chronologically. Each volume is indexed by name of State, surname of addressee, or title of official. A partial register is in entry 603.

Fair copies of letters chiefly to officials of State governments and Members of Congress relating to the status or settlement of State claims for Civil War expenses, The first volume includes copies of instructions for auditing State claims and some copies of reports submitted by States concerning their disbursements. Copies of receipts for moneys advanced and copies of powers of attorney are also sometimes included.

For later letters, see entry 618; for incoming letters, see entry 604; the claim files are described in entry 759.

618.   LETTERS SENT RELATING TO STATE CLAIMS. Aug. 4, 1877-Oct. 31, 1894. 61 cm, 2 ft. 5 boxes.

Arranged chronologically. Each volume is indexed by initial letter of addressee's surname.

Press copies of letters, chiefly to State officials and Members of Congress, relating to verification of service of persons who had been paid by States for military service, recommendations for payment of State claims, and settlement of State claims for expenses of the Indian wars.

For copies of earlier letters in this series, see entry 617; for press copies of State claims letters, November 1894-October 1895, see entry 501; the claim files are described in entry 759.

619.   LETTERS SENT RELATING TO QUARTERMASTER AND OTHER CLAIMS. Sept. 1,
1871 June 16, 1888. 2.4 m, 8 ft. 82 vols.

Arranged chronologically. The first 60 volumes are indexed by initial letter of
addressee's surname. The other volumes are not indexed.
Press copies of letters to the Quartermaster General and others relating chiefly to
claims for quartermaster property seized during the Civil War and to verification of military
service. A majority of the letters are form letters stating that the information desired had not
been located.

620.   LETTERS SENT BY THE CLAIMS DIVISION. Oct. 4, 1864-Aug. 19, 1881. 1.5 m, 5 ft.
25 vols.

Arranged chronologically. Each volume except the volume for November 19, 1875-
February 4, 1876, is indexed by initial letter of addressee's surname or party involved.
There are gaps in the date span of these records. Actual dates covered are: Oct. 4, 1864-
Feb. 4, 1876; July 27, 1880-Aug. 19, 1881.
Fair copies of letters to Government officials and private claimants and their attorneys
on various types of claims, such as Civil War property damage, transportation, commutation of
rations, claims based on military service and horse claims.
For press copies of letters sent by the Claims Division, 1878-94, see entry 621.

621.   LETTERS SENT BY THE CLAIMS DIVISION. Jan. 20, 1876-Sept. 5, 1894. 4.6 m, 15 ft.
120 vols.

Arranged chronologically. The volumes for January 20, 1876-March 20, 1882, and for
September 6, 1886-September 5, 1894, are indexed by initial letter of addressee's surname and
party involved.
Press copies of letters usually to claimants or their attorneys, relating chiefly to horse
claims, quartermaster claims, and claims based on military service. Many of the letters after
1887 are form letters.
For fair copies of letters sent by the Claims Division, October 1864-February 1876, see
entry 620. For later letters, see entry 502.

RECORDS OF SPECIAL CLAIMS COMMISSIONS

RECORDS OF THE R. B. LEE COMMISSION

An act of April 9, 1816 (3 Stat. 261), authorized the payment of claims of soldiers from volunteer military units for the loss of horses, arms , or other property damaged or destroyed while in use in the military service during the War of 1812. The act also provided for payment for property taken by the Army or for damage to houses or buildings occupied for military purposes. A commissioner was to be appointed by the President to hear claims and take evidence. The Commissioner, in turn, was authorized to appoint one or more Deputy Commissioners to assist in preparing claims. Richard Bland Lee became the Commissioner of Claims under the act.

An act of March 3, 1817 (3 Stat. 397), extended the provisions of the act to claims for property lost in Indian wars, ordered the reporting of unsettled existing claims and future claims to Congress for action, authorized the Commissioner to reopen cases by taking additional testimony and considering further evidence, and required that all proposed awards of more than $200 be reviewed by the Secretary of War, who had final authority to approve or reject the awards.

An act of March 3, 1825 (4 Stat. 123), reopened for 9 months the consideration of claims that had been presented after the original deadline of April 1818 or had not been finally settled by that date. The evidence was to be presented to the Third Auditor for his examination, review, and decision. The act also called for deducting from claims the amounts already paid to the claimants and placing a limitation on the total amount that could be allowed under the new law. Outstanding claims of the War of 1812 were again reopened by an act of 1852.

622. LETTERS RECEIVED BY RICHARD B. LEE. July 1, 1816-Nov. 5, 1817. 13 cm, 5 in.

Arranged alphabetically by name of State or Territory.

After the establishment of the Lee Commission under the act of April 9, 1816, Lee sent a circular letter to prominent citizens asking for recommendations for persons to serve as Deputy Commissioners of Claims in various parts of the country, chiefly for the purpose of taking testimony for claims to be brought before the Commission. These letters are replies received from persons in Connecticut, Delaware, Indiana, Kentucky, Maryland, Mississippi Territory, New Hampshire, New Jersey, North Carolina, Ohio, Pennsylvania, Tennessee, Vermont, and Virginia. The dates of the letters vary with each State or Territory.

623. LETTERS SENT BY THE COMMISSION. July 1, 1816-Feb. 25, 1857. 13 cm, 5 in. 3 vols.

Arranged chronologically. Each volume is indexed by addressee's surname.

There are gaps in the date span of these records; the actual dates covered are: July 1, 1816-Jan. 30, 1822; Mar. 18, 1825-Aug. 9, 1838; Feb. 17, 1852-Feb. 25, 1857.

Fair copies of letters by the Commission (later the Third Auditor) in reply to inquiries about the status of claims filed under acts of April 9, 1816; March 3, 1817; and March 3, 1825. Most letters relate to damage along the Niagara frontier. A majority of the letters are dated July 1, 1816-August 9, 1838, but each volume includes a few letters dated in the 1850's.

624. INDEX TO REGISTER OF CLAIMS. ca. 1816-18. 3 cm, 1 in. 1 vol.

Arranged alphabetically by initial letter of claimant's surname.

Index to the registers of approved claims (entry 625), showing volume and page reference in the registers, claimant's name, and claim number. At the end of the entries for "Volume 5" is a list of special claims settled later, which show claimant's name, amount of award, description of property, and date and number of settlement. Volume and page references are omitted for these claims.

625.   REGISTERS OF CLAIMS. June 7, 1816-Apr. 9, 1818. 20 cm, 8 in. 5 vols.

Arranged numerically. An index is in entry 624.

Registers contain entries that show claim number (entry 627), claimant's name, date received, description of property and its location, Commission's decision, and acknowledgment of receipt of the award. The last volume includes a statistical summary showing number of claims considered, number approved, amounts claimed, amounts awarded, and a report prepared on August 16, 1878, in the Horse Claims Division concerning 27 claims that were outstanding or disallowed at the time the Commission ceased to hear claims.

626.   REPORT OF THE DEPUTY COMMISSIONERS AT LEWISTON, N.Y. Aug. 13-Dec. 2, 1817. 1 cm, 1/2 in. 1 vol.

Arranged chronologically.

Report submitted to Lee on December 2, 1817, on claims heard at Lewiston, N.Y. The report shows the claims numbers (entry 627), claimant's name, estimate of the value of real and personal property lost, abstract of testimony received, and the Commissioner's decision on the award.

627.   SETTLED CLAIM FILES AND RELATED RECORDS. Aug. 10, 1816-Dec. 5, 1854. 7.3 m, 24 ft. 22 boxes.

Arranged in three subseries as described below.

Claim files, usually consisting of correspondence, affidavits, and proof of loss, in the following groupings: (1) cases heard by the Commission, August 10, 1816-April 4, 1818 (arranged numerically); (2) cases heard by the Deputy Commissioners of Claims at Lewiston, N.Y., August 12, 1817-July 19, 1825 (arranged numerically); and (3) miscellaneous files, arranged chiefly alphabetically, consisting of additional evidence, claims presented after the deadline set by law, petitions to Congress, copies of private bills passed for the relief of the petitioners, and a descriptive list of buildings near Buffalo and Black Rock destroyed by enemy action on December 30, 1813. Also included are documents concerning the transfer of the Commission's functions to the Third Auditor in April 1818.

628.   ABSTRACTS OF CLAIMS. Apr. 30, 1818-Feb. 11, 1820. 2 cm, 1 in. 1 box.

Arranged by type of record.

Fragmentary abstracts of action taken on claims, varying in content and date scope. One fragment is a partial abstract for Buffalo and Lewiston claims, shows claim number, claimant's name, award number, amount claimed, amounts proved, amounts deducted, amount assigned to the State of New York, and net paid to claimant. Another fragment, prepared by the Deputy Commissioners of Claims at Clinton County, N.Y., for claims of citizens of New York and Vermont, shows claimant's name, claim number, and amount awarded. A few loose pages show claimant's name, amount claimed, value proved, and value not proved. A fragmentary abstract of rejected claims, arranged by claimant's surname, shows claimant's name and address, type of property destroyed or captured, amount claimed, reason for rejection by the Commission, and date of rejection.

RECORDS OF THE DAVIS-HOLT-CAMPBELL COMMISSION

The Secretary of War appointed David Davis, Joseph Holt, and Hugh Campbell as a Board of Commissioners to examine military claims in the Department of the West. The Board heard testimony during the period November 9, 1861-March 10, 1862, and its jurisdiction was limited to hearing claims presented before January 1, 1862. Joint Resolution 18, approved March 11, 1862 (12 Stat. 615), authorized payment of sums awarded by the Davis-Holt-Campbell Commission.

629.   GENERAL CORRESPONDENCE OF THE DAVIS-HOLT-CAMPBELL COMMISSION. July 17, 1861-Mar. 29, 1862. 30 cm, 1 ft. 1 box.

Arranged by subject and thereunder chronologically.

General correspondence of the Commission, consisting chiefly of (1) letters received relating to the claims, (2) copies of correspondence with the War Department relating to various military matters and activities of the Commission, and (3) official telegrams received and sent.

630.   TRANSCRIPTS OF HEARINGS OF THE COMMISSION. Nov. 9, 1861-Mar. 10, 1862. 25 cm, 10 in. 2 boxes.

Arranged chronologically. Includes a general index.

Transcripts show date, subject, name of witness, and a record of questions and answers. Claim numbers are sometimes indicated by marginal notes.

631.   ABSTRACTS OF CLAIMS AND PURCHASES SETTLED BY COL. THOMAS J. HAINES. Jan. 7, 1862-Mar. 31, 1863. 10 cm, 4 in. 1 vol.

Arranged by type of record.

This collection of the accounts of Colonel Haines, Assistant Commissary at St. Louis, includes three types of documents: (1) abstracts of claims allowed, January 20-March 31, 1862, showing date approved, voucher number, claimant's name, and amount allowed; (2) abstracts of subsistence stores purchased, January 7, 1862-March 31, 1863, showing date of purchase, voucher number, from whom purchased, explanation, and amount paid; and (3) abstracts of contingent expenses, January 3, 1862-March 31, 1863, showing date of expense, voucher number, name of person paid, explanation, and amount paid.

632.   REGISTERS OF RECEIPTS FOR REJECTED AND WITHDRAWN CLAIMS. n.d. 5 cm, 2 in. 3 vols.

Arranged by type of action and thereunder by claim number.

Registers contain entries that show receipts for claims withdrawn (2 vols.) and claims rejected (1 vol.) showing claim number (entry 634), claimant's name, explanation, the number of vouchers, amount claimed, and signature of person withdrawing the claim. Claims rejected by the Commission were typically for rent, property damage, and commutation of rations; withdrawn claims frequently related to horses, forage, harnesses, hauling, wagons, ordnance, and other goods and services.

633.   INDEX TO ALLOWED CLAIMS PAID BY COL. ALLEN BRYAN. ca. Sept. 1861. 1 cm, 1/2 in. 1 vol.

Arranged alphabetically by claimant's surname.

A partial index to the claim files (entry 634) showing claimant's name and claim number. The index covers claim numbers 4000-6484.

634.   SETTLED CLAIM FILES. ca. Apr.-Sept. 1861. 7.3 m, 24 ft. 22 boxes.

Arranged in subseries as described below. A partial index is in entry 633.
Chiefly duplicate copies of vouchers showing voucher number, name of supplier, date of purchase, article purchased, price, certification of accuracy, and notation of approval by the Commission. The date of approval is not shown. The files are arranged in the following subseries: (1) claims under $1,000 allowed in full; (2) claims under $1,000 allowed in part; (3) claims over $1,000 allowed in full; (4) claims over $1,000 allowed in part; (5) transportation claims; and (6) "reclamation" claims (i.e., cases in which the Commission considered the claims of one or more assignees separately from the claims of the original claimant).

RECORDS OF THE STEEDMAN BOARD OF CLAIMS

The Steedman Board of Claims was established by War Department Special Field Order 329, December 8, 1863, at the headquarters of the Department of the Cumberland, to convene at Jasper, Tenn., on or about December 10, 1863. The Board was to adjust the claims of citizens of Marion County, Tenn., against the Government for damage done to their property during occupation of the county by U.S. Troops. Members named to the Board by the order were Brig. Gen. James B. Steedman; Col. P. S. Post; Lt. Col. J. P. Kerr; Capt. S. B. Moe, recorder; and William Pryor and A. Kelly, citizens of Marion County, civilian members. The Board met from December 12, 1863, to February 11, 1864, and then was abolished.

635.   TRANSCRIPT OF PROCEEDINGS OF THE STEEDMAN BOARD OF CLAIMS. Dec. 12, 1863-Feb. 11, 1864. 5 cm, 2 in. 1 vol.

Arranged chronologically.
Copy of the transcript of Board proceedings showing date, name of claimant, abstract of testimony, and summary of decisions of the Board.
Marginal notes show claim number, claimant's name, amount claimed, and references to other pages in the transcript on which the same claim is mentioned. Included are copies of War Department orders establishing the Board, modifying its membership, and instructing the Board about procedures.
Also included are a list of subjects of War Department orders relating to the Board and a summary of claims showing claim number, name of claimant, whether based on an account or voucher, amount claimed, totaled allowed, and the page in the transcript on which information about the claim first appears. This copy of the transcript was made by the Commissary General of Subsistence in 1869 from the original records borrowed from the Quartermaster General.

Records Relating to Individual Claims

636.   CLAIM FILES RELATING TO SERVICE IN THE REVOLUTIONARY WAR. Nov. 1775 - June 1851. 6.4 m, 21 ft. 50 boxes.

Arranged alphabetically by soldier's surname.
Chiefly correspondence, affidavits, and other documents relating to military service. Many of the letters were written in the early 1850s.
At the end of the file is a small group of vouchers and copies of vouchers, November 1775-May 1781. The claimants (usually heirs of veterans) hoped that claimed pay or bounty was due their ancestors for military service.

637.   REGISTER OF CLAIMS FOR MILITARY SERVICE IN THE WAR OF 1812. July 1816 -
        Mar. 1827. 1 cm, 1/2 in. 1 vol.

Arranged alphabetically by initial letter of claimant's surname.

Register contains entries that show soldier's name, rank, military unit, by whom claim
was presented, and date and type of action taken on the claim. Most entries are for pay and
bounty due the soldier.

For case files on some of the claims registered in this volume, see entry 638.

638.   CLAIM FILES RELATING TO SERVICE IN THE WAR OF 1812. 1812-50. 22.9 m, 75 ft.
        60 boxes.

Arranged alphabetically by name of soldier. A partial register is in entry 637.

Chiefly correspondence, affidavits, and other documents relating to military service.
Many of the letters were written in the 1840s and 1850s by Members of Congress and others
concerning the status of the claims. A small group of files at the end of the series consists of
claims for quartermaster and subsistence stores.

639.   INDEX TO HORSE CLAIMS. Jan. 1837-Feb. 1862. 5 cm, 2 in. 1 vol.

Arranged in part numerically and in part alphabetically.

Index shows claim number or assigned number, claimant's name and military unit, by
whom claim was presented, description of loss, amount claimed, date received, and date of
award or rejection. Some of the claims were not settled until the early 1890s.

640.   REGISTERS OF MEXICAN WAR HORSE CLAIMS. Jan. 1847-Jan. 1851. 3 cm, 1 in.
        2 vols.

Arranged alphabetically by claimant's surname.

Registers contain entries that show claimant's name and military unit, amount claimed,
date and circumstances of loss, when and by whom presented, and date of award if claim was
approved.

641.   ABSTRACT OF MEXICAN WAR HORSE CLAIMS. 1846-48. 25 cm, 10 in. 6 vols.

Arranged by designation of military unit.

Abstract of horse claims by members of Volunteer units from Arkansas, Georgia, Illinois,
Kentucky, Missouri, Tennessee, and Texas showing identity of unit, claimant's name and rank,
amounts claimed for loss of horses and equipment, date and circumstances of loss, date
remounted, and date and amount of award if the claim was approved. Most of the claims were
approved in the 1850s.

642.   INDEX TO DOCKET BOOKS OF HORSE CLAIMS. Dec. 24, 1860-July 16, 1895. 10 cm,
        4 in. 2 vols.

Arranged alphabetically by initial letter of claimant's surname.

Index to docket books (entry 643) showing name of claimant and claim number. These
volumes are also a partial index to the register of horse claims, December 24, 1860-July 31, 1865
(entry 644).

643.   DOCKET BOOKS OF HORSE CLAIMS. May 25, 1865-July 16, 1895. 61 cm, 2 ft. 12 vols.

Arranged numerically. Volumes 2-12 are indexed by surname of claimant. A separate
index is in entry 642.

Docket books of claims filed under an act of March 3, 1849, showing claim number, name of claimant, his rank and military unit, by whom claim was presented, date received, type of loss, amount claimed, and record of action taken. If the claim was approved, the award number is shown.

For copies of letters sent relating to horse claims, see entries 610 and 612; for copies of certificates of award, see entry 649.

644. REGISTER OF HORSE CLAIMS. Dec. 24, 1860-July 31, 1865. 5 cm, 2 in. 1 vol.

Arranged alphabetically by initial letter of claimant's surname.

Register contains entries that show date received, claim number, claimant's name and military unit, by whom presented, and award number or date claim was rejected. This volume partially duplicates the first volume of the docket books of horse claims (entry 643). The index described in entry 642 can be used in conjunction with this register.

645. ABSTRACT OF HORSE CLAIMS (INDEX TO HORSE CLAIM AWARDS). Oct. 3, 1861 May 29, 1865. 8 cm, 3 in. 1 vol.

Arranged alphabetically by initial letter of claimant's surname.

Abstract shows claim number, date received, claimant's name and military unit, by whom presented, type of property lost, amount claimed, and date and award number, if claim was approved.

646. REGISTER OF HORSE CLAIMS REPORTED FOR ALLOWANCE. Oct. 2, 1885-June 28, 1892. 5 cm, 2 in. 1 vol.

Arranged chronologically.

Register contains entries of approved horse claims showing date reported, docket number, claimant's name, amounts claimed and allowed, amount disallowed (if any), certificate number, and file number. This information was reported monthly to the Secretary of the Treasury.

647. REGISTER OF HORSE CLAIMS REPORTED FOR REJECTION. Jan. 28, 1888-June 28, 1892. 5 cm, 2 in. 1 vol.

Arranged chronologically.

Register contains entries of disapproved claims showing date reported, docket number, claimant's name, amount claimed, and date of concurrence with rejection. This information was reported monthly to the Secretary of the Treasury.

648. REGISTER OF APPROVED HORSE CLAIMS. Aug. 22, 1866-Dec. 23, 1873. 3 cm, 1 in. 1 vol.

Arranged numerically.

Register contains entries that show account number; claimant's name, rank, and military unit; dates reported and approved; amount for which approved; and explanation (i.e., number of horses for which payment was claimed).

649. HORSE CLAIM AWARD CERTIFICATES. Mar. 1, 1837-July 28, 1866. 61 cm, 2 ft. 10 vols.

Arranged by award number and thereunder chronologically. Each volume is indexed by claimant's surname.

There are gaps in the date span of these records. Actual dates covered are: Mar. 1, 1837-Nov. 15, 1843; June 25, 1863-July 28, 1866.

Fair copies of certificates showing award number, date, claimant's name and military unit, amount awarded, amount deducted (if any), type and circumstances of loss, and payment instructions. For copies of letters notifying claimants of awards in their favor, see entry 611.

650.   ADVERSE REPORTS ON HORSE CLAIMS. Jan. 4, 1865-July 28, 1866. 5 cm, 2 in. 1 vol.

Arranged chronologically.

Fair copies of reports to claimants on the rejection of their horse claims, showing claim number, name of claimant and his representative (if any), date, abstract of basis for claim, amount claimed, reason for rejection, and notation of the date the claimant was notified of the rejection. The first part records officers' use of horses obtained from quartermasters.

651.   DOCKET BOOK FOR STEAMBOAT AND OTHER TRANSPORTATION CLAIMS. July 23, 1863-Jan. 27, 1895. 3 cm, 1 in. 1 vol.

Arranged numerically. Indexed by name of claimant and name of steamboat.

Claim number, claimant's name, explanation, and dates and notations of action taken, including award numbers or settlement numbers (if appropriate). Claims for damage to steamboats and railroads were allowable under an act of March 3, 1849, concerning the loss of horses and other property in the military service.

For settled case files and copies of award certificates, see entries 652 and 653; for letters relating to steamboat and other claims, see entries 615 and 616.

652.   SETTLED CASE FILES FOR STEAMBOAT CLAIMS. ca. 1863-88. 4.0 m, 13 ft. 2 vols. and 11 boxes.

Arranged numerically.

Claim files for damages to steamboats during the Civil War while in use by Federal troops. A file usually consists of a statement of the claim, a copy of a favorable report by the Third Auditor, and correspondence, affidavits, and other documents submitted in support of the claim. Among the latter, for example, are a ledger and journal for the SS *James Montgomery*, which was built in Louisville, Ky., in 1856 and sunk during the Civil War while being used by the Quartermaster Department.

For a docket book relating to steamboat claims, see entry 651; copies of steamboat award certificates are described in entry 653; for related correspondence, see entries 615 and 616.

653.   STEAMBOAT CLAIM AWARD CERTIFICATES. July 23, 1863-Feb. 20, 1882. 8 cm, 3 in. 1 vol.

Arranged by award number. Indexed by name of claimant and name of ship.

Fair copies of certificates, July 23, 1863-July 26, 1866, showing award number, date, act under which award was made, claimant's name, explanation, date and circumstances of loss, amount awarded, and payment instructions. A register at the back of the book consists of cases transmitted to the Comptroller for review, September 21, 1866-February 20, 1882, showing claim number, name of ship, date reported, settlement number, and amount of settlement or of supplemental claim. For a docket book of these cases, see entry 651; for case files, see entry 652. Related correspondence is described in entries 615 and 616.

654.   REGISTERS OF ACCOUNTS AND CLAIMS RECEIVED FROM THE QUARTERMASTER GENERAL. May 1, 1884-Apr. 18, 1888. 5 cm, 2 in. 1 vol.

Arranged chronologically.

Register contains entries that generally show date received, name of claimant, and type of claim, chiefly for horses, hay and other quartermaster stores.

655.   DOCKET BOOKS OF CLAIMS RECEIVED. July 1, 1863–June 29, 1894. 1.8 m, 6 ft. 29 vols.

Arranged by type of claim and thereunder chronologically. There are no volumes numbered 2 to 5.

Dockets of claims, chiefly for quartermaster stores, commutation of rations, and subsistence stores showing claim number, date received, claimant's name, type of claim, and record of the action taken. Eight volumes, July 1, 1863–December 31, 1877, relate entirely to subsistence claims and commutation of rations; the other 21 volumes, October 6, 1864–June 29, 1894, chiefly concern quartermaster stores but include some entries for subsistence claims or commutation of rations. Most of the claims recorded in these volumes were filed under provisions of an act of July 4, 1864 (13 Stat. 381), providing for settlement of claims approved by the Quartermaster General and the Commissary General of Subsistence. If a claim was approved, the settlement number, year of settlement, and amount are shown. Claims approved between 1878-94 are among miscellaneous accounts and claims, entry 712.

656.   ADVERSE REPORTS ON ACCOUNTS AND CLAIMS. Oct. 5, 1824–July 27, 1859. 30 cm, 1 ft. 8 vols.

Arranged chronologically. Each volume is indexed by officer's or claimant's surname.

There are gaps in the date span of these records; the actual dates covered are: Oct. 5, 1824-Dec. 11, 1847; Mar. 3, 1848-Oct. 23, 1852; June 29, 1854-July 27, 1859.

Fair copies of reports from the Third Auditor to the Second Comptroller ruling against officers and claimants on a variety of matters under dispute, including damage claims for the War 1812, claims relating to construction of the Cumberland Road, repair of ships chartered for use in the Florida Indian wars, and claims for subsistence and forage during the Mexican War. These reports normally give detailed information on the evidence presented and on the reasons for the Third Auditor's decision, and they frequently include a copy of the Second Comptroller's endorsement confirming the Third Auditor's adverse report. Some entries in the last volume relate to transcripts of accounts sent to the Solicitor of the Treasury through the Second Comptroller and are dated as late as October 22, 1885.

657.   INDEX TO DOCKET BOOKS OF MISCELLANEOUS CLAIMS. May 22, 1847-Dec. 30, 1897. 61 cm, 2 ft. 10 vols.

Arranged alphabetically by claimant's surname.

Index to docket books in entry 658 showing claimant's name and claim number. The earliest volume (1847-68) includes a separate section listing claimants for a share of the award for the capture of Jefferson Davis (claim 17,728). Some of the approved claims listed in these volumes, if settled between 1847-50 or 1878-97, are among the miscellaneous accounts and claims, entry 712.

658.   DOCKET BOOKS OF MISCELLANEOUS CLAIMS. May 22, 1847-Feb. 11, 1913. 4.0 m, 13 ft. 53 vols.

Arranged numerically. The first 18 volumes and the last 3 volumes are indexed alphabetically by claimant's surname. A separate index to the first 50 volumes is in entry 657. Volume 7 appears to be missing.

There are gaps in the date span of these records; actual dates covered are: May 22, 1847-Apr. 30, 1895; Sept. 9, 1907-Sept. 29, 1908; Mar. 2, 1909-Mar. 25, 1910; Aug. 23, 1911-Feb. 11, 1913.

Claim number, claimant's name, when and from whom received, type and amount of claim, and notation of action taken. If a claim was approved, the settlement number, year of settlement, and amount are shown. Approved claims dated 1847-50 and 1878-97 are among miscellaneous accounts and claims, entry 712. The Second Comptroller's registers of these accounts are described in entry 209.

659.   REGISTER OF CLAIMS. Jan. 14, 1878-Dec. 30, 1885. 5 cm, 2 in. 1 vol.

Arranged by type of claim and thereunder chronologically.

Register contains entries of horse claims approved and rejected, January 14-December 30, 1878; State war claims, January 18-February 23, 1885; expense claims of the Bureau of Refugees, Freedmen, and Abandoned Lands, March 14, 1881-July 9, 1885; and miscellaneous claims, January 14, 1878- December 23, 1885. Although the information varies with the type of claim, the entries generally show dates received and settled, claimant's name, and amounts allowed. Many of the miscellaneous claims relate to payment for subsistence and quartermaster stores taken from loyal citizens in Northern States under provisions of an act of July 4, 1864 (13 Stat. 381).

INDIAN DIVISION

The Indian Division was established in October 1894 and assumed all functions of the former Second Auditor relating to the receipt and settlement of accounts and claims concerning Indians, including records of supplies purchased and transported to Indian agencies.

Decisions and Correspondence

660.   DIGEST OF DECISIONS RELATING TO INDIAN MATTERS. Oct. 6, 1894-Jan. 4, 1902. 3 cm, 1 in. 1 vol.

Arranged numerically and thereunder chronologically. Indexed by subject of decision.

Digest shows subject, an abstract of the Auditor's opinion, and date approved by the Comptroller. The subjects include legal age for Indians to receive annuities, jurisdiction over Indian depredation claims, surveys of Indian lands, Cherokee removal, and pay of Indian inspectors.

661.   LETTERS SENT BY THE INDIAN DIVISION. Dec. 11, 1895-Dec. 8, 1897. 18 cm, 7 in. 1 box.

Arranged chronologically. Each volume is indexed by initial letter of title or addressee's surname.

There are gaps in the date span of these records; the actual dates covered are: Dec. 11, 1895-Feb. 11, 1896; Aug. 8-Oct. 23, 1896; Jan. 9- May 10, 1897; Oct. 4-Dec. 8, 1897.

Press copies of letters to Indian agents, other Government officials, and private persons relating to settlement of accounts, settlement of claims for goods and services furnished for the Indian Service, expenses of educating Indian children, land titles, and timber sales.

For earlier letters on similar subjects, see entries 468 and 469.

Records Relating to Indian Agents' Accounts and Claims

662.   REGISTER OF BONDS OF INDIAN DISBURSING OFFICERS (BOND BOOK, INDIAN SERVICE, VOL. 1). Mar. 27, 1819-Mar. 27, 1900. 5 cm, 2 in. 1 vol.

Arranged alphabetically by initial letter of officer's surname.

Register contains entries that show officer's name and title; date of appointment, oath of office, and bond; amount of bond; and duty station or special assignment.

For a register of bonds showing the names of the officer's sureties, see entry 471. The original bonds are in Records of the Bureau of Accounts (Treasury), RG 39.

663.   INDEXES TO REGISTERS OF INDIAN AGENTS ACCOUNTS (NEW SERIES). June 1909-Sept. 1917. 5 cm, 2 in. 2 vols.

Arranged alphabetically by initial letter of name of school or surname of agent.

Indexes to volumes 5 and 6 of the registers of Indian agents accounts, new series, entry 664, showing names and page numbers.

664.   REGISTERS OF INDIAN AGENTS ACCOUNTS (NEW SERIES). July 1894-Oct. 1922. 61 cm, 2 ft. 6 vols.

Arranged alphabetically by name of agent, and thereunder chronologically. Indexed by name of agent and name of school for which he disbursed funds. A separate index to volumes 5 and 6 is in entry 663.

Registers contain entries that show officer's name and title, date and amount of bond, dates of service, names of predecessors and successors in office, dates accounts received and settled, period covered, settlement number (entry 717), adjusted balance, and summary of collections and disbursements. A few entries in volume 1 are dated as early as August 1890. Some entries in volumes 1 and 2 contain separate data for cash accounts and for property returns.

For registers of Indian agents accounts, ca. 1817-94, see entry 472.

665.   REGISTERS OF INDIAN ACCOUNTS RECEIVED. July 1, 1895-June 30, 1903. 5 cm, 2 in. 2 vols.

Arranged alphabetically by initial letter of officer's surname.

Registers contain entries that show officer's name and title or duty station, date and amount of bond, dates accounts for each quarter were forwarded and received, file location, ledger reference, and page reference to the requisition book.

666.   REGISTER OF INDIAN ACCOUNTS SETTLED. May 14, 1892-Jan. 6, 1900. 2 cm, 1 in. 1 vol.

Arranged chronologically by date reported. Indexed alphabetically by officer's surname.

Register contains entries that show number of letters written (for accounts settled before October 1, 1895); officer's name and duty station; date of bond; number and type of accounts received; dates received, reported, and confirmed; settlement number (entries 505 and 717); total disbursements; and adjusted balance.

667.   NUMERICAL REGISTERS OF INDIAN SETTLEMENTS. Oct. 1, 1894-June 13, 1911. 25 cm, 10 in. 4 vols.

Arranged by settlement number and thereunder chronologically.

Registers contain entries that show settlement number (entry 717), officer's or claimant's name, whether settlement was for an account or a claim, date settled, and amount. Beginning with the settlements for July 3, 1907, the entries show only settlement number, date approved, and volume and page references to registers of Indian agents' accounts (new series), entry 664.

668. REGISTERS OF INDIAN AGENTS ACCOUNTS, REQUISITIONS, AND CERTIFICATES OF DEPOSIT (INDIAN FISCAL OFFICERS BALANCED ACCOUNTS). Apr. 1912-July 1923. 23 cm, 9 in. 3 vols.

Arranged alphabetically by initial letter of agent's surname.

Registers contain entries that show accountable officer's name and title, date and amount of bond, disbursement limit, and appropriate information, including dates accounts were sent and received, amounts of requisitions, and sources and amounts of funds deposited.

669. NUMERICAL REGISTERS OF INDIAN FISCAL OFFICERS SETTLEMENTS. Aug. 23, 1907-Apr. 30, 1921. 8 cm, 3 in. 3 vols.

Arranged numerically.

There are gaps in the date span of these records; the actual dates covered are: Aug. 23, 1907-June 30, 1917; May 13, 1919-Apr. 30, 1921.

Registers contain entries that show dates received and settled, settlement number (entry 717), officer's name and account number, and number of accounts submitted. The entries for 1907-17 include volume and page references to registers of Indian agents accounts (new series), entry 664. The 1919-21 volume omits this reference but includes summary information on collections and disbursements reflected in the account.

670. REGISTER OF AUTHORIZED EXPENSES FOR THE INDIAN SERVICE (BOND REGISTER, INDIAN SERVICE). Mar. 11-Sept. 23, 1902. 5 cm, 2 in. 1 vol.

Arranged by initial letter of officer's surname.

Register contains entries that show date of authorization, name of authorized party (i.e., Indian agent, Indian agency, or school), authorization number, explanation, and sometimes voucher number and settlement number (entry 717) in which the expenditure was reflected.

671. REGISTER OF INDIAN DEPREDATION CLAIMS. Aug. 17, 1892-Oct. 29, 1900. 3 cm, 1 in. 1 vol.

Arranged by date of act under which claim was filed and thereunder by date of judgment.

Register contains entries that show (under each act of Congress) claim number, in whose favor, date and amount of judgment, docket number, and names of attorneys. Some entries also show amount allowed for attorneys' fees. A separate section of the book, relating to claims allowed in 1897, shows settlement number, in whose favor, amount, and name of the Indian tribe involved.

672. RECORD OF CLAIMS RECEIVED AND SETTLED. Jan. 4, 1897-Apr. 10, 1899. 2 cm, 1 in. 1 vol.

Arranged chronologically.

Register contains entries that show date received, claimant's name, settlement number (entry 717), and amount allowed. The volume also includes such additional miscellaneous information as lists of payments of claims arising from the Rogue River wars, August 14, 1854-April 2, 1890; numbers of accounts on hand, received, and settled by specific individual clerks in the Third Auditor's Office; and lists of distances between Indian schools and agencies and the military posts nearest them.

673.   REGISTERS OF CLAIMS FOR EXPENSES FOR THE INDIAN SERVICE. Oct. 2, 1900-July 23, 1907. 15 cm, 6 in. 2 vols.

Arranged by type of service (e.g., advertising) or subject (e.g., Osage Agency) and thereunder chronologically. Each volume is indexed by initial letter of subject or claimant's surname.

Registers contain entries that show claimant's name, explanation, amounts claimed and allowed, date received, and settlement number, entry 717. Additional claims for this period are included in the register of Indian claims (new series), entry 675.

674.   INDEXES TO REGISTERS OF INDIAN CLAIMS (NEW SERIES). July 1, 1907-June 30, 1913. 5 cm, 2 in. 4 boxes.

Arranged chronologically.

Indexes to volumes 14-30 of the registers of Indian claims (new series), entry 675, showing date, settlement number, and page reference to the registers.

675.   REGISTERS OF INDIAN CLAIMS (NEW SERIES). Aug. 1, 1894-Mar. 29, 1923. 1.2 m, 4 ft. 19 vols.

Arranged alphabetically by initial letter of claimant's surname.

An index to volumes 14-30 (the first 17 volumes of this series) is in entry 674.

Registers contain entries that show date received, claimant's name, explanation, amounts claimed and allowed, date confirmed, and settlement number (entry 718).

For registers of Indian claims, 1817-94, see entry 474. Other claims for expenditures for the Indian service, 1900-1907, are described in entry 673.

676.   REGISTERS OF INDIAN CLAIMS. ca. 1909-16. 20 cm, 8 in. 3 vols.

Arranged chronologically. Within each volume, entries are arranged by name of Indian tribe and thereunder chronologically. Each volume is indexed by the name of the tribe.

Registers contain entries that show name of tribe, numbers assigned to individual Indians, names of Indians, sometimes dates of birth or death, settlement numbers, notations relating to payment, and amounts due or paid.

Sometimes family relationships among various Indians are indicated. The claims appear to relate primarily to allotments and trust-fund payments.

677.   REGISTERS OF INDIAN CLAIMS. July 1, 1913-June 30, 1921. 18 cm, 7 in. 2 vols.

Arranged alphabetically by initial letter of claimant's surname.

Registers contain entries that show claimant's name, dates received and approved, explanation, claim number, settlement number (entry 718), and amount allowed.

For additional registers of settlements, see entry 675.

678.   REGISTER OF SUITS AGAINST INDIAN AGENTS. Jan. 1898. 3 cm, 1 in. 1 vol.

Arranged alphabetically by initial letter of agent's surname.

Indexed by initial letter of surname.

Register contains entries of suits against delinquent agents showing agent's name and title, date of bond, number and date of last settlement, balance remaining, and notations of efforts made to collect the balance.

For an earlier volume, see entry 478.

Records of Payments to Indian Tribes

679.   RECORD OF ANNUITY PAYMENTS TO INDIAN TRIBES. July 9, 1894-Mar. 17, 1899.
3 cm, 1 in. 1 vol.

Arranged alphabetically by name of tribe.
Date of account, name of Indian tribe and of the Indian agency at which annuity was
paid, period covered, disbursing officer's name, voucher number, period covered by account, and
date and settlement number, entry 717.
For earlier volumes, see entry 479. This volume is partially duplicated by the register
of Indian annuity payments, entry 680.

680.   REGISTER OF INDIAN ANNUITY PAYMENTS. Feb. 1894-Apr. 1923. 8 cm, 3 in. 1 vol.

Arranged by initial letter of name of tribe and thereunder chronologically. Indexed by
initial letter of surname of Indian agent responsible for paying the annuity.
Annuity payment register showing date paid, name of tribe and agency at which
payment was made, period for which paid, and settlement number, entries 717 and 718. This
volume partially duplicates the records of annuity payments to Indian tribes, entries 479 and
679.

681.   RECORD OF PAYMENTS TO INDIAN ALLOTTEES. Mar. 6, 1909-Dec. 31, 1913. 2 cm,
1 in. 1 vol.

Arranged alphabetically by name of tribe and thereunder by settlement date. Indexed
by name of tribe.
Name of tribe, balance available in the allotment fund, date and number of settlement
(entries 717 and 718), amount paid, and remaining balance. Sometimes the names of individual
Indians are shown.

682.   ALLOTMENT ROLLS FOR SIOUX INDIANS. n.d. 15 cm, 6 in. 6 vols.

Arranged by name of tribe and thereunder generally alphabetically by Indian's name.
Allotment lists compiled under provisions of acts of March 2, 1889 (25 Stat. 388), and
June 10, 1896 (29 Stat. 321), showing, in general, name of tribe, allotment number, and Indian's
name. Sometimes dates and amounts of specific payments are shown from 1891 to 1935. There are
separate volumes of allotment rolls for the following tribes of Sioux Indians: Rosebud; Standing
Rock, Lower Brule/Cheyenne River, Santee, and Flandreau.
A consolidated volume, indexed by name of tribe, includes records of payments made
primarily January 8, 1914, to October 10, 1919. Most of the individual volumes include only
occasional dates.

683.   RECORD OF PAYMENTS TO PUYALLUP ALLOTTEES. Oct. 16, 1895-Oct. 5, 1915. 5 cm,
2 in. 1 vol.

Arranged alphabetically by initial letter of allottee's surname and thereunder
chronologically by date of settlement.
Payments made by the Commission established by the acts of August 19, 1890 (26 Stat.
336), and March 3, 1893 (27 Stat. 612), to appraise the lands allotted to the Puyallup tribe and
sell the lands for the benefit of members of the tribe. Included are the name of allottee, date
and number of settlement (entries 717 and 718), date and number of certificate of deposit for sale
of the land, and number, date, and amount of revenue covering warrant issued.
For other records of land patents of Puyallup allottees, see entry 684.

684.   MEMORANDUMS OF LAND PATENT ACCOUNTS OF PUYALLUP ALLOTTEES. May 1891-Jan. 1902. 8 cm, 3 in. 2 vols.

This series appears to be missing.

Arranged numerically by land patent number.

Memorandums showing land patent number, name of allottee, name of purchaser, date of purchase, sale price, names of persons entitled to share in the proceeds, proportionate shares of each, net amounts paid, dates of payment, and settlement numbers, entries 717 and 718. Many entries in the memorandums refer to letters from the Secretary of the Interior, who had jurisdiction over the use of the funds as provided in the act of March 3, 1893. The funds raised from the sale of Puyallup lands were deposited in the U.S. Treasury for the benefit of the Indians.

For an additional record of the distribution of funds from the land patents, see entry 683.

685.   NEZ PERCE INDIAN ANNUITY PAYROLLS. Mar. 1895-Feb. 1900. 8 cm, 3 in. 1 vol.

Arranged chronologically and thereunder by initial letter of Indian's surname.

Annuity payrolls submitted by Indian agents John Lowe, S. G. Fisher, and C. T. Stranahan as part of their respective accounts. Each payroll shows annuitant's payroll number, name, age, sex, relationship to other Indians (wife, son, daughter, etc.), amount to which he was entitled, amount paid, marks and signatures of Indians and witnesses, dates payment received, and other remarks.

686.   CHOCTAW AND CHICKASAW ANNUITY PAYROLLS. Oct. 1904-Feb. 1907. 20 cm, 8 in. 3 vols.

Arranged numerically by the number assigned each Indian.

Payrolls of annuities due from the proceeds of sales of town lots in the Choctaw and Chickasaw Indian Nation and submitted to the Third Auditor as part of the accounts of Indian agents J. Blain Shoenfeldt and Dana H. Kelsey. The payrolls show name of Indian, payroll number, relationship to other Indians in the family group (usually arranged as husband-wife-sons daughters), age, sex, amount to which Indian was entitled per year, amount paid, check number, marks or signatures of Indians and witnesses, date paid and "remarks," usually to indicate changes or corrections of names.

Other Records

687.   JOURNALS OF SUPPLIES FOR THE INDIAN SERVICE. May 3, 1895-July 16, 1906. 2.1 m, 7 ft. 35 vols.

Arranged chronologically. Entries within each volume are arranged by name of contractor and thereunder chronologically. Each volume is indexed by contractor's name. Beginning with the contracts recorded for July 1901, there are four volumes per year, each covering a specific alphabetical range of contractor's names.

Journals contain entries showing contractor's name and address, date of contract, place of delivery, contract number (entry 227), settlement number (entry 717), delivery date, agency to which delivery was made, description of goods delivered (including identification and weights of various packages and quantity and type of goods delivered), and cost. Some "open market" purchases are also recorded in these journals.

For earlier journals of Indian supplies, see entry 485.

688.   RECORD OF GOODS TRANSPORTED BY WAGON. July 1898-Dec. 1899. 10 cm, 4 in.
         2 vols.

Arranged alphabetically by agency name. Each volume is indexed by agency name.
The records show agency for which shipment was intended, place and date of delivery,
from whom purchased, settlement number (entry 717), description of goods delivered, and
citation of account in which transportation expenses were paid.
For an earlier volume, see entry 489.

689.   TRANSPORTATION RECORD. July-1899-June 1900. 13 cm, 5 in. 2 vols.

Arranged by package number.
Package number, contractor's name, settlement number (entry 717), weight and contents
of each package, account in which transportation expenses were paid, and agency to which
goods were delivered.
For earlier volumes, see entry 490.

690.   RECEIPTS FROM TRANSPORTATION COMPANIES. Nov. 2-30, 1896. 3 cm, 1 in. 1 box.

Arranged chronologically.
Copies of transportation receipts showing name of the railroad or other company,
description of goods, package numbers and weights, and origin and destination of the shipment.

691.   LISTS OF SERIAL NUMBERS OF PACKAGES ASSIGNED TO INDIAN
         WAREHOUSES FOR OPEN MARKET PURCHASES. Jan. 1900-June 1909. 30 cm, 1 ft.
         9 vols.

Arranged geographically by location of warehouse and thereunder numerically.
The volumes contain lists of package serial numbers, including the location of
warehouse (usually New York City, St. Louis, Omaha, or San Francisco), date the numbers were
assigned, group of numbers assigned, name of contractor, and names of agencies or schools for
which the goods had been purchased.

692.   RECORD OF SETTLEMENT NUMBERS FOR RAILROAD CLAIMS. May 5, 1902-May
         18, 1906. 1 cm, 1/2 in. 1 vol.

Arranged numerically.
The record shows settlement number (entry 717), name of railroad company, and name of
examiner. No dates are shown in this volume, but the dates of settlement for these numbers are
shown in the numerical register of Indian settlements, 1894-1911, entry 667.

693.   REGISTER OF MISCELLANEOUS INDIAN EXPENSES. Mar. 6, 1905-June 24, 1907.
         5 cm, 2 in. 1 vol.

Arranged by name of school, agency, or accountable officer and thereunder
chronologically. Indexed alphabetically by name of school, agency, or officer.
Register contains entries that show name of school, agency, or officer; dates account was
forwarded and received; file, settlement, and voucher numbers; amount; explanation; and
period covered by expenditures.
Expenditures typically included telephone rental, dental services, wood, office
supplies, horseshoe nails, cement, and lubricating oil.

694.   REGISTER OF DEPOSITS (DEPOSITS OF COMMISSIONER OF INDIAN AFFAIRS). Dec. 12, 1904-Feb. 28, 1912. 1 cm, 1/2 in. 1 vol.

Arranged chronologically.
Register contains a record of deposits of Indian moneys that shows date and number of certificate of deposit, by whom deposited, disposition, source of funds (usually "Indian Moneys, Proceeds of Labor"), and amount deposited. These funds were covered into the Treasury.

695.   REGISTER OF INDIAN TRUST FUNDS DEPOSITED. Mar. 1908-Sept. 1909. 1 cm, 1/2 in. 1 vol.

Arranged alphabetically by initial letter of officer's surname.
Register contains entries that show name of accountable officer, quarter during which funds were deposited, and name and location of bank receiving the deposit.

696.   REGISTER OF SETTLED ACCOUNTS OF OKLAHOMA BANKS SERVING AS FISCAL AGENTS. Oct. 1911-Sept. 1918. 8 cm, 3 in. 1 vol.

Arranged alphabetically by location of bank.
Register contains entries of settled accounts of banks acting as Indian fiscal agents under provisions of an act of March 3, 1911 (36 Stat. 1058), that show bank's name and location, date and amounts of surety bonds and renewal authorizations, dates of account and receipt of accounts current, period covered, amounts of interest accrued or moneys deposited or transferred, settlement number (entry 717), and adjusted balance of account.

697.   RECORD OF INDIAN FUNDS ON DEPOSIT IN OKLAHOMA BANKS. Dec. 31, 1921-June 30, 1922. 5 cm, 2 in. 1 vol.

Arranged alphabetically by name of city.
Record of Indian deposit balances as of December 31, 1921, showing name and location of bank, name of Indian tribe, and balance of principal and interest accounts for the tribe. In a few cases, interest is posted as of June 30, 1922, and a revised total is shown. The accounts are chiefly for the Chickasaw, Choctaw, and Creek Nations.

698.   RECORD OF CHARGES AND STOPPAGES AGAINST ACCOUNTABLE OFFICERS AND CONTRACTORS. Jan. 4, 1895-Mar. 12, 1901. 1 cm, 1/2 in. 1 vol.

Arranged alphabetically by initial letter of officer's or contractor's surname.
Settlement number (entry 717), officer's or contractor's name, amount to be deducted from payments due him, explanation, titles of appropriations concerned, and number of settlement in which the deduction was actually made.

699.   REGISTERS OF INDIAN LEASES. Oct. 1895-Nov. 1905. 1.5 m, 5 ft. 46 vols.

Arranged by State. Within each volume the entries are arranged alphabetically by initial letter of surname of lessor and thereunder chronologically. Each volume is indexed by lessor's surname.
Registers contain entries that show the school or agency through which the lease was administered, the date of lease, identification of the allotment number, and legal description of the land; names of parties; purpose and terms; and usually a record of payments made under the lease.
The schools and agencies were located in Idaho, Kansas, Nebraska, Oklahoma, Oregon, South Dakota, and Washington. Leases for this period have not been located, but later leases of agricultural lands are in entry 140.

LAND, FILES, AND MISCELLANEOUS DIVISION

The Land, Files, and Miscellaneous Division was established on October 1, 1894, primarily to settle accounts relating to the Interior Department that had formerly been audited by the First and Fifth Auditors and adjusted by the First Comptroller. Among the types of accounts handled by the Division were those of Receivers of Public Moneys; both for land sales and as disbursing agents; accounts of the Surveyors General, Deputy Surveyors, and other Land Office personnel; and accounts of disbursing agents of the Department of the Interior, Geological Survey, Patent Office, Census Bureau, and all other disbursing officers of the Interior Department except pension agents and officers of the Bureau of Indian Affairs. Settled military accounts were transferred to the Office of the Auditor for the War Department (formerly Second Auditor), and military records for the Revolutionary War and for the War of 1812 were transferred to the Office of the Secretary of War. All accounts and claims settled in any Division of the Auditor's Office were sent to the Land, Files, and Miscellaneous Division for filing.

Correspondence

700. REGISTERS OF LETTERS RECEIVED. Oct. 1894-June 1908. 10 cm, 4 in. 2 vols.

Arranged alphabetically by initial letter of writer's surname and thereunder chronologically by date received.

Registers contain entries that show dates letters were written, received, and answered; writer's name and address; number assigned to the letter, and subject. Many of the letters related to the surety bonds or accounts of disbursing officers for the Geological Survey, for officials of land offices, and for institutions in the District of Columbia. A few of the entries are dated as late as February 1909.

701. LETTERS RECEIVED ACKNOWLEDGING RECEIPT OF FUNDS. Jan. 6, 1809-July 7, 1876. 15.2 m, 50 ft. 45 boxes.

Arranged chronologically. There are gaps in the date span of this series; the actual dates covered are: Jan. 6, 1809-Dec. 22, 1811; Feb. 12, 1851; Jan. 5, 1874-July 7, 1876.

Letters primarily from accountable officers reflecting amount received, number of draft, number of warrant on which draft was issued, and sometimes the purpose for which the funds were to be used. Many of the letters are from pension agents.

For related receipts, see entry 716.

702. LETTERS RECEIVED FROM THE CHIEF CLERK OF THE GEOLOGICAL SURVEY. July 1, 1905-Aug. 16, 1907. 10 cm, 4 in. 1 vol.

Arranged chronologically.

Information copies of letters from the Chief of the Geological Survey to the Director of the Survey authorizing the expenditures of funds for specific purposes requested by the Director. In many cases notations show voucher and settlement numbers in which the expenditures were recorded.

703. LETTERS SENT RELATING TO PUBLIC LANDS. Oct. 8, 1894-May 21, 1897. 13 cm, 5 in. 5 vols. in two boxes.

Arranged chronologically. Each volume is indexed by initial letter of surname of addressee or party in interest.

Press copies of letters to surveyors and other Land Office officials, including the Commissioner of the General Land Office, relating to settlement of accounts for surveying lands under contract (entry 126) and other accounts and claims; and letters to the Comptroller requesting his decision on major matters relating to public lands.

704.   LETTERS SENT BY THE MISCELLANEOUS SECTION. Oct. 1, 1894-Dec. 28, 1899. 61 cm, 2 ft. 15 vols.

Three volumes appear to be missing.

Arranged chronologically. Each volume is indexed by initial letter of addressee's surname, by name of party in interest, and by title of appropriation concerned.

Press copies of letters relating chiefly to settlement of accounts of disbursing agents for the Department of the Interior. Most are form letters.

Records Relating to Public Lands

705.   REGISTERS OF ACCOUNTS OF RECEIVERS OF PUBLIC MONEYS FOR SALE OF LANDS. July 1, 1894-June 30, 1912. 20 cm, 8 in. 3 vols.

Arranged alphabetically by location of land office and thereunder chronologically.

Registers contain entries that show location of Land Office, receiver's name and date of surety bond, period covered by accounts, dates received and approved, settlement numbers, previous balance, abstracts of debits (including cash sales, commissions, and fees) and credits (including moneys deposited), total miscellaneous debits and credits, and remaining balance.

706.   REGISTERS OF ACCOUNTS OF RECEIVERS OF PUBLIC MONEYS AND OF SURVEYORS GENERAL. Oct. 15, 1894-July 5, 1917. 18 cm, 7 in. 4 vols.

Arranged by type of official and thereunder chronologically.

Registers contain entries that show date; settlement number; name, title, and duty station of accountable officer, type of account (usually land sales, commissions, or contingent expenses), period covered, and date approved; and adjusted balance, if any. Beginning in 1907 the type of official (e.g., special disbursing agent) is shown in place of the type of account. The information on accounts of Surveyors General appears in each volume at the end of the information on accounts of receivers of public moneys.

707.   REGISTERS OF MISCELLANEOUS LAND ACCOUNTS AND CLAIMS. Oct. 4, 1894 June 11, 1913. 8 cm, 3 in. 2 vols.

Arranged chronologically.

Registers contain entries that show date received, settlement number (entry 719), name of claimant or accountable officer, explanation, period covered, date approved, and adjusted balance.

708.   REGISTERS OF ACCOUNTS OF SPECIAL DISBURSING AGENTS AND SURVEYORS GENERAL. July 1, 1894-June 30, 1912. 25 cm, 10 in. 4 vols.

Arranged by type of official and thereunder alphabetically by location of Land Office. The accounts of special disbursing agents in each State are listed before the accounts of Surveyor General for the several States.

Registers contain entries that show official's name, title, date of bond, location of Land Office, settlement number, period covered by accounts, and dates received and settled. For accounts of disbursing agents, entries show total earnings of the Land Office, amounts of cash deposited, salaries of registers and receivers, contingent expenses of the Land Office, and adjusted balance. For accounts of Surveyors General, the data shown include salaries and contingent expenses of the Surveyor General's Office, deposits by individuals for lands surveys, expenses of surveying public lands, and miscellaneous credits.

Records Relating to Bounty Land Cases

709. REGISTER OF BOUNTY LAND SCRIP ISSUED. Apr. 14, 1836-May 11, 1846. 5 cm, 2 in. 1 vol.

Arranged numerically.

Register contains entries that show number and date of certificate issued; number of acres for which issued; cash value; to whom issued; military service for which it was issued; number, date, and name of owner of original land warrant; number of acres to which owner was entitled; number of acres not claimed; date application was received from the General Land Office; application number; and net acreage for which scrip was issued. This scrip was issued for Revolutionary War service under provisions of an act of March 3, 1835 (4 Stat. 771), which extended the time limit of earlier acts relating to the claiming of land for military service.

710. REGISTERS OF BOUNTY LAND AND PENSION CLAIMS. July 1851-Feb. 1861. 5 cm, 2 in. 2 vols. in 1 box.

Arranged by initial letter of claimant's surname and thereunder by date certified to the Commissioner of Pensions.

Registers contain entries of claims received from the Commissioner of Pensions for verification, showing claimant's name, rank, and military unit; dates claim was received from and returned to the Commissioner of Pensions; and the war in which service was claimed. One volume, ca. April 1852-April 1853, concerns claims filed under the act of September 28, 1850 (9 Stat. 520); the other volume, ca. July 1851-February 1862, concerns claims filed under bounty land acts passed before the act of September 28, 1850.

For a later register of bounty land and pension claims, see entry 711 which is also contained in this box.

711. REGISTERS OF BOUNTY LAND AND PENSION CASES CERTIFIED TO THE COMMISSIONER OF PENSIONS. Aug. 7, 1875-Aug. 10, 1879. 3 cm, 1 in. 2 vols. in 1 box.

Arranged chronologically.

There are gaps in the date span of these records; the actual dates covered are: Aug. 7, 1875-Aug. 25, 1876; Sept. 18, 1878-Aug. 10, 1879.

Registers contain entries of claims for bounty land or pensions based on service in the War of 1812, showing claim number, dates claim was received from and returned to the Commissioner of Pensions, claimant's name, and whether the claim was for bounty land or for a pension.

For earlier registers of bounty land and pension claims, arranged by claimant's surname, see entry 710 which is in this box.

Settled Accounts and Claims and Related Records

712. SETTLED ACCOUNTS AND CLAIMS. Mar. 11, 1817-Dec. 27, 1897. 1,450.9 m, 4,760 ft. 2078 boxes.

Arranged numerically.

There are gaps in the date span of these records; the actual dates covered are: Mar. 11, 1817-Dec. 28, 1850 (boxes 1-2376); Feb. 4, 1878-Dec. 27, 1897 (boxes 1-609 are dated 1878-1883; boxes 610-2078 are dated 1878-1899). Boxes 1817-1850, there are boxes 1191A and 1944A. Boxes dated 1878-1833, there are boxes 64A and 231A. For boxes dated 1878-1899 there are no boxes numbered 1742-1784 or 2019 - 2020.

Settled accounts and claims of disbursing officers, other accountable officers, contractors, transportation companies, and other individuals. Each account or claim file consists primarily of a report by the Auditor, an abstract of disbursements and related vouchers, and sometimes other supporting documents or correspondence. Claim files, formerly a part of this series, include State claims (entry 759) and claims approved by the Southern Claims Commission (entry 732). Copies of audit reports and of certificates of settlement before 1850 are described in entries 714 and 715.

For indexes and docket books of miscellaneous claims dated after 1878, see entries 657 and 658; for Second Comptroller's reports of these accounts, are see entries 208, 209, and 259.

712A.   SETTLED ACCOUNTS AND CLAIMS. 1894-1908. 608 boxes.

Similar to accounts found in Entry 116. See Entry 705, 706 and 707 for registers. These accounts and claims appear to relate to land. They have not yet been described.

713.   INDEX TO AUDIT REPORTS. Mar. 11, 1817-Dec. 30, 1820. 5 cm, 2 in. 1 vol.

Arranged by initial letter of accountable officer's or claimant's surname.
Index to volumes 1-7 of the audit reports (entry 714) showing officer's or claimant's name and report number.

714.   AUDIT REPORTS. Mar. 11, 1817-Feb. 26, 1836. 1.5 m, 5 ft. 27 vols.

Arranged numerically. Volumes 5 (Feb. 15-Oct. 9, 1819) and 7-29 (May 19, 1820-Feb. 26, 1836) are each indexed by accountable officer's or claimant's surname. A separate index to volumes 1-7 is in entry 713. Volumes 2 and 3 appear to be missing.
Fair copies of Third Auditor's reports to the Second Comptroller on the examination of accounts and claims presented for settlement showing date, settlement number, officer's or claimant's name, summary of debits and credits, explanation of differences, and balance due to or from the United States.
For other copies of these reports, see the settled accounts and claims (entry 712) and the certificates of settlement (entry 715).

715.   CERTIFICATES OF SETTLEMENT. Mar. 11, 1817-Feb. 23, 1894. 39.9 m, 131 ft. Unbound records.

Arranged numerically.
There are gaps in the date span of these records; the actual dates covered are: Mar. 11, 1817-Aug. 30, 1851; Mar. 26-Apr. 23, 1872; Mar. 27-Apr. 1, 1889, Dec. 4, 1893-Feb. 23, 1894.
Reports by the Auditor on his examination of accounts and claims submitted for settlement showing date and number of settlement, name of accountable officer or claimant, explanation, summary of debits and credits, explanation of differences, and adjusted balance. Some of these reports are duplicated in the settled accounts and claims (entry 712) and the audit reports (entry 714).

716.   RECEIPTS FOR MONEYS ADVANCED. Oct. 1793-Dec. 1855. 19.8 m, 65 ft. 105 boxes.

This series appears to be missing.
Arranged chronologically.
There are gaps in the date span of these records; the actual dates covered are: Oct. 1793-Dec. 1839; Feb. 1840-May 1843; Jan. 1844-Mar. 1851; Mar. 1854-Dec. 1855.
Receipts signed by contractors, accountable officers, and others for moneys advanced for such purposes as forage, subsistence, bounty, transportation, and clothing. The receipts of quartermasters who subsequently advanced part of their funds to other officers are usually accompanied by abstracts of advances and copies of receipts of other officers. The letters in which these receipts were transmitted are described in entry 701.

717.   SETTLED ACCOUNTS OF INDIAN AGENTS. Oct. 3, 1894-Mar. 13, 1923. 3,048.0 m,
        10,000 ft. 11808 boxes.

        Arranged numerically. A register is in entry 664. Alpha boxes: 5013A, 5295A, 5419A-B,
8089A, 8418A, 9565A, 11564A, 12090A, 13107A, 13596A, 13663A. Box numbers not used: 4909,
5585.
        Chiefly audit reports, accounts current, statements of differences, statements of account,
abstracts of expenditures, and vouchers and other supporting documents.
        For earlier settled Indian accounts, see entry 525.

718.   SETTLED INDIAN CLAIMS. July 1, 1907-Mar. 29, 1923. 394.7 m, 1,295 ft. 1414 boxes.

        Arranged numerically. A register is in entry 675. Alpha boxes: 121A.
        Settled claims submitted primarily by suppliers of goods and services for Indians,
transportation companies, Indian agents, surveyors, individual Indians who had claims against
the Government, and persons who had claims for depredations caused by Indians. A typical
claim file consists of the audit report, an account current, letter to the claimant indicating
action taken on the claim, and statements, affidavits, correspondence, and other documents in
support of a claim.

719.   MISCELLANEOUS PUBLIC LAND ACCOUNTS. Jan. 28, 1895-Dec. 23, 1907. 8.5 m,
        28 ft. 28 boxes.

        Arranged numerically.
        Chiefly accounts of Special Disbursing Agents of the Interior Department for examining
surveys of public lands, and accounts for refund of moneys for lands erroneously sold. The
accounts consist, in general, of a statement of the account, reports by the Auditor and the
Bookkeepers Division, the account current, and abstracts and related supporting documents.

720.   ACCOUNTS OF RECEIVERS OF PUBLIC MONEYS FOR SALE OF INDIAN LANDS.
        July 1, 1907-Dec. 30, 1920. 2.1 m, 7 ft. 5 boxes.

        Arranged in two subseries and numerically within each.
        Accounts for sale of lands for the benefit of the Ute Indians and for the sale of lands in
Oklahoma. Accounts in both of these subseries include the statement of the receiver's account,
abstracts of receipts and disbursements, certificates of the Bookkeeper's Division concerning the
status of the receiver's account, and correspondence relating to the account.

721.   SETTLED ACCOUNTS OF PENSION AGENTS. Jan. 1813-June 1899. 1,524.0 m, 5,000 ft.
        4712 boxes.

        Arranged alphabetically by name of State, thereunder by location of pension agency,
and thereunder by type of pension. Alpha boxes: 718A, 815A, 2843A, 4359A, and 4360A.
        Accounts generally include the Auditor's report, statement of account, abstracts of
disbursements, vouchers for payment to individual pensioners, and sometimes documents
establishing the identity of the pensioner. Some warrants are included in these accounts. After
December 1894, the records consist entirely of vouchers. The accounts for Army pensions cover
the period 1818-64; accounts for Navy pensions, ca. 1818-94, are filed with the Army pensions
for the agencies at Baltimore, Boston, Chicago, Cincinnati, Detroit, New York, Norfolk, and
Philadelphia.
        For some agencies, quarterly abstracts of pension payments were separated from these
accounts and bound into volumes; these abstracts are described in entry 723. Selected vouchers
for final payment to estates of deceased pensioners, 1818-64, have also been removed and are
described in entry 722.

722.   SELECTED FINAL PAYMENT VOUCHERS. 1818-64. 167.6 m, 550 ft. Unbound records.

    Arranged alphabetically by State and thereunder alphabetically by pensioner's surname.

    Vouchers showing deceased pensioner's name and address, act under which pension was paid, and period covered by final payment. These vouchers were selected from the Army pension accounts, entry 721. Some of these records are filmed in NARA Microfilm Publication M1746, Final Revolutionary War Pension Payment Vouchers: Georgia.

723.   QUARTERLY ABSTRACTS OF PENSIONS PAID BY PENSION AGENCIES. July 1818
       Sept. 1907. 5.2 m, 17 ft. 113 vols.

    Arranged alphabetically by agency and thereunder by calendar quarter and type of pension. Abstracts show location of agency, type of pension, pensioner's name, voucher number, veteran's name and rank, rate of pension, period for which paid, amount paid, and certificate number. These abstracts were withdrawn from the pension accounts described in entry 721; unbound pension abstracts for other agencies and other periods remain a part of that series.

    Pension agencies for which there are bound abstracts in this series are:

Albany	26 vols.	Jan. 1831-June 1832;
		Jan. 1834-Sept. 1850;
		Jan. 1851-Mar. 1856;
		July 1856-Mar. 1857,
		July-Sept. 1857;
		Jan.-Mar., July-Sept. 1858;
		Jan.-Mar., July-Dec. 1859;
		Jan. 1860-Dec. 1864
Boston	1 vol.	Apr.-June 1905
Concord	2 vols.	July-Dec. 1865;
		Jan.-June 1885
Hartford	7 vols.	Jan. 1824-Dec. 1850
Indianapolis	4 vols.	July-Sept. 1892;
		July-Sept. 1907
Knoxville	34 vols.	Nov. 1865-Dec. 1884
Middletown	1 vol.	July 1818-Dec. 1823
Nashville	4 vols.	Aug. 1877-Dec. 1882
New Orleans	6 vols.	June 1879-Dec. 1882
New York City	18 vols.	Jan.-Dec. 1819;
		Apr. 1820-Dec. 1830;
		July 1832-Dec. 1835;
		Jan. 1862-Dec. 1864
Norfolk	3 vols.	Aug. 1877-Nov. 1882
Raleigh	2 vols.	Aug. 1877-Dec. 1880
Wheeling	5 vols.	Aug. 1877-Dec. 1882

724.   SETTLED ACCOUNTS FOR PAYMENT OF ACCRUED PENSIONS (FINAL
       PAYMENTS). Aug. 1838-Sept. 1865. 39.9 m, 131 ft. 144 boxes.

    Arranged numerically by account number. Alpha box: 36A

    Settled accounts for pensions claimed under provisions of an act of April 6, 1838, that allowed heirs of pensioners to claim the amount of pension accrued to a pensioner between the date of last payment and the date of death. The accounts frequently show pensioner's date and place of death and names of heirs and include supporting documents, such as proof of identity of claimant, pension certificates, power of attorney, and related correspondence.

725.   SETTLED ACCOUNTS OF AGENTS FOR PAYING INVALID PENSIONS. Apr. 30, 1816 - Apr. 17, 1819. 61 cm, 2 ft. 48 boxes.

Arranged numerically by account number.

Accounts include copies of the audit reports, abstracts of disbursements, vouchers, receipts, powers of attorney, and other supporting documents. These accounts were withdrawn from the miscellaneous Treasury accounts (entry 347) but are entered in the register of audits (entry 345) for that series.

726.   SETTLED ACCOUNTS OF PENSION AGENTS FOR PAYMENTS TO WIDOWS OR ORPHANS OF VETERANS OF THE WAR OF 1812. July 1818-Aug. 1825. 6.1 m, 20 ft. 51 boxes.

Arranged numerically by account number. Related registers are in entry 587 and 588.

Accounts for claims filed under an act of April 16, 1816, that provided for payments of half-pay pensions for 5 years to widows or orphans of soldiers who had died in the War of 1812 or had died later as a result of injuries received in that war. A typical account consists of the Auditor's report, account current, abstract of payments, pension vouchers, lists of unclaimed pensions, and correspondence. These accounts were settled by the Second Auditor and subsequently transferred to the Third Auditor.

727.   APPLICATIONS FOR PAYMENT OF CHECKS ISSUED TO DECEASED PENSIONERS. ca. Mar. 1889-Nov. 1895. 30 cm, 1 ft. Unbound records.

This series appears to be missing.

Arranged alphabetically by initial letter of pensioner's surname.

Claims of heirs of deceased pensioners for payment of pension checks issued but remaining uncashed at time of pensioner's death. The files usually consist of correspondence, affidavits, and other proof of identity of the claimant and of entitlement to the funds. These files are only for deceased pensioners whose surnames began with the letter B.

For similar records, see entry 728.

728.   APPLICATIONS FOR PAYMENT OF CHECKS ISSUED TO DECEASED PENSIONERS. Dec. 1912-Dec. 1919. 10.1 m, 33 ft. 26 boxes.

Arranged in two subseries and numerically within each.

Claims for payment of checks issued to deceased pensioners. The files usually include evidence of death, powers of attorney, affidavits, and correspondence. One group of files is for male pensioners who had died, March 1913-October 1919; the other group of files is for female pensioners who had died, December 1912-December 1919.

729.   MISCELLANEOUS PENSION ACCOUNTS AND CLAIMS (SMALL PENSION PAYMENTS). Mar. 3, 1819-Jan. 24, 1878. 28.4 m, 93 ft. 222 boxes.

Arranged numerically by account number.

There are gaps in the date span of these records; the actual dates covered are: Mar. 3, 1819-Feb. 4, 1835; Aug. 1, 1865-Jan. 24, 1878.

Settled accounts and claims primarily of five types: (1) pension payments to individual pensioners or their heirs, (2) contingent expenses of pension agencies, (3) replacement of lost pension checks, (4) reimbursement to the Quartermaster General for transportation expenses of invalid pensioners, and (5) reimbursement to the Bureau of Engraving and Printing for printing pension checks. The account numbers start over again approximately every 10,000 accounts.

730.   QUARTERMASTERS' ABSTRACTS. 1855-1898. 91.4 m, 300 ft. 195 boxes.

Arranged alphabetically by initial letter of quartermaster's surname.

Abstracts filed by quartermasters as a part of their quarterly accounts usually consisting of accounts of property purchased (abstract A) and miscellaneous disbursements (abstract B). The abstracts normally show date, voucher number, name of person paid, explanation, and amount paid. Some subsistence accounts are interfiled with the quartermaster's abstracts. Other types of abstracts occasionally found in this series are abstracts for forage issued for public animals, abstracts of funds transferred, and abstracts of expenditures for roads and other engineering projects. The various types of abstracts for a particular quartermaster are generally filed together under his name. There are two separate groups of quartermaster's abstracts for the Civil War period: one group, the 145 volumes, is arranged alphabetically by full name of quartermaster; the second group, the unbound papers is arranged by file number.

The names of quartermasters and assistant quartermasters whose abstracts are included in this series (unbound except as noted) are listed in Appendix 10.

730A.   QUARTERMASTERS' ABSTRACTS. July 1854-June 1880. 118 vols. and 59 boxes.

731.   CIVILIAN EMPLOYEES PAYROLLS. Feb. 28, 1862-Feb. 10, 1864. 3 cm, 1 in. 1 vol.

Arranged chronologically.

Payrolls for civilians employed by Capt. Treadwell Moore, Assistant Quartermaster a t Wheeling, W. Va., showing quarter, employee's name, type of work performed, period for which paid, number of days and months for which paid, rate of pay, amounts of stoppages and of income tax withheld, amount received, and signatures of employees and witnesses. Moore certified the accuracy of the rolls. The employees were typically identified as teamsters, hostlers, messengers, draymen, and laborers. A few of the rolls for 1862 and 1863 are for persons employed at New San Pedro and San Francisco, Calif. Some rolls identify the persons names as "enlisted men." The original rolls were filed as vouchers in Moore's accounts.

732.   SETTLED CASE FILES FOR CLAIMS APPROVED BY THE SOUTHERN CLAIMS COMMISSION. ca. 1871-80. 64.3 m, 211 ft. 409 boxes.

Arranged alphabetically by State, thereunder by county, and thereunder alphabetically by name of claimant. Alpha box: 215A.

Case files for approved claims of citizens of Alabama, Arkansas, Florida, Georgia, Louisiana, Mississippi, North Carolina, South Carolina, Tennessee, Texas, and Virginia who had suffered property damage or loss by Federal Troops during the Civil War. Claimants were required to prove to the Commission (established by an act of March 3, 1871) that they had remained loyal to the Union during the war. The claims were paid from appropriations for "Claims of loyal citizens for supplies furnished during the Rebellion." A typical file includes the claimant's petition, inventories of supplies and property for which compensation was desired, testimony of the claimant and others (both favorable and adverse) relating to the claim, copy of the Commission's report, and the Third Auditor's certificate of settlement. These claims were formerly a part of the main series of settled accounts and claims, entry 712. An index of claims acted upon by the Commission was published under the title Consolidated Index of Claims Reported by the Commissioners of Claims to the House of Representatives, from 1871 to 1880 (Washington, 1892).

Case files for disallowed claims are in Records of the U.S. House of Representatives, RG 233. Some claims originally disallowed by the Commission were later heard by the U.S. Court of Claims. Case files for these claims are among records of that Court in RG 123.

Additional records of the Southern Claims Commission are in General Records of the Department of the Treasury, RG 56. These records have been published as NARA Microfilm Publication M87, Records of the Commissioners of Claims (Southern Claims Commission),

1871-80 and as NARA Microfilm Publication M1658, Southern Claims Commission Approved Claims: Georgia. 1871-1880.

733.   RECORDS RELATING TO SETTLEMENT OF THE TEXAS DEBT. Dec. 27, 1850-Apr. 28, 1870. 7.3 m, 24 ft. 5 vols. and 1 box.

Arranged by type of record.

The records include: (1) settled claim files, May 22, 1856-April 25, 1870, which usually include the original canceled bond and evidence of ownership; (2) a register of claims, December 27, 1850-December 31, 1860, showing date, claim number, name of claimant, and explanation; (3) a register of warrants issued to claimants, June 2, 1856-April 8, 1861, showing date, warrant number, account number, title of appropriation, claimant's name, and amount; (4) a numerical list of settled claims, June 2, 1856-April 28, 1870, showing claim number, claimant's name, and date of settlement; (5) a register of settlements, May 23, 1856-April 27, 1870, showing payee's name, report number, claim number, to whom bonds were issued, principal and interest due, and date approved; and (6) a schedule of suspensions in settlements, May 26, 1856-January 5, 1857, showing report number, identifying the items and amounts suspended, and explaining suspensions. Only parts 4, 5 and 6 have been located; parts 1, 2, 3 appear to be missing.

734.   RECORDS OF THE WHIPPLE SURVEY. Apr. 1853-June 1855. 10 cm, 4 in. Unbound records.

This series appears to be missing.
Arranged chronologically.
Settled account of Lt. Amiel W. Whipple for expenditures under an act of March 3, 1853, that provided for the survey of proposed railroad routes from the Mississippi River to the Pacific Ocean. This account was once filed with the main series of accounts and claims, entry 712. The account consists primarily of abstracts of expenditures and related vouchers. Expenses typically included payrolls, subsistence, use of horses and mules, saddles, and shoe nails. Each abstract covers expenditures for a 3-month period.

735.   RECORDS OF THE WHEELER SURVEY. July 1873-June 1875. 61 cm, 2 ft. 2 boxes.

Arranged chronologically.
Settled accounts of Lt. George Wheeler for expenditures for surveys west of the 100th Meridian paid out of an appropriation for surveys of military defenses. The records consist of settled accounts, numbers 3797 and 7930 (both once filed with the main series of accounts and claims, entry 712). Included are audit reports, statements of differences, abstracts of expenditures, and vouchers. Expenses typically included those for payrolls, travel, office rent, subsistence, collecting material, preparing maps for publication, repairing instruments, photographic material, drawing boards, and services of photographers and geologists.

736.   MISCELLANEOUS CLAIMS. ca. 1835-1900. 1.8 m, 6 ft. 7 boxes.

Arranged roughly by year.
Claim files, some approved and some rejected, relating primarily to horse claims, 1835 - 90, and Spanish-American War Claims, 1898-1900. The files generally consist of correspondence and sometimes include evidence of loss and other supporting documents.

State Claims

737.   CLAIMS OF THE STATE OF CALIFORNIA RELATING TO INDIAN WARS. Feb. 1851-Apr. 1894. 4.0 m, 13 ft. 3 vols. 14 boxes.

Arranged generally by campaign and thereunder by type of record.

Payment of claims to California for expenses of Indian uprisings during the period 1850 - 73 was authorized by Congress in several acts and resolutions, including acts of August 5, 1854; August 18, 1856; and January 6, 1883; and resolutions dated December 19, 1889, and December 21, 1893.

The major types of documents included in the claim files (originally a part of the series described in entry 712) are: (1) copies of the accounts of Quartermaster John G. Marin, February 1-July 26, 1851; (2) copies of vouchers for quartermaster supplies and other goods and services, July 18-October 30, 1856, for which payment was not made at that time; (3) lists of bonds issued by the State of California, August 25, 1857-April 5, 1861, to raise money for paying expenses of the Indian wars in the State; (4) registers of war warrants issued by the State, March 26, 1851-July 31, 1855; (5) case files, arranged numerically, for payment of principal and interest on State bonds; (6) abstracts, vouchers, muster rolls, and related documents concerning specific Indian campaigns; (7) reports by the Auditor relating to settlement of claims of the State; and (8) published copies of congressional documents and of laws of the State of California relating to claims.

738.   CLAIMS OF DAKOTA TERRITORY RELATING TO INDIAN WARS. June 1874 - May 1877. 1.2 m, 4 ft. 4 boxes.

Arranged roughly chronologically.

Payment of claims of Dakota Territory for expenses of Indian wars was authorized under an act of March 3, 1875, and generally settled in 1878.

The major types of documents in the claim (originally filed with the series described in entry 712) include: (1) a report on June 1, 1874, on claims relating to Indian wars of 1862, accompanied by lists of claims, affidavits, and copies of Territorial records; (2) abstracts of expenditures of the Territorial government, May 8, 1875-May 22, 1877, for paying expenses of the Indian wars, with related vouchers showing date, claimant's name, explanation, and amount paid; and (3) published copies of congressional documents relating to the claim. Additional records relating to this claim are filed with the case files of State claim records relating to the Civil War (entry 759).

739.   CLAIMS OF THE STATE OF GEORGIA RELATING TO THE REVOLUTIONARY WAR AND THE WAR OF 1812. May 1793-Mar. 1859. 61 cm, 2 ft. Unbound records.

Arranged numerically by account number.

Settled accounts of the State of Georgia, filed under authority of various acts of Congress and originally a part of the settled accounts and claims described in entry 712. The records consist primarily of abstracts of expenditures for military service of State troops, with related vouchers, as well as correspondence with the Auditor relating to the claim.

For other records relating to the claims of Georgia for use of its troops during this period, see records relating to the Florida Indian wars (entry 756) and to the Mexican War (entry 757). This series has been microfilmed as NARA Microfilm Publication M1745, Final Revolutionary War Pension Payment Vouchers: Georgia.

740.   CLAIMS OF THE STATE OF ILLINOIS RELATING TO INDIAN WARS. June 1833 July 1852. 61 cm, 2 ft. 3 boxes.

Arranged by type of record.

Claims of the State of Illinois for reimbursement of expenses of the Indian wars were paid under authority of an act of June 30, 1823. A majority of the records are alphabetically arranged claim files for horses and other property lost during the Sac and Fox, and Black Hawk Indian wars; lists of the value of horses and other property furnished by individual soldiers (sometimes identified as muster rolls); and claims for personal services, such as guarding horses during the campaigns.

741. CLAIMS OF THE STATE OF MAINE RELATING TO EXPENDITURES FOR THE AROOSTOOK WAR. Feb. 1839-Dec. 1840. 3.7 m, 12 ft. 9 boxes.

Arranged by type of record.
Claims of the State of Maine for expenses arising from the Aroostook war were settled during the period 1843-50 under provisions of an act dated June 13, 1842. Some of the major documents included in the claim files are abstracts of expenditures for State militia units, including medical supplies and quartermaster stores, February 1839-December 1840, with related vouchers; muster rolls and payrolls of troops, February-July 1839; and correspondence, decisions, and accounting records relating to the settlement of the claims, ca. 1843-50.

742. CLAIMS OF THE STATE OF MARYLAND RELATING TO THE WAR OF 1812. Apr. 1813-Mar. 1854. 1.8 m, 6 ft. 1 vol. and 5 boxes.

Arranged by type of record.
Settled accounts of the State of Maryland for expenses of the War of 1812 filed under various acts and originally a part of the series of settled accounts and claims described in entry 712. The records consist chiefly of a bound abstract of action taken by the officials of Maryland on claims of its militia units in the War of 1812 approved by the State for payment. The unbound records consist primarily of case files of owners of vessels sunk by Maryland authorities for the defense of Baltimore harbor, with related correspondence; also settled claims for reimbursement of other State expenses for military activities during the war.

743. CLAIM OF THE STATE OF MASSACHUSETTS RELATING TO THE WAR OF 1812. June 1811-Jan. 1828. 61 cm, 2 ft. 15 vols. and unbound records.

Arranged by type of record.
Claim of the State of Massachusetts for expenses of the War of 1812, consisting primarily of records created by the Board of War of the Commonwealth of Massachusetts (15 vols.), including checkbooks of the Board, copies of letters sent by the Board, a journal, orders relating to the establishment and operations of militia units, and registers of supplies purchased; also an analysis by the Third Auditor of various documents included in the claim file and of their validity. Other records relating to this claim are filed with the State's Civil War claims, entry 759.

744. CLAIMS OF THE STATE OF MINNESOTA RELATING TO INDIAN WARS. 1862-65. 61 cm, 2 ft. 2 boxes.

Arranged by type of record.
Claims of Minnesota for expenses of suppressing hostilities by the Sioux Indians were settled by the Third Auditor jointly with the State's claims for expenses of raising troops for the Civil War and filed under provisions of acts of April 3, 1863; July 2, 1864; and April 10, 1869. The records relating to the Sioux expedition consist chiefly of payrolls of State troops engaged in fighting the Indians, accounting records relating to the settlement of the claim, and copies of orders issued by the State. Other Records relating to Indian war claims of Minnesota are filed with State's Civil War claim, entry 759.

745.　　CLAIMS OF THE STATE OF MONTANA RELATING TO INDIAN WARS. Oct. 1867-
　　　　Sept. 1887. 3.4 m, 11 ft. 11 boxes.

　　　Arranged by type of record.
　　　Claims of the State of Montana for expenses relating to Indian wars were approved by
Congress by acts of March 3, 1873, and August 5, 1882. The main types of records (claims records)
are numerically arranged case files, October 15, 1867-February 7, 1872, consisting chiefly of
vouchers, affidavits, and correspondence; and files of miscellaneous claims, ca. 1872-74,
arranged by initial letter of claimant's surname and relating mainly to supplies and personal
services. Many of the files are in the names of claims agents who represented several claimants.
Included are abstracts and vouchers, July-September 1877, for military service against the Nez
Perce Indians, as authorized by the act of August 5, 1882; also abstracts and vouchers, April 3,
1873-June 13, 1877, for expenditures authorized by the act of March 3, 1873.

746.　　CLAIMS OF THE STATE OF NEVADA RELATING TO INDIAN WARS. Mar. 1876-
　　　　Mar. 1877. 30 cm, 1 ft. 10 boxes.

　　　Arranged by type of record.
　　　Settled claims of the State of Nevada for expenses of the White Pine and Elko Indian
wars filed under an act of March 2, 1877. The claims were approved by the State's Adjutant
General in March 1876. The records consist chiefly of abstracts of expenditures and related
vouchers (neither group of documents in dated); a copy of the Adjutant General's report, and a
copy of the act of March 2, 1877. The Nevada claims for the Indian wars were settled jointly
with that State's claims for the Civil War, entry 759.

747.　　CLAIM OF THE STATE OF NEW HAMPSHIRE RELATING TO THE WAR OF 1812.
　　　　Dec. 9, 1815-Feb. 19, 1866. 1 cm, 1/2 in. 1 box.

　　　Arranged by type of record.
　　　Claim of the State of New Hampshire for expenses of the War of 1812, consisting of a
letter from the Third Auditor to the Second Comptroller, dated February 19, 1866, concerning
the account and enclosing copies of the State's claim as presented in December 1815; a copy of
the report of settlement, November 1, 1826; a few vouchers relating to the claim; copies of
statements of differences (undated); and a copy of a list of documents relating to the claim that
had been sent to the U.S. House of Representatives in 1852 and not returned.

748.　　CLAIMS OF THE STATE OF NEW YORK RELATING TO WAR OF 1812. Mar. 1813-
　　　　Dec. 1854. 30 cm, 1 ft. 1 box.

　　　Arranged by type of record.
　　　Settled claims of the State of New York for expenses of the War of 9 1812 filed under
various acts and once filed with the settled accounts and claims described in entry 712.
Documents in the file include an abstract of militia troops paid by the State, March 1813-April
1814; abstracts of disbursements for such items as pay of troops, subsistence, apprehension of
deserters, and moneys borrowed by the State from banks; and vouchers supporting these
abstracts. Also included are analyses of the claims, and statements of differences.

749.　　CLAIMS OF THE STATE OF NORTH CAROLINA RELATING TO THE
　　　　REVOLUTIONARY WAR AND THE WAR OF 1812. Jan. 1783-Dec. 1815. 20 cm, 8 in.
　　　　Unbound records.

　　　This series appears to be missing.
　　　Arranged by type of record. Settled claims of the State of North Carolina for expenses
of the Revolutionary War and the War of 1812, consisting chiefly of abstracts and related

vouchers of expenses of the State. Most expenses were for pay of troops, provisions furnished, and settled claims. The claim for expenses of the Revolutionary War was once filed with the miscellaneous Treasury accounts, entry 347; the claim for expenses of the War of 1812 was once part of the settled accounts and claims described in entry 712.

750.   CLAIMS OF THE STATE OF OREGON FOR EXPENSES OF INDIAN WARS. 1848-98. 37.2 m, 122 ft. 17 vols. and 90 boxes.

Arranged by campaign and thereunder by type of record. Alpha box: 6A.

The claim of Oregon (including, for a time, Washington Territory) relating chiefly to the Cayuse war, 1847-48 (settled by the Fifth Auditor, but later transferred to the Third Auditor); the Rogue River war, 1853-54; the Indian wars of 1855-56; the Modoc war, 1872-73; the Nez Perce war, 1877; and the Bannock war, 1878. Many of the claims were settled in the 1870's and 1880's under various acts. Among the more significant records in the claims are the approved claim files, September 1861-June 1890, with related docket books; bound and unbound copies of payrolls, muster rolls, and abstracts, chiefly for 1855-56; and records of the Fifth Auditor in settlement of claims of the Cayuse war. Also included are a name index to bonds issued by the State to raise money (dates not determined), miscellaneous correspondence, and copies of congressional documents and of laws and regulations of the State of Oregon.

751.   CLAIM   OF   THE   STATE   OF   PENNSYLVANIA   RELATING   TO   THE REVOLUTIONARY WAR. May 1, 1778-Aug. 20, 1804. 10 cm, 4 in. 4 vols.

Arranged by type of pensioner. Each volume is indexed by initial letter of pensioner's surname.

Claim of the State of Pennsylvania, consisting of copies of four ledgers, for payments made by the State to invalid veterans of the Revolutionary War and to orphans and widows of deceased pensioners. The copies were made by the Auditor General of Pennsylvania on February 3, 1836. This series is in the same box as entry 752.

752.   CLAIM OF THE STATE OF PENNSYLVANIA RELATING TO THE WAR OF 1812. Aug. 1812-June 1827. 15 cm, 6 in. Unbound records.

Arranged by type of document.

Evidence submitted by the State of Pennsylvania in support of claims for reimbursement of expenses of the War of 1812, relating chiefly to interest on loans made by the State for the benefit of the United States and pay and other expenses of its militia units in service near Lake Erie.

The records include copies of payrolls, vouchers, military orders, correspondence, acts of the State authorizing the borrowing of money, and copies of loan agreements between the State and banks. This entry is in the same box as entry 751.

753.   ABSTRACT OF ADDITIONAL PAY CREDITED TO SOLDIERS OF THE RHODE ISLAND MILITIA FOR SERVICE IN THE REVOLUTIONARY WAR. Apr. 1780. 5 sheets.

This series appears to be missing.

Arranged alphabetically by surname of soldier.

This abstract shows name and rank of soldier, military unit, and amount due. An act of April 10, 1780, provided that additional pay could be credited to soldiers because of depreciation of the currency.

754. CLAIM OF THE STATE OF SOUTH CAROLINA RELATING TO THE REVOLUTIONARY WAR AND THE WAR OF 1812. Sept. 1791-Jan. 1816. 13 cm, 5 in. 2 vols. and unbound records.

Arranged by type of record. Only one volume has been located.
There are gaps in the date span of these records; the actual dates covered are: Sept. 1791-Sept. 1794; Nov. 1813-Jan. 1816.
Claims of the State of South Carolina, consisting chiefly of accounts for expenditures of the State during the Revolutionary War, including expenses of fortifications, September 1791-September 1794; copies of correspondence and accounts relating to the defense of Charleston, September 1814-August 1815; and payrolls and other records relating to expenditures of the State during the War of 1812, November 1813-January 1816. Also included is an index to the records submitted by the State in support of its claim, which was settled in September 1826.

755. CLAIMS OF THE STATE OF VIRGINIA RELATING TO THE WAR OF 1812. Feb. 1813-Apr. 1814. Negligible.

This series appears to be missing.
Arranged by type of document.
Claims of the State of Virginia, consisting of a partial listing of militia units paid by the State, February 6, 1813-April 15, 1814, showing name of commanding officer; voucher number; number of commissioned officers, noncommissioned officers, and privates; period of service of the unit; number of casualties; and type of unit (e.g., rifle, artillery, or infantry). Also included are two pages of comments by the Auditor on an analysis of the account of John Woods, paymaster for the Virginia Militia during 1814, showing voucher number, whether voucher was suspended or disallowed, reason for action taken, and type of expenditure (e.g., pay, subsistence, or forage).

756. STATE CLAIMS RELATING TO THE FLORIDA INDIAN WARS. ca. Nov. 1835 - Aug. 1856. 4.9 m, 16 ft. 6 vols. and 16 boxes.

Arranged roughly by type of record.
The States of Alabama, Florida, Georgia, Tennessee, and others, furnished State troops to fight the Indians in Florida, chiefly during the late 1830's and early 1840's. The records relating to expenses for these Indian wars include journals of three boards established to consider the claims of the States. The boards met during the periods October 3, 1843- March 17, 1844; March 25-May 29, 1844; and December 28, 1844-June 20, 1845.
Each journal, arranged chronologically, is accompanied by lists of claims heard by the board and various supporting documents. Also included are two volumes of lists of claims settled by disbursing officers, 1837-50; a general index to Florida war claims (undated); abstracts and vouchers for disbursements for pay, forage, and subsistence; muster rolls of various State units; and lists of the value of horses lost. Some of the claims for the 1850 Indian wars were not settled until 1880.

757. STATE CLAIMS RELATING TO THE MEXICAN WAR. June 19, 1846-Aug. 17, 1852. 18 cm, 7 in. 2 vols. and unbound records.

Arranged by type of record. The two volumes are indexed by initial letter of claimant's surname.
Records of State claims for service of their troops in the Mexican War, consisting chiefly of copies of reports from the Third Auditor to the Comptroller, June 19, 1846-August 17, 1852, on his examination of claims filed by States under provisions of an act of June 2, 1848. The reports include statements of items allowed and disallowed, the Auditor's explanation of the action, and a copy of the Comptroller's decision. Some of the claims rejected in 1846 were

reexamined after passage of the act of 1848. Claims that were finally approved are filed with the main series of settled accounts and claims (entry 712). Also included are records of claims filed by Ohio, Tennessee, and Texas, chiefly for loss of horses by their troops; records of forage issued; records of horses and mules furnished by quartermasters; and part of a volume of registers of settled claims.

758.   REGULATIONS AND DECISIONS RELATING TO STATE WAR CLAIMS. 1863-68 and 1900-1905. 2 cm, 1 in. 1 vol.

Arranged by type of document.
Ten general regulations for guidance of accounting officers in the settlement of State claims (undated), with notations of modifications by decisions of the Second Comptroller; decisions (May 1, 1866-Nov. 14, 1868) relating to coffins, date of termination of the war, deserters, and pay of commandants; and an explanation of the laws and rulings (1900-1905) relating to claims of States for reimbursement of expenses of raising troops for service in the Spanish-American War. Many of the abstracts cite specific letters or decisions.
For some related correspondence, see entries 604, 617, and 618; for case files of State claims, see entry 759.

759.   STATE CLAIMS FOR REIMBURSEMENT OF CIVIL WAR EXPENSES. ca. 1861-1900. 189.0 m, 620 ft. 618 boxes.

Arranged alphabetically by State and thereunder by type of record. Alpha boxes: 3A, 6A, 6B, 14A, 15A, and 297A-297AH (34 boxes).
An act of July 27, 1861, authorized the Secretary of the Treasury to reimburse loyal States for expenses incurred on behalf of the United States at the outbreak of the Civil War. From time to time until the late 1890's, Congress appropriated funds for paying State claims arising under this act.
Expenses claimed typically related to pay and provisions for State troops, quartermaster and ordnance stores, either issued by the State to its own troops or furnished to Federal troops, and pay of principal and interest on bonds issued by the States to raise money for defense. The claim files, most of which were at one time part of the settled accounts and claims described in entry 712, consist of documents submitted by the State as evidence of their expenditures, correspondence of the States or their claims agents with the Third Auditor, and accounting records created in the settlement of the claims. The claim records for Dakota Territory, Massachusetts, Minnesota, and Nevada also include records relating to settlement of claims for expenses of suppressing Indian hostilities in those States.
For other records relating to the settlement of these Indian claims, see entries 738, 743, 744, and 746. Rules and regulations for the settlement of State claims are described in entry 758. Correspondence with State officials regarding the claims is described in entries 604, 617, and 618.

Other Records

760.   REGISTER OF MISCELLANEOUS SETTLEMENTS. July 1900-Nov. 1905. 3 cm, 1 in. 1 vol.

Arranged alphabetically by initial letter of claimant's surname. This volume is in very poor condition.
Register contains entries of miscellaneous Interior claims that show settlement number, dates received and settled, name of claimant, period covered, explanation, and amount allowed. Types of claims include payments to State agricultural colleges, expenses of the General Land Office, fees for examining land records, expenses of advertising, expenses of public schools in Alaska, and expenses for telephones and lighting in public - buildings.

761.   REGISTER OF PASSENGER TRANSPORTATION. Oct. 1895-June 1900. 5 cm, 2 in. 1 vol.

Arranged by subject and thereunder chronologically. Indexed by name of person, company, or administrative unit concerned.

Register contains entries that show to whom transportation requests were issued (e.g., Indian schools, railroads, or individuals), dates, number of persons to be transported, number of the Government transportation request; origin and destination of the trip, specific points between which transportation was requested, rate, amount payable, and settlement number, entry 717.

OFFICE OF THE FOURTH AUDITOR

The Office of the Fourth Auditor had its origins in an act of July 16, 1798 (1 Stat. 610), that authorized the appointment of an "Accountant for the Navy" within the Navy Department. The Accountant's duties were to settle accounts for moneys advanced and supplies and provisions issued or distributed and to report such settlements periodically to the accounting officers of the Treasury Department for review. The Accountant also countersigned warrants issued by the Secretary of the Navy for authorized disbursements.

The Accountant's office was superseded by the establishment of the-Office of the Fourth Auditor by an act of March 3, 1817 (3 Stat. 366). The Fourth Auditor was responsible for settling all accounts of or relating to the Navy Department, including those for payment of naval pensions; keeping accounts of receipts and disbursements of public moneys by the Navy Department; keeping accounts of debts due because of advances of public moneys; and filing settled accounts after final approval by the Second Comptroller. An act of May 7, 1822 (3 Stat. 688), took away the Fourth Auditor's authority to countersign warrants, but it gave the Office the function of registering warrants for disbursements for the Navy Department.

Few changes were made in the duties of the Fourth Auditor until the act of July 31, 1894 (28 Stat. 205), which transferred the responsibility for settlement of accounts for paying naval pensions from the Fourth Auditor to the Auditor for the Interior Department (formerly Third Auditor).

The Divisions of the Fourth Auditor's Office for which records are described in this inventory are the Bookkeepers Division, General Claims Division, Navy Pay and Pension Division, Paymaster's Division, and Record and Prize Division. The most significant records of the Fourth Auditor's Office are correspondence, 1795-1897, with related registers and indexes; ledgers and journals, 1798-1907; and settled accounts and claims, 1798-1922, and related records, 1800-1907. Accounts and claims for Navy pensions are described with records of the Third Auditor.

A list of names of Fourth Auditors and dates of service appear in Appendix 8.

BOOKKEEPERS DIVISION

The Bookkeepers Division was first mentioned by the Office of the Fourth Auditor in a report on the work of the Office for the fiscal year beginning July 1, 1866. The main functions of the Division were maintaining appropriation ledgers and journals, recording requisitions and warrants, and keeping a record of the balances of accounts of paymasters and other officers. The function of maintaining appropriation ledgers and journals was transferred to the Division of Bookkeeping and Warrants in the Office of the Secretary of the Treasury in 1894. These ledgers and journals are now part of Records of the Bureau of Accounts (Treasury), RG 39.

Ledgers

762.   GENERAL INDEX TO LEDGERS. ca. 1798-1921. 10 cm, 4 in. 2 vols.

Arranged chronologically. Within each volume entries are arranged alphabetically by title of account. One volume appears to be missing.

Index to general ledgers (entry 765), officer's ledgers (entry 766), defaulters' ledgers (entry 768), and pension ledgers (entry 770). Each entry shows title of account (usually the name of a person, company, or ship, sometimes with other identifying information) and volume and page reference to the ledgers. References are to the general ledgers unless identified in the index entry as "pens," "o. L.," "def. L." For separate indexes to the general ledgers and defaulters' ledgers, see entries 764 and 767.

763.   INDEX TO "AGENT OF MARINES" LEDGER. ca. 1782-87. 15 cm, 6 in. 1 vol.

Arranged by title of account.
Index to pages 1-21 of the "Agent of Marines" ledger, showing title of account (usually the name of a person, ship, or company) and a folio number. The ledger has not been located, and its dates have not been determined. The Office of Agent of Marines was established within the Navy by the Continental Congress about November 1775. Many of the accounts listed in this index are entered in the ledgers described in entry 2 during the period noted above.

764.   INDEXES TO GENERAL LEDGERS. ca. 1798-1875. 15 cm, 6 in. 10 vols.

Arranged chronologically. Within each volume the entries are arranged by title of account.
Indexes to volumes A, B, D-G, L-S, V-Z, 1, 2, 8, and 10 of the general ledgers (entry 765). The entries show title of account (usually the name of a person or title of an appropriation) and volume and page references. Some of the index volumes are for ledgers that have not been located. Some index volumes relate to several ledgers, while others relate only to one ledger.

765.   GENERAL LEDGERS. Sept. 1798-June 1900 with gaps. 9 ft. 35 vols.

Arranged chronologically. Within each volume the accounts are arranged by title of account and thereunder chronologically. Ledgers G, J, 3, 4, 6, 7, 11-13, 15, and 16 are missing. Ledgers 17 and 18, dated approximately 1895-1900, were created in the Secretary of the Treasury's Division of Bookkeeping and Warrants and transferred back to the General Accounting Office in 1921. Volumes 10, 14, 17, and 18 are each indexed by name of officer or claimant. The other volumes are not indexed.
Ledgers contain entries that show title of accounts (usually names of paymasters or claimants or titles of appropriations), dates of transactions, debits for disbursements, appropriations from which disbursements were made, journal references (see entry 771), and credits.
Numbers of settled accounts, warrants, and requisitions are also sometimes shown. Some accounts were transferred from this series of ledgers to the officers' ledgers (entry 766) when the account became inactive or the officer ceased to be accountable. Partial indexes to some of the general ledgers are in entries 762 and 764.

766.   OFFICERS' LEDGERS. 1839-1901. 91 cm, 3 ft. 9 vols.

Arranged chronologically. Within each volume the accounts are arranged by name of accountable officer and thereunder chronologically.
Ledgers 5 and 8-11 are missing. Volumes 7 and 12-14 are each indexed by name of accountable officer. The other volumes are not indexed.
There are gaps in the date span of these records; the actual dates covered are: 1839-78; 1885-1901.
Ledgers contain entries of inactive accounts showing officer's name, rank and title; balance carried forward from general ledgers, entry 765; date and number of settled account; journal reference; titles of appropriations; and debits and credits. Some accounts include later entries showing changes in the outstanding balance, final settlement of the account, or transfer of the account to the defaulters ledger (entry 768).
For a partial index to these ledgers, see entry 762.

767.   INDEX TO DEFAULTERS LEDGER. ca. 1868-1898. 1 cm, 1/4 in. 1 vol.

Arranged by name of defaulter.
Index shows name of defaulter and page reference to the ledger, entry 768.

768.   DEFAULTERS LEDGER. ca. 1868-98. 10 cm, 4 in. 1 vol.

Arranged by name of defaulter and thereunder chronologically.

Ledger contains entries showing officer's name and rank, balance carried forward from officers' ledgers (entry 766), numbers and balances of settled accounts, numbers and amounts of refund requisitions, and outstanding balances. A few accounts have entries dated as early as 1852, and some show dates of surety bonds under which the officer had been accountable. This ledger is indexed in the volume described in entry 767 and partially indexed in the volumes described in entry 762.

769.   LEDGERS FOR THE NAVY PENSION FUND. Nov. 1800-July 1829. 5 cm, 2 in. 2 vols.

This series appears to be missing.

Arranged chronologically. Within each ledger volume the accounts are arranged by title of account and thereunder chronologically. Volume 1 is indexed by title of account. The other volume is not indexed.

Ledgers contain entries showing title of account, date, explanation of transaction, and debits and credits. Warrant numbers are frequently included. Some accounts have entries dated as early as 1798. Most accounts in volume 1 are in the name of the Navy Pension Fund, the treasurer of the fund, and commissioners of loans in the several States; accounts in volume 2 are chiefly in the names of individual pensioners, titles of bank officials serving as pension agents, and specific securities held by the fund.

For a related journal, see entry 772.

770.   PENSION LEDGERS. Mar. 1849-Jan. 1896. 20 cm, 8 in. 3 vols.

Arranged chronologically. Within each volume the accounts are arranged by title of account and thereunder chronologically. Volumes 1 and 3 are indexed by title of account. The other volume is not indexed.

Ledgers contain entries showing title of account, dates of transactions, and debits and credits. Dates, numbers, amounts of settled accounts, warrants, and requisitions are frequently shown. Accounts in the names of pension agents show location of pension agency and date of surety bond. Many entries in volume 3 are in the names of surgeons employed to examine Navy pensioners to determine their continued eligibility for disability pensions. Types of pensions paid are indicated in the accounts for both pensioners and pension agents.

For a related journal, see entry 774.

Journals

771.   GENERAL JOURNALS. Sept. 7, 1798-Oct. 6, 1894. 4.0 m, 13 ft. 56 vols.

Arranged chronologically and thereunder in two subseries. In 1870 the journals were split into two groups: (1) the main journals, which continued chronologically to September 26, 1894; and (2) a second group of journals, reflecting settlement of accounts whose numbers were given an alphabetical suffix A or B, which continued to October 6, 1894. Most accounts in the A and B series were those of paymasters for pay and contingent expenses of the Navy. There is no volume 3.

Journals contain a chronological record of transactions showing date recorded, general ledger reference (see entry 765), name of accountable officer or claimant, appropriation to be charged or credited, explanation, and amount payable. Beginning with 1809, most of the journal entries include the number of the settled account noted in the margin of the page.

Many of the original settled accounts are described in entry 811. Journal 6 and two succeeding unnumbered volumes overlap each other in dates.

For certificates of settlement, see entry 778.

772.   JOURNALS FOR THE NAVY PENSION FUND. Dec. 31, 1798-Feb. 2, 1830. 8 cm, 3 in. 2 vols.

This series appears to be missing.
Arranged chronologically.
Journals contain entries showing date recorded, names of persons and titles of appropriations to be debited and credited, explanation, ledger reference (see entry 769), and amount involved. Most entries date from October 1, 1803. The transactions typically involved moneys deposited to the Navy Pension Fund from proceeds from the sale of captured ships and payments made from the fund to bank officials serving as agents for paying Navy pensions. The entry for March 3, 1817, includes a list of the titles and balances of accounts transferred from the books of the Accountant for the Navy Department to the books of the Fourth Auditor.

773.   JOURNAL FOR THE PRIVATEER PENSION FUND. Jan. 3, 1814-Jan. 28, 1830. 3 cm, 1 in. 1 vol.

This series appears to be missing.
Arranged chronologically.
Journal contains entries showing date recorded, names of persons and titles of appropriations to be debited and credited, explanation, and amount involved. A few entries date as early as September 1813, but no specific dates are shown for that period. Entries typically are for warrants issued to bank officers to enable them to pay Navy pensions and for moneys deposited in the Privateer Pension Fund from proceeds of sale of securities that had been owned by the fund.

774.   PENSION JOURNAL. Mar. 4, 1849-Apr. 27, 1869. 5 cm, 2 in. 1 vol.

Arranged chronologically.
Journal contains entries showing date recorded, number of settled account, ledger reference (see entry 770), names of persons and titles of appropriations to be debited and credited, and amount involved. Many entries debit the pension agent and credit an appropriation for specific types of pensions, such as invalid pensions; others debit the Navy Pension Fund or the Unclaimed Pension Fund and credit specific pensioners.

GENERAL CLAIMS DIVISION

The General Claims Division was first mentioned by the Fourth Auditor in a report on the work of the Office for the fiscal year beginning July 1, 1863. It is last mentioned in a similar report for the fiscal year ending June 30, 1890. The primary function of the Division was to settle all accounts and claims not settled in other Divisions of the Fourth Auditor's Office.

Records Relating to Accounts and Claims

775.   ABSTRACTS OF LETTERS RELATING TO ACCOUNTS AND CLAIMS. Nov. 12, 1860-July 30, 1908. 10 cm, 4 in. 2 vols.

Arranged chronologically. Each volume is indexed by subject.
Miscellaneous documents relating to the functions of the General Claims Division, including abstracts of letters written by the Secretary of the Navy and the Second Comptroller, circulars and general orders of the Navy Department, and abstracts of court rulings. Some of the many subjects include bounty, commutation of quarters, effects of deceased seamen, mileage and travel allowances, and sea pay; also mileage and transportation fee tables. In the case of abstracts of letters, the source of the original letter is frequently given.

776.   INDEX TO SETTLED ACCOUNTS. Mar. 13, 1817-June 30, 1824. 5 cm, 2 in, 2 vols.

Arranged chronologically. Within each volume the entries are arranged by surname of officer or claimant and thereunder chronologically.

Index entries show account number, in whose name stated, date audited, type of account, official balance, and in whose favor.

Contractors and naval officers are specifically identified as such. Many entries simply refer to "accounts closed;" others relate to military supplies furnished, freight charges, accounts of disbursing officers of the Navy, and amounts due for pay, rations, and advertising. Some of the accounts indexed in these volumes are among records described in entry 812.

777.   CERTIFICATES OF SETTLED ACCOUNTS. June 20, 1800-Aug. 24, 1907. 7.6 m, 25 ft.
        120 vols.

Arranged chronologically; within each volume the certificates are arranged numerically. The first two volumes, unnumbered (1800-1805 and 1809-13), volume 6 (Sept. 18, 1827-Nov. 1, 1828), volumes 9-13 (Mar. 13, 1830-Apr. 20, 1838), volumes 17-36 (Apr. 24-June 6, 1845, and Jan. 1, 1859-June 25, 1874), and volumes A1-A4 (Oct. 4, 1870-June 23, 1874) are each indexed by surname of official or claimant. In 1870 the certificates were split into two groups: the main group, which continued in numerical sequence to December 20, 1883, and a second group with the numbered reports given an alphabetical suffix (A, B, or C), which continued to August 24, 1907. Volume 3 appears to be missing.

Reports showing settlement number, date reported, titles of appropriations to be charged, name of accountable officer or claimant, adjusted balance, and explanation. The numbers were assigned at the time the Auditor reported the account for approval.

For the accounts to which these certificates relate, see entry 812; for registers of action taken by the Second Comptroller, see entries 242 and 244; for journals of the Fourth Auditor, see entry 771.

778.   CERTIFICATES OF SETTLEMENT OF CLAIMS. Aug. 22, 1831-June 19, 1882. 3.7 m, 12 ft.
        49 vols.

Arranged chronologically. Volumes 1 (Aug. 22, 1831-Aug. 31, 1832), 3 (Sept. 6, 1833-Dec. 24, 1834), and 5-49 (July 9, 1836-June 19, 1882) are each indexed by name of claimant. Volumes 2 and 4 are not indexed. There is not volume 2.

Certificates showing date audited, title of appropriation to be charged, claimant's name, type of claim (usually pay, bounty, or rations), amount payable, and name of paymaster or location of pay office at which payment was to be made. Beginning with July 1886, the certificates are assigned a number consisting of the initial letter of the claimant's surname and the number assigned to the certificate. This number corresponds to the number in the registers of claims, entry 780. The numbers were repeated for each letter of the alphabet.

For a register of action by the Second Comptroller on these claims, see entry 242.

779.   ABSTRACTS OF ACCOUNTS OF OFFICERS OF THE FREEDMEN'S BUREAU.
        Feb. 28, 1874-June 28, 1882. 5 cm, 2 in. 1 vol.

Arranged by name of officer. Indexed by name of officer.

Abstracts show name and rank of officer representing the Freedmen's Bureau, titles of appropriations from which he disbursed funds on behalf of naval personnel, debits and credits, explanation, and number of settled account. Most of the money was disbursed from appropriations for pay of the Navy, bounty, prize money, and bounty for destruction of enemy ships. The accounts were to repay the Freedmen's Bureau for funds spent on behalf of naval personnel. Loosely inserted in the front of the volume is a list of payments to Gen. O. O. Howard by Navy Paymasters C. C. Jackson and Edwin Stewart, May 4, 1867-March 6, 1872, showing date paid, claimant's name, and amount paid. General Howard receipted for the moneys paid.

780.   REGISTERS OF CLAIMS. Jan. 2, 1863-June 30, 1895. 1.5 m, 5 ft. 21 vols.

Arranged chronologically. Within each volume the entries are arranged by initial letter of claimant's surname and thereunder chronologically. Volume 14 is bound in two parts (A-L and M-Z).
Registers contain entries that show certificate number; dates claim was received, stated, approved, and paid; claimant's name; by whom submitted; type of claim (bounty, arrearages, travel expense, indemnity, or allotment); amount allowed; when paid; and by whom paid. Some of these volumes are identified as "claims registered for settlement." For certificates of settlement of some of these claims, see entry 778.

781.   REGISTERS OF INDEMNITY CLAIMS SETTLED. May 1864-June 1899. 10 cm, 4 in. 2 vols.

Arranged chronologically and thereunder by type of claimant.
Within each volume the entries are arranged by initial letter of claimant's surname and thereunder by date paid. One volume is for enlisted men; the other for officers.
Registers contain entries for enlisted men that show dates received and paid, claimant's name, name of ship or pay office at which payment was made, amount paid, how paid (usually by certificate), and name of ship on which claimant was stationed. Entries for warrant officers show dates received and paid, claimant's name and rank, name of ship on which he served, name of disbursing officer or location of pay office, amount paid, and officer's address. Most claims were paid under an act of July 4, 1864 (13 Stat. 389), that provided for pay for personal effects of enlisted men on ships sunk or lost during the war and for determining the amount of additional pay due them for service on the ship between the date of the last payroll and the date of loss.

NAVY PAY AND PENSION DIVISION

The Navy Pay and Bounty Division was first mentioned by the Fourth Auditor in a report on the work of his Office for the fiscal year beginning July 1, 1888. It resulted from a revision of the duties of the Navy Pension Division and the Navy Pay and Allotment Division, both of which had been established in July 1876. The initial functions of the Division were to record allotments authorized by naval personnel from their pay and to handle allotment and pension claims. The Division was substantially changed in October 1894 when its pension functions were transferred to the Auditor for the Interior Department (formerly the Third Auditor). Pension accounts and claims, plus some related records, are described with records of the Third Auditor. Some correspondence relating to pensions is described as part of the records of the Record and Prize Division of the Fourth Auditor's Office.

Records Relating to Allotments

782.   INDEXES TO REGISTERS OF ALLOTMENTS. Jan. 1886-Mar. 1900. 13 cm, 5 in. 5 vols.

Arranged by name of grantor.
Indexes to registers (entry 783) showing name of grantor, page reference, name of ship on which grantor was stationed, and location of the pay office at which deduction was to be made.

783.   REGISTERS OF ALLOTMENTS. Mar. 1838-Mar. 1900. 3.7 m, 12 ft. 61 vols.

Arranged chronologically. Within each volume entries are arranged by surname of grantor and thereunder chronologically. Five volumes relate only to officers, nine only to enlisted men, and the balance relate to both.

Registers contain entries that show grantor's name and rank, when and by whom registered, amount of allotment, date of first payment, number of months, and record of allotments. Most volumes also show grantor's duty station, name of person to whom allotment was to be sent, and the pay office at which it was to be deducted. Allotments are also recorded in the abstracts of Navy Pay Office accounts (entry 798).

For an index to the allotment registers, see entry 782.

Records Relating to Pensions

784.   INDEX TO PENSION AGENTS' ACCOUNTS. Sept. 1816-Mar. 1895. 3 cm, 1 in. 1 vol.

Arranged by location of pension agency and thereunder chronologically.

Index entries show location of pension agency, account number, name of pension agent, where account was filed, and period covered by account.

The dates vary considerably from one agency to another.

For some of the accounts listed in this index, see entry 721; some of the accounts are also listed in the pension ledgers (entry 770) and pension journals (entry 774).

785.   CERTIFICATES OF SETTLEMENT OF PENSION ACCOUNTS. Jan. 3, 1824-June 4, 1870. 10 cm, 4 in. 3 vols.

Arranged chronologically. The first two volumes are indexed by surname of pension agent or pensioner. The other volume is not indexed.

There are gaps in the date span of these records; the actual dates covered are: Jan. 3, 1824-June 16, 1829; Jan. 4, 1844-June 4, 1870.

Certificates show title of appropriation, date audited, in whose name stated, explanation, balance, and payment instructions if the balance was in favor of the agent or pensioner. Volume 1 includes a section of certificates on accounts involving the privateer pension fund. One certificate in volume 3 is dated July 6, 1874.

786.   INDEXES TO PENSION ROLLS B-D. n.d. 3 cm, 1 in. 3 vols.

Arranged chronologically. Within each volume, the entries are arranged by initial letter of pensioner's surname.

Indexes to unidentified pension rolls showing pensioner's name, whether pension was payable from Navy Pension Fund or Privateer Pension Fund, whether arrears of pension had been paid, and page references to the pension rolls. Some of the pensioners listed in index B died in 1850.

Index C identified the arrearages of pension as having been paid under an act of March 3, 1837. Index D includes a newspaper clipping referring to appointments to the Navy "prior to 1853." No definite relationship has been established between these three indexes and other pension records described in this preliminary inventory.

787.   RECORD OF PENSION PAYMENTS. 1859-1901. 2.7 m, 9 ft. 37 vols.

Arranged chronologically. Within each volume the entries are arranged by location of pension agency and alphabetically thereunder by surname of pensioner.

The entries generally show location of pension agency, name of pensioner, veteran's name and rank (if other than pensioner), rate of pension, act under which payable, date of first payment, and record of subsequent payments. Other information sometimes included is date of death, date of widow's remarriage, date and amount of final payment, number of the pension certificate, and whether the certificate was original or reissued. Many accounts of Navy pension agents are among the records described in entry 721.

788.   ABSTRACT OF PENSION AGENTS' REPORTS. July 1864-June 1883. 61 cm, 2 ft. 10 vols.

Arranged chronologically. Within each volume the entries are generally arranged geographically by location of agency and thereunder by type of pension.

A majority of the volumes consist of reports prepared by the Interior Department's Pension Office, based on monthly and quarterly reports from pension agencies, showing names of pensioners, veteran's name and rank, act under which the pension was paid, period covered by payment, amount paid, and voucher number. Reports of payments to invalid pensioners frequently show type and degree of disability. One volume consists primarily of bound copies of reports received by the Pension Office from local pension agencies, mostly relating to transfers of pensioners from the rolls of one agency to the rolls of another agency.

For similar reports on Army pensions, see entry 591; for Navy pension accounts, see entry 721.

PAYMASTERS DIVISION

The Paymasters Division was first mentioned by the Fourth Auditor in a report on the work of the Office for the fiscal year beginning July 1, 1866. The primary function of the Division was to settle accounts of Navy paymasters, pay agents, and transportation and telegraph claims.

Settled accounts and claims were sent to the Record and Prize Division.

Correspondence

789.   REGISTERS OF LETTERS RECEIVED FROM PAYMASTERS. July 1906-June 1910. 8 cm, 3 in. 3 vols.

Arranged chronologically. Within each volume the entries are arranged by surname of paymaster and thereunder chronologically.

There are gaps in the date span of these records; the actual dates covered are: July 1906-Oct. 1907; Mar. 1909-June 1910.

Registers contain entries that show paymaster's name, paymaster's identifying number, and dates and subjects of letters received. The identifying numbers are the same in all three volumes and correspond to the numbers in the registers of letters sent to paymasters and others (entry 791). Some of the letters registered in these volumes are filed with the accounts described in entry 811.

790.   INDEXES TO LETTERS SENT TO PAYMASTERS, NAVY AGENTS, AND RECRUITING OFFICERS. Jan. 21, 1860-Apr. 5, 1867. 18 cm, 7 in. 2 vols.

Arranged chronologically. Within each volume the entries are arranged alphabetically by subject or name of addressee and thereunder chronologically.

Indexes to volumes 28-62 of the letters sent to paymaster, Navy agents, and recruiting officers (entry 792) showing name and rank of addressee or about whom letter was written, volume number, date span of volumes, and page references to letters to or about the person named.

791.   REGISTERS OF LETTERS SENT TO PAYMASTERS AND OTHERS. Jan. 4, 1869 - Oct. 7, 1910. 30 cm, 1 ft. 6 vols.

Arranged chronologically. Within each volume entries are arranged by name of addressee and thereunder chronologically.

Registers contain entries that show date of letter, name and residence of addressee, and subject of letter. Most of the letters are routine acknowledgments of receipt of accounts.

Beginning with January 1902, entries for letters to paymasters include an identifying number that is the same as the number for the paymaster in the registers of letters received from paymasters, entry 789. Some letters registered in the first volume of this series are copied in volumes 69-94 of letters sent to paymasters, Navy agents, and recruiting officers, entry 792.

792.   LETTERS SENT TO NAVY AGENTS, PURSERS, AND RECRUITING OFFICERS.
        Jan. 1, 1835-Apr. 30, 1875. 6.7 m, 22 ft. 94 vols.

Arranged chronologically. Each volume except volumes 86 and 87 (covering the period May 20-Dec. 18, 1873) is indexed by name of addressee and by subject of letter.

Fair copies of letters relating chiefly to the receipt and settlement of accounts and claims, allotments, certificates of deposit, and approval of requisitions. Beginning with volume 30 (July 6, 1861), the word "paymaster" was substituted for the word "purser" in the title of the series. Beginning with volume 37 (Nov. 26, 1862), letters to Navy agents were dropped from this series and made part of a new series (see entry 793).

Beginning with volume 69 (Jan. 2, 1869), the series includes letters to Cabinet-level officers, and the title of the series was changed to "Paymasters and Executive Letters Sent." For related indexes and registers, see entries 790 and 791; for a continuation of these letters, see entry 809.

793.   LETTERS SENT TO NAVY AGENTS. Oct. 1, 1862-Dec. 31, 1866. 61 cm, 2 ft. 7 vols.

Arranged chronologically. Each volume except 1 and 2 (Oct. 1, 1862-June 3, 1863) is indexed by subject of letter and name of addressee.

There are gaps in the date span of these records; the actual dates covered are: Oct. 1, 1862-Feb. 23, 1864; Sept. 21, 1864-Dec. 31, 1866.

Fair copies of form letters to Navy agents, relating chiefly to the settlement of their accounts. The "text" of these letters usually consists of only a few unrelated words.

For copies of other letters to Navy agents, see entry 792.

Records Relating to Accounts

794.   INDEXES TO NAVY PAYMASTERS ACCOUNTS. Jan. 1798-Mar. 1896. 30 cm, 1 ft. 7 vols.

Arranged chronologically. Within each volume the entries are arranged by name of paymaster and thereunder chronologically.

Partial index to settled accounts described in entry 811 showing paymaster's name, account number, name of ship or station, and period covered by the account. Also included are some entries for accounts of railroads, fiscal agents, and contractors. There are relatively few entries before 1820. The volumes overlap and somewhat duplicate one another in date coverage. Several have the notation, "copied April-July 1902 as opportunity offered." For an index of paymasters' accounts arranged by name of ship, see entry 813.

795.   INDEX TO NAVY PAY AGENTS ACCOUNTS. Jan. 1798-Dec. 1908. 3 cm, 1 in. 1 vol.

Arranged by location of pay office and thereunder chronologically.

Partial index to quarterly abstracts of Navy pay accounts (entry 793) and original pay accounts (entry 811) showing account number, location of pay office, name of pay agent, and period covered by account. The dates of accounts vary considerably from one pay office to another.

796.   CERTIFICATES OF SETTLEMENT OF MARINE CORPS ACCOUNTS. June 23, 1855-
        July 19, 1869. 8 cm, 3 in. 2 vols.

        Arranged chronologically. Each volume is indexed by name of person submitting
account.
        Date reported, title of appropriation to be charged, in whose name stated, explanation,
balance due from the United States, and payment instructions. The certificates also include a
notation of approval by the Comptroller for payment.

797.   CERTIFICATES OF SETTLEMENT OF PAYMASTERS ACCOUNTS. Mar. 30, 1872 -
        Mar. 29, 1877. 8 cm, 3 in. 1 vol.

        Arranged chronologically. Indexed by name of paymaster.
        Date reported, account number, title of appropriation to be charged, paymaster's name,
amount due him by the United States, explanation, and payment instructions.

798.   QUARTERLY ABSTRACTS OF NAVY PAY ACCOUNTS. Apr. 1827-Dec. 1922. 36.0 m,
        118 ft. 1,438 vols.

        Arranged chronologically and thereunder by name of city in which Navy pay office
was located. Within the volumes for each office the entries are arranged by type of expenditure
and thereunder chronologically. Alpha boxes: 450A, 889A, 1242A, and 1293A.
        Abstracts show period covered, name of pay agent, title of appropriation, and summary
of disbursements from that appropriation.
        Disbursements typically include salaries, purchases of supplies and equipment, and
authorized allotments from pay of naval personnel. The volume described in entry 795 serves as
an index to pay offices and names of pay agents. The vouchers and supporting documents that
accompanied these abstracts are described in entry 811. Pay office abstracts are included for:

        Annapolis, Sept. 1921-Sept. 1922, 2 vols.
        Baltimore, Jan. 1843-Aug. 1921, 145 vols.
        Boston, July 1842-Sept. 1922, 200 vols.
        Brooklyn, Apr.-Dec. 1921, 3 vols.
        Charleston, July 1909-Dec. 1922, 34 vols.
        London, July 1865-Dec. 1896, 2 vols.
        Manila, Apr. 1907-Mar. 1917, 48 vols.
        Memphis, June 1845-Mar. 1856, 1 vol.
        Newport, July 1910-Sept. 1922, 29 vols.
        New York, Oct. 1842-Sept. 1921, 255 vols.
        Norfolk, Aug. 1829-Sept. 1922, 68 vols.
        Pensacola, Oct. 1841-Sept. 1860, 3 vols.
        Philadelphia, Apr. 1841-Sept. 1922, 182 vols.
        Portsmouth, Jan. 1847-Dec. 1922, 32 vols.
        Puget Sound, May 1917-Sept. 1922, 18 vols.
        San Francisco, Jan. 1847-Sept. 1922, 169 vols.
        Seattle, July 1907-May 1917, 45 vols.
        Washington, D.C., Apr. 1827-Sept. 1922, 202 vols.

RECORD AND PRIZE DIVISION

The Record and Prize Division was first mentioned by the Fourth Auditor in a report on the work of the Office for the fiscal year beginning July 1, 1887. It was a successor to the Prize Money, Record, and Files Division, which had been established in July 1881. The functions of the Division were to register, index, and record general correspondence; to settle claims for prize money; to prepare reports on naval personnel and reports requested by Congress, courts, or the Secretary of the Treasury; to handle personnel matters within the Fourth Auditor's Office; and to maintain the files of the Office.

Correspondence

799.   REGISTERS OF LETTERS RECEIVED. Jan. 2, 1836-Jan. 15, 1898. 7.0 m, 23 ft. 95 vols.

Arranged chronologically. Beginning with September 2, 1861, the entries are arranged by initial letter of writer's surname or title and thereunder chronologically. From June 1864 to December 1867 there are two sets of registers; one for persons whose surnames begin with the letters A-L (vols. 6, 8, 10, 12, 14, 15, and 17) and one for persons whose surnames begin with the letters M-Z (vols. 7, 9, 11, 13, and 16).

Registers contain entries that show date received, name of writer, subject, and date of letter. Subjects include pay, allotments, pensions, certificates of deposit, claims for prize moneys, requests for transfer, and information on the service of seamen. These registers are reproduced on rolls 1-62 of NARA Microfilm Publication M1187, Letters Received by the Fourth Auditor.

For the original letters, see entries 800-806; for copies of replies, see entries 809 and 810.

800.   LETTERS RECEIVED FROM THE SECRETARY OF THE NAVY. Dec. 19, 1817-Dec. 31, 1865. 1.2 m, 4 ft. 19 vols.

Arranged chronologically, usually by date of Auditor's action on the letter. Each volume is indexed by surname of person concerned.

There are gaps in the date span of these records; the actual dates covered are: Dec. 19, 1817-June 3, 1845; June 15, 1848-July 6, 1850; Jan. 5-Dec. 27, 1853; Jan. 6, 1855-Dec. 31, 1865.

The letters relate to the distribution of prize moneys, approvals of expenditures, allotments from pay of officers and men, and promotions or resignations of officers. These letters are reproduced on rolls 63-71 of NARA Microfilm Publications M1187, Letters Received by the Fourth Auditor.

For a register, see entry 799; for additional letters from the Secretary of the Navy, see entries 804 and 805; for copies of replies, see entry 809.

801.   LETTERS RECEIVED FROM THE SECRETARY OF THE TREASURY AND OTHER TREASURY DEPARTMENT OFFICIALS. Feb. 17, 1848-Sept. 8, 1868. 23 cm, 9 in. 5 vols.

Arranged chronologically by date of Auditor's action on the letter. Each volume is indexed by surname of person concerned.

The letters concern personnel actions, instructions, orders, major decisions, and the preparation of reports. These letters are reproduced on rolls 72 and 73 of NARA Microfilm Publication M1187, Letters Received by the Fourth Auditor. Part of this series is in the same box as entry 802.

For a register, see entry 799; for additional letters from the Secretary and other Treasury officials, see entry 804; for copies of replies, see entry 809.

802.　LETTERS RECEIVED FROM THE SECOND COMPTROLLER. Apr. 4, 1849-Dec. 30, 1865. 8 cm, 3 in. 2 vols.

Arranged chronologically by date of Auditor's action on the letter. Each volume is indexed by surname of person concerned.

There are gaps in the date span of these records; the actual dates covered are: Apr. 4, 1849-Nov. 19, 1862; Jan. 5-Dec. 30, 1865.

The letters relate to the status of accounts, filing of surety bonds, receipt of certificates of deposit, and decisions on appeals. The 1865 volume includes one letter from the Postmaster General to the Fourth Auditor. These letters and those in entry 803 are reproduced on roll 74 of NARA Microfilm Publication M1187, Letters Received by the Fourth Auditor. Part of this series is filed in the same box as entry 801 and 803.

For a register, see entry 799; for other letters from the Second Comptroller and Postmaster General, see entry 804; for copies of replies, see entry 809.

803.　LETTERS RECEIVED FROM THE COMMISSIONER OF PENSIONS. May 18, 1849-Aug. 16, 1858. 5 cm, 2 in. 1 vol.

Arranged chronologically by date of Auditor's action on the letter. Indexed by surname of person concerned.

Chiefly letters about verification of naval service of persons claiming pensions or bounty land based on such service or concerning changes in pension rolls. Included is one letter for June 4, 1861, and one for December 29, 1862. These letters and those in entry 802 are reproduced on roll 74 of NARA Microfilm Publication M1187, Letters Received by the Fourth Auditor. This series is filed in the same box as part of entry 802.

For a register, see entry 799; for additional letters from the Commissioner of Pensions, see entry 804; for copies of replies, see entry 809.

804.　LETTERS RECEIVED FROM GOVERNMENT OFFICIALS (EXECUTIVE LETTERS). Nov. 21, 1801-Dec. 31, 1868. 1.8 m, 6 ft. 25 vols.

Arranged chronologically, chiefly by date of Auditor's action on the letter. Those for 1866-68, however, are arranged by office of administrative origin, in no particular order, and thereunder chronologically by date of Auditor's action. Each volume is indexed by surname of person concerned.

There are gaps in the date span of these records; the actual dates covered are: Nov. 21, 1801-Dec. 19, 1864; Jan. 1, 1866-Dec. 31, 1868.

Letters from the Secretaries of the Navy and the Treasury, auditors, heads of Navy bureaus, the First and Second Comptrollers, and the Commissioner of Pensions relating to such subjects as supplies, personnel, and settlement of accounts and claims. These letters are reproduced on rolls 75-91 of NARA Microfilm Publication M1187, Letters Received by the Fourth Auditor. Box 17 contains the end of entry 804 and the beginning of entry 805.

For a register, see entry 799; for additional letters from Navy officials, see entry 805; for additional letters from other Government officials, see entries 800-803; for copies of replies, see entry 809.

805.　LETTERS RECEIVED FROM NAVY DEPARTMENT OFFICIALS. Jan. 2, 1869-Dec. 29, 1895. 3.7 m, 12 ft. 49 vols.

Arranged chronologically, generally by date of Auditor's action on the letter. Each volume is indexed by surname of writer and surname of person concerned.

Letters about settlement of accounts and claims, requests for rehearing cases, verification of naval service, personnel actions, and allotments from pay of officers and enlisted men. These letters are reproduced on rolls 92-122 of NARA Microfilm Publication M1187, Letters Received by the Fourth Auditor. The beginning of this series is found in box 17 of entry 805.

For a register, see entry 799; for additional letters from heads of Navy bureaus, see entry 804; for copies of replies, see entry 809.

806. MISCELLANEOUS LETTERS RECEIVED. Jan. 12, 1795-Dec. 31, 1897. 128.0 m, 420 ft. 1,575 vols.

Arranged chronologically, primarily by date of Auditor's action on the letter. Many letters before 1829, however, are arranged either by date letter was written or date received. The letters for 1829-33 are arranged by year only, and those for 1894-97 are arranged by month only. Most volumes after 1830 are indexed by surname of writer and surname of person concerned, but there are a few indexed volumes before that date.

Letters from seamen, ordinary citizens, attorneys, heirs of sailors, and accountable officers on such subject as settlement of claims, pay, transfer from one ship or shore station to another, entitlement to prize moneys, and verification of naval service. Some of these letters are reproduced on rolls 123-1330 of NARA Microfilm Publication M1187, Letters Received by the Fourth Auditor.

For a register, see entry 799; for copies of replies, see entries 809 and 810.

807. INDEXES TO MISCELLANEOUS LETTERS SENT. June 7, 1859-Aug. 10, 1864. 15 cm, 6 in. 2 vols.

Arranged chronologically. Within each volume the entries are arranged by surname of addressee and thereunder chronologically.

Indexes to volumes 66-84 of the miscellaneous letters sent (entry 810) showing name and rank of addressee, volume number, date span of the volume, and page references to the letters to or about the person named.

808. REGISTERS OF LETTERS SENT. Sept. 2, 1861-Jan. 15, 1898. 5.5 m, 18 ft. 70 vols.

Arranged chronologically. Within each volume entries are arranged by surname of addressee and thereunder chronologically.

Registers contain entries of letters sent to Government officials (entry 809) and miscellaneous letters sent (entry 810). The entries show date of letter, name and address or title of addressee, and subject. If the person was a naval officer, his rank is also shown. Included are letters to accountable officers, naval personnel, Government officials, and claimants relating to such subjects as settlement of accounts and claims, decisions on bounty and prize money payable, requisitions, and allotments.

809. LETTERS SENT TO GOVERNMENT OFFICIALS (EXECUTIVE LETTERS). Apr. 28, 1820-Dec. 31, 1868. 91 cm, 3 ft. 15 vols.

Arranged chronologically. Each volume is indexed by name or title of addressee.

Fair copies of letters to Auditors and Navy and Treasury officials relating primarily to verification of naval service, settlement of accounts and claims, explanation of decisions, and submission of prize lists for approval.

For a register, see entry 808; for replies, see entries 800-805.

810. MISCELLANEOUS LETTERS SENT. May 3, 1800-Aug. 21, 1896. 22.6 m, 74 ft. 309 vols.

Arranged chronologically. Each volume is indexed by name or title of addressee and party in interest.

There are gaps in the date span of these records; the actual dates covered are: May 3, 1800-Jan. 22, 1811; Aug. 26, 1812-Aug. 21, 1896.

Fair copies of letters to naval personnel, claimants, and Government employees relating to the settlement of a wide variety of accounts and claims for whose settlement the Auditor was responsible. Volume 5 was not used. Because of the large number of letters written between October 1863 and May 1864, several volumes were used in which letters to persons with surnames beginning with particular letter of the alphabet (e.g., A-G) were copied. Two volumes are identified as volume 81. A special unnumbered volume consists of letters dated December 20-30, 1878.

For indexes, see entry 807; for registers, see entry 808; for replies, see entry 806.

Accounts and Claims

811.   SETTLED ACCOUNTS OF NAVY PAYMASTERS AND PAY AGENTS. ca. 1798-1915. 1,341.1 m, 4,400 ft. Unbound records.

Arranged alphabetically by name of accountable officer and thereunder chronologically. Alpha boxes (1st group): 184A, 225A, 285A, 454A, 485A, 497A. Alpha boxes (2nd group): 185A, 263A, 334A, 374A, 490A, 583A, 716A, 797A, 876A-B, 1793A, 1803A, 2016A, 2046A, 2274A, 2295A, 2325A, 2674A, 2735A, 2982A.

These original pay accounts usually consist of the Auditor's certificates, a statement of the account, abstracts of expenditures, and such supporting documents as muster rolls, payrolls, and vouchers. The registers described in entries 794 and 795 serve as indexes to the names of paymasters and pay agents whose accounts are included in this series.

For abstracts of Navy pay agent's accounts, see entry 798; for copies of Auditor's certificates, see entry 777.

812.   SETTLED MISCELLANEOUS ACCOUNTS AND CLAIMS. Mar. 29, 1817-Aug. 31, 1911. 213.4 m, 700 ft. 287 boxes.

Arranged by account number.

Each file generally consists of a statement of the account, abstract of disbursements, and vouchers. Sometimes birth and marriage certificates, pension certificates, court decisions, correspondence, wills, and powers of attorney are included as supporting documents. Types of accounts and claims include those for purchase of supplies; of military storekeepers; for moneys owed deceased seamen; of surgeons and recruiting officers; for transportation, prize money, and arrears of pay; and of consular officials for care of seamen.

For certificates of settlement of these accounts and claims, see entry 778.

Records Relating to Ships and Crews

813.   INDEXES TO SHIPS AND STATIONS. May 8, 1798-Dec. 31, 1907. 25 cm, 10 in. 4 vols.

Arranged chronologically. Within each volume the entries are arranged by name of ship or shore unit and thereunder chronologically.

Indexes to accounts, showing name of ship or shore unit, account number, period covered by account, and name of paymaster. Few entries date before 1840, and each of the volumes overlaps the other in date span. Some of the accounts are among the records described in entry 811.

For an additional index arranged by name of paymaster, see entry 794.

814.   MISCELLANEOUS DATA ON THE SERVICE OF SHIPS. Jan. 1846-Aug. 1905. 5 cm,
        2 in. 2 vols.

        Arranged chronologically, thereunder by type of information, and thereunder
        alphabetically by name of ship. The first volume includes the first four lists described below,
        and the part of volume 1 pertaining to Civil War service is indexed by name of ship. Volume 2
        includes only the fifth list described below. One volume appears to be missing.
        Data on Navy ships: (1) list of ships in New Orleans during 1846; (2) list of ships in the
        Western Gun Boat Flotilla; (3) list of ships whose crews were paid by Paymaster Hollabird
        during 1862-63; (4) list of ships in the Civil War, including information on their date of
        purchase or capture, military actions, circumstances of destruction (if pertinent), numbers and
        periods covered by payrolls and pay accounts, and the names of paymasters; and (5) lists of
        ships commissioned and decommissioned from April 1898 to August 1905.

815.   REGISTERS OF PERSONNEL ACTIONS AFFECTING THE STATUS OF NAVAL
        OFFICERS. Jan. 15, 1861-Nov. 28, 1902. 23 cm, 9 in. 4 vols.

        Arranged chronologically. Within each volume the entries are arranged by officer's
        surname. Volume 4 (Sept. 1890-Nov. 1902) is indexed by surname of officer. The other volumes
        are not indexed. One volume appears to be missing.
        Registers contain entries that show date and type of action, officer's name and rank,
        and effective date of action. Most entries record death or resignation of the officer although
        some show dates of commissions, promotions, or leaves of absence. Volumes 2 and 3 overlap in
        date span and largely duplicate one another.

816.   SERVICE RECORDS OF NAVY ENLISTED MEN AND WARRANT OFFICERS. July 7,
        1825-Sept. 15, 1892. 61 cm, 2 ft. 9 vols.

        Arranged chronologically. Within each volume entries are arranged by surname of
        person. Each volume is indexed by name.
        The entries show seaman's name and rank, ship on which he first enlisted, period of
        service, dates of transfers to other ships or shore units, names of other units with which he saw
        service, date of death or discharge, and rank at time of discharge if different than original
        rank.
        Most entries relate to Civil War service.

817.   CARD INDEX TO MUSTER ROLLS AND PAYROLLS FOR NAVY SHIPS AND
        SHORE UNITS. Jan. 1, 1828-July 9, 1907. 15 cm, 6 in.

        Arranged alphabetically and thereunder chronologically.
        Index, on 5 by 8-inch cards, to some of the muster rolls and payrolls described in entry
        818. Cards show the name of ship or shore unit, inclusive dates of muster rolls or payrolls for
        the ship or station, number of the volume in which they are bound, and names of pursers or pay
        agents of the units for the period covered by the rolls.

818.   MUSTER ROLLS AND PAY AND RECEIPT ROLLS FOR SHIPS AND SHORE UNITS.
        Nov. 1, 1820-Aug. 31, 1898. 41.5 m, 136 ft. 686 vols.

        Arranged by name of ship or station and thereunder chronologically.
        There are gaps in the date span of these records; the actual dates covered are: Nov. 1,
        1820-Dec. 31, 1873; Apr. 1-Aug. 31, 1898.
        The rolls show name of unit; period covered; names and ranks of officers, recruits,
        enlisted men, and others making up the crew; dates of enlistment; signature; base pay; amounts
        credited; amounts deducted (including allotments); and net pay. Some of the rolls also show

amounts of overpayments or amounts due but not paid. Some of the rolls are for Coast Survey ships and revenue cutters operating as part of the Navy, and some are for civilian personnel of Navy yards and other shore units.

For a partial index to these rolls, see entry 817.

819.   RECORD OF PERSONS ENTITLED TO EXTRA PAY FOR SERVICE IN THE MEXICAN WAR. ca. Apr. 1842-Mar. 1855. 5 cm, 2 in. 1 vol.

Arranged chronologically and thereunder by type of information.

This volume was compiled under provisions of an act of February 19, 1879 (20 Stat. 316), which extended to the officers, seamen, and marines of the U.S. Navy and the Revenue-Cutter Service the same additional 3 months extra pay for service in the Mexican War that had previously been granted to officers and soldiers of volunteer units and of the Army. The volume contains four sections: (1) vouchers of officers, April 1847-August 1848, showing officer's name and rank, period covered by pay account, and amount paid; (2) copies of requisitions on the Secretary of the Navy by the Paymaster of the Marine Corps, June 2-September 25, 1851; (3) list of persons in the Gulf Squadron entitled to 3 months extra pay; and (4) list of persons in the Pacific Squadron entitled to 3 months extra pay.

Sections 3 and 4 each show the name of the ship and claimant; date claimant enlisted, reenlisted, and was discharged; amount due; and when, where, and by whom paid.

820.   REGISTER OF COURT-MARTIAL SENTENCES. Feb. 13, 1871-Sept. 30, 1878. 5 cm, 2 in. 1 vol.

Arranged by initial letter of defendant's surname and thereunder chronologically.

Register contains entries that show date sentence was imposed, defendant's name and rank, name of ship on which he served, summary of sentence, and amount of penalty.

821.   INDEX TO PRIZE CASES. 1862-73. 3 cm, 1 in. 1 vol.

Arranged by name of captured ship and thereunder chronologically.

The entries show year of capture, name of captured ship, location of court in which case was tried, and case number. Sometimes cross-references to other cases are also shown. The records indexed by this volume have not been located.

822.   INDEX TO CIVIL WAR PRIZE LISTS. May 27, 1863-June 1, 1868. 3 cm, 1 in. 1 vol.

Arranged by name of "captor" (i.e., capturing ship).

The entries show volume and page references to the Second Comptroller's registers of prize cases (entry 168), names of "captor" and prize or description of property captured (e.g., cotton), value of captured ship or property, date of court's decree, and date of payment. Some pages in the back of the book list Navy ships destroyed during the Civil War and sometimes include information on date and place of destruction and notations as to whether officers and crew were entitled to compensation for loss of personal property.

823.   ABSTRACTS OF PRIZE ACCOUNTS, ca. 1815-98. 1.2 m, 4 ft. 15 vols.

Arranged chronologically. Within each volume the entries are arranged by name of captor. Each volume is indexed by name of captor.

The abstracts show names of captor and prize, date of capture, amounts available for distribution as prize money, names and ranks of persons entitled to payment, percentages and amounts due, and, frequently, when and where paid. Most abstracts relate to ships captured during the Civil War, but many in the first volume relate to ships captured during the 1815 Algerian Expedition and to slave ships captured in the 1850s.

For original prize cases, see entry 824; for certificates of settlement of prize claims, see entry 825.

824.   PRIZE LISTS. 1862-65. 4.3 m, 14 ft. 11 boxes.

Arranged by initial letter of name of captor.

Each list shows names of captor and prize or description of property captured, date of capture, and names and ranks of all persons assigned to the captor ship at the time of the capture. For abstracts of prize accounts, see entry 823; for certificates of settlement of prize claims of individual crew members, see entry 825.

825.   CERTIFICATES OF SETTLEMENT OF PRIZE CLAIMS. May 12, 1863-Oct. 22, 1884. 4.9 m, 16 ft. 75 vols.

Arranged chronologically. Each volume is indexed by claimant's name.

The certificates show date and number of report, title of appropriation to be charged, claimant's name and rank, amount due claimant, names of capturing and captured ships, and payment instructions. For prize lists, see entry 824; for abstracts of prize accounts, see entry 823.

826.   REGISTERS OF PRIZE CLAIMS PAID. Jan. 5, 1875-Feb. 9, 1903. 10 cm, 4 in. 2 vols.

Arranged chronologically. Entries within the second volume (which is primarily a duplicate copy of the first volume) are arranged by claimant's name and thereunder chronologically.

Registers contain entries that show date of claim, name of claimant, name of ship on which claimant served, to whom paid, amount paid, and date paid. The second volume also shows name of captured ship or description of captured property.

827.   LISTS OF PERSONS OMITTED FROM PRIZE LISTS. Nov. 22, 1862-Feb. 26, 1873. 3 cm, 1 in. 2 vols.

Arranged chronologically. Volume 1 is indexed by name of ship.

The entries show, in general, name of capturing ship, seaman's name and rank, amount due seaman, and date paid. The second volume, in addition, shows name of captured ship and the citation of authority for adding the claimant to the prize list.

OFFICE OF THE FIFTH AUDITOR

The Office of the Fifth Auditor was established by an act of March 3, 1817(3 Stat. 366), which assigned to the Auditor the functions of settling all accounts of the Department of State, the Post Office Department, and accounts arising out of Indian affairs; also certifying the balances of the accounts and claims to the First Comptroller for his decision. Responsibility for Indian accounts and claims was transferred from the Fifth Auditor to the Second Auditor by an act of February 24, 1819 (3 Stat. 487). The functions relating to accounts of the Post Office Department were transferred to the Sixth Auditor when that Office was created by an act of July 2, 1836 (5 Stat. 80). The duties of the Fifth Auditor that relate to the general superintendence of the lighthouse system began in January 1820 and were formalized by an act of March 3, 1845 (5 Stat. 762), which provided for the Fifth Auditor to continue performing that function. The Fifth Auditor became responsible for the settlement of internal revenue accounts under provisions of an act of June 30, 1864 (13 Stat. 223). No further major changes in the duties of the Office were made until an act of July 1, 1894 (28 Stat. 205), made the Fifth Auditor (renamed Auditor for the State and Other Departments) responsible for the settlement of accounts of the State and Justice Departments and other accounts not specifically assigned by the act to another Auditor.

The main operating Divisions of the Fifth Auditor's Office were the Diplomatic and Consular Division, the Internal Revenue Division, the Division of Judicial Accounts, and the Miscellaneous Division. Records dealing with the functions of more than one Division and with personnel matters are described under general records. The most important records of the Office of the Fifth Auditor are accounts, 1817-52; audit reports on several series of accounts, 1817-94; and copies of letters sent, 1817-99.

A list of names of Fifth Auditors and their dates of service appear in Appendix 9.

GENERAL RECORDS

Correspondence

828.   MISCELLANEOUS LETTERS SENT. Mar. 18, 1817-Apr. 30, 1869.1.5 m, 5 ft. 27 vols.

Arranged chronologically. Each volume, except the one identified as volume 18 1/2 is indexed by name or title of addressee.

There are gaps in the date span of these records; the actual dates covered are: Mar. 18, 1817-June 11, 1856; Aug. 12, 1856-Apr. 30, 1869.

Fair copies of letters relating chiefly to diplomatic, consular, internal revenue, and judicial accounts; also to drawback claims. Volumes 1-11 and 13-15 (ending Feb. 14, 1862) include letters on all of these types of accounts and claims. There is no volume 12. An attempt was apparently made after February 1862 to separate the letters by type. Volumes 17-20 contain only internal revenue and drawback letters; volumes 18 1/2, 19 1/2, and 22, plus two unnumbered volumes, contain only letters relating to diplomatic and consular accounts. Volumes 16 and 21 include all types of letters; volumes 23 and 24 relate entirely to the settlement of drawback claims. Beginning in May 1869, two separate series were maintained: internal revenue letters (new series) and consular and miscellaneous letters (new series). These two series of letters are described in entries 868 and 839, respectively. There is no volume 2.

829.   MISCELLANEOUS LETTERS SENT. Nov. 23, 1855-June 17, 1869. 91 cm, 3 ft. 25 vols.

Arranged chronologically. Each volume is indexed by name or title of addressee. There are gaps in the date span of this series; the actual dates covered are: Nov. 23, 1855-Aug. 12, 1856; Feb. 7, 1862-June 17, 1869.

Press copies of letters to diplomatic and consular officials, internal revenue officials, and private persons, relating to such subjects as diplomatic, consular, and internal revenue expenses, settlement of drawback claims, and accounts for transportation of destitute seamen. The volume that includes letters dated November 23, 1855-August 12, 1865, fills a gap in the fair copies of letters described in entry 828; some of the others supplement or duplicate copies of letters in other volumes of that series.

Records Relating to Accounts

830. INDEX TO AUDIT REPORTS ON MISCELLANEOUS ACCOUNTS AND CLAIMS. Mar. 17, 1817-Dec. 2, 1848. 5 cm, 2 in. 1 vol.

Arranged by initial letter of officer's or claimant's name and thereunder chronologically.

An index to volumes 1-15 of audit reports on miscellaneous accounts and claims (entry 832) showing account number, date approved, officer's or claimant's name, type of account or claim, and period covered. Entries include accounts for diplomatic and consular salaries and expenses, for contingent expenses of the State Department, for expenses of taking the census, and for expenses of public printing. Also included are accounts of the Postmaster General, accounts of the disbursing agent of the Post Office Department for contingent expenses of the Department, and accounts and claims relating to Indian affairs. The accounts of the Postmaster General were withdrawn from the series of accounts described in entry 833 and transferred to the Post Office Department. Accounts and claims relating to Indian affairs were transferred to the Second Auditor and are described as part of entry 525.

831. REGISTER OF MISCELLANEOUS ACCOUNTS RECEIVED. July 31, 1839-July 21, 1859. 5 cm, 2 in. 1 vol.

Arranged chronologically.

Register contains entries that show account number, name of accountable officer, date approved, and by whom received.

For an index to these accounts, see entry 830; for copies of audit reports, see entry 832. Some of the accounts are described in entry 833.

832. AUDIT REPORTS ON MISCELLANEOUS ACCOUNTS AND CLAIMS. Mar. 17, 1817 Apr. 26, 1895. 3.1 m, 10 ft. 47 vols.

Arranged chronologically. Within each volume the reports are arranged numerically. Each volume is indexed by surname of accountable officer or claimant.

Fair copies of reports showing date audited, number of account, name of officer or claimant, type of account or claim, period covered, debits and credits, statement of differences, and adjusted balance. The original reports are filed with the settled accounts (entry 833).

For an index to volumes 1-15, see entry 830.

833. MISCELLANEOUS SETTLED ACCOUNTS AND CLAIMS. Mar. 17, 1817-Mar. 4, 1851. 99.1 m, 325 ft. Unbound records.

Arranged numerically by account number. Alpha boxes: 7A, 7B, 66A, 181A, and 236A.

An account usually consists of the Auditor's report, a statement of the account or claim as submitted, lists of outstanding warrants, abstracts of expenditures, and vouchers, bills, or other supporting evidence of the validity of the account or claim. Types of accounts include diplomatic and consular expenses, contingent expenses of the State Department, expenses of taking the census, accounts of the Postmaster General, accounts of the disbursing agent of the Post Office Department for contingent expenses, and expenses of the Patent Office. The accounts of the Postmaster General later were withdrawn from this series and transferred to the Post

Office Department. Accounts and claims for Indian affairs, originally a part of this series, were withdrawn and transferred to the Second Auditor; they included in entry 525.

For additional copies of the audit reports, see entry 832; for an index to the accounts, covering the period March 17, 1817-December 2, 1848, see entry 830.

834. COPIES OF VOUCHERS FOR DISBURSEMENTS FOR SUBSISTENCE OF DESTITUTE AMERICAN SEAMEN AT LONDON. Nov. 1, 1816-Oct. 7, 1819. 3 cm, 1 in. 1 vol.

Arranged chronologically.

The entries show date of payment, amount paid, name of seaman, his signature, and sometimes an explanation of the reason for the payment. This volume was compiled at a later date from the original accounts of Thomas Aspinwall, consul at London (included in the records described in entry 833).

835. JOURNAL OF THE AMERICAN AND BRITISH COMMISSIONERS APPOINTED UNDER THE SIXTH AND SEVENTH ARTICLES OF THE TREATY OF GHENT. Nov. 18, 1816-Oct. 27, 1827. 5 cm, 2 in. 1 vol.

Arranged chronologically.

This journal consists of copies of the oaths and credentials of the American and British Commissioners, minutes of meetings of the Commissioners, copies of reports considered and resolutions adopted, and an abstract of joint expenses of the Commissioners. This journal became part of the account of American Commissioner Peter B. Porter, settled July 13, 1829, and originally was included in the accounts described in entry 833.

Other Records

836. PAYROLLS OF EMPLOYEES IN THE FIFTH AUDITOR'S OFFICE. Jan. 1817-Aug. 1900. 15 cm, 6 in. 3 vols.

Arranged chronologically.

There are gaps in the date span of these records; the actual dates covered are: Jan. 1817-Mar. 1831; Apr.-June 1832; Jan.-Sept. 1833; Oct. 1839-Mar. 1844; July-Sept. 1845; Jan.-Mar. 1848; Jan.-Mar. 1849; Apr. 1850-June 1851; July 1853-Sept. 1857; Jan.-Mar. 1858; Jan. 1859-July 1896; Nov. 1896-Mar. 1899; May-Aug. 1899; Oct. 1899; Dec. 1899-Jan. 1900; Mar. 1900; Aug. 1900.

Copies of rolls usually signed by the employees showing period covered, employee's name and title, annual salary rate, and amount paid during the month and/or quarter. Employees are usually listed in order of importance of their position. Sometimes personnel actions are noted on the payrolls. Original payrolls through September 1894 are among the First Auditor's miscellaneous Treasury accounts, entry 347.

DIPLOMATIC AND CONSULAR DIVISION

The Diplomatic and Consular Division was first specifically mentioned by the Fifth Auditor in a report on activities of the Office for the fiscal year beginning July 1, 1882. It may have been a Division in the Office as early as 1868. Among the major types of accounts settled by the Diplomatic and Consular Division were those for salaries, fees, and contingent expenses of diplomatic and consular officers; expenses for care and transportation of destitute American seamen; expenses relating to deceased seamen; and contingent and other expenses of the State Department.

Correspondence

837.   REGISTERS OF LETTERS RECEIVED. Nov. 22, 1883-Apr. 30, 1909. 61 cm, 2 ft. 9 vols.

Arranged chronologically. Within each volume, except that for 1883-87, the entries are arranged by initial letter of writer's surname and thereunder chronologically.
There are gaps in the date span of these records; the actual dates covered are: Nov. 22, 1883-May 14, 1887; July 13, 1896-Apr. 30, 1909.
Registers contain entries that show dates letters were written and received, writer's name and address or title, subject of letter, and to whom assigned for reply. Reference is also made to referral of letters to or from other offices. Typical subjects are explanations of differences in diplomatic and consular accounts, verification of dates of service, value of foreign currency, relief of seamen, and settlement of estates of deceased Americans overseas.

838.   LETTERS RECEIVED. Sept. 9, 1856-Dec. 16, 1858. 1 cm, 1/2 in. 1 vol.

Arranged chronologically.
Letters, chiefly from U.S. consuls and commercial agents, relating to the settlement of their accounts and answering questions raised by the Auditor relating to accounts. Some of these letters are in reply to the letters sent described in entry 828.

839.   CONSULAR AND MISCELLANEOUS LETTERS SENT (NEW SERIES). May 1, 1869-May 2, 1891. 91 cm, 3 ft. 16 vols.

Arranged chronologically. Each volume is indexed by name or title of addressee.
Fair copies of letters to State Department and consular officials, to the Secretary of the Treasury, and to private persons relating to such matters as verification of leave of absence of consular officials, eligibility of consuls for travel pay, crediting deposit of consular fees into the Treasury, advances to consular officials, and replies to requests for copies of annual reports and other publications. One letter for May 14, 1891, is included.
For letters sent for the period 1817-69, see entry 828. Other letters relating to consular officials and expenses of consuls and other officials are described in entries 840 and 841.

840.   LETTERS SENT RELATING TO DIPLOMATIC AND CONSULAR OFFICIALS. Oct. 4, 1894-Dec. 30, 1899. 1.8 m, 6 ft. 24 vols.

Arranged chronologically. Each volume has a separate index for the letters for each month; each index is arranged by name or title of addressee.
There are gaps in the date span of these records; the actual dates covered are: Oct. 4, 1894-Mar. 31, 1896; July 1, 1896-Dec. 30, 1899.
Press copies of letters relating chiefly to verification of service of diplomatic and consular officials and to their eligibility for travel pay and pay for leave of absence.
For copies of similar letters, see entries 828 and 839; for copies of letters relating chiefly to consular and miscellaneous expenses, see entry 841.

841.   LETTERS SENT RELATING TO CONSULAR AND MISCELLANEOUS EXPENSES. Jan. 18, 1893-Dec. 31, 1896. 61 cm, 2 ft. 12 vols.

Arranged chronologically. Each volume is indexed by name or title of addressee.
Letters relating chiefly to settlement of accounts for salaries and contingent expenses, consular fees, relief and transportation of seamen, and bills of exchange. Included are a few miscellaneous letters relating to such subjects as personnel actions, drawback claims, printing and binding for the Government, and purchase or repair of furniture and equipment.
For similar letters, see entries 828 and 839.

841A. DIGEST OF COMPTROLLER & OTHER DECISIONS APPLICABLE TO THE OFFICE OF THE AUDITOR FOR THE STATE & OTHER DEPTS. 1 vol. Compiled by C. H. Butler, 1909.

841B. DECISIONS OF THE COMPTROLLER OF THE TREASURY. AUDITOR STATE & OTHER DEPARTMENTS; DIPLOMATIC & CONSULAR DIVISION. Oct. 1, 1894 - Dec. 31, 1914. 2 vols.

Records Relating to Accounts and Claims

842. ALPHABETICAL REGISTERS OF DIPLOMATIC AND CONSULAR ACCOUNTS. Nov. 1854-May 1896. 28 cm, 11 in. 6 vols.

Arranged chronologically. Within each volume the entries are arranged by initial letter of accountable officer's surname and thereunder chronologically.

The entries show officer's name, title, and duty station, type and period of account, and date received. Among the types of accounts included are those for salaries and contingent expenses of U.S. diplomatic and consular officials, relief of destitute seamen, and such other special expenses as those of representatives on the Mexican Boundary Commission.

843. NUMERICAL REGISTERS OF DIPLOMATIC AND CONSULAR ACCOUNTS. July 21, 1859-Dec. 3, 1896. 30 cm, 1 ft. 10 vols.

Arranged chronologically. Within each volume the entries are arranged by account number. There are gaps in the date span of this series; the actual dates covered are: June 21, 1859-Apr. 2, 1885; Sept. 6, 1888- Dec. 3, 1896.

The entries show account number, name of accountable officer, usually the type of account, and date received. A new sequence of account numbers was begun in October 1894.

For copies of audit reports on many of these accounts, see entries 845-847.

844. GEOGRAPHICAL REGISTERS OF DIPLOMATIC AND CONSULAR ACCOUNTS. Jan. 1890-Feb. 1914. 61 cm, 2 ft. 9 vols.

Arranged chronologically. Within each volume the entries are arranged by location of diplomatic or consular post and thereunder chronologically. Each volume is indexed alphabetically by location.

The entries show location of diplomatic or consular post, accountable officer's name, type and period of account, and date received.

845. AUDIT REPORTS ON DIPLOMATIC ACCOUNTS. Mar. 11, 1865-Sept. 29, 1894. 1.2 m, 4 ft. 16 vols.

Arranged chronologically. Within each volume the reports are arranged by account number. Each volume, except volume 1 (Mar. 11, 1865- Nov. 30, 1868), is indexed by name of official.

There are gaps in the date span of these records; the actual dates covered are: Mar. 11, 1865-June 22, 1885; Sept. 13, 1886-Sept. 29, 1894.

Copies of reports showing date audited; account number; official's name, title, and duty station; period covered; debits and credits; explanation of differences; adjusted balance; and payment instructions. A continuous set of numbers was assigned for all different types of diplomatic and consular accounts. For this reason the numbers assigned to the diplomatic accounts are not consecutive.

846.   AUDIT REPORTS ON ACCOUNTS FOR SALARIES OF CONSULAR OFFICIALS. Apr. 22, 1857-Sept. 24, 1894. 5.2 m, 17 ft. 80 vols.

Arranged chronologically. Within each volume the reports are arranged by account number. Each volume is indexed by surname of consular official.

There are gaps in the date span of these records; the actual dates covered are: Apr. 22, 1857-Feb. 9, 1882; May 17, 1882-Sept. 24, 1894.

Copies of reports showing date audited; account number; official's name, title, and duty station; period covered; salary due; other debits and credits; explanation of differences; adjusted balance; and payment instructions. Salaries of consuls were frequently paid to persons other than the consuls themselves. A continuous set of numbers was assigned for all different types of diplomatic and consular accounts. For this reason the numbers assigned to consular salary accounts are not consecutive.

847.   AUDIT REPORTS ON CONTINGENT EXPENSES OF CONSULATES. Oct. 18, 1883 - Sept. 26, 1894. 2.1 m, 7 ft. 35 vols.

Arranged chronologically. Within each volume the reports are arranged by account number. Each volume is indexed by surname of consular official.

There are gaps in the date span of these records; the actual dates covered are: Oct. 18, 1883-June 12, 1890; Sept. 27, 1890-Sept. 26, 1894.

Copies of reports showing date audited; account number; official's name, title, and duty station; period covered; type and amount of expense; debits and credits; explanation of differences; adjusted balance; and payment instructions. These accounts were most often for hiring clerks, rent, postage, stationery, blank forms, and loss by exchange. A continuous set of numbers was assigned for all different types of diplomatic and consular accounts. For this reason the numbers assigned to accounts for contingent expenses of consulates are not consecutive.

848.   REGISTERS OF ACCOUNTS FOR RELIEF OF SEAMEN. Jan. 1845-Aug. 1908. 61 cm, 2 ft. 9 vols.

Arranged chronologically. Within each volume the entries are arranged by location of consulate and thereunder chronologically. The last five volumes (July 1881-Aug. 1908) are each indexed by location of consulate.

Registers contain entries that show the location of consulate, name of consular official, period covered, account number (except in the first volume), type of service provided, expense, and the number of seamen assisted.

849.   AUDIT REPORTS ON CONSULAR ACCOUNTS FOR RELIEF OF SEAMEN. Apr. 24, 1871-Apr. 26, 1895. 91 cm, 3 ft. 17 vols.

Arranged chronologically. Within each volume the reports are arranged by account number. Each volume is indexed by surname of consular official.

Copies of reports showing date audited; account number; name, title, and duty station of consular official; period covered; type and amount of expenditures in behalf of destitute American seamen; other debits and credits; explanation of differences; adjusted balance; and payment instructions. The account numbers begin again in October 1894. A continuous set of numbers was assigned for all different types of diplomatic and consular accounts. For this reason the numbers assigned to accounts for relief of seamen are not consecutive.

850.   AUDIT REPORTS ON ACCOUNTS FOR PASSAGE OF SEAMEN. Mar. 20, 1857-
       Apr. 23, 1895. 61 cm, 2 ft. 10 vols.

       Arranged chronologically. Within each volume the reports are arranged by account
number. Each volume is indexed by surname of the master of the ship on which transportation
was furnished.
       Copies of reports showing date audited, account number, name of master, name and
nationality of ship, amount payable, number of seamen transported (and sometimes their
names), points between which transportation was furnished, date of transportation, and
payment instructions. Payment was usually made to the owner of the ship or his agent, or to
assignees of the ship's master. The account numbers begin again in October 1894. A continuous set
of numbers was assigned to all different types of diplomatic and consular accounts. For this
reason the numbers assigned to accounts for passage of seamen are not consecutive.

851.   RECORD OF ACTION TAKEN BY THE COURT OF COMMISSIONERS FOR THE
       ALABAMA CLAIMS. July 21, 1874-Dec. 31, 1885. 28 cm, 11 in. 18 vols.

       Arranged chronologically.
       There are gaps in the date span of these records; the actual dates covered are: July 22,
1874-Dec. 14, 1876; July 13, 1882-Dec. 31, 1885.
       The entries show case number, title, date of judgment, name of claimant, amount of
principal and interest awarded, date from which interest was to accrue, total judgment, and
names and addresses of attorneys. In a few cases the claims were rejected. The name of the ship
sometimes is shown.
       For related audit reports, see entry 852.

852.   AUDIT REPORTS ON APPROVED AWARDS OF THE COURT OF COMMISSIONERS
       FOR THE ALABAMA CLAIMS. Apr. 11, 1876-Oct. 9, 1894. 1.2 m, 4 ft. 24 vols.

       Arranged chronologically. Each volume is indexed by surname of claimant and name of
ship.
       There are gaps in the date span of these records; the actual dates covered are: Apr. 11,
1876-Jan. 18, 1877; July 26, 1884-Oct. 9, 1894.
       Copies of audit reports showing claim number; date reported; claimant's name; date,
number, and amount of judgment; amounts of principal and interest due; and payment
instructions. One report is dated February 1, 1895.
       For a list of judgments, see entry 851.

853.   REGISTERS OF MISCELLANEOUS CONSULAR ACCOUNTS. Nov. 1885-Mar. 1902.
       8 cm, 3 in. 2 vols.

       Arranged chronologically. Within each volume the entries are arranged by type of
account and thereunder chronologically. The first volume is indexed by location of consulate.
       Registers contain entries that show account number, date audited, name of accountable
officer, type and period of account, title of appropriation to be charged, and amount payable.
Expenses include salaries, fulfilling treaty obligations, transporting remains of deceased
diplomatic and consular officers, and national defense. Many of the accounts relate to consulates
in China.

854.   REGISTER OF ACCOUNTS FOR CONTINGENT EXPENSES OF MINISTERS. July 1,
       1874-June 30, 1883. 1 cm, 1/2 in. 1 vol.

       Arranged by location of legation and thereunder chronologically.

Register contains entries that show location of legation, maximum salary and expenses allowable, account number, name of minister, period covered, amounts charged for rent and contingent expenses, amounts disallowed, and explanation.

855.   REGISTERS OF ACCOUNTS FOR SALARIES AND EXPENSES OF LEGATIONS. July 1, 1885-June 30, 1899. 10 cm, 4 in. 2 vols.

Arranged chronologically. Within each volume the entries are arranged by location of legation. Each volume is indexed by location of legation.
Registers contain entries that show location of legation, accountable officer's name and title, type of account, amounts reported for each type of account, and account numbers.

856.   RECORD OF CONSULAR EMOLUMENTS. Jan. 1882-Dec. 1887. 1 cm, 1/2 in. 1 vol.

Arranged alphabetically by name of consular official.
The entries show official's name, account number, amount of emoluments, and year in which received. The account numbers are for the salaries covered by the audit reports described in entry 846.

857.   REGISTERS OF ACCOUNTS FOR CONSULAR FEES AND SALARIES. July 1862-June 1881. 23 cm, 9 in. 3 vols.

Arranged chronologically. Within each volume entries are arranged by location of consulate and thereunder chronologically.
Registers contain entries that show consular official's name and duty station, period covered, account number (except in the first volume), amount of salary and fees reported for partial and/or complete quarters, loss by exchange, tax, and sometimes explanations, such as "additional salary" or "receiving instructions," if the amount reported was different than normal.

858.   REGISTER OF ACCOUNTS FOR SALARIES, FEES, AND CONTINGENT EXPENSES OF CONSULATES. Oct. 1868-Sept. 1875. 5 cm, 2 in. 1 vol.

Arranged by location of consulate.
Register contains entries that show location of consulate, date reported, officer's name, type and period of account, fees reported, account number, and debits and credits. The salaries and contingent expenses were included in the accounts of consular officials and are covered in the audit reports described in entries 846 and 847.

859.   ABSTRACTS OF FEES, COMPENSATION, AND CONTINGENT EXPENSES OF CONSULATES. July 1881-June 1899. 20 cm, 8 in. 6 vols.

Arranged by location of consulate.
The entries show location of consulate, name of official, amounts reported as compensation, fees, rent, hiring clerks, consular agent's fees and contingent expenses, and numbers of accounts in which the moneys were reported. These accounts are covered by the audit reports described in entries 846 and 847.

860.   RECORD OF HIRING CLERKS AND CONTINGENT EXPENSES OF CONSULATES. Jan. 1883-Mar. 1886. 1 cm, 1/2 in. 1 vol.

Arranged chronologically and thereunder by type of information.
This volume consists of three types of lists: (1) maximum allowance for hiring clerks showing location of consulate, maximum amount allowed by law for hiring clerks, actual

expenses, and total expenses for hiring clerks for the year; (2) additional allowances for hiring clerks approved by the Secretary of State showing location of consulate and total additional allowance approved and its distribution among the several consulates; and (3) abstract of contingent expenses showing account number, name of officer, duty station, and type and amount of expense.

861.   ABSTRACT OF CONTINGENT EXPENSES OF CONSULATES. July 1877-June 1881.
       5 cm, 2 in. 1 vol.

Arranged by location and thereunder chronologically. Indexed by location.
The entries show location of consulate, year, name of consular officer, expenses each 3 months, and total expenses for the year.

862.   REGISTER OF CONSULAR FEES RECEIVED. Jan. 1, 1857-Dec. 31, 1857. 3 cm, 1 in.
       1 vol.

Arranged by location of consulate.
Register contains entries that show location of consulate, period covered, type of services performed, fees received for the services, and summary figures for the entire year.

863.   REGISTER OF FEES RECEIVED. July 1881-June 1882. 1 cm, 1/2 in. 1 vol.

Arranged by location. Indexed by location.
Register contains entries that show location of consulate, name of officer, account number, type of services performed, and fees received for the services. These fees were included in salary accounts of consular officers and are covered in the audit reports described in entry 846.

864.   RECORD OF FEES RECEIVED AT THE CONSULATE AT BREMEN AND THE
       CONSULAR AGENCIES AT BREMERHAVEN AND GEESTEMUNDE. Jan. 10, 1864-
       June 30, 1872. 10 cm, 4 in. 2 vols.

Arranged chronologically and thereunder by location in the order listed.
The entries show location of consulate or consular agency, date of payment, receipt number, name of ship, by whom fees were paid, service performed, amount of fee, and explanation. Most fees for were certifying invoices or issuing landing certificates. These volumes were a part of diplomatic account No. 68,743, settled on July 11, 1872.

865.   REGISTERS OF DISBURSING AGENTS AND MISCELLANEOUS ACCOUNTS. Nov.
       8, 1894-July 7, 1909. 10 cm, 4 in. 3 vols.

Arranged chronologically. Within each volume the entries are arranged by type of account and thereunder chronologically. Each volume is indexed by title of appropriation or type of account.
Registers contain entries that show type of account, disbursing agent's or claimant's name, and account number. Accounts of disbursing agents are both for funds disbursed and funds received and deposited; the entries for claims are generally for foreign indemnity awards.

866.   AUDIT REPORTS ON ACCOUNTS OF DISBURSING AGENTS FOR THE
       DEPARTMENT OF STATE. Jan. 14, 1892-July 24, 1894. 8 cm, 3 in. 1 vol.

Arranged chronologically and thereunder by account number. Indexed by title of appropriation.
Copies of reports showing date audited, account number, name of disbursing clerk, title of appropriation, period covered, debits and credits, explanation of differences, and adjusted

balance. A continuous set of numbers was assigned for all different types of diplomatic and consular accounts. For this reason the numbers assigned to accounts of disbursing agents are not consecutive.

INTERNAL REVENUE DIVISION

The Internal Revenue Division was first specifically mentioned by the Fifth Auditor in a report on activities of the Office for the fiscal year beginning July 1, 1882. The report mentions activities of the Division "for the past six years," and was probably a separate Division as early as the 1860s. The Internal Revenue Division received and settled accounts for assessing and collecting the internal revenue, for salaries and contingent expenses of collectors, and for salaries of storekeepers. All other types of internal revenue accounts were settled in the Miscellaneous Division.

Also included in the Internal Revenue Division are records (received by the Fifth Auditor as Commissioner of the Revenue) relating to the final collection of the 1814 direct tax and records created under the "Act for collection of direct taxes in insurrectionary districts within the United States," June 7, 1862 (12 Stat. 422).

Correspondence

867.   REGISTERS OF LETTERS AND ACCOUNTS RECEIVED FROM INTERNAL REVENUE COLLECTORS AND ASSESSORS. Dec. 1862-Mar. 1876. 8 cm, 3 in. 3 vols.

Arranged chronologically. Within volumes 2 and 3 the entries are arranged by internal revenue district and thereunder chronologically. The dates of entries vary considerably from one district to another. Volume 3 is indexed by name of State.

Registers contain entries that show internal revenue district, name and title of official, date letter or account was received, and type of account or subject of letter. Volume 1 includes entries for both collectors and assessors, volume 2 is for letters and accounts from collectors, and volume 3 for letters and accounts from assessors. A few entries are dated as late as 1881.

For copies of replies to some of the letters registered in these volumes, see entry 868.

868.   INTERNAL REVENUE LETTERS SENT (NEW SERIES). May 1, 1869-Jan. 19, 1891. 30 cm, 1 ft. 6 vols.

Arranged chronologically. Each volume is indexed by surname of addressee.

Fair copies of letters from the Fifth Auditor to the Commissioner of Internal Revenue and to collectors, assessors, and stamp agents relating chiefly to the settlement of accounts and claims and to expenses of collecting the revenue. Some of these letters were sent in reply to the registered letters described in entry 867.

For earlier and later letters on internal revenue matters, see 828 and 869. The last two volumes of this series overlap in date span.

869.   LETTERS SENT BY THE INTERNAL REVENUE DIVISION. Oct. 1, 1885-May 7, 1894. 5 cm, 2 in. 2 vols.

Arranged chronologically. Each volume is indexed by name of addressee.

Press copies of letters to the Commissioner of Internal Revenue or to collectors and other officials relating to settlement of accounts and claims. Many of the letters to the Commissioner list the numbers of internal revenue accounts settled the previous month and the names and districts of the officials whose accounts had been approved. Some letters returned vouchers for explanation or correction.

For earlier letters on internal revenue subjects see entries 828 and 868.

Records Relating to Accounts

DIRECT TAXES BEFORE 1817

870.   ABSTRACTS OF INTERNAL DUTIES DEPOSITED BY REVENUE COLLECTORS. Jan.
        1, 1815-Dec. 31, 1816. 5 cm, 2 in. 2 vols.

Arranged chronologically. Within each volume the entries are arranged by State.
Entries show account number, collector's name and district, balance from previous
settled account, abstract of revenues and expenses, amount paid into the Treasury, and
remaining balance.

871.   MISCELLANEOUS RECORDS RELATING TO DEPOSIT OF DIRECT TAXES. ca. 1801-
        24. 3.1 m, 10 ft. 3 vols.

Arranged alphabetically by State and thereunder chronologically.
Records, primarily for the period 1816-18, showing amounts of taxes collected and
related expenses. Sometimes these are accompanied by receipts and letters of transmittal. The
tax records for Massachusetts include copies of property valuation reports (including names of
owners, street addresses and description of houses and other buildings) in the 9th and 10th
wards of Boston (2 vols.) and a record of property sold for nonpayment of taxes, March 11, 1816-
July 7, 1817 (1 vol.).

DIRECT TAX OF 1862

872.   DIRECT TAX LEDGER. 1868-93. 5 cm, 2 in. 1 vol.

This series appears to be missing.
Arranged by title of account and thereunder chronologically.
Some ledger accounts are in the names of Direct Tax Commissioners and concern revenue
collected by them and their administrative expenses.
Other accounts are in the names of States and reflect the refunding of the Civil War
direct taxes as authorized by an act of March 1891 (26 Stat. 822). Entries normally show title of
account, dates of transactions, numbers and balances of previous settled accounts, and debits and
credits.

873.   ASSESSMENT BOOKS FOR ALABAMA. n.d. 25 cm, 10 in. 22 vols.

Arranged alphabetically by name of county.
Lists of lands assessed for taxes under the Act of June 7, 1862, showing legal description
of the land, acreage, assessed value, and name of owner. These volumes were probably
submitted in support of an account (not located) of the Direct Tax Commission for Alabama.
Correspondence and other records of the Commission are in Records of the Internal Revenue
Service, RG 58.

874.   ACCOUNTS OF THE DIRECT TAX COMMISSION FOR ARKANSAS. Jan. 1866 -
        Apr. 30, 1886. 3.4 m, 11 ft. 153 vols.

Arranged chronologically.
There are gaps in the date span of these records; the actual date covered are: Jan.-Sept.
1866; Oct. 21, 1874-Apr. 30, 1886.
Accounts for receipts and expenses of the Arkansas Direct Tax Commission, consisting of
account numbers 6, 25, and 30. These accounts were approved by the Fifth Auditor on October 21,
1874; June 11, 1884; and April 30, 1886, respectively. The accounts include the audit report,

abstracts and vouchers for expenses of the Commissioners, and summary statements of assessments and collections.

Account Number 6 was accompanied by receipt books, January-September 1866 (68 vols.), and lists of assessments for the same period (85 vols.).

Both sets of books are arranged alphabetically by name of county and thereunder chronologically. Both sets show names of taxpayer and owner of land, legal description, acreage, valuation, and date tax was paid. Included in box 1 is a part of entry 877 and entry 882.

875.   ADMINISTRATIVE RECORDS OF THE DIRECT TAX COMMISSIONER FOR ARKANSAS. Apr. 20, 1865-Aug. 1, 1866. 5 cm, 2 in. 3 vols.

Arranged chronologically and thereunder by type of record.

These records consist of two cashbooks, April 20, 1865-May 9, 1866, and a receipt book, May 8, 1865-August 1, 1866. Receipts recorded in the cashbooks were primarily from taxes paid to the Commission, and show name of person paying the taxes and date and amount paid. Expenses reflected in the cashbooks and the receipt book are chiefly for payment of salaries and office rent, payment of bills for newspaper advertising, and similar expenses. Also recorded are the deposit of tax collections and the refund of taxes. The receipt book was signed by the persons receiving payment from the Commission. Correspondence and other records of the Arkansas Direct Tax Commission are in Records of the Internal Revenue Service, RG 58.

876.   DIARY OF CHARLES E. STODDARD. Dec. 12, 1864-Feb. 7, 1865. 1 cm, 1/2 in. 1 vol.

Arranged chronologically.

Charles E. Stoddard was one of the members of the Direct Tax Commission for Arkansas. This diary is his personal account of the early activities of the Commission in that State.

877.   ACCOUNT OF THE DIRECT TAX COMMISSION FOR FLORIDA. Mar. 3, 1866-Feb. 19, 1887. 1 cm, 1/2 in. 1 vol. and 1 box.

Arranged chronologically.

Assessment book showing the ownership and valuation of lands in Nassau County, as determined by the Commissioners on March 3, 1866, and a record of lands of the Florida Railroad Co. sold for nonpayment of taxes; also an audit report on account Number 33, dated February 19, 1887. The assessment book accompanied account Number 7, which has not been located. This entry shares a box with entry 874 and entry 882.

No vouchers or other supporting documents have been found that relate to account Number 33. Other records of the Florida Direct Tax Commission are in Records of the Internal Revenue Service, RG 58.

878.   MISCELLANEOUS RECORDS RELATING TO ASSESSMENTS ON LANDS IN FLORIDA. 1855-Mar. 1867. 20 cm, 8 in. 6 vols.

Arranged chronologically and thereunder by type of information.

These volumes include information of the following types: (1) alphabetical lists of persons assessed, 1855-61; (2) valuation of lands in St. Johns County, St. Augustine, and Fernandina; (3) lists of lands sold at tax sales in Fernandina and St. Augustine, including lands purchased by the United States at such sales; (4) lists of lands redeemed after sale; and (5) lists of Spanish grants in Clay, Duval, Nassau, and Volusia Counties. The dates and nature of the records vary considerably, but information on valuation of lands usually includes location, legal description, value, taxes and costs due, and name of owner; information on land sales or redemptions also shows date of sale or redemption, name of purchaser or redeemer, and amount. Two volumes appear to be missing.

879.   RECORDS RELATING TO LAND SALES IN FERNANDINA, FLA. June 1863-Feb. 1866.
        8 cm, 3 in. 2 vols.

Arranged chronologically by month. The first volume, tax sale certificates, is indexed by name of purchaser.

This series comprises two volumes: (1) copies of tax sale certificates, June 18, 1863-February 21, 1865; and (2) abstract of lands owned by the Florida Railroad Co. in Fernandina that were sold for nonpayment of taxes and later redeemed, December 1864-February 1866. The copies of tax sale certificates show the certificate number, name of purchaser, description of the land, and price paid. The abstract shows the location and valuation of railroad lands in Fernandina, land sale records, and a record of applications of the company to redeem the lands. Other records relating to efforts of the company to recover its lands are in Records of the Internal Revenue Service, RG 58.

880.   RECORD OF U.S. LAND IN FERNANDINA, FLA. 1863-82. 5 cm, 2 in. 2 vols.

Arranged chronologically. Indexed by name of occupant.

Record of the use of lands purchased by the United States at tax sales in Fernandina showing lot and block number, description of land, year bid in (usually 1863-65), information on terms on which lands were leased, lists of lands redeemed in November 1877, and lists of permits granted by the United States in July 1882 for use of its lots in Fernandina.

881.   RECORD OF CASH RECEIVED FROM LAND SALES IN FERNANDINA AND
        ST. AUGUSTINE, FLA. Dec. 1863 - Jan. 1867. 3 cm, 1 in. 1 vol.

Arranged by city and thereunder chronologically.

The entries for each city show date received, amount received as taxes, penalty, interest, and cost; also amount bid in excess of the total of these figures.

882.   ACCOUNTS OF THE DIRECT TAX COMMISSION FOR GEORGIA. Dec. 1865 - Apr.
        1884. 1.2 m, 4 ft. 69 vols. and unbound records.

Arranged chronologically. Alpha box: 1A.

Direct tax accounts, number 5 (approved Sept. 3, 1874) and number 23 (approved Apr. 23, 1884), including audit reports, abstracts of expenditures with related vouchers, abstracts of taxes collected, and circulars and orders of the Commission. Account number 5 was accompanied by receipt books, December 1865-July 1866 (22 vols.), and undated assessment books (47 vols.). Both sets of volumes are arranged alphabetically by name of county and show description and location of land, its valuation, and name of owner and taxpayer. Other records of the Georgia Commission are in Records of the Internal Revenue Service, RG 58. This series shares a box with entry 874 and 877.

883.   ACCOUNTS OF DIRECT TAX COMMISSION FOR LOUISIANA. Feb. 1865 - June 1884.
        2.4 m, 8 ft. 159 vols. and unbound records.

Arranged chronologically. Within each of the bound volumes, the entries are arranged by name of parish or ward.

Assessment lists, February 1865-February 1866, submitted as part of direct tax accounts, numbers 10 and 11 by the Direct Tax Commissioners for Louisiana; and direct tax account number 26, approved June 12, 1885.

The assessment lists show location and description of land, name of owner, valuation of the land, and amount due or paid. The audit reports and other documents relating to account numbers 10 and 11 have not been located.

Account number 26 consist of the audit report, abstracts of disbursements by the Commissioners, August 1865-June 1866, and original and duplicate vouchers. Other records of the Louisiana Commission are in Records of the Internal Revenue Service, RG 58. This entry shares box 1 with entry 884, 885, and 886.

884.   ACCOUNTS OF THE DIRECT TAX COMMISSION FOR MISSISSIPPI. Jan. 1866 - Nov. 1883. 1.5 m, 5 ft. 100 vols. and unbound records.

Arranged chronologically. Within each of the bound volumes the entries are arranged alphabetically by name of county.
Receipt books, January-August 1866 (25 vols.), and assessment books, March-June 1866 (75 vols.), accompanying direct tax account Number 8; and direct tax account number 18 (approved Jan. 20, 1877) and number 22 (approved Nov. 19, 1883). The receipt and assessment books show location and description of land, valuation, taxes due or paid, and names of taxpayer and owner. The audit report for account number 8 has not been located.
Account numbers 18 and 22 consist of audit reports, abstracts of expenditures with related vouchers, and correspondence relating to expenses of the Commission. This entry shares box 1 with entry 883, 885, and 886.

885.   ACCOUNTS OF THE DIRECT TAX COMMISSION FOR NORTH CAROLINA. Dec. 1865-Dec. 1873. 7.0 m, 23 ft. 295 vols. and unbound records.

Arranged chronologically.
Direct tax account numbers 3 and 4, both approved December 5, 1873, include audit reports, abstracts of disbursements, related vouchers, and abstracts of taxes assessed and collected by the Commission. Account number 4 is accompanied by receipt books (138 vols.) and assessment books (157 vols.), both groups covering the period December 1865-August 1866. They show location and valuation of lands, names of owners and taxpayers, and amounts of taxes paid. Both groups of volumes are arranged alphabetically by name of county. Also included is the approved claim of North Carolina, March 31, 1891, for refund of the taxes. Other records of the North Carolina Commission are in Records of the Internal Revenue Service, RG 58. This entry shares box 1 with entry 883, 884, and 886. This entry shares box 17 with entry 886.

886.   ACCOUNTS OF THE DIRECT TAX COMMISSION FOR SOUTH CAROLINA. Apr. 1865-May 1885. 1.5 m, 5 ft. 50 vols. and unbound records.

Arranged chronologically.
Direct tax account number 12 (approved Feb. 29, 1876), number 15 (approved Aug. 26, 1876), number 28 (approved May 4, 1885), and number 29 (approved May 29, 1885) include audit reports, abstracts of disbursements of the Commissioners in behalf of the school system in South Carolina, and receipts for rents paid to the Commissioners. Account number 12 is accompanied by receipt books, April-December 1865 (22 vols.), and assessment books, December 1865-February 1866 (28 vols.). They show location, description, and valuation of land, names of owners and taxpayers, and amounts of taxes paid. Other records of the South Carolina Commission are in Records of the Internal Revenue Service, RG 58. This entry shares box 1 with entry 883, 884, and 885. This entry shares box 17 with entry 885.

887.   JOURNAL OF THE DIRECT TAX COMMISSION FOR SOUTH CAROLINA. Feb. 28, 1871-Aug. 30, 1876. 3 cm, 1 in. 1 vol.

Arranged chronologically.
Entries for funds received relate typically to sale or rental of lands or buildings and show name of purchaser or renter, location and description of property, and amounts paid. Entries for disbursements are chiefly for administrative expenses and show names of persons

paid and explanation of services furnished. Other entries relate to the transfer of funds, applications for redemption of land, and delivery of leases.

888.   RECORDS OF THE BEAUFORT, S.C., TAX DISTRICT. Nov. 3, 1862-Mar. 27, 1872. 28 cm, 11 in. 6 vols.

Arranged chronologically.

(1) A record of the assessed value of lands in the Beaufort District as determined by the Commission during the period November 3-25, 1862, and in a few cases showing actual payment of taxes; (2) applications for redemption of plantations sold for taxes, April-May 1863, December 1865, and October 1866; (3) land maps annotated to show the township, range, and section of surveyed lands in the District, surveyors field notes, and such topographical features as swamps and such landmarks as houses and graveyards; and (4) copies of leases by the Commissioners, December 26, 1863-March 27, 1872, including name and address of person leasing the land, location and description of the property, and terms and special conditions of the lease.

889.   LIST OF SOUTH CAROLINA TAX SALE CERTIFICATES. Dec. 30, 1875-Jan. 12, 1876. 1 cm, 1/2 in. 1 vol.

This entry appears to be missing.
Arranged chronologically.
The entries show number and date of certificate, name of purchaser, purchase price, and description of the property. The information in the volume was certified to be correct on August 12, 1876, by Charles W. Eldridge, superintendent of sales of direct tax lands in South Carolina.

890.   ACCOUNTS OF THE DIRECT TAX COMMISSION FOR TENNESSEE. May 1864-Apr. 1876. 2.1 m, 7 ft. 105 vols. and unbound records.

Arranged chronologically.

Direct tax account numbers 9 and 15 (approved Apr. 6, 1875, and Apr. 15, 1876, respectively). The accounts include audit reports; abstracts of disbursements of the Tennessee Direct Tax Commission, with related vouchers; copies of tax sale certificates; applications for redemption of land; and monthly summaries of receipts and disbursements. Account number 9 was accompanied by assessment books, August-November 1865 (102 vols.), arranged alphabetically by name of county and showing location and description of land, name of owner, number of acres, assessed value, and amount due or paid. Similar records for Davidson County, May 17-June 10, 1865 (2 vols.), are also included. Account number 13 was accompanied by a record of land sales and redemptions in Shelby County, 1864-72 (1 vol.). Box 2 also contains part of entry 893. In part, reproduced on NARA Microfilm Publication T227, Civil War Direct Tax Assessment Lists: Tennessee.

891.   LEDGERS OF THE DIRECT TAX COMMISSION FOR TENNESSEE. July 1, 1865 - Aug. 30, 1876. 5 cm, 2 in. 2 vols.

Arranged chronologically. Within each ledger the entries are arranged by title of account and thereunder chronologically. Each volume is indexed by title of account, which is sometimes the name of a county.

There are gaps in the date span of these records; the actual dates covered are: July 1, 1865-Apr. 30, 1867; Feb. 1, 1871-Aug. 30, 1876.

Account titles are usually tax collections in specific counties, administrative expenses, refund of taxes, proceeds of sale of lands, and collection of rent. Entries within an account show the date of transaction, explanation (including names of persons from whom funds were received), and debits and credits.

892.   ACCOUNTS OF THE DIRECT TAX COMMISSION FOR TEXAS. Nov. 1865-Aug. 1866.
        2.4 m, 8 ft. 125 vols.

Arranged by name of county and thereunder chronologically.
Receipt books (62 vols.) and assessment books (63 vols.) that accompanied direct tax
account number 7 of the Texas Direct Tax Commission.
The entries show location and description of land, assessed valuation, names of owners
and taxpayers, taxes and other costs due, and dates and amounts of payments. The audit report
for account number 7 and supporting documents have not been located. Other records of the Texas
Commission are in Records of the Internal Revenue Service, RG 58.

893.   ACCOUNTS OF THE DIRECT TAX COMMISSION FOR VIRGINIA. Sept. 1865 -
        Sept. 1887. 9.1 m, 30 ft. 662 vols. and unbound records.

Arranged chronologically.
Direct tax account numbers 1 and 2 (both approved July 23, 1873), number 21 (approved
March 9, 1881), and numbers 35 and 36 (approved Sept. 12-13, 1887). Accounts include audit
reports, abstracts of disbursements, vouchers, tax receipts, and tax sale certificates. Account
numbers 1 and 2 are accompanied by receipt books, September 1865-August 1866 (142 vols.), and
undated assessment books (520 vols.). Both groups of books are arranged by county and show
location and description of land, assessed valuation, name of owner and taxpayer, and amount
paid. Other records of the Virginia Commission are in Records of the Internal Revenue Service,
RG 58. Box 2 also contains part of entry 890.

894.   RECORD OF TAXES RECEIVED IN ALEXANDRIA, VA. Sept. 1863-Feb. 1864. 5 cm,
        2 in. 1 vol.

Arranged chronologically and thereunder by location of land.
The entries show name of owner; location, description, number of acres, and assessed
value of land; taxes, penalties, and costs due; and when by whom, and to whom paid. Lists of
city lots, which precede the lists of rural lots, show the distance and direction of the lot from
the Alexandria Courthouse.

895.   LISTS OF LOTS IN ALEXANDRIA AND IN ACCOMACK AND NORTHAMPTON
        COUNTIES IN VIRGINIA SOLD AND LATER REDEEMED. Jan. 29, 1864-Aug. 15, 1866.
        15 cm, 6 in. 2 vols.

Arranged chronologically.
The entries in the volume for lands sold for nonpayment of taxes, January 29-June 14,
1864, show location, description, and number of acres; assessed valuation; tax, penalty, costs,
and interest due; date of sale; name of purchaser; and purchase price. Entries in the volume for
lands redeemed after sale, February 9, 1864-August 15, 1866, also show the number of each
redemption certificate and when and by whom redeemed.

DIVISION OF JUDICIAL ACCOUNTS

The Division of Judicial Accounts was established on October 1, 1894, when the function
of settling judicial accounts was transferred from the Office of the First Auditor to that of the
Auditor for the State and other Departments (formerly the Fifth Auditor). In addition to
handling accounts for judicial officers and for disbursing clerks of the Department of Justice for
salaries and other expenses, the Division of Judicial Accounts was responsible for payment of
salaries of Territorial Governors and retired judges.

Correspondence

896.	REGISTERS OF LETTERS RECEIVED. Jan. 2, 1895-May 3, 1920. 61 cm, 2 ft. 9 vols.

Arranged chronologically. Within each volume the entries are arranged by initial letter of writer's surname or title and thereunder chronologically. There are gaps in the date span of this series; the actual dates covered are: Jan 2, 1895-Sept. 30, 1901; July 1, 1903-Dec. 23, 1907; Sept. 4, 1909-May 3, 1920.

Registers contain entries that show date received, writer's name and address or title, and subject. Most letters enclosed accounts or emolument returns or responded to inquiries from the Auditor. The letters and accounts registered in the volumes have not been located.

897.	LETTERS SENT. Oct. 5, 1894-Dec. 30, 1899. 3.7 m, 12 ft. 61 vols.

Arranged chronologically. Each volume is indexed by surname or title of addressee.
There are gaps in the date span of these records; the actual dates covered are: Oct. 5, 1894-July 31, 1895; Sept. 3, 1895-Dec. 30, 1899.

Press copies of form letters to judicial officers in the several States and Territories relating to receipt and adjustment of their accounts and requests for information needed in the adjustment of the accounts. Also included are letters to the Attorney General requesting information on the status of pending suits and cases.

For earlier letters on similar subjects, see entry 314.

897A.	UNPRINTED DECISIONS OF THE COMPTROLLER OF THE TREASURY, U.S. MARSHALS. Oct. 1, 1894 - June 30, 1920. 5 vols.

Volumes are numbered 1 - 4, & 6.

897B.	UNPRINTED DECISIONS OF THE COMPTROLLER OF THE TREASURY, U.S. ATTORNEYS, DISTRICT CLERKS, ETC. July 1, 1895 - June 30, 1915. 3 vols.

897C.	UNPRINTED DECISIONS OF THE COMPTROLLER OF THE TREASURY, CLERKS, U.S. COURTS. Jan. 1 1896 - June 30, 1916. 2 vols.

897D.	DIGEST OF DECISIONS, OPINIONS, AND PRECEDENTS, 1896 - 1914. 1 box.

Records Relating to Accounts and Claims

898.	REGISTER OF SETTLED ACCOUNTS OF DISBURSING CLERKS OF THE DEPARTMENT OF JUSTICE. Sept. 9, 1899-Dec. 13, 1906. 5 cm, 2 in. 1 vol.

Arranged by title of appropriation and thereunder chronologically.
Register contains entries that show title of appropriation, account number, period covered, date approved, adjusted balance, and total disbursements reflected in the account. Appropriations include salaries, fees, and contingent and regular expenses of the Department; salaries and expenses of Territorial Governors; and rental, repair, and construction of buildings.

MISCELLANEOUS DIVISION

The Miscellaneous Division was first mentioned by the Fifth Auditor in a report on the operations of the Office for the fiscal year beginning July 1, 1882. Its initial functions were to settle all miscellaneous revenue accounts and claims, including salaries and expenses of agents, surveyors, gaugers, and stamp agents; expenses of the Office of the Commissioner of Internal Revenue; accounts and claims for drawbacks and tax refunds; contingent expenses of the State and Post Office Departments and of the Census and Patent Offices; and expenses of the Smithsonian Institution. In 1894 many functions formerly exercised by the First Auditor were transferred to the Miscellaneous Division, including settlement of accounts for the District of Columbia, the U.S. Senate and House of Representatives, Library of Congress, and Public Printer; expenses of Territorial governments; and accounts of independent agencies and boards.

Correspondence

899.   REGISTERS OF LETTERS RECEIVED. July 5, 1884-June 30, 1911. 25 cm, 10 in. 5 vols.

Arranged chronologically. Entries in the 1884-91 volume are arranged chronologically; entries in each of the other volumes are arranged by initial letter of writer's surname or title and thereunder chronologically.

Registers contain entries that show dates letter was written and received, writer's name and address or title, subject, and remarks on the disposition of the letter. Most of the entries in the earliest volume relate to drawback claims and expenses of taking the census; entries in the later volumes are from disbursing clerks for various departments or agencies or officials of States and Territories and relate chiefly to requests for decisions, information on the status of accounts, and deposit of funds.

900.   LETTERS SENT. May 14, 1883-Mar. 31, 1898. 18 cm, 7 in. 4 vols.

Arranged chronologically. Each volume is indexed by surname or title of addressee.

There are gaps in the date span of these records; the actual dates covered are: May 14, 1883-Feb. 29, 1896; Jan. 1, 1897-Mar. 31, 1898.

Press copies of letters relating to rebate and drawback claims, accounts of gaugers, refund of moneys, and status of accounts of disbursing officers for various departments and agencies.

Records Relating to Accounts and Claims

901.   REGISTERS OF ACCOUNTS RECEIVED. Feb. 5, 1870-Oct. 27, 1904. 61 cm, 2 ft. 10 vols.

Arranged chronologically. The last two volumes (Jan. 1898-Oct. 1904) are indexed by name of official.

Registers contain entries that show account number, name of official or claimant, type of account or claim, period covered, and date received or adjusted. Most entries are for revenue stamps; accounts of disbursing agents for various departments, agencies, and the District of Columbia; expenses of public printing and binding; and salaries and expenses of Territorial Governors. Account numbers are omitted from the last three volumes.

902.   AUDIT REPORTS ON DEPARTMENTAL AND MISCELLANEOUS ACCOUNTS. Aug. 23, 1860-Sept. 12, 1894. 61 cm, 2 ft. 9 vols.

Arranged chronologically. Each volume is indexed by name of official.

Copies of reports on accounts of disbursing agents for various departments showing account number, date approved, name and title of accountable officer, type of account, period covered, debits and credits, statement of differences, and adjusted balance. Reports of accounts of disbursing agents are dated August 23, 1860-July 2, 1873, and September 22 1879-September 12, 1894. A separate volume is used for reports on accounts of expenses of taking the census, July 3, 1873-May 7, 1892.

903.   LIST OF INTERNAL REVENUE AGENTS AND INSPECTORS. n.d. 3 cm, 1 in. 1 vol.

This entry appears to be missing.
Arranged alphabetically by name of employee and thereunder by title.
List showing employee's name, where stationed, whether an agent or inspector, and usually salary rate. Sometimes date of appointment or dismissal is shown, usually in the period August 2, 1866-September 28, 1868.

904.   AUDIT REPORTS ON MISCELLANEOUS INTERNAL REVENUE ACCOUNTS AND CLAIMS. Jan. 11, 1872-Aug. 16, 1894. 30 cm, 1 ft. 5 vols.

Arranged chronologically. Each volume is indexed by surname of officer or claimant.
Copies of reports showing account number, date approved, name of officer or claimant, type of account or claim, debits and credits, adjusted balance, statement of differences, and payment instructions if the balance was in favor of the officer or claimant. Types of accounts included furnishing and selling tax stamps and stamped foil wrappers; expenses of the Office of the Commissioner of Internal Revenue; accounts for deposit of proceeds of fines, penalties, and forfeitures; and pay of teachers in the South Carolina free school system.

905.   SETTLED ACCOUNTS OF THE COMMISSIONER OF INTERNAL REVENUE. Feb. 11, 1891-June 22, 1892. 13 cm, 5 in. Unbound records.

This entry appears to be missing.
Arranged chronologically.
Five accounts of the Commissioner of Internal Revenue relating chiefly to refund of taxes erroneously collected in the 1870 s. The accounts consist of the audit reports and related vouchers and claim forms.
Some of the claims represented in these accounts, for example, were for refund of taxes withheld from interest on bonds owned by nonresident aliens.

906.   SETTLED TERRITORIAL JUDICIAL ACCOUNTS. ca. 1894-1911. 152.4 m, 500 ft. 505 boxes.

Arranged alphabetically by name of Territory and thereunder chronologically.
Accounts of marshals, Governors, and other Territorial officials for judicial and administrative expenses. Accounts usually consist of the audit report, abstracts of disbursements with related vouchers, statements of warrants involved in the account, an account current, and a summary statement of the account. Oversize accounts for Territories are filed at the end of the regular accounts for the same Territory. The judiciary ledgers (entry 24) serve as a finding aid to these accounts.

907.   DECISION MEMORANDUM FILE, 1921 - 1922. 8 boxes.

908.   ADMINISTRATIVE AND DECISION FILES OF THE COMPTROLLER OF THE TREASURY AND THE COMPTROLLER OF THE UNITED STATES. 1912 - 1921. 45 boxes.

909.   ADMINISTRATIVE AND DECISION FILES OF THE COMPTROLLER OF THE TREASURY AND THE COMPTROLLER GENERAL OF THE UNITED STATES. 1920 - 1924. 84 boxes.

910.   RECORDS RELATING TO CUSTOMS REPORTS AND CLAMS, 1920 - 1925. 1 box.

911. LEGISLATIVE HISTORY FILES, 1921 - 1978.

This series appears to be missing.

912. PRESIDENTIAL PAY FILES, 1923 - 1963. 1 box.

NOTES

UNDESCRIBED MATERIALS

The following is material that may belong in Record Group 217 located during the reorganization of the record group in 1995. Descriptions of this material have not yet been developed by the National Archives staff. In order to obtain these materials an archivist mus be consulted.

1.   FIRST COMPTROLLER'S GENERAL LAND OFFICE; RECEIVER'S ACCOUNTS, 1872 89. 3 boxes

2.   ALPHABETICAL CARD FILE RELATING TO WARRANTS, ca. 1910-11. 6 boxes.

3.   LOOSE PAGES OF UNIDENTIFIED LEDGERS. 1 box.

4.   NOTICES TO BANKS, 1830-34. 1 vol.

5.   PAPERS REFERRING TO INTERNAL REVENUE, 1866-68. 1 vol.

6.   REGISTER OF MISCELLANEOUS RECEIPTS FROM BANKS AND INDIVIDUALS, 1833-38. 1 vol.

7.   REGISTER OF LISTS OF DEPOSITS, 1882-86. 1 vol.

8.   WITHDRAWN DOCUMENTS FROM RG 217. 4 boxes.

9.   REGISTER OF CUSTOMS COVERING WARRANTS, 1805-55. 5 vols.

10.   REGISTER OF CUSTOMS PAY WARRANTS, 1849; 1855-60. 3 vols.

11.   REGISTER OF CUSTOMS WARRANTS, 1861-69. 2 vols.

12.   REGISTER OF WARRANTS ON BANKS, 1810-36. 3 vols.

13.   TREASURY APPROPRIATION JOURNALS, 1870-73. 2 vols.

14.   WAR DEPARTMENT APPROPRIATION JOURNALS, 1869-74. 3 vols.

15.   REGISTER OF TREASURY NOTES RECEIVED FROM LAND OFFICERS AND COLLECTORS OF CUSTOMS, 1840-47. 1 vol.

16.   WAR DEPARTMENT APPROPRIATION JOURNAL: CIVIL EXPENSES, 1870-72. 1 vol.

17.   WAR DEPARTMENT AUXILIARY APPROPRIATION LEDGERS, 1868-96. 2 vols.

18.   WARRANT LEDGERS, 1819-25. 7 vols.

      Volumes are numbered 29 to 35.

19.   INTERIOR (CIVIL) APPROPRIATION JOURNAL, 1870-74. 1 vol.

20.   CUSTOMS APPROPRIATION JOURNAL, 1870-73. 1 vol.

21.   REGISTER OF REPAY WARRANTS DRAWN PURSUANT TO REQUISITIONS OF THE SECRETARY OF WAR, 1835-67. 3 vols.

22. REGISTER OF WARRANTS ON INDIVIDUAL, 1866-69. 1 vol.

23. REGISTER OF INTERNAL REVENUE COVERING WARRANTS, 1867-68; 1889-94. 2 vols.

24. REGISTER OF INTERNAL REVENUE WARRANTS, 1862-68. 2 vols.

25. REGISTER OF WARRANTS DRAWN BY THE SECRETARY OF THE TREASURY ON OFFICERS OF THE CUSTOMS AND OTHERS, 1851-53. 1 vol.

26. INTERIOR "MEMORANDUM" JOURNALS: CIVIL EXPENSES, 1891-97. 3 vols.

27. EXPENDITURES - REGISTER OF WARRANTS, 1858-61. 1 vol.

28. COPIES OF APPROPRIATION WARRANTS, 1869-73. 5 vols.

29. COPIES OF MISCELLANEOUS LETTER SENT BY THE REGISTER, 1884-85. 1 vol.

30. LETTER BOOK, 1828-43. 1 vol.

31. BLOTTER OF COVERING WARRANTS FOR COLLECTING THE DIRECT TAX, 1862-67. 1 vol.

32. REGISTER OF WARRANTS DRAWN ON RECEIVERS OF PUBLIC MONIES, 1848-49. 1 vol.

33. REGISTER OF REPAY AND MISCELLANEOUS WARRANTS, 1870-72. 1 vol.

34. REGISTER OF WAR WARRANTS, 1863-67. 1 vol.

35. INTERNAL REVENUE LEDGER "A," 1867. 1 vol.

36. WEEKLY REGISTER OF NATIONAL BANK BALANCES, 1894-1900; 1905-6. 3 vols.

37. REGISTER OF APPROPRIATION WARRANTS, 1833-56. 1 vol.

38. REGISTER OF REPAY WARRANTS, 1913. 1 vol.

39. REGISTER OF WAR PAY WARRANTS, 1874-75. 1 vol.

40. RECORD OF INTEREST PAID ON PUBLIC DEBT, 1862-72. 1 vol.

41. PRELIMINARY RECORD OF BALANCES OF ACCOUNTS OF GEORGE W. EVANS, 1897-99. 1 vol.

42. PRELIMINARY RECORD OF ACCOUNTS RECEIVED FROM DISBURSING AGENTS FOR THE TREASURY DEPARTMENT, 1904-10. 1 vol.

43. REQUISITIONS FOR PAPER FOR TREASURY BUREAUS, 1868-70. 1 vol.

44. REGISTER OF ACCOUNTS FOR RECEIPTS AND DISBURSEMENTS OF THOMAS J. HOBBS, 1865-75. 1 vol.

45. REGISTER OF BONDS ISSUED IN LONDON, 1876-77. 1 vol.

46. REGISTER OF WEIGHT OF PAPER RECEIVED, 1866-69. 1 vol.

47. REGISTER OF VESSEL REGISTERS ISSUED AT PHILADELPHIA, 1815-42, AND REMAINING UNACCOUNTED FOR, 1847. 1 vol.

48. REGISTER OF INTERIOR (CIVIL) PAY WARRANTS, 1865-66. 1 vol.

49. REGISTER OF WARRANTS ISSUED PAYABLE IN COIN, 1861-63. 4 vols.

50. LIST OF AWARDS MAKE TO INDIVIDUALS BY THE COMMISSION FOR SETTLING THE BRAZILIAN INDEMNITY, JULY 1852. 1 vol.

51. RECORD OF INTEREST PAID ON BOUNTY LAND STOCK, 1847-48. 4 vols.

52. REGISTER OF INTERIOR WARRANTS, 1865-68. 1 vol.

53. STATE OF ARKANSAS IN ACCOUNT WITH THE SECRETARY OF THE TREASURY AS TRUSTEE FOR THE SMITHSONIAN FUND, 1838-75. 1 vol.

54. RECEIPTS FROM CUSTOM HOUSES, 1859-65. 1 vol.

55. JOURNAL OF THE U.S. COMMISSIONER'S U.S. CUSTOM HOUSE INVESTIGATION, 1841. 1 vol.

56. COUNTER ENTRIES, 1884-1892. 1 vol.

57. LIST OF PERSONNEL EMPLOYED IN THE NOTE AND BOND DIVISION OF THE REGISTER'S OFFICE, 1868. 1 box.

58. STATEMENT OF THE ACCOUNT OF JOHN CAMPBELL, 1831. 1 vol.

59. UNIDENTIFIED ACCOUNTS LEDGER, 1892-96. 1 vol.

60. REGISTER OF WARRANTS ISSUED 1877-79. 1 vol.

61. NAME INDEX TO UNIDENTIFIED LEDGER. 1 vol.

62. MILITARY - THIRD AUDITOR, LETTERS, ca. 1845-70. 1 box.

63. REGISTER OF WARRANTS FOR THE TRANSFER OF THE FUNDED 6% STOCK OF 1814, 1814-29. 1 vol.

64. INTERIOR APPROPRIATION JOURNAL: INDIAN EXPENSES, 1870-74. 1 vol.

65. REGISTERS OF APPROPRIATION WARRANTS, 1809-32; 1870-80. 3 vols.

66. INDEX, "VOL. 13," 1897-98. 1 vol.

67. INDEX, "VOL. 9," 1893-94. 1 vol.

68.   REGISTER OF LETTERS AND PAPERS RECEIVED RELATING TO CAPTURED AND ABANDONED PROPERTY ACCOUNTS OF SPECIAL AGENTS OF THE TREASURY DEPARTMENT, 1868-72. 1 vol.

        The first 142 pages are missing.

69.   REGISTERS OF PAID AND UNPAID WARRANTS DRAWN ON THE TREASURER OF THE UNITED STATES, 1872. 1 vol.

70.   RECORD BOOK OF DRY SUBSTANCE TESTS, 1902-3. 1 vol.

71.   CIRCULARS OF TREASURY DEPARTMENT, 1872-94. 1 vol.

72.   REGISTER OF WARRANTS ISSUED FOR REFUND OF DUTY ON WINE, 1833-36. 1 vol.

73.   INVENTORY OF OFFICE SUPPLIES, 1884-85. 1 vol.

74.   ABSTRACT OF DECISIONS ON MISCELLANEOUS CLAIMS, 1898-1904. 1 vol.

75.   INDEX, "VOL. 3," 1880. 1 vol.

76.   INDEX, "VOL. 17," 1901. 1 vol.

77.   INDEX, "VOL. 17," 1901. 1 vol.

78.   REPORT OF COMMITTEE AND SCHEDULES FROM AMERICAN BANK NOTE CO. 1 vol.

79.   RECORD OF WORK DONE IN AUDITOR'S OFFICE, 1895-98. 1 vol.

80.   INDEX TO TREASURY LEDGER NO. 44. 1 vol.

81.   LETTERS RECEIVED - PUBLIC LAND, 1805-1833. 1 vol.

82.   UNIDENTIFIED INDEX. 1 vol.

83.   UNIDENTIFIED INDEX TO CIRCULARS. 1 vol.

84.   CHIEF CLERK - LETTERS. 5 vols.

85.   CHIEF CLERK - INVOICES. 1 vol.

86.   CHIEF CLERK - INSTRUCTIONS. 1 vol.

87.   UNIDENTIFIED REGISTER. 1 vol.

88.   INDEX TO CORRESPONDENCE RELATING TO CUSTOMS CARTAGE AND GENERAL ORDER BUSINESS AT THE PORT OF NEW YORK, 1869-70. 1 vol.

89.   ABSTRACTS OF ARTICLES PURCHASED; PURCHASES, CLOTHING, & C.; AND BY CAPT. GEO. D. WISE, A.Q.M., 1861-62. 1 box.

90.   STATEMENT AND REPORTS OF THE ACCOUNT OF CALHOUN BENHAM, U.S. ATTORNEY FOR THE NORTHERN DISTRICT OF CALIFORNIA (ACCOUNT NO. 109502), 1852. 1 vol.

91.   CHECKS AND BALANCE BOOKS , 1865-71. 1 box.

92.   LOOSE PAPERS - UNIDENTIFIED FILES. 1 box.

93.   LOOSE PAPERS - ABSTRACTS OF DISBURSEMENTS. 1 box.

94.   VOUCHERS FOR DISBURSEMENTS AND PAYMENTS TO OFFICERS AND EMPLOYEES IN THE DISTRICT OF NEW YORK (ACCOUNT NO. 110473), 1890. 17 vols.

95.   VOUCHERS FOR DISBURSEMENTS AND PAYMENTS TO OFFICERS AND EMPLOYEES IN THE DISTRICT OF NEW YORK (ACCOUNT 113165), 1891. 29 vols.

96.   RECORDS OF THE VIRGINIA LOAN OFFICE, ca. 1778-1796. 3 boxes.

97.   REGISTER OF CERTIFICATES ISSUED FROM THE TREASURY FROM THE 15TH JULY TO 15TH SEPT. 1786. 1/2 box.

      Shares box with entry 98.

98.   LOAN OFFICE FORMS (SAMPLES) FOR THE 1790 LOAN (SOME ANNOTATED BY THE VA. LOAN OFFICE COMMISSIONER.). 1/2 box.

      Shares box with entry 97.

99.   EXCESS OF DEPOSITS (FILE NO. 11912), 1892 AND 1894. 6 vols.

100. MILITARY - QUARTER MASTER RETURNS, ca. 1820-1850. 2 boxes.

101. MILITARY - FLORIDA CLAIMS - INDIANS. 3 boxes.

102. VOUCHERS FOR DISBURSEMENTS AND PAYMENTS TO OFFICERS AND EMPLOYEE IN THE DISTRICT OF NEW YORK (ACCOUNT NO. 117593), 1893. 36 vols.

103. VOUCHERS FOR DISBURSEMENTS AND PAYMENTS TO OFFICERS AND EMPLOYEE IN THE DISTRICT OF NEW YORK (ACCOUNT NO. 113877), 1892. 3 vols.

104. FRED MANNING COLLECTION OF DOCUMENTS DRAWN FROM VARIOUS SERIES IN RG 217. 69 boxes.

      Alpha boxes: 16A, 16B. There is no box 16.

105. RECORDS RELATING TO THE ALABAMA CLAIMS, ca. 1865-69. 1 box.

106. PUBLIC DEPARTMENT A/C, TREASURY NOTES, WAR OF 1812. 1 box.

107. SCHEDULES OF SPANISH INDEMNITY CERTIFICATES AND RELATED RECORDS, 1888-1908. 1 box.

108.   PAPERS RELATIVE TO DISTILLATION OF LIQUOR IN THE STATES OF OHIO AND KENTUCKY, 1797-1805 (1802-1805). 1 box.

109.   UNCLAIMED DIVIDENDS, 1807-08; U.S. LOAN OFFICES. 1 box.

110.   U.S. PATENT OFFICE BUILDING, FLOOR PLANS AND PHOTOGRAPHS, 1875. 1 box.

111.   CONTRACTS AND PLANS, TREASURY BUILDING EXTENSION, 1855-56. 1 box.

112.   CIVIL WAR RECRUITING POSTER. 1 tube.

113.   DISTRICT OF PUERTO RICO - CUSTOMERS DIVISION - LETTERS SENT, 1899-1901. 2 vols.

114.   RECORDS RELATING TO FRENCH SPOLIATION CLAIMS, ca. 1838-1900. 1 box.

115.   PUBLIC DEBT - MISCELLANEOUS RECORDS, 1785-1875. 1 box.

116.   POWERS OF ATTORNEY. 1 box.

117.   RECORD OF CONTINGENT EXPENSES FOR THE TREASURY DEPARTMENT, 1871-81; 1888-90. 3 vols.

118.   PENSION LEDGER. 1 vol.

119.   DIPLOMATIC LEDGERS. 3 vols.

120.   INTERNAL REVENUE LEDGERS. 8 vols.

121.   JUDICIARY LEDGERS. 4 vols.

122.   NAVY LEDGERS. 22 vols.

123.   CIVIL, DIPLOMATIC & C. LEDGERS. 52 vols.

124.   WAR LEDGERS. 22 vols.

125.   INDEX TO ACCOUNTS FOR RECEIPT OF INTERNAL REVENUE STAMPS, 1877-79. 1 vol.

126.   INDEX TO FIRST AUDITOR'S ACCOUNTS. 3 vols.

127.   INDEX TO FIFTH AUDITOR'S REPORTS. 14 vols.

128.   REGISTER OF ACCOUNTS RECEIVED FROM FIRST AUDITOR. 2 vols.

129.   REGULATIONS, DECISIONS, ETC. - ARMY. 1 vol.

130.   INDEX TO DISBURSING AGENT'S ACCOUNTS, 1879-80. 1 vol.

131.   LETTER BOOK, 1890-94. 1 vol.

132.   REGISTER OF CUSTOMS COVERING WARRANTS, 1850-52, 1904-12. 5 vol.

133. REGISTER OF WARRANTS DRAWN ON COLLECTORS OF CUSTOMS, 1808-49. 4 vols.

134. CASH WARRANTS - CUSTOMS, 1849-1869. 16 vols.

135. CASH WARRANTS - INTERIOR, 1849-1869. 20 vols.

136. REGISTER OF WARRANTS ISSUED BY AUTHORITY OF THE SECRETARY OF WAR FOR PAYMENTS OF CLAIMS AGAINST THE INTERIOR DEPARTMENT, ca. 1849-82. 4 vols.

137. REGISTER OF INTERNAL REVENUE COVERING WARRANTS FOR COLLECTION OF TAXES, 1862-1912. 7 vols.

138. REGISTER OF INTERNAL REVENUE PAY WARRANTS, 1862-1867. 5 vols.

139. WARRANTS ON RECEIVERS OF PUBLIC MONEY AND OTHERS, 1840-48. 1 vol.

140. REGISTER OF MISCELLANEOUS COVERING WARRANTS, 1828-48. 3 vols.

141. REGISTER OF COVERING WARRANTS FOR RECEIPTS FROM SALES OF PUBLIC LANDS AND FOR MISCELLANEOUS RECEIPTS, 1848-1912. 14 vols.

142. MISCELLANEOUS REVENUE WARRANTS, 1870-78. 6 vols.

143. MISCELLANEOUS COVERING WARRANTS, 1849-69. 7 vols.

144. MISCELLANEOUS REPAY WARRANTS. 9 vols.

145. BOOK 25 FROM JANUARY 13, 1885 TO MAY 25, 1885. 1 vol.

146. REGISTER OF NAVY WARRANTS PAY, 1830-38. 2 vols.

147. REGISTER OF NAVY WARRANTS REPAY, 1830-69. 4 vols.

148. REGISTER OF APPROPRIATION WARRANTS. 8 vols.

149. RECORD OF WARRANTS ISSUED ON REQUISITIONS, 1834. 1 vol.

150. REGISTER OF CASH WARRANTS, 1845-82. 38 vols.

151. REGISTER OF WARRANTS FOR PAYMENT OF SALARIES TO JUDICIAL AND TERRITORIAL OFFICIALS, 1882-88. 1 vol.

152. REGISTER OF WAR WARRANT REPAY, 1822-1869. 5 vols.

153. REGISTER OF PUBLIC WARRANTS, 1862-64. 1 vol.

154. REQUISITIONS - THIRD AUDITOR, VOL. 4. 1 vol.

155. REGISTER OF CLAIMS, 1871. 1 vol.

156. INDEX TO WAR AND INTERIOR LEDGER NO. 3, n.d. 1 vol.

157.   UNIDENTIFIED LOOSE PAPERS. 1 box.

158.   REGISTER OF DIPLOMATIC REPAY WARRANTS. 1 vol.

159.   REGISTER OF AGRICULTURE REPAY WARRANT. 1 vol.

160.   ABSTRACTS OF DECISION, 1896-1900. 2 vols.

161.   NAVY ACCOUNTS, ETC., ca. 1837-51. 1 vol.

162.   APPEALS, BRIEFS, AND DECISIONS REGARDING CLAIMS, 1886-1907. 1 vol.

163.   REGISTER OF ACCOUNTS, 1851-66. 1 vol.

164.   STOREKEEPER LEDGER, 1881-82. 1 vol.

165.   REGISTER OF ACCOUNTS (PRINTING), 1862-72. 1 vol.

166.   REGISTER OF WARRANTS. 1 vol.

167.   NAVY ACCOUNTS. 1 vol.

168.   REGISTER OF CERTIFICATE OF SETTLEMENT WITH CONTRACT PHYSICIAN. 2 vols.

169.   QUARTERMASTER REGISTER. 1 vol.

170.   REGISTER OF APPLICATIONS FOR REVIEW BY THE COURT OF DECISIONS OF THE BOARD OF U.S. GENERAL APPRAISERS, 1891-1905. 1 vol.

171.   INDEX OF SUBJECTS OF REPORTS FROM JAN. 1, 1899 TO DEC. 31, 1902. 1 vol.

172.   UNIDENTIFIED INDEX (COMM. OF CUSTOMS). 1 vol.

        First 22 pages are missing.

173.   REGISTER OF BALANCES OF ACCOUNTS OF U.S. MARSHALS, 1892-94. 1 vol.

174.   INDEX SHOWING NAMES OF RECEIVERS OF PUBLIC MONEY. 1 vol.

175.   REGISTER OF PUBLIC OFFICERS (OUT OF OFFICE) WHO HAVE BALANCES STANDING AGAINST THEM ON THE BOOKS OF THE TREASURY, 1826-35. 1 vol.

176.   DAY BOOK, 1869-78. 1 vol.

177.   NAME INDEX TO LETTERS OF EMPLOYMENT - U.S. GEOLOGICAL SURVEY. 1 vol.

178.   "STOCK." 1 vol.

179.   REGISTER LISTING EXPENSES OF COLLECTOR OF THE REVENUE, 1850. 1 vol.

180.   MARINE HOSPITAL & LIGHT HOUSE CERTIFICATES. 1 vol.

181. BOOK CONTAINING ABSTRACTS, REPORTS, AND ACCOUNTS REGARDING THE PAYMENT OF DUTIES ARISING ON SPIRITS DISTILLED FROM FOREIGN MATERIALS, AND IN CITIES, TOWNS & VILLAGES FROM DOMESTIC MATERIALS, 1791-95. 1 vol.

182. INDEX TO VOL. 1, IMMIGRATION. 1 vol.

183. RECORD OF BONDS, 1871-1907. 1 vol.

184. DECISIONS OF THE U.S. TREASURY DEPARTMENT. 1 vol.

185. RECORD OF BONDS OF TERRITORIAL SECRETARY, STEAMBOAT INSPECTORS, ETC., ca. 1871-94. 1 vol.

186. CUSTOM ACCOUNTS, AUG. 25, 1896 (PART) TO AUG. 19, 1899. 1 vol.

187. NAME INDEX TO LETTERS OF EMPLOYMENT - U.S. GEOLOGICAL SURVEY. 1 vol.

188. CUSTOM HOUSE BONDS, 1830-41. 1 vol.

189. ACCOUNT OF BONDS TAKEN AND LIQUIDATED FOR DUTIES ON MERCHANDISE, 1815-30. 2 vols.

190. RECORD BOOK OF MANUFACTURES BONDS, 1873-89. 1 vol.

191. REGISTER OF WARRANTS ON THE SUPERVISORS, 1800-47. 1 vol.

192. REGISTER OF LETTERS SENT, JULY 1901 - JULY 1902. 1 vol.

193. INDEX TO OFFICIAL COMMUNICATIONS SENT, 1877-79. 1 vol.

194. FIRST AUDITOR'S OFFICE, CUSTOM DIVISION, REPAY WARRANTS, 1889. 1 vol.

195. LETTERS, OCT. 2, 1899 TO NOV. 29, 1899. 1 vol.

196. UNIDENTIFIED NAME INDEX. 1 vol.

197. WARRANTS ON COLLECTORS OF INTERNAL DUTIES, 1817-47. 1 vol.

198. LIST OF TAXES ON LANDS, LOTS, DWELLING HOUSES AND SLAVES, WITHIN THE COUNTY OF SUFFOLK, IN THE STATE OF MASSACHUSETTS, 1814-17. 1 box

This may be a part of entry 871.

199. ARSENALS - MISCELLANEOUS LETTERS, 1816-19. 1 box.

200. 2ND AUDITOR, RECORDS PERTAINING TO HARPER'S FERRY, 1817-1851. 62 rolls, 1861-69. 1 box.

201. RECORD BOOK OF PAYMENTS MADE, 1853-61. 1 vol.

202. U.S. STOCKS REDEEMED BY LOT. 1 vol.

203.   REGISTER OF COUNTER ENTRIES IN THE RECEIPTS OF NATIONAL BANKS OF THE U.S., 1868-75. 1 vol.

204.   CALIFORNIA STATE CLAIMS - CIVIL WAR, 1861-1900. 1 box.

205.   PAY & MILEAGE, HOUSE OF REPRESENTATIVES, 1813-1889. 69 vols.

206.   CLAIMS FOR SIOUX DEPREDATIONS, 1863. 1 vol.

207.   LIST OF WARRANTS DRAWN ON AND IN FAVOR OF TREASURER OF THE U.S. DURING THE QUARTER ENDING 30TH SEPTEMBER 1870. 1 vol.

208.   JOURNAL "B", 1892-93. 1 vol.

209.   REQUISITIONS ON THE CIVIL SERVICE, 1896-1900. 1 vol.

210.   INDEX TO NAMES OF SEAMEN REMAINING IN MARINE HOSPITALS. 1 vol.

211.   CONTINGENT EXPENSE ACCOUNT BOOK, 1855-66. 1 vol.

212.   REGISTER OF AUDITOR'S CERTIFICATES PAID (VOL. 8 1/2). 1 vol.

213.   REGISTER OF PAYMENTS TO COLORED TROOPS. 1 vol.

214.   NUMERICAL REGISTER OF PENSION SETTLEMENTS - REIMBURSEMENTS, 1907-13. 1 vol.

215.   INDEXING CHARTS SHOWING SAMPLE ALPHABETICAL ARRANGEMENTS FOR GENERAL LEDGERS AND WAR REQUISITIONS - DEBIT & CREDIT. 1 box.

216.   RECORD OF SEMI-ANNUAL PAYMENTS TO WIDOWS - MILWAUKEE, WIS., AGENCY. 1 vol.

217.   REGISTER OF CERTIFICATES PAID. 1 vol.

218.   RECEIPTS AND EXPENDITURES, 1791-1940; 1954. 129 boxes.

219.   STATEMENT OF THE PUBLIC DEBT OF THE UNITED STATES FROM 1789 TO 1885 AND RECEIPTS AND EXPENDITURES FROM 1855 TO 1885. 2 vols.

220.   EXPENDITURES OF THE DEPARTMENT OF THE STATE FROM MARCH 4, 1789 TO JUNE 30, 1876. 1 vol.

221.   ANNUAL REPORTS OF THE AUDITOR FOR THE TREASURY, POST OFFICE, STATE AND OTHER DEPARTMENTS, 1865-66; 1868-69; 1881-84; 1891-92; 1897-98; 1900-2; 1906-16. 1 box.

222.   NAMES & RANK OF OFFICERS WHO ISSUED FORAGE TO VOLUNTEERS IN THE MEXICAN WAR TOGETHER WITH THE PLACES AND DATES OF THE DISBURSEMENTS, 1846-48. 1 vol.

223.   RECORD OF PAYMENTS - EASTERN. 5 vols.

224.   PAYMENTS TO DISCHARGED SOLDIERS - EASTERN. 14 vols.

This is probably part of entry 860.

225. PAYMENTS TO DISCHARGED SOLDIERS - MIDDLE. 9 vols.

This is probably part of entry 860.

226. PAYMENTS TO DISCHARGED SOLDIERS - WESTERN. 18 vols.

This is probably part of entry 860.

227. PAYMENTS TO DISCHARGED SOLDIERS - MISCELLANEOUS. 3 vols.

228. PAYMENTS TO DISCHARGED SOLDIERS - VETERANS RESERVE CORPS. 2 vols.

229. PAYMENTS TO GENERALS - SURGEONS - PAYMASTERS CLERKS AND MISCELLANEOUS, 1866-69. 1 vol.

230. EFFECTS BOOK, ca. 1861-87. 1 vol.

231. ABSTRACTS OF PAYMENTS BY MAJOR OLIVER HOLMES, U.S. ARMY, JUNE-NOV. 1862. 1 vol.

232. AUDITOR'S ACCOUNTS, 1870'S-1880'S. 1 box.

233. REGISTER AND RECORD OF LONGEVITY SERVICE. 4 vols.

234. REGISTER OF PAYMENTS-HOSPITALS AND MISCELLANEOUS. 1 vol.

235. LEDGER OF EXPENDITURES, 1824. 1 vol.

236. RECORD OF PAYMENTS OF PERSONS IN UNITS FOR OHIO AND MICHIGAN. 1 vol.

237. REGISTER OF CLAIMS, 1842-45. 1 vol.

238. RECORD OF PAYMENTS TO VOLUNTEER UNITS, 1861-65. 2 vols.

239. REGISTER, RECORDING DATES AND NUMBER OF SETTLEMENTS, 1815-61. 1 vol.

This is probably part of entry 1014.

240. REGISTER LISTING OLD CASES FROM DIFFERENT SHEET FILE, ACCOUNTS WITH OFFICERS. 1 vol.

241. DISBURSING BOOK. 1 vol.

242. UNIDENTIFIED REGISTERS OF VOLUNTEERS. 1 vol.

243. CLAIMS BOOK, 1ST-20TH U.S. INFANTRY, 1867-68. 1 vol.

244. COMPARATIVE TABLE OF OLD AND NEW FILE NUMBERS, n.d. 1 vol.

245. LIST OF ACCOUNTS, 1862-69. 1 vol.

246. CLOTHING ACCOUNTS, TREASURY REGIMENT, 1864. 1 vol.

247. LIST OF OFFICERS AND THEIR SETTLEMENTS, 1863-65. 1 vol.

248. REGISTER OF BONDS, 1823-76. 1 vol.

249. UNIDENTIFIED ACCOUNT BOOK, ca. 1861-72. 1 vol.

250. RECORD OF VOLUNTEERS & SUBSTITUTES ACCOMPANYING LEDGER NO. 2, 1864-65. 1 vol.

251. MUSTER ROLLS, 1846-48. 1 box.

252. DRAFT RENDEZVOUS - LIST OF BONDS. 1 box.

253. COPIES OF LETTERS SENT BY THE AUDITOR FOR WAR DEPARTMENT, MARCH 1896 TO JAN. 1898. 1 box.

254. MISCELLANEOUS LETTERS RECEIVED, COLLECTION DIVISION, 1883-91. 4 vol.

255. INDEX-OREGON WAR DEBT. 1 vol.

256. APPROPRIATION LEDGER NO. 1, THIRD AUDITOR'S OFFICE. 1 vol.

257. LEDGER NO. 28, 3RD AUDITOR'S OFFICE. 1 vol.

258. COMMISSARY LEDGER NO. 26. 1 vol.

259. COMMISSARY AND PENSIONS LEDGER NO. 1, 1873. 1 vol.

260. THIRD AUDITOR'S REPORT BOOKS. 2 vol.

261. INDEXES. 1 box.

262. REGISTER: COMMUTATION OF RATIONS, 1866-94, AND INDEX, 1901. 1 vol.

263. REGISTER OF ACCOUNTS, PENSION AGENTS. 4 vols.

This is probably part of 786.

264. OFFICE OF COMMISSARY GENERAL OF PRISONERS, LETTER BOOKS, 1814. 2 vols.

This is probably part of 1403.

265. RECORD OF MILITIA CLAIMS FOR THE EASTERN SHORE OF MARYLAND, 1813-15. 1 vol.

This is probably part of 1401.

266. ABSTRACTS "A" AND "B", 1862-67. 7 vols.

267. BALANCES, MAY 1792 TO JULY 1, 1815. 1 vol.

This is probably part of entry 1445.

268.   REGISTER OF ACCOUNTS AND CLAIMS RECEIVED FROM QUARTERMASTER. GENERAL, 1863-66. 2 vols.

This is probably part of entry 654.

269.   REGISTER OF CLAIMS, SUBSISTENCE BUREAU, WASHINGTON D.C., 1863-86. 2 vols.

This is probably part of entry 655.

270.   TREASURY SETTLEMENTS, PENSION CLAIMS, 1864-68. 1 vol.

271.   EXPENDITURES, OREGON AND WASHINGTON INDIAN WARS, 1855-56. 1 vol.

272.   REGISTER OF INDIAN WAR CLAIMS, 1855-56. 4 vols.

Volumes are numbered 2 to 5.

273.   REGISTER OF CLAIMS OF OREGON AND WASHINGTON VOLUNTEERS, 1855-56. 3 vols.

274.   3RD AUDITOR, HORSE CLAIMS NOS. 490-606, 1839-40. 1 box.

275.   STATEMENT OF THE CONTRACTS FOR THE PURCHASE AND CHARTER OF VESSELS FOR TRANSPORTATION PURPOSES IN THE WAR WITH MEXICO, 1846-47. 1 vol.

276.   STATE CLAIMS LETTERS, 1861-1862. 1 vol.

277.   STATEMENTS OF CLAIMS IN PENSION ROLLS, 1832-36; 1844-47. 1 box.

This is probably part of entry 1032.

278.   MISCELLANEOUS-LETTERS SENT, PENSION BUREAU TO AGENTS, AUG. 25 & 27, 1816. 1 box.

279.   REGISTER OF REVOLUTIONARY WAR PENSIONERS, ca. 1818-1822. 2 boxes.

280.   INDEX TO BOOK ONE. 1 vol.

281.   LOOSE DOCUMENTS BELONGING IN THE 3RD AUDITOR'S OFFICE. 1 box.

282.   REGISTER OF DIPLOMATIC AND CONSULAR ACCOUNTS, 1863-1913. 1 vol.

283.   UNIDENTIFIED REGISTERS OF THE THIRD AUDITOR'S OFFICE. 1 box.

284.   ABSTRACTS OF DISBURSEMENTS ON ACCOUNT OF CONTINGENCIES BY COL. T. J. HAINES, 1865. 1 box.

285.   STATEMENT SHOWING THE PARTICULARS OF THE ITEM OF THE $240,759.59 WHICH APPEARS ON THE REPORT OF THE 30TH OF JANUARY 1828, ON THE

CLAIM OF THE STATE OF MASSACHUSETTS, UNDER THE HEAD "MISCELLANEOUS." 1 box.

286. UNIDENTIFIED ACCOUNT LEDGER "NO. 18." 1 vol.

This is probably part of entry 1378.

287. LETTERS RECEIVED, CLAIM FILES, PROPERTY RETURNS, ABSTRACTS, AND OTHER RECORDS FILED UNDER ENTRIES 991, 1276, 1277, 1420, 1421, 1422, 1423, 1424, 1425, 1426, AND 1427. 3 boxes.

288. REPORTS FROM AUGUST 1ST 1847, TO DECEMBER 31ST 1849. 1 vol.

289. MISCELLANEOUS LETTERS RECEIVED, 1862. 3 boxes.

290. LETTERBOOKS - GENERAL CORRESPONDENCES, 1864. 3 vols.

Volumes are numbered 82, 83, and 84.

291. WESTERN GUNBOAT FLOTILLA-CONSOLIDATED INDEX. 1 vol.

292. WESTERN GUNBOAT FLOTILLA-GENERAL MUSTER BOOK AND PAY & RECEIPT ROLL, 1862. 9 vols.

293. WESTERN GUNBOAT FLOTILLA-VOUCHERS, FINAL RETURNS, EVIDENCE, AND OTHER PAPERS, 1862. 7 boxes.

294. HOUSE DOCUMENT NO. 446, HISTORICAL REGISTER AND DICTIONARY OF ARMY, 1789-1903. 1 box.

295. THIRD AUDITOR'S ACCOUNTS AND CLAIMS, 1850-1910. 81 boxes.

296. ABSTRACTS LIST-INDEX QUARTERMASTER, MONEY ACCOUNTS, CIVIL WAR PERIOD. 1 vol.

297. INDEMNIFICATION FOR ITALIANS LYNCHED IN NEW ORLEANS, 1891. 1 box.

298. FIRST AUDITOR'S OFFICE; LETTERS RECEIVED, 1ST COMPTROLLER, DISTRICT OF COLUMBIA GOVERNMENT, 1878-94. 1 box.

299. LIGHTHOUSE LETTERS, 1790-1835. 2 boxes.

300. CLAIMS FILES; INDIAN HOME GUARDS, ca. 1862-78. 2 boxes.

301. CERTIFICATES OF THE FIFTH AUDITOR ON THE ACCOUNT OF JOHN LOWELL, JR.; "PAYMENT OF FRENCH SPOLIATION CLAIMS", 1905. 1 box.

302. ACCOUNTS AND CLAIMS OF THE 3RD AUDITOR, 1823-99. 1 box.

303. ACCOUNT REPORT OF WILLIAM BLOUNT, GOVERNOR OF TENNESSEE, ca. 1812-1856. 1 box.

304. STATEMENTS, VOUCHERS, AND RELATED RECORDS PERTAINING TO PUBLIC DEBT, ca. 1801-25. 1 box.

305. RECORDS OF THE COLLECTORS OF CUSTOMS, ca. 1803-39. 1 box.

306. RECORDS PERTAINING TO PITTSBURGH DEFENSE CLAIMS, 1863-1905. 2 boxes.

307. LAND ACCOUNTS, 1829-39. 1 box.

308. MILITIA ROLLS AND CORRESPONDENCE, WAR OF 1812. 1 box.

309. LETTERS OF 1ST COMPTROLLER, 1ST AUDITOR'S OFFICE AND 5TH AUDITOR'S OFFICE. 1 box.

310. RECORDS OF CONSTANTINE MAGUIRE, INTERNAL REVENUE COLLECTOR AND DISBURSING AGENT, RE: MISSOURI LIQUOR FRAUD, 1873-75. 1 box.

311. MISCELLANEOUS GAO - RECORDS OF CHARLES W. FORD, INTERNAL REVENUE COLLECTOR AND DISBURSING AGENT, RE: MISSOURI LIQUOR FRAUD, 1872-73. 1 box.

312. DIRECT TAX, CIVIL WAR. 1 box.

313. RAINCOAT CONTRACTS. 1 box.

314. RECORDS REGARDING BOSTON DEFENSE, WAR OF 1812. 1 box.

315. ACCOUNTS AND CLAIMS OF THE SECOND AUDITOR'S OFFICE, ca. 1817-89. 1 box.

316. NEWSPAPERS. 1 box.

317. FIFTH AUDITOR'S ACCOUNTS, SALARY AND FEES FOR DIPLOMATS AND CONSULS, ca. 1872-85. 1 box.

318. CLAIMS OF THE STATE OF TEXAS; ca. 1845-1908. 1 box.

319. RECORDS OF THE 3RD AUDITOR REGARDING THE PURCHASE OF CAMELS, 1855-57. 1 box.

320. CLAIMS OF THE STATE OF FLORIDA, ca. 1851-93. 1 box.

321. CLAIMS OF UTAH MILITIA FOR EXPENSES INCURRED IN SUPPRESSING INDIAN HOSTILITIES, ca. 1850-53. 1 box.

322. CLAIM OF JAMES W. MAGOFFIN, SECRET AGENT-MEXICAN WAR, 1848-1967. 1 box.

323. ACCOUNTS OF THE COMMISSION OF INDUSTRIAL RELATIONS. 1 box.

324. CLAIMS OF THE REVERE COPPER CO., BOSTON; MASSACHUSETTS, AND THE WINCHESTER REPEATING ARMS CO., NEW HAVEN CONNECTICUT, 1862-93. 1 box.

325. CLAIMS OF THE STATE OF VIRGINIA, WAR OF 1812. 1 box.

326. PENSION FRAUD (REVOLUTIONARY WAR), 1816-28. 1 box.

327.   LETTERS BY STATE. 1 box.

328.   SURVEYOR GENERAL AND DEPUTY SURVEYOR'S ACCOUNTS - FLORIDA; 1831-35; 1840; 1842. 1 box.

329.   SURVEY 3 - COLUMBIAN EXPOSITION IN CHICAGO, 1893. 2 boxes.

330.   SURVEY 4 - INLAND WATER, MISSISSIPPI RIVER COMMISSION, 1882. 3 boxes.

331.   SURVEY 6 - EXPENSES OF FREEDMAN'S BUREAU, 1866-70. 2 boxes.

332.   SURVEY 12 - BUILDING LIBRARY OF CONGRESS, 1884-96. 3 boxes.

333.   SURVEY 14 - PACIFIC RAILROAD EXPLORATION, 1853-62. 1 box.

334.   SURVEY 15 - JOHN SIMPSON SURVEYS - UTAH TERRITORY, 1857-59. 1 box.

335.   SURVEY 18 - CLARENCE KING SURVEY - EXPLORATION OF THE 40TH PARALLEL, 1867-78. 2 boxes.

336.   SURVEY 21 - MARK H. CARLETON, AGRONOMIST, 1891-1901. 1 box.

337.   SURVEY 23 - VESSELS OF FISH AND WILDLIFE SERVICES, 1881-1924. 1 box.

338.   SURVEY 24 - CLEVELAND ABBS, METEOROLOGIST, 1863-1916. 2 boxes.

339.   SURVEY 28 - U.S. INDUSTRIAL COMMISSION, 1898-1902. 2 boxes.

340.   SURVEY 30 - 1ST PAN AMERICAN CONFERENCE, WASHINGTON, D.C. 1889. 1 box.

341.   SURVEY 32 - PARIS UNIVERSAL EXPOSITION, 1867. 1 box.

342.   FOURTH AUDITOR'S OFFICE, LETTERS RECEIVED, 1843-61. 10 vols.

343.   UNIDENTIFIED ACCOUNT REGISTER, 1888. 1 vol.

344.   FOURTH AUDITOR'S OFFICE, CERTIFICATES, 1855-57. 1 vol.

345.   APPROPRIATION JOURNALS, 1810-1822. 3 vols.

346.   WARRANTS BOOK, 1799-1910. 1 vol.

347.   APPROPRIATION LEDGERS, 1809-1822. 4 vols.

348.   REGISTER OF ACCOUNTS, FOR CLAIMS DUE FROM AND TO THE UNITED STATES, 1843-51. 1 vol.

349.   COPIES OF PRIZE LIST, 1859-61. 1 box.

350.   REQUISITION BLOTTERS, 1827-29; 1831-39. 3 vols.

       Volumes are numbered 6, 8, and 9.

351.   ACCOUNT LEDGER OF ISAAC HENDERSON, NAVY AGENT OF NEW YORK, 1861-62. 1 vol.

352.   LEDGER OF OFFICERS' ACCOUNTS, 1839-1850. 1 vol.

353.   GENERAL INDEX TO LEDGERS. 1 vol.

       This is probably part of entry 762.

354.   RECORD OF PAYMENTS MADE TO PERSONS LEFT OFF OF PRIZE LISTS OR RANKED WRONG, 1864-1877. 1 vol.

355.   UNIDENTIFIED NAME INDEXES. 18 vols.

356.   REGISTER OF CLAIMANTS, 1872-74. 1 vol.

       This may be part of entry 1935.

357.   UNIDENTIFIED LEDGER SHOWING DATES OF SALARIES AND FEES TO BE PAID, 1882. 1 vol.

       This may be part of entry 1729.

358.   REGISTER OF LETTERS RECEIVED, OFFICE OF AUDITOR FOR THE STATE & OTHER DEPARTMENTS (BLANK PAGES). 1 vol.

359.   INDEX - MENS PAY ROLL, U.S. RECEIVING SHIP "GREAT WESTERN", 1864. 1 vol.

360.   "PRIVATE MATTER," 1897. 1 vol.

361.   PAY TABLE, U.S. NAVY, 1860. 1 vol.

362.   O.K. BOOK, U.S. TREASURY DEPARTMENT, STOCK NO. 24. 1 vol.

363.   LEDGER FOR OFFICERS. 1 vol.

364.   BOOK OF INDICES - GENERAL CORRESPONDENCE. 1 vol.

365.   INDEX OF NAMES OF CREW, MARINES, AND OFFICERS. 9 vols.

366.   NAVY MISCELLANEOUS LEDGERS AND PAPERS. 1 box.

367.   REPORT BOOK NO. 9, ALABAMA JUDGMENTS, 1886. 1 vol.

368.   REGISTER OF REMARKS OF THE ACCOUNTS CURRENT OF THE GENERAL POST OFFICE WITH THE UNITED STATES, 1810-1834. 1 vol.

369.   REGISTER OF CONTINGENT EXPENSES OF CONSULATES THAT WERE EXHAUSTED, 1897. 1 vol.

370.   LEDGER OF THE TREASURER'S OFFICE RE: REDEMPTION NOTES, 1892-93. 1 vol.

       This may be part of entry 2029.

371.   LETTER SENT REGARDING COLLECTION OF DEBTS UNDER INTERNAL REVENUE LAWS, 1829-44. 1 vol.

372.   REGISTER OF THE ACCOUNTS REPORTED UPON BY THE FIFTH AUDITOR, 1833-44; 1863-69. 5 vols.

373.   MISCELLANEOUS RECORDS OF THE FIFTH AUDITOR. 1 box.

374.   DAY BOOK (EXHIBIT 92-SAN ANTONIO CRIMINAL BLOTTER). 1 vol.

375.   INDEX - COLLECTORS. 1 vol.

376.   REGISTRATION OF ACCOUNTS, 1869-70. 1 vol.

377.   INDEX - REGISTRATION ACCOUNTS, 1869. 1 vol.

378.   INDEX TO PAYMASTERS SETTLEMENTS. 1 vol.

379.   MARSHAL'S CRIMINAL BLOTTER. 1 vol.

380.   FIFTH AUDITOR'S REPORTS. NO. 8, 1855-58. 1 vol.

381.   BILLS OF N.Y. CORDING & SEALING CO., MEMO OF THEIR AMOUNT AND DATA OF PAYMENTS, 1873. 1 vol.

382.   UNIDENTIFIED REGISTER OF BONDS, 1866-67. 1 vol.

383.   CERTIFIED STATEMENTS, JANUARY 1885 TO 1892. 1 vol.

384.   INDEX TO REGISTER OF ACCOUNTS "D." 1 vol.

385.   CENSUS ROLL. 1 vol.

386.   "NO. 16," 1894-1983. 1 vol.

387.   ACCOUNT BOOK - UNION AND CENTRAL PACIFIC RAILROAD COMPANY AND SIOUX CITY RAILROAD COMPANY, OPENED JANUARY 1, 1883, 1885. 1 vol.

388.   INDEX TO VOUCHER BOOK. 1 vol.

389.   INDEX - RAIL BOOK. 1 vol.

390.   LEDGER (EXHIBIT 96). 1 vol.

391.   BENCH DOCKET, LEON COUNTY, FLORIDA, 1841-42. 1 vol.

        This may not belong in RG 217.

392.   CLAIM OF ILLINOIS CENTRAL RAILROAD COMPANY (ACCOUNT NO. 18,327), 1876. 1 vol.

393.   CLAIM OF ALIEN STOCKBROKERS OF ILLINOIS CENTRAL RAIL ROAD COMPANY, ca. 1876. 1 vol.

394.   UNIDENTIFIED INDEX. 1 vol.

395.   UNIDENTIFIED ACCOUNT LEDGER, 1886. 1 vol.

396.   LEDGER RELATING TO INDIAN AFFAIRS, n.d. 1 vol.

397.   INDEX TO LEDGER, ca. 1828-49. 1 vol.

398.   FIFTH AUDITOR'S ACCOUNTS; ACCOUNT NO. 9718 - TREATY WITH MEXICO - FIRST INSTALLMENT, 1847. 1 box.

399.   MISCELLANEOUS RECORDS. 2 boxes.

400.   LETTER AND DOCKET OF CLAIMS - GARFIELD BOARD OF AUDIT, 1882-83. 1 vol., 1 vol.

        This is probably part of entry 347.

401.   "2107 - U.S. TREASURY DEPARTMENT," 1933. 1 vol.

402.   UNIDENTIFIED REGISTER NO. "3." 1 vol.

403.   RECORD BOOK OF EMPLOYEES REPORTED FOR DUTY AT OFFICE OF AUDITOR FOR WAR, 1899-1903. 1 vol.

404.   ALPHABETICAL LIST OF POST, 1846-48. 1 vol.

405.   VOUCHER CHECK (COPIED), 1862-65. 1 vol.

406.   ACCOUNTS IN ROOM 1 AND AT SECOND AUDITOR'S 1865-67. 1 vol.

407.   REGISTERS (BLANK PAGES). 2 vols. (all pages are blank).

408.   NEWSPAPER CUTTINGS, R. A. BAYLEY, PERSONAL, 1880. 1 vol.

409.   CIVIL ESTABLISHMENT LETTER BOOK, 1869-1886. 1 vol.

410.   ACCOUNT LEDGER LISTING AMOUNTS PAID ON THE SEVERAL INSTALLMENTS OF THE FRENCH INDEMNITY, ca. 1838. 1 vol.

411.   PRINTED LETTERS & C. OF THE COMMISSIONER OF THE REVENUE, 1815-23. 1 vol.

412.   INDEX TO FILES OF THE AUDITOR FOR THE INTERIOR DEPARTMENT, 1907. 1 vol.

413.   LIST OF CLAIMS FOR POST PROPERTY IN THE EXPEDITION AGAINST THE SEMINOLE INDIANS, 1818. 1 vol.

413A.   ACCOUNT LEDGER OF FORTS AND ORDNANCES, 1809-1814. 1 vol.

414.   LIST OF INDIAN DEPREDATION CLAIMS, 1819-72. 1 vol.

415. REGISTER OF SEMINOLE CLAIMS. 1 vol.

416. STATEMENT OF 217 AWARDS MADE PAYABLE TO THE AGENT OF THE UNITED STATES... UNDER THE 7TH ARTICLE OF THE LATE TREATY BETWEEN THE UNITED STATES AND GREAT BRITAIN, 1804. 1 vol.

417. UNIDENTIFIED REGISTER LISTING CLAIMS (INCLUDING MEMORANDUMS OF THE AUDITOR ON WHETHER TO ALLOW AWARDS TO BE MADE). 1 vol.

418. MISCELLANEOUS RECORDS (NEED TO BE IDENTIFIED AND/OR REFILED). 6 boxes.

419. MISCELLANEOUS RECORDS - WAR CLAIMS, 1898. 1 box.

420. MISCELLANEOUS RECORDS - RETURN, 1845-67; 1876. 6 boxes.

421. MISCELLANEOUS RECORDS - RETURN OF SUBSISTENCE STORES, 1891. 1 box.

422. "SPECIAL POWERS" OF ATTORNEYS, 1842-50. 1 box.

423. PUBLISHED ITEMS. 1 box, 1 box, 6 boxes, 1 box.

424. PACIFIC RECORD INDEX NO. 2. 1 vol.

425. ORDERS-ANNUAL REPAIRS, 1892-94. 1 vol.

426. "VOL. 19," COMMENCING JULY 1, 1904 WITH #28774 - AND ENDING WITH #31528. 1 vol.

427. INDEX TO VOL. 19 (NEW BOOK). 1 vol.

428. REQUISITIONS FOR PRINTING, BINDING, 1879-87. 1 vol.

429. REGISTER OF LAND OFFICES - NAMES AND DATES OF BONDS, 1846-87. 1 vol.

430. RECOMMENDATIONS FOR RETENTION AND APPOINTMENTS, 1885-87. 1 vol.

431. "VOL. 8," COMMENCING WITH #8175, AUG. 25, 1892. 1 vol.

432. "VOL. 10," COMMENCING SEPT. 18, 1894, WITH #10753, TO AUG. 24, 1895. 1 vol.

433. "VOL. 12," COMMENCING JUNE 1, 1896 (WITH #14,302 TO # 15,884), MAY 29, 1897. 1 vol.

434. "VOL. 14," COMMENCING MARCH 7, 1898, WITH #17,418. 1 vol.

435. "VOL. 15," COMMENCING WITH JANUARY 25, 1899 - #19, 308, ENDING WITH #21,230. 1 vol.

436. "VOL. 16," COMMENCING WITH FEB. 1, 1900, WITH #21,231, ENDING FEB. 9, WITH #23,744. 1 vol.

437. APPOINTMENT LEDGER, 1898. 1 vol.

438.   REPAYMENTS TO IMPORTERS AND DEBENTURES OR DRAWBACKS. 1 vol.

439.   CONTRACT BOOK. 1 vol.

440.   INDEX TO LAND LEDGER "F." 1 vol.

441.   U.S. FRACTIONAL CURRENCY DESTROYED, 1837-86. 1 vol.

442.   BOOK OF THE 2ND NATIONAL BANK. 1 vol.

443.   RIBBONS (REFUNDS ON RIBBONS UNDER TREASURY DECISIONS), 1873-74. 1 vol.

444.   INDEX OF MISCELLANEOUS CASES. 1 vol.

445.   INDEX TO ARTICLES - APPEALS. 2 vols.

446.   GENERAL INDEX TO LETTER BOOKS. 4 vols.

447.   INDEX OF EMPLOYEES. 1 vol.

448.   INDEX - CUSTOMS APPROPRIATION LEDGER NO. 13. 1 vol.

449.   INDEX TO TREASURY LEDGER, 1886-87. 1 vol.

450.   BRIEFS, W.F.C., 1868-74. 2 vols.

451.   PRESS COPIES, W.F.C., 1871-74. 1 vol.

452.   CIVIL - INDIAN LEDGER NO. 2121, 1922-23. 1 vol.

453.   RECEIPT BOOK OF ITEMS SENT BY MAIL EXPRESS AND RAILROAD, 1882. 1 vol.

454.   UNIDENTIFIED REGISTER OF CLAIMS, 1867-80. 1 vol.

455.   RECORD OF RECEIPTS OF COLLECTORS, MONTHLY REPORTS OF INVOICES, AND LANDING CERTIFICATES, 1886. 1 vol.

456.   ABSTRACTS - SALE OF UNCLAIMED MERCHANDISE, DEC. 1895. 1 vol.

457.   BALANCE BOOK - U.S. BULLION FUND ("MINT"), 1893. 1 vol.

458.   REGISTER OF TREASURY DEPARTMENT EMPLOYEES. 1 vol.

459.   ACCOUNT LEDGER OF THE COLLECTORS, ENGINEERS, AND INSPECTORS, 1895-98. 1 vol.

460.   GENERAL LAND OFFICE - ACCOUNT LEDGER, 1897-1900. 1 vol.

461.   MISCELLANEOUS AND UNSORTED RECORDS - CIVIL. 12 boxes.

462.   UNIDENTIFIED LEDGERS, REGISTERS, AND INDEXES. 23 vols. and 5 boxes.

463.   TREASURER'S ACCOUNTS, 1837; 1839; 1862. 8 vols.

464.   UNIDENTIFIED NAME INDEXES. 2 vols.

465.   TREASURY DAILY STATEMENT, 1866. 1 vol.

466.   1ST AUDITOR INDEX. 1 vol.

467.   REGISTER OF ACCOUNTS RECEIVED FROM DISBURSING AGENTS OF LAND OFFICES, ca. 1890-96. 1 vol.

468.   REPAY WARRANTS. 1 vol.

469.   BOOK "C", 1819, '20 & '21. 1 vol.

470.   REGISTER OF TREASURY INTERIOR WARRANTS. 1 vol.

471.   LEDGER - RAILROAD SINKING FUND ACCOUNTS, 1869. 1 vol.

472.   RECORD OF SALARIES PAID, 1870-72. 1 vol.

473.   CLAIMS FOR EXTRA PAY UNDER ACT APPROVED FEBRUARY 19, 1879. 1 vol.

474.   "DOCKET NO. 1, NOS. 1 TO 221." 1 vol.

475.   RECORD BOOK LISTING APPLICANTS APPLYING FOR POSITIONS. 1 vol.

476.   INDEX TO THE LEDGER OF THE PUBLIC DEBT. 1 vol.

477.   INDEX TO INTERIOR LEDGER NO. 2. 1 vol.

478.   JOURNAL - STATISTICAL DESTRUCTIONS, 1868-70. 1 vol.

479.   INDEX TO REGISTER OF MISCELLANEOUS ACCOUNTS. 1 vol.

480.   INDEX - FIRST AUDITOR. 1 vol.

481.   CONTRACTS VOL. V, COMMISSARY GENERAL, 1814. 1 vol.

482.   INDEX TO WAR LEDGER NOS. 25 AND 24. 1 vol.

483.   BRIEF OF CLAIM OF WM. J. CHANDLER ON HAY CONTRACT, FT. SMITH, ARKANSAS, JUNE 1864. 1 vol.

484.   REGISTER OF OFFICERS, 1868-69. 1 vol.

485.   INDEX TO LEDGER NO. 2. 1 vol.

486.   LEDGER SHOWING NAMES AND AMOUNT OF WAGES PAID UNDER THE EIGHT HOUR LAW (ACT OF MAY 1872). 1 vol.

487.   LEDGER NO. 26. 1 vol.

488.   INDEX - HOSPITAL PINKNEY. 1 vol.

489.   REGISTER OF APPLICATIONS AND PAYMENTS - SOLDIERS' CLAIMS, 1815-1830. 1 vol.

490.   MEMORANDUM BOOK OF P. Y. DOLAN, ca. 1887-88. 1 vol.

491.   RECORD BOOK OF SHIPMENTS BY RAILROAD COMPANIES, 1864-65. 1 vol.

492.   DUPLICATE BOOK NO. 4, SPECIAL SETTLEMENTS, JULY 1888. 1 vol.

493.   LEDGER NO. 23. 1 vol.

494.   LIST OF CONTRACTS APPROVED BY THE SECOND COMPTROLLER, 1884-85. 1 vol.

495.   BOOK NO. 1 - TRANSFERRED CASES TO COL. R. P. DODGE, 1866. 1 vol.

496.   CERTIFICATES ISSUED TO CLAIMANTS IN MODOC WAR CLAIMS, 1856. 1 vol.

497.   INDEX, NOS. 1926 TO 4000. 1 vol.

498.   INDEX - WAR DEPARTMENT, 1885. 1 vol.

499.   REPORT OF PROCEEDINGS OF BOARDS OF SURVEYS, FORT LEWIS, COLORADO, 1892. 1 vol.

500.   NUMERICAL REGISTER OF CERTIFICATES. 1 vol.

501.   LIST OF PENSIONERS, 1832. 1 vol.

502.   LEDGER NO. 2. 1 vol.

503.   LEDGER NO. 6. 1 vol.

504.   LEDGER NO. 7. 1 vol.

505.   "TICKLER NO. 5." 1 vol.

506.   RECORD BOOK OF THE THIRD AUDITOR'S OFFICE, WASH., D.C. 1 vol.

507.   BALANCE SHEET, MILITARY ESTABLISHMENT, 1837. 1 vol.

508.   LEDGER NO. 24. 1 vol.

509.   REGISTER OF CLAIMS FROM COURT OF CLAIMS RECEIVED AND ANSWERED FROM JULY 1903 TO 1909. 1 vol.

510.   MISCELLANEOUS AND UNSORTED RECORDS - MILITARY. 16 boxes.

511.   REGISTER SHOWING THE DISPOSITION OF PAID AND CANCELLED CHECKS OF U.S. DISBURSING OFFICERS, 1866-87. 1 vol.

512.   RECORDS OF THE GENERAL COUNSEL OFFICE RELATING TO SECTION 102 OF THE REVENUE ACT OF 1936, 1937-38. 1 box.

513.   LETTERS RECEIVED, 1854-64. 3 boxes.

514. LETTERS RECEIVED FROM Q. M. REGARDING ADVANCES, 1855. 1 box.

515. ACCOUNT CURRENT ADVANCES, 1863-65, 1869. 6 boxes.

516. SUBSISTENCE ACCOUNT CURRENT (COMMISSARY), 1867-69. 8 boxes.

517. Q. M. ACCOUNT CURRENT, 1868-69. 1 box.

518. ABSTRACTS OF PURCHASES (ABSTRACTS "D"), 1858-87. 35 boxes.

519. QUARTERMASTER RETURNS, 1861-64. 6 boxes.

520. Q. M. SETTLEMENT, JOHN H. MORRIS, A.Q.M., LEXINGTON, KY. 1865. 2 box.

521. QUARTERMASTER SETTLEMENTS {FY 1868, 1888, AND 1890}. 9 boxes.

522. SUBSISTENCE SETTLEMENTS, FY 1890. 1 box.

523. DEPOSIT RECEIPTS, 1887-1893. 2 boxes.

524. NAVY DEPARTMENT, COVERING WARRANTS, 1909-10. 2 boxes.

525. OFFICE OF INTERNAL REVENUE, DAILY REPORTS, 1890. 1 box.

526. MISCELLANEOUS ACCOUNTS AND UNIDENTIFIED RECORDS. 14 boxes.

527. REIMBURSEMENTS LETTERS, JAN. 2 - MAR. 6, 1909. 1 box.

528. MISCELLANEOUS CLAIMS, 1856-86. 2 boxes

529. ACCOUNTS OF CLAIMS GROWING OUT OF THE FLORIDA WAR, 1836-38. 1 box.

530. PAYMASTER ACCOUNTS OF MAJ. WILLIAM SMITH, DEPARTMENT OF THE DAKOTAS, 1876-1877. 1 box.

531. CALIFORNIA STATE CLAIMS; CIVIL WAR; MISCELLANEOUS, UNARRANGED RECORDS. 1 box.

532. ABSTRACT BOOKS RELATING TO THE STATE CLAIMS OF THE STATE OF CALIFORNIA. 20 vols.

533. WAR CLAIMS OF STATE OF CALIFORNIA RELATING TO THE EXPENDITURES ON ACCOUNT OF INDIAN WARS, 1851-57. 1 vol.

534. REGISTER OF BONDS (ISSUED FOR THE RELIEF OF THE CALIFORNIA VOLUNTEERS), 1864-75. 1 vol.

535. STATE OF CALIFORNIA, REGISTER OF CLERKS. 1 vol.

536. CALIFORNIA WAR CLAIMS, SOLDIER'S COUPONS. 4 vols.

537. CALIFORNIA INDIAN WARS, LISTS OF STATE BONDS AND PAYROLLS. 1 box.

538.   ACCOUNTS AND CLAIMS SETTLED BY THE SECOND AUDITOR OF THE TREASURY DEPARTMENT RELATING TO ARSENAL AT HARPER'S FERRY, 1817-1852. 42 boxes.

539.   U.S. PENITENTIARY CHECKBOOKS, ca. 1829-1861. 1 box, 1 box.

540.   MILITARY WARRANTS, 1813-1814. 3 boxes.

541.   LEDGERS OF ACCOUNTS PAID, 1848-1857. 2 boxes.

542.   MISC. LETTERS, VOUCHERS, AND CLAIMS, 1800'S - 1850'S. 1 box, 3 boxes.

543.   RECORDS RELATING TO CUSTOMS ACCOUNTS AND CLAIMS. 1 box.

544.   OFFICE OF THE FOURTH AUDITOR; NAVY PENSION PAYMENTS, 1815-73. 3 vols.

545.   RECORDS RELATING TO MILITARY CONTRACTS AND LEASES. 1 box.

546.   ABSTRACTS OF UNCLAIMED MERCHANDISE SOLD AT PUBLIC AUCTION IN NEW YORK, 1884-98.

547.   PAY WARRANTS - CUSTOMS (1851-54). 4 vols. (vols. are 17 1/2″ high; these vols. may be an accretion to A-1, entry 48 "Warrants").

548.   MISCELLANEOUS UNIDENTIFIED RECORDS. 1 box, 1 box, 2 boxes.

549.   OFFICE OF THE THIRD AUDITOR; RECORD OF MISCELLANEOUS SETTLEMENTS, BOOK NO. 1, 1847-78. 1 vol.

550.   OFFICE OF THE THIRD AUDITOR; REMITTANCES, 1853. 2 boxes.

551.   OFFICE OF THE THIRD AUDITOR; CLAIMS REPORTED FOR SETTLEMENT, 1894-1900. 1 vol.

552.   OFFICE OF THE THIRD AUDITOR; STATE & HORSE CLAIMS DIVISION; MEMORANDUM OF HORSE CLAIMS FILED LATE AND OF INFORMAL CLAIMS, 1883-84. 1 vol.

553.   OFFICE OF THE THIRD AUDITOR; LIST OF ACCOUNTS UNSETTLED AGAINST THE QUARTERMASTER GENERAL'S DEPARTMENTS IN DISTRICT 7, 1815. 1 vol.

554.   OFFICE OF THE FOURTH AUDITOR; LETTERS RECEIVED, 1836-43. 4 vols.

555.   OFFICE OF THE FIFTH AUDITOR; VOUCHERS FOR ELECTION OFFICIALS, 1890-1907. 2 boxes.

556.   OFFICE OF THE FIRST COMPTROLLER; INDEX TO INTERNAL REVENUE LEDGER, 1872-79. 1 vol.

557.   ACCOUNTS OF PAYMASTER - ARMY, 1812-19. 1 vol.

558.   PAYMASTER LEDGER - SOUTH CAROLINA MILITIA (BAILEY'S CORPS) , 1813-16. 1 vol.

559. SETTLEMENTS AND APPEALS, 1896. 1 vol.

560. TREASURY SETTLEMENTS - PENSION CLAIMS, 1864-68. 1 vol.

561. RECORD OF REDEMPTION OF U.S. GOVERNMENT STOCK CERTIFICATES, 1818-36. 4 vols.

562. ALPHABETICAL NAME INDEX, n.d. 1 vol.

563. INDEX TO LETTER BOOKS, 1866-67. 1 vol.

564. MISCELLANEOUS PENSION RECORDS, ca. 1798-1900. 9 boxes.

565. MISCELLANEOUS UNIDENTIFIED RECORDS FOUND DURING THE MOVE TO ARCHIVES II RELATING TO RG 217. 6 vols. and 1 box.

1001. COMMISSARY RETURNS 3RD AUDITOR, 1861-1894. 1029 boxes.

1002. ARMY SUBSISTENCE ACCOUNTS 3RD AUDITOR., 1865-1877. 563 boxes.

       Alpha box: 402A.

1003. 3RD AUDITOR - SUBSISTENCE RETURNS, 1879-1894. 472 boxes.

       Boxes 373 and 457 were not located. Alpha box: 33A.

1003A. 3RD AUDITOR'S OFFICE DRAFT RECEIPTS - U.S. TREASURY OFFICE, NEW YORK ASST. TREASURER, 1867-1868. 1 box.

1004. MISCELLANEOUS PAPERS - INDIAN. 13 boxes.

1005. UNNUMBERED ACCOUNTS, 1797-1813. 3 boxes.

1006. 2ND AUDITOR ACCOUNTS, 1821. 4 boxes.

1007. 5TH AUDITOR ACCOUNTS, 1817-24. 16 boxes.

1141. CIVIL DEPARTMENTS AND AGENCIES; STATE DEPARTMENT AND VARIOUS INDEPENDENT AGENCIES, 1922. 1 box.

APPENDIX 1

REGISTERS OF THE TREASURY, 1789-1897

Name	Dates of Service
Joseph Nourse	Sept. 17, 1789-May 31, 1829
Thomas L. Smith	June 1, 1829-Mar. 31, 1845
Ransom H. Gillett	Apr. 1, 1845-June 3, 1847
Daniel Graham	June 4, 1847-Mar. 5, 1849
Allen A. Hall	Apr. 9, 1849-Jan. 17, 1850
Townsend Haines	Feb. 13, 1850-Oct. 31, 1851
Nathan Sargent	Nov. 1, 1851-Apr. 19, 1853
Finley Bigger	Apr. 20, 1853-Apr. 16, 1861
Lucius E. Chittenden	Apr. 17, 1861-Aug. 10, 1864
S. B. Colby	Aug. 11, 1864-Sept. 21, 1867
Noah L. Jeffries	Oct. 5, 1867-Mar. 15, 1869
John Allison	Apr. 3, 1869-Mar. 23, 1878
Glenni W. Scofield	Aug. 1, 1878-May 20, 1881
Blanche K. Bruce	May 21, 1881-June 5, 1885
William S. Rosecrans	June 8, 1885-June 19, 1893
James Fount Tillman	July 1, 1893-Dec. 2, 1897

APPENDIX 2

FIRST COMPTROLLERS, 1789-1921

Note: From September 11, 1789, to March 3, 1817, the First Comptroller had the title "Comptroller of the Treasury," and resumed that title in October 1, 1894. In July 1921, the First Comptroller became the Comptroller-General of the United States.

Name	Dates of Service
Nicholas Eveleigh	Sept. 11, 1789-Mar. 3, 1791
Oliver Wolcott, Jr.	June 17, 1791-Feb. 2, 1795
David Lennox (acting)	Feb. 20-Mar. 31, 1795
Henry Kuhl (acting)	Apr. 9-Sept. 7, 1795
John Davis	Sept. 7, 1795-June 30, 1796
John Steele	July 1, 1796-Dec. 14, 1802
Gabriel Duvall	Dec. 15, 1802-Nov. 21, 1811
Richard Rush	Nov. 22, 1811-Feb. 10, 1814
Ezekiel Bacon	Feb. 11, 1814-Feb. 28, 1815
Joseph Anderson	Feb. 28, 1815-June 30, 1836
George Wolf	July 5, 1836-Feb. 28, 1838
James N. Barker	Feb. 28, 1838-Apr. 2, 1841
Walter Forward	Apr. 6-Sept. 13, 1841
James W. McCulloch	Apr. 1, 1842-May 31, 1849
Elisha Whittlesey	May 31, 1849-Apr. 30, 1857
William Medill	May 1, 1857-Apr. 30, 1861
Elisha Whittlesey	May 1, 1861-Dec. 13, 1862
William Hemphill Jones (acting)	Dec. 14, 1862-Apr. 20, 1863
Robert W. Taylor	Apr. 20, 1863-Feb. 25, 1878
Albert G. Porter	Mar. 8, 1878-July 10, 1880
William Lawrence	July 15, 1880-Mar. 18, 1885
Milton J. Durham	Mar. 20, 1885-Apr. 22, 1889
Asa C. Matthews	May 13, 1889-Mar. 6, 1893
Robert B. Bowler	May 6, 1893-July 2, 1897
Robert J. Tracewell	Aug. 5, 1897-Mar. 11, 1913
George E. Downey	May 12, 1913-Aug. 31, 1915
Walter W. Warwick	Sept. 1, 1915-July 1, 1921

APPENDIX 3

SECOND COMPTROLLERS, 1817-94

Name	Dates of Service
Richard Cutts	Mar. 6, 1817-Mar. 17, 1829
Isaac Hill	Mar. 21, 1829-May 24, 1830
James B. Thornton	May 27, 1830-June 30, 1836
Albion K. Parris	Aug. 1, 1836-Nov. 28, 1850
Hiland Hall	Nov. 30, 1850-Sept. 10, 1851
E. J. Phelps	Oct. 1, 1851-Feb. 13, 1853
J. M. Brodhead	Feb. 14, 1853-Oct. 8, 1857
James M. Cutts	Oct. 8, 1857-May 11, 1863
J. M. Brodhead	May 29, 1863-Jan. 23, 1876
Cyrus C. Carpenter	Jan. 25, 1876-Aug. 29, 1877
W. W. Upton	Sept. 30, 1877-June 25, 1885
Isaac H. Maynard	July 1, 1885-Apr. 6, 1887
Signouri Butler	May 6, 1887-May 23, 1889
Benjamin F. Gilkeson	June 4, 1889-May 6, 1893
Charles H. Mansur	June 20, 1893-Sept. 30, 1894

APPENDIX 4

COMMISSIONERS OF CUSTOMS, 1849-94

Name	Dates of Service
Charles W. Rockwell	Mar. 16, 1849-Dec. 31, 1852
Hugh J. Anderson	Mar. 23, 1853-Dec. 4, 1857
Samuel Ingham	Dec. 5, 1857-May 19, 1861
Nathan Sargent	May 20, 1861-May 31, 1871
William T. Haines	June 29, 1871-Apr. 14, 1874
Henry C. Johnson	Apr. 15, 1874-Mar. 28, 1885
John S. McCalmont	Apr. 8, 1885-June 7, 1889
Samuel V. Holliday	June 17, 1889-May 31, 1893
William H. Pugh	June 1, 1893-Sept. 30, 1894

APPENDIX 5

FIRST AUDITORS, 1789-1921

Note: From September 12, 1789, to March 3, 1817, the First Auditor had the title "Auditor for the Treasury." Beginning October 1, 1894, his title was "Auditor for the Treasury Department."

Name	Dates of Service
Oliver Wolcott	Sept. 12, 1789-June 17, 1791
William Smith	July 16-Nov. 28, 1791
Richard Harrison	Nov. 29, 1791-Oct. 31, 1836
Jesse Miller	Nov. 1, 1836-May 14, 1842
Tully R. Wise	June 17, 1842-July 22, 1844
William Collins	July 24, 1844-Sept. 3, 1849
John C. Clark	Sept. 4-Nov. 4, 1849
Thomas L. Smith	Nov. 5, 1849-Nov. 14, 1871
David W. Mahon (acting)	Nov. 15-Dec. 21, 1871
David W: Mahon	Dec. 22, 1871-Mar. 23, 1878
Robert A. Reynolds	Apr. 18, 1878-Apr. 30, 1885
James Q. Chenowith	May 1, 1885-May 20, 1889
George P. Fisher	June 12, 1889-Mar. 25, 1893
Ernest P. Baldwin	Mar. 28, 1893-June 8, 1897
William E. Andrews	June 10, 1897-Apr. 30, 1915
Samuel Patterson	May 12, 1915-June 30, 1921

APPENDIX 6

SECOND AUDITORS, 1792-1921

Note: From May 8, 1792, to March 3, 1817, the Second Auditor had the title "Accountant for the War Department." Beginning October 1, 1894, his title was "Auditor for the War Department."

Name	Dates of Service
Joseph Howell	May 8, 1792-Apr. 10, 1795
William Simmons	Apr. 11, 1795-Aug. 27, 1804
Peter Hagner	Aug. 28, 1804-Oct. 29, 1810
William Simmons	Oct. 30, 1810-June 6, 1814
Peter Hagner (acting)	June 7-Aug. 5, 1814
Tobias Lear	Aug. 8, 1814-Oct. 8, 1816
Willian Lee	Jan. 13, 1817-Mar. 21, 1829
William B. Lewis	Mar. 21, 1829-Mar. 20, 1845
John M. McCalla	Mar. 29, 1845-Apr. 8, 1849
Philip Clayton	Apr. 9, 1849-Mar. 14, 1857
Thomas J.D. Fuller	Apr. 15, 1857-July 31, 1861
Ezra B. French	Aug. 3, 1861-Apr. 26, 1880
Orange Ferriss	May 13, 1880-June 18, 1885
William A. Day	July 2, 1885-June 15, 1889
J.N. Patterson	June 18, 1889-Apr. 8, 1893
T. Stobo Farrow	Apr. 13, 1893-June 8, 1897
William W. Brown	June 9, 1897-Aug. 4, 1899
Frank M. Morris	Aug. 10, 1899-Dec. 22, 1900
Frederick E. Rittman	Jan. 7, 1901-May 1, 1905
Benjamin F. Harper	May 2, 1905-Apr. 19, 1911
Elton A. Gongwer	May 18, 1911-May 7, 1913
James L. Baity	May 9, 1913-June 30, 1921

APPENDIX 7

THIRD AUDITORS, 1816-1921

Note: From May 8, 1816, to March 3, 1817, the Third Auditor had the title "Additional Accountant for the War Department." Beginning October 1, 1894, his title was "Auditor for the Interior Department."

Names	Dates of Service
Peter Hagner	May 8, 1816-Oct. 22, 1849
John S. Gallagher	Oct. 22, 1849-Apr. 24, 1853
Frances Burt	Apr. 25, 1853-Sept. 15, 1854
Robert J. Atkinson	Sept. 16, 1854-July 17, 1864
Elijah Sells	July 19-Oct. 29, 1864
John Wilson	Oct. 31, 1864-Mar. 15, 1869
Reader W. Clarke	Mar. 26-Dec. 7, 1869
Allan Rutherford	Mar. 29, 1870-Jan. 14, 1876
Horace Austin	Jan. 17, 1876-Apr. 25, 1879
Edwin W. Keightley	May 1, 1879-Mar. 28, 1885
John S. Williams	Apr. 29, 1885-Aug. 25, 1889
William H. Hart	Aug. 26, 1889-May 23, 1893
Samuel Blackwell	May 27, 1893-Apr. 19, 1897
William Youngblood	Apr. 26, 1897-June 15, 1901
Robert S. Person	June 16, 1901-Dec. 20, 1909
Howard C. Shobart	Dec. 21, 1909-Apr. 28, 1913
Robert W. Woolley	Apr. 30, 1913-Mar. 2, 1915
Oscar A. Price	Mar. 10, 1915-Dec. 31, 1917
David C. Reay	Feb. 19, 1918-Dec. 30, 1919
John E. R. Ray	Feb. 21, 1920-June 30, 1921

APPENDIX 8

FOURTH AUDITORS, 1798-1921

Note: From September 7, 1798, to March 3, 1817, the Fourth Auditor had the title "Accountant for the Navy Department." Beginning October 1, 1894, his title was "Auditor for the Navy Department."

Name	Dates of Service
William Winder	Sept. 7, 1798-Jan. 25, 1800
Thomas Turner	Jan. 26, 1800-Mar. 5, 1817
Constant Freeman	Mar. 6, 1817-Feb. 27, 1824
William Lee	Mar. 12-June 23, 1824
Tobias Watkins	June 23, 1824-Mar. 22, 1829
Amos Kendall	Mar. 24, 1829-Apr. 30, 1835
John C. Pickett	May 1, 1835-June 25, 1838
Aaron O. Dayton	June 26, 1838-Oct. 4, 1858
A.J. O Bannon	Oct. 5, 1858-July 13, 1860
Taliafero Hunte	Aug. 15, 1860-Apr. 20, 1861
Hobart Berrian	May 4, 1861-May 1, 1863
Stephen J.W. Tapor	June 1, 1863-July 31, 1879
Charles Beardsley	Aug. 9, 1879-May 10, 1885
Charles M. Shelley	May 11, 1885-May 17, 1889
John R. Lynch	May 21, 1889-June 29, 1893
Charles B. Morton	Aug. 2, 1893-June 5, 1895
William H. Pugh	June 7, 1895-May 3, 1897
Frank H. Morris	June 26, 1897-Aug. 4, 1899
William W. Brown	Aug. 10, 1899-May 30, 1907
Ralph W. Tyler	June 1, 1907-May 30, 1913
Edward Luckow	June 1, 1913-June 30, 1921

APPENDIX 9

FIFTH AUDITORS, 1817-1921

Note: On October 1, 1894, the Fifth Auditor's title was changed to "Auditor for the State and Other Departments."

Name	Dates of Service
Stephen Pleasonton	Mar. 6, 1817-Jan. 20, 1855
Josiah Minot	Jan. 24-July 30, 1855
Murrey McConnell	Sept. 3, 1855-Feb. 28, 1859
Bartholomew Fuller	Mar. 4, 1859-Apr. 29, 1861
John C. Underwood	Aug. 6, 1861-Aug. 31, 1863
Charles M. Walker	Sept. 1, 1863-Apr. 30, 1869
Henry D. Barron	May 1, 1869-Dec. 31, 1871
Jacob H. Ela	Jan. 1, 1872-June 3, 1881
DeAlva S. Alexander	June 9, 1881-July 28, 1885
Anthony Eickhoff	Aug. 1, 1885-May 17, 1889 I
L.W. Habercom	May 18, 1889-June 16, 1892 I
Ernest G. Timme	July 15, 1892-Mar. 18, 1893
Thomas Holcom	Mar. 28, 1893-Mar. 21, 1897
Ernest G. Timme	Apr. 14, 1897-Apr. 30, 1906
Caleb R. Layton	May 1, 1906-Nov. 9, 1910
Frank H. Davis	Mar. 6, 1911-June 9, 1913
Edward D. Hearne	June 10, 1913-June 30, 1921

APPENDIX 10

LIST OF QUARTERMASTERS AND ASSISTANT QUARTERMASTERS WHOSE ABSTRACTS ARE INCLUDED IN ENTRY 730.

Name	Date of Service
Abbey, Seth A.	1862
Allen, Abner J.	1862-64
Allen, John T.	1863-64 1864-65 (2 vols.)
Allen, Robert	1863-66 1861-65 (4 vols.)
Anderson, George W.	1863-65
Armor, George F.	1862-64
Armstrong, Charles D.	1864
Armstrong, George A.	1863-66
Armstrong, William B.	1863-65
Ashmead, A. S.	1863-65
Avis, Samuel	1865
Bailhache, William A.	1862-65
Bainbridge, E. C.	1862
Baker, Edward D.	1862-64 1864-66 (1 vol.)
Barringer, Augustus V.	1863-64
Batchelder, Richard N.	1861-65
Bean, S. B.	1865-66
Belcher, John H.	1865-66
Bell, David	1862-64
Biggs, Herman	1861-65
Bingham, Judson D.	1861; 1864-67 1862-64 (1 vol.)
Black, Samuel	1862-1862-63 (1 vol.)
Blanchard, C. D.	1862-63
Blanchard, Osias	1864-65
Bliss, Alexander	1863-64
Bliven, Charles E.	1865-66 (1 vol.)
Blodgett, Gardner S.	1864-65
Blood, Henry B.	1862-64
Boggess, Henry H.	1861-65
Bohn, Herman J.	1862-65
Bosbyshell, William	1863
Botts, Randolph	1864-65
Bowles, Thomas C.	1864-66
Bowman, Henry	1864
Boyd, Augustus	1861-62
Boyd, J. F.	1862-65 (1 vol.) 1865-66
Boyle, John R.	1865-66
Bradford, G. P.	1865
Bradley, George W.	1865-66
Bradley, Jerome	1863-64
Bradley, Luther	1864-65
Bradshaw, Albert M.	1864-65
Bradshaw, John M.	1861-65
Brinkerhoff, Roeloff	1862-66
Brooks, James	1862-66
Brown, Simon B.	1862-65
Brown, S. Lockwood	1861-65 (2 vols.)

Brown, William H.	1862-65
Browning, George T.	1864-65
Buck, Isaac N.	1864-65
Buntin, Touissant C.	1863-65
Burr, Arthur G.	1862-65 (1 vol.)
Burr, Raymond	1862-65
Cadwalleder, George B.	1863-66
Camp, Elisha E.	1861-67
Campbell, John B.	1864-66
Carlile, Thomas J. .	1864-66 (1 vol.)
Carling, Elias B.	1864-65
Carr, Byron O.	1862-65 (1 vol.)
Carrington, J. F.	1865
Case, Theodore S.	1862-65
Chamberlain, H. S.	1863-65 (1 vol.)
Champlin, Edward P.	1864
Chandler, John G.	1862-65
Chapman, Edmund D.	1861-65 (1 vol.)
Chew, T. J.	1863-64
Churchill, James O.	1865-66
Clark, George F.	1862-65 (2 vols.)
Clark, James F.	1862-66
Clark, John Warren	1863-64
Clary, Robert E.	1863-64 1864-65 (1 vol.)
Clemens, Gilbert H.	1864-65
Cloury, Robert C.	1864-65
Clubb, Henry S.	1862-66
Coffin, Oliver S.	1863-65
Colburn, Webster J.	1864-66
Colby, C. A.	1862
Constable, Nathaniel S.	1862-65
Corning, James	1862-63
Coryell, Ingham	1862-65 (5 vols.)
Coulter, T. J.	1863
Coverdale, Robert T.	1862-63
Craig, John R.	1861-65
Craig, William	1862-64
Crane, John C.	1862-65 (1 vol.)
Crawford, E.	1863-65
Crilly, Francis J.	1863-64, 1864-66 (1 vol.)
Crossman, George H.	1861
Crowell, John H.	1864-66
Croxton, Lafayette J.	1863-65
Currie, William	1862-65
Curtis, Walter	1863
Cushing, George W.	1865-66
Dana, James J.	1861-62
Dandy, George B.	1866
Daniels, William H.	1863-64
Darling, George	1865
Davis, E. M.	1861-62
Day, Deming W. H.	1863-64
Del Veccio, James R.	1863-66
Dewey, Archibald S.	1862-65

De Wolf, David O.	1863-65 (1 vol.)
Dexter, John B.	1862-66
Dickerson, John H.	1862, 1863-64 (1 vol.)
Dodge, Nathaniel S.	1863-64, 1864-65 (2 vols.)
Donaldson, James L.	1862 1862-64 (1 vol.)
Drake, Q. J.	1863-64
Drennan, John P.	1865
Dunbar, G. E.	1864-65
Du Puy, Horatio A.	1863-65
Durbin, Greene	1864-65
Dutton, Carlos	1862-63
Dyer, George R.	1862-65
Earnest, William D.	1861-64
Easton, L. C.	1861; 1865-66 1862-64 (2 vols.)
Eaton, Alonzo	1862-65
Eddy, Asher R.	1861-62; 1866 1862-65 (1 vol.)
Edwards, Arthur	1863-65
Ekin, James	1862-65
Ernst, Frank	1862-64
Farnsworth, John G.	1863-64
Farnum, Edwin J.	1864-65
Ferry, John H.	1862-64 (1 vol.)
Finch, A.	1862-63
Finch, H. B.	1862
Finkler, William	1862-65
Finley, James A.	1863-64
Finney, Charles G.	1863-65
Fisher, Adam	1863-66
Fitch, Enoch P.	1861-64
Fitch, Henry S.	1862
Fitch, Thomas D. .	1862-65 (3 vols.)
Flagg, George A.	1861 1862-66 (1 vol.)
Flagg, Newton	1862-65
Flanigan, Patrick	1864-66
Fleming, John E.	1865-66
Forsyth, Lewis C.	1862-66 (3 vols.)
Fort, Greenberry S.	1862-63, 1864 (1 vol.)
Fry, Thomas W., Jr.	1863-66 (1 vol.)
Fuller, F.	1862-64
Garber, Michael C.	1862-66 (1 vol.)
Gardner, R. S.	1861-66
Garretson, Charles	1862-64
Garrett, Charles F.	1862-64
Garvens, H.	1862-65
Gaster, William	1862-63
Gaubert, Charles H.	1862-65 (1 vol.)
Gilley, C. M.	1862-64
Goff, Willis C.	1863
Goldie, William	1862-63
Goodman, Charles	1862-65
Goodrich, Moses P.	1862-65 (1 vol.)
Goulding, C. N.	1862-64
Green, Joseph A.	1863-65
Greene, Elias M.	1862-64 (1 vol.)

Grierson, John C.	1865-66
Grimes, Edward B.	1863-64 (1 vol.) 1864-65
Gross, William L.	1864-66
Hade, Emanuel	1864-65
Hall, Theron E.	1862-64 (2 vols.)
Hamill, Samuel R.	1863-65, 1866-67 (2 vols.)
Hancock, Frederick	1865-66
Harper, R. J.	1863-64
Harris, W. F.	1861-64
Harrison, George W.	1862-66
Hart, Isaac W.	1864-66
Hartz, Edward L.	1861-64
Haskell, John G.	1862-65 (1 vol.)
Hatch, Reuben B.	1861-65
Heaney, Daniel	1862-65
Heaton, Grore L.	1864-65
Henry, Charles A.	1864-65
Herr, John	1864-65
Hibbard, George B.	1864-65
Hinchman, J. R. W.	1864-65
Hipple, Samuel	1864-65
Hodges, Henry C.	1862-63 (1 vol.) 1864
Hoge, Holmes	1864-65
Holabird, Samuel B.	1861-64
Hollowbush, Jacob R.	1862-64
Holman, B. F.	1863-64
Hooker, A. E.	1869
Hopkins, Nelson J.	1864-65
Hopkins, Woolsey R.	1864-66
Hosmer, James R.	1863
Howard, J. B.	1862-65
Howell, William F.	1863-65
Howland, Henry	1862-64, 1864-65 (1 vol.)
Hoyt, Charles H.	1862-64
Hull, Gustavus A.	1864-66
Humphreys, R. H.	1863-64
Hunt, Thomas B.	1864-67
Hunter, William A.	1863-65
Huntington, John M.	1861-64
Hurtt, Francis W.	1862-63 (1 vol.)
Insley, Merritt H.	1861-65
Irvin, Charles H.	1862-65 (1 vol.)
Isenstein, George	1863-66
Isom, J. F.	1863-64
Jacobson, Gustav	1863
James, John H.	1864-66 (1 vol.)
James, William L.	1865-66
Jenkins, Walworth	1861-63 (2 vols.)
Jennings, John R.	1864-65
Joel, E. M.	1861-64
Johnson, James G.	1864-65
Johnson, Richard P.	1861-65
Johnson, William H.	1863-65
Johnston, Thomas P.	1865-66

Jones, Henry L.	1863-65
Kelley, B. F., Jr.	1864-66
Kennedy, William K.	1863-65
Kirk, Ezra B.	1864-66 (2 vols.)
Klinck, John G.	1861-65 (1 vol.)
Lacy, Henry B.	1861-65
Laird, George A.	1864
La Porte, Samuel McKean	1862-65
Le Blond, E. C.	1864
Lee, James G. C.	1863-66
Leffingwell, Cristopher W.	1862-65
Levering, John	1862-63
Lewis, John V.	1862-64 (1 vol.)
Lloyd, Alford J.	1864-65
Loomis, Moses D. W.	1862
Lott, George G.	1865
Loury, Fielding	1861-65
Ludington, Marshall J.	1863-68
Lunt, Sam H.	1862-64 (2 vols.)
Lyman, Charles W.	1862-64
Lynch, John A.	1863-64
Mackay, Aeneas J.	1861-65
Mahler, Jacob	1863-65
Maize, William R.	1866-67
Mann, James C.	1862-65
Mark, C. K.	1862-65
Marsh, Thomas B.	1863-64
Marshal, B. F.	1863
Marshall, George W.	1866
Mason, Albert	1864-65
Maupin, A. T.	1863-64
Mayall, Samuel	1862-64 (1 vol.)
McCall, F. C.	1865
McCann, Thomas K.	1864
McClung, David W.	1862-65 (2 vols.)
McClure, John W.	1863-65
McCormick, Reuben A.	1865-66
McFerran, John C.	1862-64,1865-68 (1 vol.)
McGonigle, Andrew J.	1865-66
McHarg, John	1862-65
McKay, James H.	1862-64
McKim, William W.	1864-66
Meigs, Samuel E.	1862-63
Metcalf, Lyne S.	1862-65
Miller, Morris S.	1861-65
Mills, William	1862-64 (1 vol.), 1864-65
Moer, Samuel H.	1862-65
Monroe, George	1864
Moore, James M.	1865-67
Moore, Treadwell	1860-61 (1 vol.), 1861-64; 1866-67
Morford, William E.	1864-66
Morlan, Jonah	1864-65
Morris, John A.	1863-64 (1 vol.)
Morse, Edward A.	1862-65

Morton, Prince G.D.	1862
Moulton, Charles W.	1861-63, 1863-65 (1 vol.)
Mullin, Loudon	1864
Myers, William	1861, 1862-67 (8 vols.)
Neale, William L.	1865
Nelson, George F.	1864-65
Nigh, Elias	1861-64 (1 vol.)
Norcross, Frederick M.	1864-66
Norton, George A.	1863-65
Norton, Joshua	1862-64
Oakley, Franklin W.	1864-65
O Brien, Thomas	1862-63
Owens, R. B.	1862-66 (1 vol.)
Parker, Gilbert L.	1863-64
Parsons, Charles	1863-64
Parsons, Lewis B.	1862-64
Patton, Henry D.	1862-64
Peck, S. C.	1862-65
Perkins, F. W.	1862-65
Perkins, Simon	1862-64 (2 vols.)
Persing, Henry W.	1864-65
Phelps, Abner S.	1863-64 (1 vol.)
Phelps, Vincent	1863-64
Pierce, G. A.	1862-65
Pierce, G. W.	1861
Pierce, Luther H.	1862-63
Pinckard, William G.	1862-64
Pitkin, Pearly P.	1862-64
Platt, Samuel K.	1863-64
Potter, Joseph A.	1864-67
Power, John	1864-65
Pratt, James H.	1862-64
Prime, Mark	1862-63
Quier, Levi	1863-64
Raisin, H.	1863-65
Rankin, William A.	1863-64
Rankin, W. G.	1863-64
Ransom, Hyatt C.	1862-64 (1 vol.), 1862-65
Rapelje, John T.	1862-65
Reichenback, E. D.	1862-64
Remington, J. E.	1863-66
Reno, Benjamin F.	1863
Restreaux, E. B. W.	1864-67
Reynolds, Charles A.	1861-66
Reynolds, Charles H.	1865
Robb, A. W.	1865
Robinson, Henry L.	1864-66
Rucker, Daniel H.	1861-67, 1861-62 (1 vol.) 1862-65 (1 vol.)
Rugar, Francis H.	1863-65
Rundle, Samuel E.	1863-65
Rusling, James F.	1863-65
Russell, John K.	1862
Rutherford, John P.	1862-66

Sawtelle, Charles G.	1862-66
Schenck, James W.	1862-65
Schmidt, Charles D.	1861-64
Seelye, Edgar	1864-66
Sevier, A. M.	1864
Shaffer, J. W.	1861-62
Shannon, A. J.	1862-63
Shaw, Joel K.	1864-65
Shepherd, Leven W.	1864-65
Sheridan, P. H.	1862
Shimmel, Augustus	1861-64
Shipley, Alexander N.	1862-64
Smith, Charles K., Jr.	1862-64, 1865-66 (1 vol.)
Smith, Hiram M.	1864-65 (1 vol.)
Smith, John Condit	1862-64 (1 vol.)
Smith, W. H.	1863-64
Smith, W. Willard	1862-64
Spangler, Basil L.	1864-65
Stager, Anson	1862-64
Starkweather, Frederick T.	1863-64
Stealey, George J.	1862-64
Steiner, David C.	1862-64
Steven, J. V.	1862
Stewart, Frederick V.	1862-63
Stone, James	1863-64
Strang, Edward J.	1864-65
Stubbs, Joseph D.	1862-66
Suydam, S. P.	1863-65
Swain, James A.	1861-63
Swigart, D. W.	1862-64
Swords, Thomas	1862-63
Sympson, Alex	1862-63
Taylor, John W.	1862-64
Thayer, H. L.	1864-66
Thomas, Charles W.	1864-67, 1864 (1 vol.)
Thompson, Charles	1863-65
Thorne, G. R.	1865
Tighe, John H.	1862-66
Tompkins, Charles H.	1862-67
Treat, Richard B.	1863-64
Trumbull, J. L.	1865
Tucker, Alba M.	1863-65 (1 vol.)
Tyler, Charles R.	1861-65
Van, W. A.	1862-64
Van Duzer, John C.	1865
Van Ness, William W.	1862-64
Van Vleit, Leonard S.	1863-66 (1 vol.)
Wagner, Charles B.	1862-63
Wainwright, William A.	1863-68 (1 vol.)
Walker, William N.	1862-63
Warren, Samuel P.	1865
Warren, William A.	1862-64
Webster, George P.	1862-66
Weeks, George H.	1862-64

Welch, Deming N.	1864-66 (2 vols.)
West, C. L.	1861-62
Wetherell, R. W.	1862-65
Wheeler, Phineus A.	1863-65
White, George O.	1864-65
Whitman, Edmund B.	1866-68, 1862-65 (3 vols.)
Whittelsy, Henry M.	1862-66
Wickersham, Morris D.	1864-66
Wickizer, John H.	1864-65
Wills, George W.	1864-66
Wilmot, E.	1865
Wilson, James H.	1863-66
Wing, Charles T.	1862-68 (6 vols.)
Winslow, Frederick S.	1861-62, 1862-64 (4 vols.)
Winslow, Geo. C.	1863-66
Winslow, John B.	1862-65
Wise, George D.	1861-63
Woods, Charles R.	1861-62
Woods, John L.	1863-66
Woods, William M.	1865
Woolfolk, Austin C.	1862-66
Worms, Charles	1864-65
Wright, John W.	1863

NOTES

APPENDIX 11

MICROFILM PUBLICATIONS

M235   Miscellaneous Treasury Accounts of the First Auditor Treasury Department. (formerly the Auditor) of the 1790-1840. 1170 rolls

M497   Letters Sent by the Commissioner of Customs Relating to Smuggling. 1865-1869. 1 roll

M498   Letters Sent by the Commissioner of Customs Relating to Captured and Abandoned Property. 1868-1875. 1 roll

M520   Records of the Board of Commissioners for the Emancipation of Slaves in the District of Columbia. 1862-1863. 6 rolls DP

M1014 Central Treasury Records of the Continental and Confederation Governments. 1775-1789. 23 rolls DP

M1015 Central Treasury Records of the Continental and Confederation Governments Relating to the Military Affairs. 1775-1789. 7 rolls DP

M1658 Southern Claims Commission Approved Claims, 1871-1880: Georgia. 1871-1880. 1100 fiche

M1678 Accounts and Claims Settled by the Second Auditor of the Treasury Department Relating to the Arsenal at Harper's Ferry, 1817-1851. 62 rolls

M1745 Claims for Georgia Militia Campaigns Against Indians on the Frontier, 1792-1827. 5 rolls. DP

M1746 Final Revolutionary War Pension Payment Vouchers: Georgia. 4 rolls. DP

T135   Selected Records of the General Accounting Office Relating to the Fremont Expeditions and the California Battalion. 1818-1890. 3 rolls

T227   Civil War Direct Tax Assessment Lists: Tennessee. No date. 6 rolls

T718   Ledgers of Payments, 1818-1872, to U.S. Pensioners Under Acts of 1818 Through 1858 From Records of the Office of the Third Auditor of The Treasury. 23 rolls

T899   Register of Audits of "Miscellaneous Treasury Accounts" (First Auditor's Office). No date. 1 roll

T909   Fiscal Records of the United States. 1776-1789. 1 roll.

T964   Day Book of the Register's Office of the Treasury. 1789-1791. 1 roll.

NOTES

Index

—A—

www.ingramcontent.com/pod-product-compliance
Lightning Source LLC
Chambersburg PA
CBHW061717270326
41928CB00011B/2012